ICONS OF AFRICAN AMERICAN PROTEST

**Recent Titles in
Greenwood Icons**

Icons of Horror and the Supernatural: An Encyclopedia of
Our Worst Nightmares
Edited by S.T. Joshi

Icons of Business: An Encyclopedia of Mavericks, Movers, and Shakers
Edited by Kateri Drexler

Icons of Hip Hop: An Encyclopedia of the Movement, Music, and Culture
Edited by Mickey Hess

Icons of Evolution: An Encyclopedia of People, Evidence, and Controversies
Edited by Brian Regal

Icons of Rock: An Encyclopedia of the Legends Who Changed Music Forever
Scott Schinder and Andy Schwartz

Icons of R&B and Soul: An Encyclopedia of the Artists Who Revolutionized
Rhythm
Bob Gulla

African American Icons of Sport: Triumph, Courage, and Excellence
Matthew C. Whitaker

Icons of the American West: From Cowgirls to Silicon Valley
Edited by Gordon Morris Bakken

Icons of Latino America: Latino Contributions to American Culture
Roger Bruns

Icons of Crime Fighting: Relentless Pursuers of Justice
Edited by Jeffrey Bumgarner

Icons of Unbelief: Atheists, Agnostics, and Secularists
Edited by S.T. Joshi

Women Icons of Popular Music: The Rebels, Rockers, and Renegades
Edited by Carrie Havranek

Icons of Talk: The Media Mouths That Changed America
Donna L. Halper

ICONS OF AFRICAN AMERICAN PROTEST

Trailblazing Activists of the Civil Rights Movement

VOLUME 2

Gladys L. Knight

Greenwood Icons

GREENWOOD PRESS
Westport, Connecticut · London

Library of Congress Cataloging-in-Publication Data

Knight, Gladys L., 1974–
    Icons of African American protest: trailblazing activists of the civil rights movement /
Gladys L. Knight.
        p. cm.
    Includes bibliographical references and index.
    ISBN 978-0-313-34062-8 ((set) : alk. paper)—ISBN 978-0-313-34063-5 ((vol.1) : alk. paper)—
ISBN 978-0-313-34064-2 ((vol.2) : alk. paper)
    1. African American civil rights workers—Biography. 2. Civil rights workers—United States—
Biography. 3. African Americans—Civil rights—History. 4. African Americans—Civil rights—
History. 5. Civil rights movements—United States—History. 6. Political activists—United States—
History. I. Title.
    E185.96.K56 2009
    323.092′2—dc22
    [B]   2008034739

British Library Cataloguing in Publication Data is available.

Library of Congress Catalog Card Number: 2008034739
ISBN: 978-0-313-34062-8 (set)
        978-0-313-34063-5 (Vol 1)
        978-0-313-34064-2 (Vol 2)

First published in 2009

Greenwood Press, 88 Post Road West, Westport, CT 06881
An imprint of Greenwood Publishing Group, Inc.
www.greenwood.com

Printed in the United States of America

The paper used in this book complies with the
Permanent Paper Standard issued by the National
Information Standards Organization (Z39.48–1984).

10 9 8 7 6 5 4 3 2 1

Contents

Volume 2

Photos

Ella Baker (page 1), between 1942 and 1946. Courtesy of the Library of Congress.

Black Panther Party members, leader Elaine Brown (page 27; center) and co-founder Huey P. Newton (right), pose with their lawyer Charles R. Garry (left) on the campus of Yale University, New Haven, Connecticut, probably in April 1970. Photo by David Fenton/Getty Images.

Stokely Carmichael (page 53), 1966. Courtesy of the Library of Congress.

Poster of Angela Davis (page 79), 1971. Courtesy of the Library of Congress.

W.E.B. Du Bois (page 105), between 1930 and 1950. Courtesy of the Library of Congress.

James Farmer (page 131) at Foley Square in New York, speaking at a memorial for four African American girls killed in a church bombing in Birmingham, Alabama, 1963. Courtesy of the Library of Congress.

Louis Farrakhan (page 155) told a Washington news conference he has no doubt that Libyan leader Moammar Khadafy was sincere in offering to help train and arm black Americans for an uprising against the U.S. government. "I cannot accept the carnal weapons of this world," Farrakahn said, 1985. AP Photo/Scott Stewart.

Marcus Garvey (page 181), 1924. Courtesy of the Library of Congress.

Fannie Lou Hamer (page 207) at the Democratic National Convention, Atlantic City, New Jersey, 1964. Courtesy of the Library of Congress.

Dorothy Height (page 233; right) presents the Mary McLeod Bethune Human Rights Award to Eleanor Roosevelt (left) at the council's silver anniversary lunch, 1960. Courtesy of the Library of Congress.

Jesse Jackson (page 259) surrounded by marchers carrying signs advocating support for the Hawkins-Humphrey Bill for full employment. Courtesy of the Library of Congress.

Martin Luther King, Jr. (page 285) delivering a speech at Girard College, Philadelphia, 1965. Courtesy of the Library of Congress.

Director Spike Lee (page 311) shown on the set of his 1996 film *Get on the Bus*. Courtesy of Photofest.

Composite of two photographs: bottom photo shows the Selma Montgomery civil rights march, with Dr. Martin Luther King, Jr. (front/center), Coretta Scott King (behind Dr. King), and John Lewis (page 337; right of Mrs. King); top photograph shows five white segregationists, two with confederate flags, 1965. Courtesy of the Library of Congress.

Malcolm X (page 365) during a rally in Harlem, New York, 1963. Courtesy of the Library of Congress.

Thurgood Marshall (page 391) shown in front of the Supreme Court, 1958. Courtesy of the Library of Congress.

A Black Panther poster featuring Huey Newton (page 417). Text beneath this image read: "The racist dog policemen must withdraw immediately from our communities, cease their wanton murder and brutality." Courtesy of the Library of Congress.

Rosa Parks (page 443) seated toward front of bus, Montgomery, Alabama, 1956. Courtesy of the Library of Congress.

A. Philip Randolph (page 467) standing before the statue at the Lincoln Memorial, during the 1963 March on Washington. Courtesy of the Library of Congress.

Al Sharpton (page 493) on *Saturday Night Live*, 2003. Courtesy of Photofest.

Ida B. Wells (page 519), 1891. Courtesy of the Library of Congress.

Roy Wilkins (page 545), 1963. Courtesy of the Library of Congress.

Robert F. Williams (page 571) living in exile. Lynn Pelham/Time Life Pictures/ Getty Images.

Whitney Young (page 597) reading a book, 1963. Courtesy of the Library of Congress.

Series Foreword

Worshipped and cursed. Loved and loathed. Obsessed about the world over. What does it take to become an icon? Regardless of subject, culture, or era, the requisite qualifications are the same: (1) challenge the status quo, (2) influence millions, and (3) impact history.

Using these criteria, Greenwood Press introduces a new reference format and approach to popular culture. Spanning a wide range of subjects, volumes in the Greenwood Icons series provide students and general readers a port of entry into the most fascinating and influential topics of the day. Every two-volume title offers an in-depth look at approximately 24 iconic figures, each of which captures the essence of a broad subject. These icons typically embody a group of values, elicit strong reactions, reflect the essence of a particular time and place, and link different traditions and periods. Among those featured are artists and activists, superheroes and spies, inventors and athletes—the legends and mythmakers of entire generations. Yet icons can also come from unexpected places: as the heroine who transcends the pages of a novel or as the revolutionary idea that shatters our previously held beliefs. Whether people, places, or things, such icons serve as a bridge between the past and the present, the canonical and the contemporary. By focusing on icons central to popular culture, this series encourages students to appreciate cultural diversity and critically analyze issues of enduring significance.

Most importantly, these books are as entertaining as they are provocative. Is Disneyland a more influential icon of the American West than Las Vegas? How do ghosts and ghouls reflect our collective psyche? Is Barry Bonds an inspiring or deplorable icon of baseball? Designed to foster debate, the series serves as a unique resource that is ideal for paper writing or report purposes. Insightful, in-depth entries provide far more information than conventional reference articles but are less intimidating and more accessible than a book-length biography. The most revered and reviled icons of

American and world history are brought to life with related sidebars, time-lines, fact boxes, and quotations. Authoritative entries are accompanied by bibliographies, making these titles an ideal starting point for further research. Spanning a wide range of popular topics, including business, literature, civil rights, politics, music, and more, books in the Greenwood Icons series provide fresh insights for the student and popular reader into the power and influence of icons, a topic of as vital interest today as in any previous era.

Preface

According to Dictionary.com, an icon is a sign or representation, an important and enduring symbol, or one who is the object of great attention and devotion. Protest is defined as an expression or declaration of objection, disapproval, or dissent.

The twenty-four individuals featured in this book, *Icons of African American Protest: Trailblazing Activists of the Civil Rights Movement,* are worthy of renown (and sometimes notoriety) because of their extraordinary contributions to the enduring fight against racism, injustice, and discrimination. Many are recognizable, such as Dr. Martin Luther King, Jr., Rosa Parks, and Malcolm X. Others, like Al Sharpton and Jesse Jackson, remain at the forefront of black protest in the twenty-first century. The fact that others, such as Ida B. Wells-Barnett, James Farmer, and Elaine Brown, are less well known does not diminish the magnitude of their contribution; it simply illuminates the need to reexamine the heroes from the past.

The purpose of the present work is therefore two-fold. First, it fills in the gaps on the shelf by focusing on lesser-known individuals like Ida B. Wells-Barnett, an urbane "lady" who launched an unprecedented crusade against lynching in the early twentieth century. Second, it provides background and corollary material on truly famous individuals such as King and Parks. School textbooks highlight achievements and experiences of some African American leaders, but, due to space limitations, they often lack the depth that makes these figures come alive. These life stories, when told in detail as these two volumes strive to do, accomplish much: they reveal the extraordinary strength and sacrifice displayed by courageous men and women for the cause of freedom and civil rights; they provide in-depth information on the century-long battle that was waged against gross injustice to supplement the more general information that is available elsewhere; and they help insure that these incredible individuals are never forgotten.

The exploration of the lives of these great men and women was, for me, alternately alarming, extremely difficult to stomach, inspiring, and spellbinding. I often felt as if I were mingling with mythic heroes from some strange, frightening, and tumultuous past. At other times, their humanity—their insecurities, weaknesses, fears, ideological shifts, problematic marriages and divorces, illnesses, and exhaustion—exposed them as flawed and fragile. The climate in which they toiled, the obstacles they faced, were intensely harrowing, and their victories were all too infrequent. Still, they persevered.

The personalities of these leaders cover a broad spectrum of descriptors—vibrant, tame, intense, aggressive, and diffident—and their politics run the gamut from conservative to ultra-radical. Nevertheless, whatever techniques, modes, or tactics employed—Thurgood Marshall's legal fights in the courtroom, Dr. King's reliance on nonviolent civil disobedience and direct action, or Huey P. Newton's advocacy of armed self-defense—they were all, in their time, radicals who strove against a climate of racism, discrimination, exclusion, oppression, violent abuse, ignorance, and neglect.

Many surprising commonalities are revealed by a comparison of the individual essays. A. Philip Randolph, James Farmer, Martin Luther King, Dorothy Height, and Angela Davis were academic superstars—well-educated and raised in relatively advantaged families. Others, like Fannie Lou Hamer and Malcolm X, epitomized the greater portion of African Americans: people with little formal education who hailed from the troublous regions of the South or the ghettos of the North. Due to societal expectations and traditions, most of the well-known activists were male. Most, if not all, had extremely supportive parents who stressed self-esteem, dignity, and pride, and were iconoclasts in their own right and, frequently, leaders in their communities.

In appearance, these icons of African American protest were as diverse as any group of twenty-four in the general population. The conservatives, like Roy Wilkins, wore immaculate suits; the young-adult activists, like Stokely Carmichael, wore overalls with sleeves rolled above the elbows. The rebels of the late 1960s and 1970s wore afros and dashikis, adopted Afrocentric names, and walked with a commanding strut and saluted with a clenched fist.

Despite their differing temperaments, tactics, and ideologies, what most leaders wanted can be summed up by the following statement: We may have a different color skin, but we are still American and deserve and demand the same rights, protection, justice, freedoms, and opportunities as you. These leaders yielded their lives to those who criticized their protestations—or worse, threatened, harassed, beat, jailed, or even martyred them for it. In exchange for their manifold sacrifices, these courageous men and women engendered unparalleled progress.

Protest has always been a catalyst for change, reform, and critical development in society. Indeed, protest is at the cornerstone of America's own birth. Did not the first immigrants help America take its first steps upon the road to greatness when they long ago protested against the oppression of their native government and established new edicts promoting the ideals of freedom and opportunity?

Likewise, since the first African slave was forced to board a ship bound for America, protest has been a major motif in the African American experience. Protest was a critical weapon during the raging violence against blacks following the end of Reconstruction and throughout the Jim Crow years, and against the grisly conditions in the ghettos of the North. It was used to combat economic and political oppression, racism, discrimination, and exclusion from mainstream America.

I believe this text will prove to be user-friendly and of interest and value to students, teachers, researchers, and the general public. To that end, the introduction summarizes the history of African American protest and the conditions that called for remonstration. It is followed by a timeline of relevant events. Entries are presented in alphabetical order, each containing simple sub-headings that introduce childhood, young adulthood, and other milestones in the lives of the activist. Sidebars provide background information on key events, individuals, and organizations. Symbols are provided for important themes such as the freedom song "We Shall Overcome," the clenched fist of the Black Power Movement, and the lynching noose. At the end of each entry, there is a "See also" section and a "Further Resources" section to provide additional sources of information—both print and electronic—for each icon.

Also provided are several appendices, including historical documents, quotes from the icons of protest themselves, a bibliography, a chronology, a glossary, and a detailed subject index. Words defined in the glossary are boldfaced the first time they appear in any of the essays.

Acknowledgments

Special thanks go to so many people who have made this encyclopedia possible. I deeply appreciate Greenwood Publishing for their commitment to important subjects such as this one. This is the opportunity of a lifetime. I have been a voracious student of African American history since Mrs. Wotton facilitated a high school course on U.S. History, where I learned about slavery, the Civil War, Reconstruction, and the Civil Rights Movement. It was Mrs. Wotton who helped a group of us take a trip to the nation's capital, where we stood on the very steps where Martin Luther King thundered out his famous "I Have a Dream" speech before an enthralled sea of some 250,000 people at the March on Washington for Jobs and Freedom in 1963.

I am deeply thankful to Michael Hermann and Shana Grob-Jones, with whom I have had the great pleasure to work since 2002. Editors Kristi Ward and John Wagner have been extraordinarily helpful every step of the way of this project. I would also like to extend my heartfelt appreciation to editors of other Greenwood books: Hans Ostrom, J. David Macey, Anand Prahlad, Richard Zuczek, Walter Rucker, James Nathaniel, and all the behind-the-scenes players who have facilitated the publication and promotion of this volume. To Ellen Larson, a brilliant writer and indispensable adviser, encourager, and friend, I say thank you, thank you, thank you. You are absolutely the best.

Special thanks to Teri Knight, a graduate of Spelman College and University of Michigan, who currently teaches high school English in Chicago, for writing the compelling introduction.

To the remarkable individuals and activists I have known: the Black Student Union (BSU) president, who constructed a list of demands—including an appeal to diversify our predominately white campus—and gave them to the dean at a BSU meeting; the dean, who was at that meeting and listened patiently and responded accordingly; my mother, who participated in boycotts and sit-ins; Ursula, who wrote a paper on Malcolm X and received a failing grade because the teacher did not like her subject choice; Jackie Coard, who founded the first African American Museum in the state of Washington; the courageous museum board that gave of their time, energy, and ideas; Jessica and Najja, who protested against the blackface performances on their university campus; the University of Puget Sound, which hosted the 2006 National Race and Pedagogy Conference; the chair of that conference and acclaimed author, Dexter Gordon; and the mother who challenged an entire public school system to be more inclusive of other cultures and address racially charged incidents. To all of you, I say thank you for your contributions and bravery.

My parents, Larry and Mary Gipson, my sisters Ursula and Teri, and countless prayers were a boundless source of strength, encouragement, and inspiration. Thank you to all the friends who provided support and patiently accepted rain checks for dinners and movie outings; to Derrick Pinckney, a great artist and sounding board; to my undergraduate advisor, David Droge, one of the best thinkers, doers, and professors I know; and to so many, many more, including you, the reader, whom I hope will be as profoundly moved as I was by the lives of these extraordinary icons.

Introduction: Icons and Protestors of the Twentieth Century

> The need for change bulldozed a road down the center of my mind.
> From Maya Angelou's *I Know Why the Caged Bird Sings*

Any living soul—sighted or blind—at any point in the twentieth century has been an eyewitness to protest. Yet what does protest sound like? How does it taste? Can you smell it in the air? Or feel it in your bones? In her 1969 autobiographical work, *I Know Why the Caged Bird Sings*, Maya Angelou recalls the moment when protest awakened her to act upon the racial injustices that she faced growing up in Stamps, Arkansas. Angelou poetically asserts this universal truth: Activism is a powerful inherent force that seeks to eliminate obstacles and create paths. Protest intersects oppositional elements to effect change: visibility and invisibility, external and internal influences, immediacy and patience, force and nonviolence. Civil disobedience is the road that leads to equality.

African American protest, as all African American history, has its roots in slavery. In *The People Could Fly*, Virginia Hamilton recounts a version of the African folktale about slaves who desired freedom from an oppressive master. In Hamilton's version, an old African slave whispers words to help other African slaves fly to freedom. When he is caught, the old African slave flies away, unable to help all the slaves escape; however, he leaves the witnesses with a story to tell their children.

In the folktale, the destination of the flying Africans is freedom in Africa; in the mind of black America's greatest activists, freedom is equality and dignity. Traditionally, the greatness of any protest begins with the magic of words from one who possesses the keen insights of the universe. Few are bestowed with this knowledge; furthermore, the opportunities for change must be taken in an instant with a simple action of grand consequence. It was this way for the flying Africans who escaped the fields of the brutal overseer, and it has been this way for African Americans in the twentieth century seeking justice in their communities, workplaces, schools, prisons, and courts.

EARLY TWENTIETH-CENTURY PROTEST

Protest grew up watching his parents being cheated in the game of share-cropping. The white man permitted his absence from school to help on the farm. He might eventually drop out of school to work in the field alongside his parents; in the evening, Activism listened to his grandparents tell stories about slavery. Protest made clothes out of flour sacks, and when the sole black doctor's penicillin was not enough, Activism used the leaves of a peach tree to draw out fever. As a young man, Protest looked for the words to help free the souls of black folk as he fought to expose and end brutal lynching, which claimed thousands of freedom seekers each year. Leaving Injustice to chirp in the warm, damp night, those who could flew north. In great numbers, they filled southern cities in the North, where Injustice lived in cramped spaces in tall buildings and walked surreptitiously down crowded avenues. Black Activism looked back to Africa. He wrote about the crisis. Protest organized labor unions for his brothers and watched his sisters fight for women's rights. He founded associations and leagues to assist his brothers and sisters in every fight. At night, Activism dreamt about the mule's burden and of peeling back the husk of the sorghum cane and sucking out the sweetness of molasses.

MID-CENTURY PROTEST: JIM CROW AND THE CIVIL RIGHTS ERA

Halfway through the century, the restlessness of Activism increased. Jim Crow told blacks to order and eat their meals in the back of the restaurant, drink from different fountains, use dirty restrooms, and defer to whites in all situations. For many African Americans, segregated schools held secondhand textbooks and insufficient materials. To read and write, black students borrowed one of the school's encyclopedias and wrote reports about English heroes like Sir Walter Raleigh. The white man said to teach black girls to cook and clean and teach black boys to farm; however, many black teachers knew the secret of the old African slave and taught their students more than just the curriculum. Black students learned that they were not inferior to whites. High school graduates of the middle decades could dream of traveling the world, practicing law or medicine, and teaching, but the wake-up reality was fraught with institutional racism and blatant and subtle prejudice.

Increasingly frustrated with the raw end of Jim Crow's deal, Protest aggressively sought school integration, formed committees, held conferences, and relied on the foundation of the association and the league. In 1961, Activism soared down the nation's interstates singing spirituals in the key of militancy, seeking the elusive balance of peace, equality, and unity. Protest cooked breakfast for little black kids on their way to school. Protest marched, was beaten and jailed, all the while singing freedom's songs, wearing an afro and straightened hair with waves and tight curls, a dashiki, a dress, or a suit with a bow-tie. The face of freedom wore sideburns, seldom smiled, and declared, "By any means necessary."

Activism became one of the greatest leaders to teach nonviolence. He was a brave king who traveled the streets blacks were not supposed to travel and sat at counters where blacks were not supposed to sit. From the Lincoln Memorial in Washington, Protest shouted the words of the old African slave that lifted his ancestors in the sky, and watched the hundreds of thousands before him ascend from the lawn surrounding the reflecting pool. The great granddaughters of slaves looked white people in the eye and refused to say "yes ma'am" or "yes suh" and sat wherever they wanted on the bus. When these civil descendents went to lunch downtown, they were told, "We don't serve niggers." They replied, "Well, we don't eat niggers either." Protest raised a sole fist and shed his and her own blood for dignity.

Activism worked hard just to survive; Protest worked harder to survive *and* get an education. Continually ignored for promotions and raises, Activism helped create jobs and demand federal aid for social programs. Activism moved to predominantly white neighborhoods. While her little black children played with white neighbor children, Protest kept a gun in her apron and watched the white parents. In an integrated school, Black Activism astonished her white teacher and classmates, who thought she was inept, when she recited British poet William Ernest Henley's "Invictus." Protest is unconquerable; it is the grass that grows through the crack in the sidewalk.

Up North, if you were a black man or woman, Injustice might smile in your face and stab you in the back, but you were *North* where promised advantages and expectations hovered just within a fight's reach; down South, you knew where you stood, and you also knew you did not have to stand there—and with a mustard seed's faith, you moved to your rightful place. Activism was not born with second-class spirits. As Jim Crow staggered out and Integration pressed in, Protest took a glimpse of freedom's face.

END-OF-THE-CENTURY PROTEST

Near the close of the twentieth century, urban blight, poverty, and a host of political issues—including the Vietnam War—collided with the noble objectives of the Civil Rights Movement and produced a kaleidoscope of detrimental social problems.

Growing up during the middle of the twentieth century, Protest had known that his future held prison or death at the hands of a white man, so Protest bulldozed his way through the ranks of the military, serving his country in Vietnam as an officer in the Marines. While stationed in Germany, Private Protest fought unequal treatment from white officers. Using the Army's own chain of command, Protest stated his case in appropriate sequence to each officer, breaking one shackle at a time. Protest knew someone had to listen. Meanwhile, back home, Activism enraged the Old Boys Network when he was elected as mayor of his hometown and encouraged his friend Protest to become a member of the city council. Multifarious firsts in many corporate and political arenas inspired Activism; at the same time, the imprisoned and economically disadvantaged demanded Protest's energy.

Constructive, affirmative, realistic, and injurious images of African Americans blazed across televisions, movie screens, and theater stages. The alphabet organizations of the Civil Rights Movement seemed archived in history's black-and-white photographic memory as the complexity of Modern Injustice attempted to disown his Jim Crow roots. The materialistic lullaby of the late twentieth century provided a false comfort and a divisive—too often violent—element that turned black on black in ways that had not been seen before.

Heartened by Amiri Baraka's "Wise 1," Protest carves another Baraka title, "SOS," into the wooden desk that holds his young mind in history class. For this offense, he finds himself in detention writing a film script. His desire to share those flying words rattles off his tongue with lightning speed. Activism professes flying stories to college students and pushes a coalition around the world advocating, mediating, and encouraging others with the words of the old African slave. Although February celebrates freedom's heroes in twenty-eight or twenty-nine days a year, Activism rides the bus to the state capital on black legislature day and fights for juvenile justice every day. Protest's spark still burns and marches against police brutality and gang violence.

PROTEST IN THE NEW MILLENNIUM

At the dawn of the twenty-first century, technology has expanded Protest's means of communication and audiences; thus, the need for social change, too, grows exponentially. African Americans continue to respond to the voices of their predecessors in struggle, using every available medium: film, fiction, philanthropy, and even the information highway. Activism lives in the voices of university professors, community organizers, ministers, artists, presidential candidates, CEOs, and judges. The "who," "what," "when," "where," and "how" may be different, but the "why" remains the same—justice. The ability to acknowledge the essential equality of each human being is honorable, noble, and good; the ability to help others recognize that innate sameness is most honorable, the noblest, the purest good.

As Americans continue to see barriers broken in all areas from city officials to the highest elected positions in the country, we must remain diligent in our responsibility to share these stories of protest and activism with our children. If we are to survive, the spirit of protest that resides within all of us must be nourished in our children. The cost of passive assimilation and complacency is too high. We must teach our children to identify and follow the voice within that seeks positive change and inspires others to seek the same. We must encourage our children to develop the strength to admonish naysayers with an unavoidable truth: freedom elevates all of humanity.

Teri Knight

Chronology of African American Protest

SLAVERY AND RESISTANCE TO 1877

1619	First record of Africans brought to North America as indentured servants.
1644	Black slaves successfully petition for freedom in New Netherlands (later New York).
1708	African slaves revolt in Newton, Long Island, and are punished by death.
1738	Fugitive slaves from the southern English colonies live with the Creek Indians in Georgia and the Spanish in Florida.
1739	Following the Stono slave rebellion in South Carolina, thirty enslaved Angolans elude capture for up to thirty years.
1780	Elizabeth Freeman sues for her freedom in Massachusetts.
1787	Richard Allen and Absalom Jones establish the Philadelphia Free African Society, one of the first free all-black societies formed to advocate black separatism and self-help programs.
	Slavery is made illegal in the Northwest Territory, i.e., the territory soon to comprise the states of Ohio, Indiana, Illinois, Michigan, and Wisconsin.
1793	Fugitive slave law enacted that requires escaped slaves to return to their slave owners.
1800	Gabriel Prosser leads a slave revolt in Richmond, Virginia.
1804	New Jersey is the last state in the North to abolish slavery.
	Ohio becomes one of the first northern states to enact discriminatory black laws against free blacks.
1808	Congress bans the importation of African slaves.
1812–1840s	More than three decades of white riots against African Americans and abolitionists in the North.
1814	Paul Cuffee, one of the earliest proponents of the Back-to-Africa Movement, transports thirty-four blacks to Sierra Leone.

1816	Richard Allen founds the African Methodist Episcopal Church in Philadelphia.
1817	African Americans in Philadelphia protest the American Colonization Society (ACS), an organization formed to transport blacks back to Africa.
1820	The Missouri Compromise bans slavery north of the southern boundary of Missouri.
1821	The ACS establishes the colony of Liberia in West Africa for blacks.
1822	Denmark Vessey leads a slave revolt in South Carolina.
1830	The first national black convention is held in the North to address issues such as slavery, voting rights, and integration.
1831	Nat Turner leads a slave revolt in Southampton County, Virginia.
1839	Africans revolt on the Spanish schooner *Amistad* but are recaptured during their attempt to return to Africa. Slave revolts, as well as suicide, were common forms of African resistance to slavery during the Middle Passage.
1841	Abolitionists play an instrumental role in freeing the Africans of the *Amistad* after they had been recaptured.
1843	Henry Highland Garnet, a militant abolitionist, delivers "Address to the Slaves" at the National Convention of Colored Citizens in Buffalo, New York.
1845	Frederick Douglass publishes *The Narrative of the Life of Frederick Douglass: An American Slave,* the first of three autobiographies.
1846	Frederick Douglass, a former slave and prominent African American abolitionist, founds *The North Star.*
1849	Harriet Tubman escapes slavery and becomes a major leader in the Underground Railroad Movement.
1851	A large migration of African Americans to Canada begins and lasts eight years.
1857	U.S. Supreme Court rules in the Dred Scott case that African Americans are not citizens.
1861	Civil War begins.
1863	President Abraham Lincoln issues the Emancipation Proclamation, bestowing freedom to all slaves within Confederate territory.
1865	Civil War ends with the defeat of the Confederacy. Following the end of the Civil War, embittered southerners violently attack newly freed slaves. President Abraham Lincoln is assassinated. Major General Gordon Granger announces in Galveston, Texas, that the slaves are free.

	Congress ratifies the Thirteenth Amendment to the United States Constitution, officially abolishing slavery.
1866	Black codes are established throughout the South, severely restricting the rights of African Americans. African Americans, known as the Exodusters, migrate to Kansas in response to the violence, racism, and oppression of the South. Other migrations occur from the rural South to the Urban South, to the West, and to the North. In Tennessee, ex-Confederates establish the Ku Klux Klan, one of numerous racist white organizations in the South.
1866–1868	During Reconstruction, schools for blacks are established and civil rights acts are passed. The South is divided into five military districts. African American politicians are elected for the first time ever in the South. Congress ratifies the Fourteenth Amendment to the United States Constitution, granting citizenship, due process, and equal protection to former slaves. Following a fiery speech of protest against the passing of a bill to remove African Americans from political office, Henry McNeil Turner leads a walkout from the capitol building in Georgia.
1870	Congress ratifies the Fifteenth Amendment to the United States Constitution, giving black men the right to vote.
1875	Congress enacts the Civil Rights Act of 1875, guaranteeing African Americans the right to equal access to public accommodations.

BLACK NADIR, 1877–1901

1877	Reconstruction ends in the South. Most of the gains received during Reconstruction are eliminated when political power is returned to conservative Democrats.
1878	Martin R. Delany is one of the sponsors for the Liberian Exodus Joint Stock Steamship Company, which is formed to help transport black Southerners to Liberia.
1886	A race riot occurs in Washington County, Texas.
1890	The beginning of the era of the black women's club movement.
1892	The lynching of three African American owners of the People's Grocery Company is the impetus for Ida B. Wells' anti-lynching campaign.
1896	The Supreme Court rules in *Plessy v. Ferguson* that racial segregation is constitutional. The Jim Crow era begins. The National Association of Colored Women is formed.

1898	Race riots break out in Phoenix, South Carolina and Wilmington, North Carolina.

EARLY CIVIL RIGHTS MOVEMENT, 1901–1955

1905	W.E.B. Du Bois, William Monroe Trotter, and others found the Niagara Movement.
1906	Race riot in Brownsville, Texas.
	Race riot in Atlanta, Georgia.
1908	Race riot in Springfield, Illinois.
1909	The National Association for the Advancement of Colored People (NAACP) is founded in New York.
1910	W.E.B. Du Bois founds *The Crisis,* the official magazine of the NAACP.
	The National Urban League is founded in New York.
	The Great Migration, a mass exodus of blacks from the South to cities in the North, begins.
	Ida B. Wells founds the Alpha Suffrage Club of Chicago, the first African American suffrage association.
1914	Marcus Garvey establishes the Universal Negro Improvement Association.
1915	D.W. Griffith releases the *Birth of a Nation.* The NAACP is among the protesters of this film.
1917	United States enters World War I.
	Race riot in East St. Louis, Illinois and Houston, Texas.
	Marcus Garvey delivers the address "The Conspiracy of the East St. Louis Riots."
	A. Philip Randolph and Chandler Owen establish the *Messenger.*
1918	Marcus Garvey establishes the *Negro World.*
1919	Race riots in Chicago, Illinois and Elaine, Arkansas.
1920	Congress ratifies the Nineteenth Amendment to the United States Constitution, giving women the right to vote.
	Harlem, New York is the birthplace of the Harlem Renaissance, a period of intense developments in African American art, literature, and music.
1921	Race riot in Tulsa, Oklahoma.
1923	Race riot in Rosewood, Florida.
1930	The *Chicago Tribune* reports that 3,437 black men and 76 black women were lynched in America between the years 1882 and 1930.
1931	Nine black youths are accused of raping two white women in the Scottsboro case.

1941	President Franklin D. Roosevelt signs Executive Order 8802, mandating equal employment in defense plants and federal jobs. A. Philip Randolph plays a leading role in this victory.
1941	United States enters World War II.
1942	James L. Farmer and others found the Congress of Racial Equality (CORE).
1947	CORE participates in the Journey of Reconciliation.
1948	A. Philip Randolph plays a leading role in the protests that lead to President Harry S. Truman issuing an executive order to integrate the U.S. Armed Forces and the creation of a Fair Employment Board.
1952	Malcolm X becomes a minister of the Nation of Islam and advocates black nationalism, black separatism, and militancy.
1954	Thurgood Marshall is one of the attorneys in *Brown v. Board of Education of Topeka*, which declares that racial segregation in schools is unconstitutional.
1955	Roy Wilkins is named executive director of the NAACP.

MODERN CIVIL RIGHTS MOVEMENT, 1955–1965

1955	Fourteen-year-old Emmett Till is lynched for allegedly whistling at a white woman in Mississippi. The two men charged with the crime are acquitted by an all-white jury.
	Following Rosa Parks' refusal to give up her seat to a white passenger on a bus in Montgomery, Alabama, Dr. Martin Luther King, Jr. leads a triumphant bus boycott.
1957	The Southern Christian Leadership Conference (SCLC) is formed.
	Ella Baker and Bayard Rustin co-organize the Prayer Pilgrimage.
	Eleven hundred paratroopers and the state national guard provide protection for the first black students to integrate Little Rock Central High School in Arkansas.
	Dorothy Height becomes President of the National Council of Negro Women.
1960	Four African American students conduct a sit-in at a Woolworth's in Greensboro, North Carolina.
	The Student Nonviolent Coordinating Committee (SNCC) is founded.
1961	President John F. Kennedy issues Executive Order 10925, creating the Committee on Equal Employment Opportunity and mandating affirmative action to ensure that hiring and employment practices are nondiscriminatory.

CORE and SNCC conduct freedom rides to test the new laws that prohibit segregation in interstate travel facilities.

1962   James Meredith is the first African American to enroll at the University of Mississippi. Rioting ensues, and President Kennedy sends 5,000 federal troops in response.

1962   Robert F. Williams' _Radio Free Dixie_ airs from Cuba.

1963   During civil rights demonstrations in Birmingham, Alabama, fire hoses and police dogs are used against activists.

Martin Luther King, Jr. writes the famous "Letter from Birmingham Jail."

Children are attacked and arrested at a "Children's Crusade."

Medgar Evers, a field secretary for Mississippi's NAACP, is murdered outside his home.

Martin Luther King, Jr. delivers his famous "I Have a Dream" speech at the March on Washington for Jobs and Freedoms.

Four young African American girls are killed when a bomb explodes at the Sixteenth Street Baptist Church in Birmingham, Alabama.

President John F. Kennedy is assassinated.

1964   Fannie Lou Hamer assists with the Freedom Summer project for voter registration, involving the Council of Federated Organizations (CORE, SNCC, SCLC, and NAACP).

Three civil rights workers are murdered by the Ku Klux Klan.

Deacons for Defense and Justice is founded.

President Lyndon B. Johnson signs the Civil Rights Act of 1964, eradicating segregation laws.

Martin Luther King, Jr. receives the Nobel Peace Prize.

President Lyndon B. Johnson presents War on Poverty Program in his State of the Union Address.

Congress ratifies the Twenty-Fourth Amendment, abolishing the poll tax, which was created to deter black voting.

BLACK POWER MOVEMENT, 1965–1976

1965   American military involvement in the Vietnam War begins.

Malcolm X is assassinated.

State troopers violently attack demonstrators led by Martin Luther King, Jr., as they march to Selma. This incident is known as "Bloody Sunday."

LeRoi Jones establishes the Black Arts Repertory Theater, prompting the Black Arts Movement and inspiring a massive appeal to Black Consciousness.

Congress passes the Voting Rights Act of 1965, eliminating discriminatory voting laws.

African Americans riot in Watts, California.

President Johnson issues Executive Order 11246, establishing affirmative action.

President Johnson proposes the Great Society Program during his State of the Union Address.

1966 Stokely Carmichael presents his first "Black Power" speech.

Huey Newton and Bobby Seale found the Black Panthers.

1967 Fifty-nine riots erupt in cities in the North.

Major race riots take place in Newark, New Jersey and Detroit, Michigan.

The Supreme Court rules in *Loving v. Virginia* that prohibiting interracial marriage is unconstitutional.

President Johnson appoints Thurgood Marshall to the U.S. Supreme Court.

The first National Black Power Conference is held in Newark, New Jersey.

1968 The Kerner Commission releases a report on their findings of what caused African American rioting.

Martin Luther King, Jr. is assassinated in Memphis, Tennessee. Riots erupt soon after in more than 100 U.S. cities.

President Johnson signs the Civil Rights Act of 1968, prohibiting discrimination in the sale, rental, and financing of housing.

1969 Student strikes result in the first black studies program at San Francisco State College.

1969 James Forman of SNCC interrupts worship services at Riverside Church in New York to present the Black Manifesto.

1970 Black feminism emerges.

1971 Jesse Jackson founds People United to Save Humanity (PUSH).

1972 First National Black Political Convention in Gary, Indiana.

Angela Davis is acquitted of kidnapping, murder, and conspiracy concerning an escape attempt at Marin County Hall of Justice.

1974 Elaine Brown becomes the first and only woman leader of the Black Panthers.

1976 A riot takes place in Pensacola, Florida.

MODERN PROTESTS, 1980–

1980 African Americans riot in Miami.

Molefi Kete Asante publishes *Afrocentricity*.

1982	African Americans riot in Miami.
1989	Spike Lee releases *Do the Right Thing*.
1992	African Americans riot in south-central Los Angeles after a jury acquits four white police officers for the videotaped beating of African American Rodney King.
	Maxine Waters, Democratic member of the United States House of Representatives, is a voice for rioters in Los Angeles.
	Spike Lee releases *Malcolm X*.
1995	Louis Farrakhan holds Million Man March in Washington, D.C.
1996	California becomes the first of several states to ban affirmative action in college admissions and state contracts.
1997	John Singleton releases the film *Rosewood*, based on the race riot that occurred there in 1923.
	Spike Lee releases the documentary *4 Little Girls* about the 1965 bombing of the Sixteenth Street Baptist Church in Birmingham.
	Million Woman March takes place in Philadelphia.
2000	Tavis Smiley and Tom Joyner co-host the first of annual town hall meetings called "The State of the Black Union."
2005	Millions More March is held in Washington, D.C. to commemorate the tenth anniversary of the Million Man March.
2006	Spike Lee releases *When the Levees Broke: A Requiem in Four Acts*, a documentary on the Hurricane Katrina tragedy in New Orleans.
	Jesse Jackson leads campaign against the use of the N-word.
	Jesse Jackson leads a rally and march in New Orleans. The theme is "The Right to Return, Vote, and Rebuild."

Spike Lee (1957–)

Spike Lee is a film director, producer, writer, and actor. Spike Lee speaks his mind. He also produces controversial films, several of which deal with **racism**, skin color prejudice, racial violence, and radical activists like Malcolm X and Huey P. Newton. One of his films explores the tragedy of the four little black girls who died in the 16th Street Baptist Church in Birmingham, Alabama when it was bombed during the tumultuous Civil Rights Movement. Lee asserts that he is not a "spokesperson" for African Americans, but he certainly is ever ready to defend them. For example, in the spring of 2008 he criticized Clint Eastwood, director and longtime actor famous for his squinty-eyed, husky-voiced portrayals, for not including African Americans in his 2006 World War II movie *Flags of Our Fathers*. At the time he brought Eastwood's omission to light, Lee's latest film, *Miracle at St. Anna,* about African American soldiers who fought in Italy during the same war, was still in production. It was due to premiere in the fall of 2008.

Lee's dedication to bringing the black experience and its legacy of protest to the big screen calls to mind the words of Ida B. Wells-Barnett. The aging activist met a twenty-five-year-old African American woman who knew the name "Ida B. Wells" but did not know what made people revere her. Wells-Barnett wrote, in her autobiography, "I realized that one reason she did not know me was because the happenings about which she inquired took place before she was born. Another was that there was no record from which she could inform herself." And so Wells-Barnett set out to chronicle her life and achievements, most notably as the pioneer of a spectacular anti-lynching campaign (Duster, 3, 4). There are reasons for the lack of information. Patricia A. Schecter, a Wells-Barnett scholar, determined that writing about resistance in Wells-Barnett's day, "seemed to invite disregard, misunderstanding, or even punishment" (Schecter, 7). Indeed, when Wells-Barnett wrote an article castigating the lynching of the three black men who owned the People's Grocery Store, in Memphis, Tennessee, in 1891, she became a marked woman and eventually chose to settle in the North rather than face the potentially fatal consequences of living in the South.

Lee too faces repercussions, both for his remarks and his radical films. For instance, in response to Lee's criticism of *Flags of Our Fathers* (2006), Eastwood told him to "shut his face," explaining that the film was historically accurate, "that black troops were not involved in raising the flag at Iwo Jima." Lee would also contend that his radicalness has cost him in others ways, such as the biting reviews he has received, the lack of recognition by the powers-that-be in Hollywood, and, sometimes, the trouble he has experienced trying to secure funding for his films. And yet he is one of only a few African Americans to have attained great fame, influence, and status as a moviemaker and in popular culture, especially considering his track record of controversy and his almost exclusive focus on black life.

Like Wells-Barnett, Lee's crusade appears to be to educate blacks as well as America as a whole. But he has other objectives. For example, he strives to spark dialogue, to raise critical issues, and to bring to light those historical events that have shaped today's America that have been neglected or glossed over. Lest we forget or are too young to know what so many sacrificed and fought for, he makes his films. He has also inspired an array of books that describe his personal struggles during the process of moviemaking and how he became the giant he is.

GROWING UP IN THE CIVIL RIGHTS ERA

When Shelton Jackson Lee was born, on March 20, 1957, in Atlanta, Georgia, African Americans were anything but powerful and influential. Although the famous *Brown v. Board of Education* ruling in 1954 prohibited segregated schools in the South, real change came about slowly and not without struggle and hardship.

In the South, conservative whites prevented blacks from voting through discriminatory laws and practices such as poll taxes, literacy tests, and other means—not excluding violence and intimidation. Blacks who registered to vote lost their jobs, or were harassed and threatened. In the South, Jim Crow laws segregated blacks from whites. There were separate parks, restrooms, hospitals, and other facilities for blacks and whites. In department stores, blacks could not try on clothes before they purchased them. In the North, segregation was generally prohibited, but it did not stop some whites from practicing Jim Crow when they could. In the North and South, rampant discrimination affected housing, job opportunity, and advancement. In the South, blacks could only attain top positions within the all-black segregated communities. In a world dominated by whites, blacks were relegated to second-class status, limited to menial jobs, and made less money than whites working in the same field. Unlike twenty-first–century America, blacks could not advance into positions of power, such as mayors, doctors (in mainstream hospitals), police chiefs, or run for president of the United States. In 2008, Barack Obama, the third black U.S. senator since **Reconstruction** (1862–1877), became the first African American to win the Democratic nomination for president and the first serious black candidate in either mainstream party.

In this context, Shelton was not like most other blacks. His parents had college degrees, and so did their parents, and at least one great-grandparent before them. His mom, Jacquelyn, was a schoolteacher, and his dad, Bill, was a jazz composer who played in various clubs. Bill had graduated from Morehouse College, a black college (known as an HBCU, for historically black colleges and universities). He was a freshman there when Dr. Martin Luther King, Jr. was a senior. King was only fifteen years old when he entered Morehouse and just nineteen when he graduated with a B.A. in sociology. King went on to graduate from Crozer Theological Seminary and

Historically Black Colleges and Universities

Historically black colleges and universities (HBCUs) are institutions that were established specifically for African Americans prior to the enactment of the Higher Education Act of 1965. HBCUs were created to fill the need for educational institutions for blacks, since Jim Crow laws prohibited African Americans from attending white colleges and universities. Many HBCUs were funded by private individuals and organizations, churches, and federal grants.

The first black college, the Institute for Colored Youth, was founded by a Quaker named Richard Humphreys in Philadelphia, Pennsylvania in 1837. However, the majority of black colleges and universities are located in the South and were established after the Civil War (1861–1865). Indeed the creation of the HBCUs, as well as schools for children, was arguably the most substantial action undertaken to assist freed slaves during Reconstruction (1863–1877). There are currently 110 historically black institutions of higher learning in the United States.

The HBCUs have had an uneven relationship with black activism. Many professors advanced social activism and played a part in inspiring future black leaders. A large number of black activist leaders attended historically black colleges and universities for undergraduate study. At Fisk University in Tennessee, W.E.B. Du Bois developed his concept of the Talented Tenth, i.e., the need for gifted black leaders to guide the black community toward racial, economic, and social improvement. Du Bois later taught for several years at Atlanta University, an HBCU. Others who attended HBCUs include Dr. Martin Luther King, Jr., president of the Southern Christian Leadership Conference; Jesse Jackson, founder of Rainbow/Push; and Robert F. Williams, who headed an armed self-defense organization and led demonstrations in North Carolina. One of the most famous associations with an HBCU was the landmark sit-in by North Carolina Agricultural and Technical students Ezell Blair, Jr., Franklin McCain, Joseph McNeil, and David Richmond.

Notwithstanding the legacy of activism and HBCUs, administrators at black universities and colleges were often leery of getting involved with the Civil Rights Movement. Wealthy conservative whites who helped fund the institutions or served on the boards of directors frequently thwarted activism on campus. When Whitney Young, executive director of the National Urban League, taught at Atlanta University in Georgia in the 1960s, the then-president was anxious to quell student sit-in demonstrations.

HBCUs remain an integral part of the history and traditions of African Americans. Black institutions still rank high with black youths considering college, although blacks from outside the South sometimes have trouble transitioning due to differences and perceptions associated with blacks living in predominately white communities.

(continued)

Black students who choose to attend predominately white institutions also have a host of issues to contend with in terms of racial tolerance and sensitivity, and of simply fitting in. For instance, in the 1960s and 1970s, black students led protests to employ black professors, as well as to include diversity (such as black studies programs) in the academic curriculum. Substantial progress in this area has been made at some institutions, but still languishes at others to this day.

Boston University. In 1955, he would lead his first major civil rights campaign, the Montgomery Bus Boycott. Other demonstrations followed in towns in the South, such as Albany, Georgia, Birmingham, Alabama, and St. Augustine, Florida. He also initiated campaigns in the North beginning in 1966, a few years before his assassination on April 4, 1968.

Of the two parents, Jacquelyn appeared to be the most racially conscious. Her initial understanding of race pride came from her mother, Zimmie Shelton. In the early twentieth century, when the only race that mattered or was represented in the American media was the white race, this was no easy task. When blacks were represented, say, on television or in a song, it was in a derogatory way. Jacquelyn's mom only permitted her to play with black dolls, even though they were made to look less attractive than the white dolls. She also painted the white faces on cards brown so it would reflect her own color. In this way, Zimmie Shelton demonstrated to her daughter that she was of value too.

Jacquelyn and Shelton lived in Atlanta with Jacquelyn's grandmother, while Bill worked in Chicago, where there was more work to be found for a bass player than in Georgia. It was around this time, while still a baby, that Shelton received his moniker, Spike. Jacqueline attributed his nickname to his toughness, and it stuck.

In 1958, mother and son moved to Chicago, thus circumventing Jim Crow and the perilous South. In the following year, his brother Chris was born, and Bill convinced Jacquelyn that New York was the place to be. Most of his music friends and others he had heard about had moved to New York. Undoubtedly, he believed that New York promised better and more opportunities than Chicago. So the Lees packed up their belongings and headed east, settling in Crown Heights, a neighborhood in the borough (as it is called) of Brooklyn, in New York City. The Lees were the first African American family to live there. Most everyone else was Italian, which, in those days, was not unusual. Despite the fact that Jim Crow was unlawful, the North was still heavily segregated in most aspects of life. Generally, when blacks moved into previously all-white communities, trouble, harassment, and calamity were sure to follow.

As a toddler, Spike was not aware of what those early days, months, and years were like for his parents in the predominately Italian neighborhood. The few incidents, like when his parents were called "niggers" by neighbors, that did occur were relatively mild compared to events in the South, or in other, more racially hostile, areas in New York. Spike's brother David and sister Joy were born in 1961 and 1962, respectively. In those years, blacks in the South, especially those activists who tried to force integration upon conservative whites using the new tactics of sit-ins and **picketing,** lived in daily peril of harassment and violence. They endured heckling, being spat upon, and having food thrown at them. Some blacks who lived too close to white neighborhoods were regularly terrorized by nightriders.

In other parts of New York, the enmity between blacks and whites (and other racial groups such as Italians and Jews) was so intense that neither side dared enter the other's neighborhood (except to provoke a fight) for fear of physical assault or harassment. In this atmosphere, black and white gangs frequently formed. These tensions extended back to the early days of the **Great Migration** (1910–1950), when waves of blacks left the South in search of better jobs and the greater freedoms of the North. Black enclaves known as ghettos sprang up on the outskirts of many northern cities. Whites and other immigrants were exasperated over their presence. Competition over resources, housing, and work (especially given the fact that blacks were paid less than any other race and were, as a result, frequently hired over others) made for explosive encounters.

Spike made friends with young Italian boys in the neighborhood. He went to public school without incident, although he was not allowed to join the Cub Scouts because of the color of his skin. His early years were happy and serene. Jacquelyn and Bill made sure to expose their children to varied and rewarding experiences. All the children received music lessons. Spike learned how to play the violin and the piano. His mother took them to concerts and museums and supplemented his education with lessons in African American history. She brought home books on important black men and women for her children to read so that they would grow up with a strong understanding of their history, and America's history. At school, African American history was barely addressed.

Trips to the South to visit his grandparents added to Spike's awareness of black life and social conditions in the 1960s. Family road trips each summer entailed long drives to Georgia and Alabama, where Spike saw Jim Crow up close. He saw the signs that read "blacks only" and "white only." And he learned about slavery from his relatives, who remembered the tales that had been passed down to them through the generations. Spike's maternal great-great grandparents had been slaves.

Most African American family histories can be traced back to slavery. The first slave ship, carrying human cargo, arrived in America in 1619. By 1804, slavery had been abolished in all northern states. But in the South, white landowners continued to practice slavery. At the end of the Civil War (1861–1865), blacks celebrated their freedom, though some were apprehensive of the future—and for good reason. Civil rights gains and progress for the newly freed slaves turned out to be ephemeral.

A hundred long years later, as Spike and his siblings played games and battled over space in their parent's cramped car heading to and fro on the highways from the North and South, violence erupted throughout the South, a brutal backlash directed at nonviolent demonstrators. Spike was not yet six years old when President John F. Kennedy was assassinated on November 22, 1963. It seemed to many as if nothing had changed. But change was coming, though at great cost and sacrifice for blacks and whites.

Spike was seven years old when President Lyndon B. Johnson signed the landmark Civil Rights Act of 1964 into existence, destroying Jim Crow. The old black- and white-only signs were dismantled across the South, but blacks and whites continued to live in two separate worlds. And the tumult persisted. On February 21, 1965, Malcolm X was assassinated by members of the Nation of Islam.

One of Spike's childhood visits included a trip to Snow Hill, Alabama, where his paternal grandparents lived. Nearby, in Selma, Martin Luther King, Jr. waged a voter registration campaign. But he was absent the day that white mobs and police brutally attacked demonstrators on a Sunday on March 7, 1965. That day, known as "Bloody Sunday," was one of a string of civil rights tragedies that led to the pivotal Voting Rights Act of 1965. Thirteen days after Bloody Sunday, Spike celebrated his eighth birthday, back in New York, where blacks were free to vote. He played baseball and other games with his Italian friends and did not feel the magnitude of these privileges. When King was a boy growing up in Atlanta, Georgia, white racism prevented him from making friends with whites.

Spike did, at least for a time, have to contend with another plight for African Americans: poverty. There were times when his father could not find any work, partly because he refused to transition to the new electric instruments like everyone else. And yet, Spike recalled that there was still food to eat, and the poverty that was so omnipresent in other neighborhoods was not felt. Neither was the crime, though in so many impoverished black ghettos throughout the North, life was hard, the crime rate was high, and violence was deeply entrenched. To be sure, there were bullies, but Spike learned how to cope with them: he gave up his lunch money without a fight.

In 1968, the Lees' financial situation took a turn for the better. Bill began playing with folk singers, and Jacquelyn took a job teaching at a prestigious private school, St. Ann's in Brooklyn Heights. The Lees moved to a brownstone house across from a housing project. In the summers, the family went to Newport, Rhode Island for folk festivals where Bill performed with mostly white artists, many of whom were activists. Spike heard the black singer Odetta; Pete Seeger, who was affiliated with the Highlander

Afrocentricism

Afrocentricism refers to a philosophy or cultural expression that is based on the African experience. Afrocentricism is not a new concept, although the term was coined by Molefi Asante in the 1980s. Afrocentricism can take many forms and has been expressed in various ways by leaders in African American protest since post-slavery times. W.E.B Du Bois, one of the first black activists of the twentieth century, battled racism, discrimination, and anti-black violence dressed like a distinguished professor. But he advanced African American culture in a time when many blacks strove to distance themselves from the trappings of their African and slave past. When Angela Davis and Jesse Jackson grew out their hair in "naturals" and sported *dashikis*, they exhibited black pride, defying the structure that promulgated white concepts of beauty.

Other black leaders have fused Afrocentricity into the ideology of their organizations. Louis Farrakhan, of the Nation of Islam, and Marcus Garvey, early twentieth-century founder and leader of the Universal Negro Improvement Association and African Communities League, allowed only blacks to join their organizations. Garvey, in particular, endorsed the idea that God was black and that black ambition and ability was boundless. He attempted to demonstrate this by launching his own black-owned businesses and a spectacular shipping line. Stokely Carmichael, a one-time activist in the Student Nonviolent Coordinating Committee, embraced Afrocentricity to the degree that he took on an African name, Kwame Ture, and moved to Africa in 1969.

Afrocentricism was often instilled into leaders during childhood. For example, to counteract society's negative image of blacks, the mother of Fannie Lou Hamer, a prominent activist in Mississippi during the 1960s, gave her daughter a black doll to play with. In those days racist black paraphernalia was abundant. Modern day Afrocentric shops specialize in dolls, gifts, and books that celebrate blackness. Spike Lee's mother gave him and his siblings books about blacks to read. She also braided his little sister's hair and decorated it with cowry shells, a tradition based in Africa. Through natural hairstyles and Afrocentric clothes and accessories, blacks affirmed, celebrated, and embraced their racial identities.

Folk School (an activist training institution) in Tennessee; Joan Baez, who participated in civil rights demonstrations; Peter, Paul, and Mary; and Bob Dylan.

Bill Lee was not the only family member to move into a predominately white arena. Jacquelyn was the only African American teacher at St. Ann's, and she was the first to introduce black history into the curriculum. David,

Joy, and later Cinque were enrolled there. Cinque, born in 1966, was named after a slave revolt leader named Joseph Cinque.

Joseph Cinque was born Sengbe Pieh in Mani, Sierra Leone, circa 1817. He was a husband and father of three children when he was captured by a rival African tribe, who sold him to slave traders. Only one-half of the African slaves survived the difficult **Middle Passage** to Cuba. The rest died along the way. To cover up the fact that they were slaves (slavery was unlawful in Cuba), he and the others were given Spanish names. En route to his new master's plantation, aboard another vessel called *La Amistad*, Cinque led a slave revolt. It was an attempt to force his captives to return the Africans home, but the ship's navigator steered them to the United States, where, in New Haven, Connecticut, the Africans were put on trial for the slave rebellion. In 1840, with the help of abolitionist and former president John Quincy Adams, Cinque and the others were set free. After lecturing throughout the North about his daring revolt, he returned, in 1842, to Sierra Leone. In 1997, Steven Spielberg would produce the movie, *Amistad*.

During Lee's pre-teen years, he enjoyed going to the movies. There were few movies with black casts, and fewer still that offered positive roles for black actors. Blacks in power positions such as director, producer, or writer were virtually nonexistent. These power positions in the movie industry were crucial, as they controlled the choice of content and the manner in which that content was presented, thus wielding the ability to influence perception. Lee remembered the first film he saw featuring a black actor. The movie was *Lilies of the Field* (1963), and it cast Sidney Poitier as Homer Smith, a worker who is persuaded to help Catholic nuns build a new chapel. Lee was unimpressed. Smith's character was one-dimensional and too nice.

Lee was in junior high school when he discovered *The Autobiography of Malcolm X* (1965). The book was compelling, brutally honest, and eye-opening. Spike immediately took to the embittered, radical, and flawed man revealed in the book. It appears that Malcolm X's outspokenness was an especially appealing trait. Spike liked the rawness of Malcolm and his life, and the way he brought out the blatant ugliness and subtleties of racism. Lee had learned about racism vicariously through his parents, and through discussions at the family dinner table. Later, his friends experienced problems while attending Fort Hamilton High School and Franklin Delano Roosevelt High School, which were in a predominantly white neighborhood. White youths were hostile to the blacks who attended those schools and frequently chased after them.

Notwithstanding Lee's enjoyment in movie-going during this period, he preferred sports. He especially liked baseball, though in high school he became enamored with basketball. Lee went to professional games and dreamed of becoming an athlete when he grew up.

Lee turned down his mother's offer to enroll him in the Catholic school where she taught; he did not want to go to an all-white school. His siblings had experienced bouts of racism while attending the predominately white school, St. Ann's, where their mother taught. Because of Lee's good grades, he was able to attend John Dewey High School in Coney Island. A student could receive a good education there, as well as enjoy the diverse environment. As he grew toward manhood, Spike developed a keen sensitivity toward racism, though he was not yet the outspoken and assertive critic he would soon become. All in all, high school was a pleasant experience. But Lee was small in stature, even after growing an afro, reaching only five feet six inches as an adult, which meant that professional sports were out of the question. He would have to look elsewhere for a career.

MOREHOUSE COLLEGE

Not attending college was not an option. In the fall of 1975, Lee entered the all-black and all-male Morehouse College in Atlanta, Georgia. The other two major black institutions in Atlanta are Spelman College, a private institution for black women, and Clark Atlanta University.

Spike's experiences at Morehouse were troublesome. One can imagine that Morehouse, an all-black school in the South, would be an ideal institution for someone who would be known for his **race consciousness**. However, while attending Morehouse, Spike encountered a problem that was rampant on campus: skin-color prejudice.

Skin prejudice is a centuries-old issue, stemming from slavery, where black slave women were subjected to abuse from white slave masters, producing biracial children. Generally, these children had lighter skin and straighter hair, along with other white features. The slave master frequently separated these offspring from the general slave population. In a few cases, the master treated the children as his own. Generally, the biracial men and women worked in his home, wore castoffs of the white family, and were made to feel "better" than the black population of "field slaves" who worked outdoors and lived in coarse shacks. This phenomenon later manifested itself into elitist black bourgeoisie communities, where light skin, education, polite manners, and money were among the keys to admission.

Skin color prejudice is not unique to the South. Most anywhere, blacks are sometimes affected by this internalized racism, falling into the trap of thinking that black is "ugly" and "bad" and white is "attractive" and "good." As such, some blacks have differentiated between "good hair" and "bad hair" with regard to hair texture. Hair that is naturally straight, as a result of racial mixing, is considered "better."

At Morehouse, Spike did not fit the mold. He stood out. Although not dark complected, he was not "fair enough" to pass the test of color attractiveness. He was small, lanky, and wore oversized glasses and an afro. He did not own a car—he did not even have a driver's license. In New York, one could catch a taxi or the subway. As he had in New York, Spike rode his bike everywhere, while the cool fair-complected crowd drove around in flashy cars. Spike was a loner and out of his element.

Making matters worse, Spike was homesick. He wrote home often and spent as much time as possible with his grandmother, who lived nearby. This helped a little, but during his sophomore year, Spike found out that his mother had liver cancer. She died in 1976.

Spike's pain was great, but he did not permit himself to wallow in it or show grief. He felt he had to be the anchor of the family, to carry his siblings through their deep sorrow. And he felt all the more compelled to make something of his life to make his mother proud. In the summer of 1977, he purchased his first video camera.

Lee's Junior year at college was a busy one. In addition to deciding to major in mass communications and taking classes in journalism, radio, and television, he wrote articles for the college newspaper. He also hosted a radio show at a local jazz station. And he continued to go to the movies. A friend at Morehouse said that Spike first relayed to him his dream of moviemaking after a trip to the movies to see *The Deer Hunter* (1978). That movie, like others, had him spellbound.

In the late sixties and seventies blacks finally asserted themselves in the movie industry as producers. Until then, black producers had been few and far between. Pioneers like Emmett J. Scott produced several films, including *The Birth of a Race* (1918), an unsuccessful attempt to counter the racist movie *The Birth of a Nation* (1915), which vilified blacks and glorified the Ku Klux Klan. Black filmmaker Oscar Micheaux, who owned his own production company, produced a number of important "race movies," a term used to denote films with all-black casts. Micheaux broke ground as a writer, director, and producer. He produced forty-four films and wrote seven novels between 1913 and 1948. Micheaux's characters defied the rampant stereotypical images of mainstream white films and featured blacks in exciting roles that black audiences appreciated and enjoyed.

Gordon Parks, Ossie Davis, and Sidney Poitier directed movies in Hollywood during the sixties and seventies. All were also activists. Gordon Parks was a photographer, musician, and journalist, as well as a film director. His films include *Diary of a Harlem Family* (1968), *The Learning Tree* (1969), *Shaft* (1971), and *Solomon Northup's Odyssey* (1984). The latter film was based on a true story about a free black man who was kidnapped and sold into slavery. He was enslaved for twelve years before his whereabouts were discovered and he was allowed to return to his wife in New York. Ossie Davis, who got his start in Hollywood as an actor, sat in the director's seat for several movies, including *Kongi's Harvest* (1970), *Cotton Comes to Harlem* (1970), *Black Girl* (1972), *Gordon's War* (1973), and *Countdown at Kusini* (1976). Sidney Poitier, one of the first black actors to gain fame portraying positive and leading roles in white films, directed *Buck and the*

Preacher (1972), *A War December* (1973), *Uptown Saturday Night* (1974), and *Let's Do It Again* (1975).

Some movies, like Davis' *Cotton Comes to Harlem* (1970) and Gordon's *Shaft* (1971), contributed to a stereotype of blacks. This new genre was called "blaxploitation," a combination of the words "black" and "exploitation." Critics argue that the films glamorized a black urban underworld, criminal activity, drug use, and the degradation of women (who were frequently scantily clad). These films were produced by blacks as well as whites. The National Association for the Advancement of Colored People, the Southern Christian Leadership Conference, and the Urban League established the Coalition Against Blaxploitation to protest the films. By the eighties, blaxploitation was a thing of the past.

Spike made his own films while he was still an undergraduate at Morehouse. His first was *Black College: The Talented Tenth* (1977). The term "talented tenth" refers to a term coined by scholar and activist W.E.B. Du Bois. Du Bois started life in an isolated, mostly white, New England community in the late nineteenth century. His first experience at an all-black southern school, at Fisk University in Tennessee, was inspiring; it inflamed his interest in black culture and life. And he was surrounded by like-minded progressives who, like him, felt the intense desire to use their education and gifts to uplift the race. However, Du Bois was aware that many of his school fellows did not appreciate his interest in the blacks who lived in impoverished rural settings, many of whom retained precious culturisms going back to slavery and Africa. Du Bois hoped that what he called "the Talented Tenth," or the best minds among African Americans, would take up leadership roles in the black community.

Spike's film was not about that noble goal; it was instead about a love relationship. However, the title was an example of how he would enmesh bits of black history into his films.

Neither this film, nor the next, *Last Hustle in Brooklyn* (1978), were major productions; they were only amateur films. The latter combined scenes from a disco and shots of people looting stores (and also rioting) Spike caught in a blackout in New York in 1977.

In 1979, Spike graduated from Morehouse. That summer he interned at Columbia Pictures in Burbank, California. In the fall he began studying at the New York University Institute.

NEW YORK UNIVERSITY INSTITUTE OF FILM AND TELEVISION

Spike Lee and New York have become almost synonymous. His love for New York is as well-known today as is his passion for basketball. However, in 1979, coming back home was not an easy transition. For one thing, his mother was not there. For another, his father had moved on; he was in a relationship with another woman, named Susan Kaplan, and it bothered Spike that she was Jewish. Evidently, he was the only one of the siblings to object. Bill eventually married Susan and they had a son.

Though his home life distressed him, Spike flourished at the New York University Institute of Film and Television, after a bumpy start. He was one of only a handful of blacks who sat in the auditoriums listening to lectures, scrutinizing films, camera angles, and *mis-en-scenes*. This presented a new set of challenges. For instance, when he presented a counterattack to D.W. Griffith's *Birth of a Nation* (1915) in the spirit of Emmet J. Scott with the title *The Answer*, his professors were critical. The professors "did not charge him with disrespect for Griffith. Rather, they criticized the film for being overambitious: First-year student films are only ten minutes long ... they also criticized Spike for not having yet mastered 'film grammar,' or the techniques of filmmaking." Spike believed otherwise, sensing "they thought he was an upstart to criticize Griffith, the 'father of cinema' " (Haskins, 25). Spike showed his movie to the public anyway, screening it at a black dance club in Manhattan.

Despite the early criticism, Spike returned to the New York film program for a second year. This was no small accomplishment, since many students were let go after their first year. Spike received a teaching assistantship and a job working in the equipment room to cover his tuition. His grandmother provided him with money to make films. Also pivotal to Spike's start in filmmaking was the relationship he formed with another student, Ernest Dickerson.

Born on June 25, 1951, in Newark, New Jersey, Dickerson attended Howard University, an HBCU, and New York University Graduate School of Film, emerging as a gifted cinematographer. He and Spike would team up for several films, and Dickerson would go on to direct films of his own. It was no wonder the two became fast friends: both were from the East Coast, attended historically black colleges in the South, and found themselves back in New York to engage in the magic of moviemaking.

Dickerson was in charge of cinematography for Spike's second film assignment, *Sarah* (1981). This one featured a black family in Harlem on Thanksgiving Day. His father wrote the score. To produce this film, Lee established Forty Acres and a Mule Filmworks. The name of Spike's production company referred to the part-fact, part-fable rumor that circulated after the Civil War (1861–1865) that blacks would receive **reparations** in the form of forty acres of property and a mule. However, the reparations were to be granted only to former black slaves living in the Charleston, South Carolina area. In any event, General William Tecumseh Sherman's order was overturned by President Andrew Johnson, and the land confiscated by the Union was returned to the white landowners.

The name was a none-too-subtle way for Spike to address the issue of slave reparations. Every time his movies were shown the credits featured the name of his production company. On the one hand, this would play out as an inside understanding among many blacks, who know the term and its meaning. And to others, especially generations of blacks further removed from such racial issues, "Forty Acres and A Mule" might at least spark questions that led to a search for the answer. Spike understood the power of words, as well as that of images.

Spike's next movie, *Joe's Bed-Stuy Barbershop: We Cut Heads*, his master's thesis, was a stellar success. It captured the private world of black life in a barbershop, where black men go to discuss politics and local gossip, as well as get a haircut. Zach, the manager, runs into trouble with a local gangster who wants to use the barbershop as a cover for illegal gambling. But Zach wants no part in the gangster's lawless schemes. The former owner, Joe, was killed by the gangster. Spike received a student Academy Award from the Academy of Motion Picture Arts and Sciences for that film, and it was shown on public television's *Independent Focus* and at film festivals in California, Georgia, and Switzerland.

Spike graduated from film school in 1982, at the beginning of a decade that would see a host of evocative black movies, including *A Soldier's Story* (1984), *Purple Rain* (1984), and *The Color Purple* (1985). However, all three films were directed by whites. Spike was confident, with the success of his thesis film, that he would have no problem penetrating the movie industry.

STARTING OUT

Starting out was not as easy as Spike had thought it would be. Although he signed on with several agencies, the phone did not ring. He had to make a living until he got a break, so he cleaned and shipped out film for First Run Features. Thanks to that job, he was able to move into his own place. He also began writing. His first script after graduating was *The Messenger*. This film bore some resemblance to Lee's own life. It was about a bicycle messenger who must then bear the responsibility of leading the family when his mother dies.

Spike faced several new challenges trying to make this film. Raising funds was one grueling aspect of moviemaking. But there were other tasks, such as hiring a crew and finding actors. Lee amped up his responsibilities by insisting that he "control all aspects of his films" (Haskins, 31). About this time he hit upon the idea of selling T-shirts to market his film.

There were many filmmaking entities he had to answer to—not only the organizations funding the film, but the Screen Actors Guild, which he hoped would waive the rule that he had to employ union actors (who were more expensive). They denied him the waiver, stating that "the film was too commercial" (Haskins, 32). Lee was crushed. He could not afford union actors, and so he had to terminate production and confront the friends and associates who had contributed their own money. His girlfriend, Cheryl Burr, who had lent Lee money, broke up with him over this failure. But he learned his lesson: his ambition had exceeded his budget. The film was never shot.

She's Gotta Have It

Lee's next film, released in 1986, was his first feature-length motion picture. In it are some of the trademarks that would become famous in future films: the jazzy and soulful score, the monologue scenes in which characters rail into the camera, and the subtle reminders of Lee's radicalism such as the fact that the main character, Nola Darling, has the same birthday as his hero Malcolm X and broaches the subject of police brutality against blacks. The movie revolves around a female protagonist, Nola Darling, an independent African American woman in Brooklyn, New York who's pursued by three men. One of her love interests is Spike Lee, who plays the quirky Mars Blackmon.

Lee (and his sister Joie, who had by this time changed the spelling of her name) appeared in the movie to save money. For the same reason, he filmed the movie in black and white and limited the cast. The film was shot in twelve days on a modest budget of $175,000. Lee sold paraphernalia and a book that chronicled the making of the film, *Spike Lee's* She's Gotta Have It: *Inside Guerrilla Filmmaking* (1987).

Despite the all-black cast and the frugality of the production, the movie grossed an impressive $7,137,502, received glowing recognition, and won the Young Director's Prize at the Cannes Film Festival on the French Riviera. Perhaps even more significant, he piqued the interest of a white audience. Historically, "race films" had appealed almost exclusively to a black audience. Lee would change that paradigm, as he moved blackness out of the symbolic corner in the back of the room into the mainstream.

Spike's film was praised for his groundbreaking portrayal of upbeat, urban black professionals and the community of Brooklyn, New York. Indeed, the large influx of progressive young adults and artists into the neighborhood was attributed to his film. Others recognized Spike's influence and capitalized on it. Nike featured Spike, along with famed basketball player Michael Jordan, in advertisements and commercials. Lee's career opened up to new and exciting opportunities.

RADICAL BLACK FILMS

School Daze

Beginning with his next movie, Lee showed America that he liked to shake things up, that he was not one to back down from controversy (in fact, he was drawn to it), and that he felt no obligation to propose resolution to the conundrums he constructed. In this way, Lee is tantamount to the student who is not afraid to tell on the classroom bully, but will leave it up to the teacher to deal (or not) with the wayward youth. Like Louis Farrakhan, the leader of the Nation of Islam, he has a tendency to hold up a mirror so that blacks can see problems within their own cultural community. *School Daze* (1988) is a case in point.

School Daze is a musical that explores the tumultuous relationships between dark-skinned and light-skinned blacks at a fictional historically black college named Mission. During the opening scenes, Lee educates the audience with a brief pictorial history of African Americans, beginning with slavery. He then moves straight to the real-life topic of skin-color prejudice and the conflict it produces. His material is clearly based on what he observed while attending Morehouse College, though he creates make-believe characters and exaggerated situations. Laurence Fishburne plays Vaughn "Dap" Dunlap (who is "dark-skinned"), the campus activist who launches demonstrations against the South African apartheid system. Dap is also anti-fraternity. The Gamma Phi Gamma fraternity is home to all the "light-skinned" blacks with supposedly "good hair." To accentuate the conflict, Lee uses the offensive term "Jigaboo" to label the dark-skinned blacks, and has Dap call the light-skinned blacks "Wannabes" or "Oreos" (i.e., black on the outside, white on the inside). Lee plays Half Pint, Dap's cousin. Lee disappoints Dap when he announces that he wants to pledge for Gamma Phi Gamma.

Word got out that Morehouse was not happy about the parody. Lee was "criticized … for airing dirty laundry" (Aftab, 58). But Lee did well. He popularized the song and dance routine, "Da Butt," gave Columbia Pictures the biggest profit-making film of the year, and launched the careers of a number of previously unknown actors. Admissions of HBCUs reportedly shot up.

Do the Right Thing

Lee's 1989 film about racism and a race riot turned him into a household name. It was his most controversial film yet; indeed, it is possible that he has yet to make another film as radical as *Do The Right Thing*. Adding to the disquieting tone of the movie was the fact that the movie came in the wake of an actual white-on-black incident and the belief that Lee had a political motive for making it.

The real-life incident took place in 1986. Three black friends—Michael Griffith, Cedric Saniford, and Timothy Grimes—drove into a predominately Italian neighborhood in Howard Beach, Queens, New York. After their car broke down, they went into a pizza parlor to use the telephone to get help. Shortly thereafter, a white mob chased the three black men out of the pizzeria. Saniford and Griffith were beaten. Grimes had a knife, so he was able to escape. In an attempt to escape, Griffith ran onto a busy street and was hit by a car and killed. Reverend Al Sharpton, a civil rights activist, helped launch rallies and a march to protest the event.

New York was fraught with racial violence and frightening incidents such as this. Police brutality was an especially troublesome problem in the black communities of the North. Anytime a black person was abused or murdered, especially by a white person or persons, it was not uncommon for rioting to break out in black communities. A number of riots had occurred in cities across the nation during the 1960s.

Anti-black violence was not the only causal factor involved in race riots, though it was usually the triggering event. A host of problems exacerbated the tensions blacks living in impoverished communities felt. Studies and investigations by the federal and state authorities concluded that racism, as well as the lack of opportunities, general neglect, and overcrowded and in-imical housing environments played a role as well.

A year after the Howard Beach tragedy, Tawana Brawley, a fifteen-year-old African American girl, was found in a garbage bag. Her body was covered with feces and racist epithets. Her clothes were torn and burned, and she claimed that she had been sexually assaulted by six white men, including a police officer. Evidence gathered showed that Brawley had not been sexually assaulted, which led authorities to believe that the state in which she was found had been concocted by herself. Still, Reverend Sharpton continued to publicize the case, and many blacks rallied to support her. Not everyone believed that Brawley fabricated her story.

Such racially charged incidents, as well as Lee's long-time desire to make a film about a riot, were behind Lee's desire to make *Do the Right Thing*. The other reason was that Lee wanted to do something to thwart New York's then-mayor from getting re-elected. Lee saw Ed Koch as one of the main reasons why New York was so racially volatile. He planned that "when the film came out it would be right before the Democratic primary for mayor. We felt that we could have a little bit of influence ... and every time we could nail Koch, we would' " (Aftab, 76). Koch's last year as mayor coincided with the year *Do The Right Thing* was released.

Lee fused a lot of vitriol into this film. He "decided that his forthcoming film would feature graffiti proclaiming 'Tawana Told the Truth'" (Aftab, 75). The tension in the film was exacerbated by the oppressive heat that almost everyone in the film commented on and suffered from. This tidbit alluded to the idea that actual riots tended to erupt in the hottest days of summer. There are also several allusions to real-life situations in the movie. For example, one of the main settings of the movie takes place in a pizzeria (which had been where the trouble started for the three black youths in Howard Beach) in Bedford-Stuyvesant (a neighborhood known for its racial problems), where Mookie (Spike Lee) is the only black employed by the Italian owner named Sal (Danny Aiello) and his two sons.

During one part of the movie, people of different ethnicities face the camera and take part in a racial epithet-spewing session. The scene is unorthodox, shocking, and vintage Lee. What Lee seemingly attempts to show is that racism is alive and well, though individuals may hide behind a guise of political correctness. The tension and sweltering heat are palpable, and the situation erupts after two black characters stage a sit-in because there are no black celebrity portraits on the walls of the pizzeria, only Italians. When the two men do not leave, the owner destroys the boom box of the character named Radio Raheem. A fight ensues between the Italian owner, his sons, and the two blacks. Cops arrive and Radio Raheem is killed when he is roughly handled by an officer. Mookie throws a trashcan through the window of the pizzeria and a riot erupts. The movie concludes with quotes form Dr. Martin Luther King, Jr. denouncing violence, and Malcolm X advocating **self-defense**.

Among the cast members are Ossie Davis, who plays Da Mayor, a neighborhood drunk, and Ruby Dee, as Mother-Sister, a local who sits perched on a stoop. These two were legendary actors whose careers began in the 1950s. In real life, the couple was married and had been civil rights activists, friends, and supporters of leaders like Dr. Martin Luther King, Jr. Davis and Dee played in several of Lee's films. Their presence was a silent homage to nonviolent black protest. Lee's films were stock-full of such symbols, and of tidbits of African American history, as well as racism and racial conflict at its worst.

Do the Right Thing was one of the most talked about movies of the year. The Public Enemy song "Fight The Power," featured in the film, became the new anthem for resistance. But the critics were harsh on Lee. Reviews in *New York* magazine and *Today* "argued that *Do The Right Thing* was of no value except as agit-prop to incite the black community to riot" (Aftab, 96). Lee may not have started any riots, but he did influence popular culture in other ways.

Jungle Fever

Interracial relationships used to be one of the most taboo subjects in America. For years spanning the late nineteenth century into the early twentieth century, black males were lynched over real and imagined sexual relationships with white women. In fact, interracial marriage was unlawful throughout America due to miscegenation, which did not begin to be lifted until 1967.

Whether in television or the big screen, romantic relationships between blacks and whites have been a subject that producers and directors have handled with a heightened awareness of the potential scandal involved. In 1968, a *Star Trek* episode featured the first kiss between a white man, Captain James T. Kirk (William Shatner), and a black woman, Lieutenant Uhura

(Nichelle Nichols), in television history. The actors were deluged with favorable letters from fans in response. In the same year, Plymouth Motors, the sponsor of an NBC television special, was outraged when, during a song number, singer Petula Clark, a white woman, touched the arm of Harry Belafonte, a black singer and actor. Plymouth Motors wanted the scene edited out, but Clark protested. When the special was aired, it received high ratings.

But the movie to pioneer relationships between blacks and whites was *Guess Who's Coming to Dinner* (1967). Produced by George Glass and Stanley Kramer, this movie was especially controversial considering that seventeen states in the South still upheld miscegenation laws. The movie stars Sidney Poitier as Dr. Prentice and Katharine Houghton as Joanna Drayton. The two meet while vacationing in Hawaii and fall in love. The movie focuses on their sudden engagement and the reactions of both their families back home in San Francisco, California. The movie was well received and was a positive, uplifting take on the theme of love conquers all—including racism.

When Spike Lee produced his version of black-and-white love, he explored a controversial aspect of it, one that is the antithesis of racism: loving (rather than hating) another solely because of the skin color. *Jungle Fever* (1991) paid homage to interracial love based on race obsession. The idea was inspired by the murder of Yusef Hawkins in the predominately Italian neighborhood of Bensonhurst. Hawkins was an innocent victim of an Italian who was reportedly provoked to seek vengeance on any black man because his girlfriend told him that she had a black boyfriend. Lee wanted to find a way to dramatize the conundrum of interracial love and the animosity between two ethnic groups.

"Jungle fever" is a slang term that refers to a white person's infatuation with blackness as a sexual turn-on. Lee also addresses the subject of black men's fixation with white women as "being on a pedestal, the universal standard of beauty" (Aftab, 123). This was a subject few would openly discuss, particularly not on a movie screen for the whole world to see. But Lee did it, making his movie under the tension of rumors that a riot would occur to protest the filming in Bensonhurst, though nothing came of it.

The film was not only about the misdirected ulterior motives of romantic love between races and the anger it produced in two communities, one Italian and one black (not to mention that Wesley Snipes' character, Flipper Purify, is married). There are subplots involving an Italian man who falls in love with an African American woman for apparently genuine reasons and the heartwrenching story of Purify's brother, a crack addict, played by Samuel L. Jackson, which Lee asserts is the crux of the story. Indeed, that subplot received kudos. But the romantic relationship was heavily criticized for being negative.

Another theme of the film was the selling out of the black middle class. This has been a complaint of some blacks against other blacks who pursue "whiteness" (e.g., stereotypical white diversions and interests, behavior, white friends and spouses, etc.) as opposed to "blackness" as they scale the heights of economic success. At least one other black filmmaker has criticized Lee for not being "authentically" black. Matty Rich, who wrote and directed *Inkwell* (1994), charged Lee with being "a phony. He's a middle-class third-generation college boy.... I'm a street kid. I think and talk street." Lee countered with the following: "This is one of the things that is messed up now—that if black people are educated and speak correct English, they get accused of 'trying to be white,' selling out ... so a lot of these young kids, they equate ignorance with 'being black,' 'keeping it real'" (Aftab, 136, 137).

Jungle Fever had company; black filmmakers were finally getting the chance to produce their films. Beginning in 1990, more than a dozen black films were produced by black directors and producers, including Mario Van Peebles' *New Jack City* (1991) and John Singleton's *Boyz N the Hood* (1991).

Malcolm X

Lee was still in production for his epic movie, *Malcolm X* (1992), when he started a promotional trend that swept the country. Michael Jordan began wearing "X" caps, and so, it appeared, did most everyone else in the black community. The modern surge of black consciousness was fueled by Spike's marketing savvy with the establishment of his Joint shops, which carried clothes inspired by his movies.

It was fitting that someone as radically minded as Lee would tackle the movie of the man deemed the most radical activist of his time. For the making of such a movie itself was fraught with danger. Lee risked being labeled a racist and being ostracized by the Hollywood community. Malcolm X was no Martin Luther King, Jr. At the start of his tenure with the Nation of Islam, Malcolm called whites "devils." He said things that were racially divisive and provoked strife and anger. And unlike King, he was not so well received by liberal whites.

But Malcolm X was a personal hero of Lee's, one who had not received equal treatment in the history books. According to many mainstream sources, his claim to fame was his hate-filled, angry invective. But there was a complex life history behind the divisive image commonly portrayed in schools and in the media.

In three hours and twenty-odd minutes (which in the movie business ranks as a substantial chunk of time), Lee explored the many divergent phases of Malcolm X's life: the troubled childhood, an early adulthood in which he plunged into crime, the angry black Muslim, the devoted husband and father, and the ultimate transformation. Shortly before his assassination (which some alleged might have occurred because of Malcolm X's

X

X is the chosen surname for male and female members of the Nation of Islam (NOI). According to Elijah Muhammad's *Message to the Blackman in America* (1965), new converts to NOI must change their last name to X. In the case of individuals with the same first name, a number is added to distinguish each person, i.e., "Michael 5X." Eventually, black Muslims are given an Islamic name. This name is considered a "holy name of God." The most famous black Muslim to take on the "X" name was Malcolm X, formerly Malcolm Little.

The "X" was a symbol of black protest to the slave names blacks received from their slave owners. Most slaves were referred to by their first name only. However, to distinguish one group of slaves from another, it was the custom for slave owners to bestow their own surnames upon them. This is true today for most African Americans who are descended from slaves.

Spike Lee popularized the X symbol by wearing hats bearing the "X." Malcolm X had been one of Lee's heroes since he first read the *Autobiography of Malcolm X* (1965) when he was in junior high school. In 1992, Lee produced the movie, *Malcolm X*, which was based on that book. Along with the movie, Lee marketed a plethora of paraphernalia—T-shirts and hats, for example—featuring the X. Blacks of all ages took to wearing clothing that featured the X, commemorating a man who, in life, had been the most radical black leader in American history.

However, some contended that this was an ephemeral fashion statement and, as such, did not go beyond that. In Arthur Magida's *Prophet of Rage: A Life of Louis Farrakhan and His Nation* (1996), he visits this issue. He recalls a situation when an African American woman asked black youths, in a Boston ghetto in 1994, if they knew the man who was represented on the clothes they wore. They did not know, thus demonstrating that fashion and black history knowledge are not always one and the same.

transformation), he took a pilgrimage to Mecca and returned to America transfigured. He no longer called white people devils, and believed that it was possible for blacks and whites to live in harmony. He broke from the Nation of Islam and took steps to assume a new role in black protest.

Lee inserted footage of the infamous Rodney King beating into the film. In 1991, King was stopped by Los Angeles police for speeding and beaten by four officers while several other officers stood by and watched. A witness taped the beating and the four officers were brought to trial. When they were acquitted of wrongdoing, riots in the city ensued.

The movie almost did not get made. Lee ran out of money near the end of production and Warner Brothers would not give him any more. They wanted him to cut the duration of the film to save money. Lee interpreted this as a racist offense: "Warner Brothers don't view black people as important," he said, and started calling them "the plantation" (Aftab, 148). But Lee forged ahead and got several black celebrities—Bill Cosby, Oprah Winfrey, Magic Johnson, Tracy Chapman, Prince, Peggy Cooper-Cafritz, Michael Jordan, and Janet Jackson—-to donate the $1.3 million that was needed to complete the movie. After this demonstration of generous support, Warner Brothers provided Lee with more money.

When the movie was released in November 1992, Spike Lee encouraged youth to skip school to see his film. "Who said that the only place that you can learn is within the four walls of a school?" (Aftab, 166). However, many in the public were none too pleased that Lee would call for mass truancy and, in effect, challenge the importance of school.

The movie only made $48 million at the box office. Some have surmised that the newness and intrigue of Lee had eroded some, or that the timing of the movie's release was off. But the fact remains that it is a landmark motion picture and Spike Lee's greatest accomplishment.

MARRIAGE AND FAMILY

Despite the box-office disappointment of his masterpiece, Lee continued to make movies. He also found time to fall in love with a woman named Tonya Linette Lewis, a practicing attorney in Washington, D.C., whom he met at the annual Congressional Black Caucus. They dated for a year or so and then decided to get married.

The wedding occurred in the fall of 1993 at the Riverside Church in New York City, famously known as the location where James Forman, a former executive secretary of the Student Nonviolent Coordinating Committee, interrupted services to read the Black Manifesto, a demand for reparations, in 1969. Spike, who was thirty-six at the time, was in the middle of shooting *Crooklyn* (1994), a semiautobiographical movie, and Tonya was thirty-two. They had a daughter named Satchel (after the famous African American baseball player, Leroy "Satchel" Paige) in 1994 and a son, Jackson Lewis, in 1997. Jackson is Lee's middle name.

Get on the Bus

Marriage and fatherhood did not slow Lee down—at least not much. In 1996, he produced *Get on the Bus*. The movie portrays fictional events leading up to Louis Farrakhan's Million Man March, which had taken place the year before. The march was considered controversial because whites feared what might come of an all-black male gathering coordinated by the radical Farrakhan. Farrakhan's radicalism was as extreme as it gets, tantamount to that of pre-Hajj Malcolm X. Farrakhan admits to being a religious leader, a separatist, and a fiery critic of white America. Critics call him a racist, anti-Semitic, and a rabble-rouser. Many black women were none too pleased when they were told that they could not attend the march. But the event ultimately was a success. Black men from all walks of life, all levels of economic and social status, rallied at the nation's capitol in Washington D.C. They met at the historic location of the legendary March on Washington for Jobs and Freedom, where Dr. King had had risen to superstardom.

Black men left the Million Man March invigorated, inspired, and—in spite of the differences among them—with a sense of solidarity. This was what Lee wanted to capture when he made *Get on the Bus*. The cast of characters included a senior citizen, an estranged father and son, a gay couple, a self-absorbed actor, a bi-racial police officer, a film student, a Muslim, a conspiracy theorist, and others—along with a Jewish bus driver. The men talk and debate as they travel to the Million Man March. By the end of the film, the men are transformed in a positive way.

4 Little Girls

Lee's next film (1997), his first documentary, delved into the tragic murder of four African American girls in a church bombing in Birmingham, Alabama in 1963. The victims were Denise McNaire (age 11), Cynthia Wesley (age 14), Carole Robertson (age 14), and Addie Mae Collins (age 14). The documentary opened with a song by folk singer and activist Joan Baez and featured several interviews with the girls' parents, as well as whites and others who recalled the tragedy and its aftermath.

Lee's film exposed the violence that was so prominent during the Civil Rights Movement. The Ku Klux Klan was responsible for the bombing of the 16th Street Baptist Church. At the public funeral of three of the girls, more than 8,000 people attended and Dr. King spoke. Robert Chambliss was convicted of the four murders in 1978, and he died in prison seven years later. Forty-five years after the murders, two others, Bobby Frank Cherry and Thomas Blanton, were convicted and sentenced to life in prison. The fourth suspect was never charged due to weak evidence.

Tragedies such as this created a crisis in America. They also helped propel the federal government toward intervention and meaningful civil rights legislation.

Bamboozled *and* A Huey P. Newton Story

In back-to-back projects, Lee explored racism and another radical figure. *Bamboozled* (2000) is a term Malcolm X once used in a speech that includes the popular refrain, referring to the powerlessness of blacks in America, "Ya been had, ya been took, ya been hoodwinked, led astray, ran amok." The film is a satire of blackface minstrel shows. Every mercifully forgotten racist epithet and image is conjured up. Characters in blackface cavort in a watermelon patch. Prominent actors such as Ving Rhames and Will Smith lampoon stereotypical black roles. Al Sharpton plays himself and voices disapproval at these images.

In the following year, Lee directed a one-man film: Roger Guenveur Smith's reprisal of *A Huey P. Newton Story* (2001). Newton and Bobby Seale co-founded the Black Panther Party for Self-Defense in 1966. Newton created a program for the organization that included social-reform programs and armed patrols of black communities to act as a buffer against police abuse. However, Newton was a conflicted man whose mind eventually becoming ravaged from his drug addiction. He was ultimately murdered during a drug deal in 1989. The film was commended by several, including the NAACP, which nominated it for the Image Awards.

OTHER FILMS

Over the years, Lee has demonstrated his versatility as well as his refusal to be pigeonholed or typecast as a maker of "race films." His films, centering around black life, black characters, and black experiences, are a significant addition to the canon of American cinema. Lee's films cover a broad range of subject matter. *Mo' Better Blues* (1990) deals with an African American musician who grapples with balancing his music and romantic relationships. Black love is an important theme for Lee. In *Crooklyn* (1994), Lee paints an intimate portrait of his childhood growing up in Brooklyn, preceding the death of his mother. In *Clockers* (1995), he explores crime and the tough choices that are made in black inner-city communities. Lee looks into the father–son dynamic and the world of basketball in *He Got Game (1997)*.

Other films, like *Summer of Sam* (1999), *25th Hour* (2000), and *Inside Man* (2006), depart from the themes of racism and controversy. *Summer of Sam* takes place in a predominately Italian neighborhood in New York during the real-life Son of Sam serial murders, which occurred in 1976 and 1977. *25th Hour* is based on the novel of the same name and features a white protagonist: a drug dealer on his last day of freedom before he serves a seven-year prison sentence.

Inside Man is a movie that, at first glance, comes across as a mainstream thriller. But it has a twist at the end that bears Lee's signature. Another Lee trademark is the fact that the two protagonists are black detectives investigating a bank robbery and hostage situation in progress. Near the end of the film, Lee reveals that the bank robbers are bribing the chairman of the board of directors and founder of the bank, whose wealth was built upon his involvement in the Holocaust during World War II.

Lee returned to full-blown controversy with *When the Levees Broke: A Requiem in Four Acts* (2006), a documentary that was aired on HBO. The film deals with the tragedy—which many consider to be the gross neglect—of primarily lower-class blacks whose lives and homes were devastated due to the levees that failed during Hurricane Katrina in 2005.

Lee's most recent film, *Miracle at St. Anna* (2008), centers around four African American Buffalo Soldiers in Italy during World War II. This film fills in another gap in the untold story of the black experience in America.

Currently, Lee is fashionably bearded, a husband, and father of two children. He is also a man with a lot of ideas and issues still to explore. Who knows what shrewd, illuminating—though often emotionally uneasy—and groundbreaking filmmaking the coming years will bring.

See also W.E.B. Du Bois; Louis Farrakhan; Martin Luther King, Jr.; Malcolm X; Huey P. Newton; Al Sharpton; and Ida B. Wells-Barnett.

FURTHER RESOURCES

Aftab, Kaleem. *That's My Story and I'm Sticking to It.* New York: W.W. Norton, 2005.

Duster, Alfreda M., ed. *Crusade for Justice: The Autobiography of Ida B. Wells.* Chicago: The University of Chicago Press, 1970.

"Eastwood Hits Back at Lee Claims." *BBC News* (June 2008). See http://news.bbc.co.uk/2/hi/entertainment/7439371.stm.

Haskins, Jim. *Spike Lee: By Any Means Necessary.* New York: Walker Publishing, Company, 1997.

Schecter, Patricia A. *Ida B. Wells-Barnett and American Reform, 1880–1930.* Chapel Hill: The University of North Carolina Press, 2001.

John Lewis (1940–)

John Lewis was the chairman of the Student Nonviolent Coordinating Committee in the 1960s. During the civil rights era he shared a leadership role with James Forman as a member of the Civil Rights Big Six. He has been a U.S. Congressman since 1986.

John Lewis was supposed to be a preacher. That was what he wanted to be as a child. While he was growing up, his family—mother, father, and nine siblings—called him "Preacher," and he would daily visit the wooden henhouse to play preacher with the hens and chicks. He preached sermons to his "flock," baptized and buried them, and presided over their funerals with solemnity.

As a youth, Lewis stuttered a little and spoke with the heavy southern drawl of his native Troy, Alabama. He was also incredibly reticent and shy—at least, until he got comfortable. Perhaps that is one reason why he came to idolize Dr. Martin Luther King, Jr., a Baptist preacher and masterful orator. He also admired what King said—how he spoke about social activism in the same context as Christianity. As Lewis listened to him over the static of the family radio, he nursed a new aspiration. His parents—sensible, law-abiding, and churchgoing—were crushed when, after attending American Baptist Theological Seminary, he started participating in civil rights demonstrations and then told them that he did not want to be a preacher after all. He wanted to be an activist.

Although small and boyish-looking, John Lewis was tough. He made a name for himself in 1963 as the quiet, strong chairman of the Student Nonviolent Coordinating Committee. Lewis' toughness was constantly tested as he encountered vitriolic crowds, violence, and arrest. He was removed from the SNCC leadership in 1966 by militants who overturned the organization's pacifist philosophy. Building upon his activist experiences, Lewis devoted his energies to encouraging African Americans to register to vote and strengthening black communities that suffered from years of neglect and abuse. In the late 1970s he entered politics, and in 1986 he was elected to a seat in the U.S. House of Representatives from the state of Georgia.

CHILDHOOD

John Robert Lewis was born on February 21, 1940. His parents, Eddie and Willie Mae Lewis, were sharecroppers who brought up their ten children in the small, isolated, rural community of Troy, Alabama. In describing Troy, Lewis wrote "it was a small world, a safe world, filled with family and friends" (Lewis, 17). Troy, like any southern town, was segregated. As a result, all the blacks lived in one side of town, while the whites lived, worked, shopped, and worshipped in another. Lewis recalled that he did not see many white people while growing up. Elsewhere, southern blacks had violent and humiliating contact with whites, but Lewis was spared this. And so his memories of childhood, of growing up, were tranquil.

Home was a three-bedroom abode to which the family moved, arriving on a mule-drawn wagon, when John was four years old. Few African Americans actually owned their own home. Lewis' parents were fortunate. They purchased this home, along with 110 pristine acres, for $300. They were lucky to be left to live in peace, because racists in many southern communities contrived ways to run blacks from their homes. This phenomenon was called **whitecapping**.

Lewis' world centered on the home, caretaking the hens, working in the fields, worship, and school. Life was simple, basic, and earthy, ensconced as in a warm blanket by family and friends. His family's vast plot meant that they could grow plenty of food for daily meals and canning. Among the cornucopia of produce were southern delicacies like okra, collared greens, sweet potatoes, peaches, and watermelon. John's father and big brothers had rifles with which they hunted for game to supplement the family meals. Laundry was washed in a cast-iron pot with soap that was made by hand. The clothes that hung on the clothesline dried crisp under a pale yellow sun.

There was a lot to do if you were a member of the Lewis family. On Saturdays, the younger children pulled weeds from the yard. The older children learned how to plow and pick cotton. John's favorite chore was taking care of the hens and the chicks. At night the family gathered around the radio. Twice a month, the family enjoyed worship services at the Macedonia Baptist or Dunn's Chapel African Methodist Church. Each church only held one service a month. Without songbooks, blacks sang a capella. From the beginning, Lewis was riveted by these church services.

When it came to those hens, Lewis was just as passionate as he was about Sunday worship. If a bird was needing to be sold for money or killed for food, Lewis would stage his own quiet protest. He would either forgo eating or refrain from talking. His tactics did not reform his family, but it was something Lewis felt compelled to do.

When Lewis turned six and was forced to take his turn in the field, he complained bitterly to anyone who would listen about the wrongness of sharecropping. Sharecropping usually came with permanent debt. He wondered why no one else resisted. Lewis had a vague memory of his mother imploring his father not to do something. His father was visibly angry about something and was going to take his hunting rifle and handle some crisis. The crisis was never revealed, but the fact was that he relented, and that his mother begged him not to go. Indeed, most African Americans were prudent in that respect. The blacks in Troy at that time did not experience a lot of racial duress, and they wanted to keep it that way. To stir up trouble was to rouse dreaded attention that might end in death.

Though comforting, home was in many ways confining. Lewis longed for a glimpse of life beyond the puffy white clouds that rolled listlessly above the treetops; beyond the unpaved paths of red soil that on a rainy day could trouble the most robust of horses. Only once in his childhood did Lewis leave Troy, traveling with an uncle to Montgomery, Alabama, fifty miles away. School represented a way out for Lewis. Not only did he enjoy learning, but the bus that carried him to the one-room school took him to another section of town, away from grueling chores. The school library was another of Lewis' favorite places. Through books, he would be transported to other times and locations. This was all well and good, but during harvest season, John was supposed to stay home and work in the fields. Undeterred, young John hid under the broad porch, waiting anxiously and breathlessly for the bus to rumble down the unpaved road. When it came, he hustled over and climbed aboard before he was discovered skulking under the porch and forced to work in the fields.

Montgomery, Alabama became the center of attention in 1955 during the momentous Montgomery Bus Boycott. Dr. Martin Luther King, Jr., a local Baptist preacher, was nearing twenty-six years of age at the start of the boycott in early December, when he became the leader of the demonstration. The entire black community in Montgomery participated, refusing to ride on public buses for almost an entire year.

Fifteen-year-old Lewis, sitting transfixed by the radio, was spellbound by the words and the distinctive melodic thunder of Dr. King. Everything in him was attuned to the sonorous voice that rose and fell like a swelling ocean wave. The title of the sermon was "Paul's Letter to the American Christians." The sum of his message was that African Americans should concern themselves not with the afterlife, but with life on earth. He pushed his listeners to think radically; to protest against the system that barred them from mainstream life, from full freedom and equality. To many, his words were almost scandalous. Lewis once overheard his parents talking about King, and their response was a mixture of admiration and fear. Mostly fear. For Lewis, hearing King speak was a life-changing event.

But Lewis' parents could not shelter him forever. As he grew older and was able to discern for himself the realities of life, the truth was unmistakable. And the truth disturbed him. He read in the papers how Emmett Till, a fourteen year old, was lynched for whistling at a white woman. He was gripped by the events of the Montgomery Bus Boycott and its aftermath.

The Lynching of Emmett Till

The tragic murder of fourteen-year-old Emmett Till remains one of the most well-known of the all-too-many tragic events that nevertheless helped to propel civil rights activism. Indeed, it was Mamie Till, his mother, who courageously toured the nation to expose her son's brutal lynching, demanding that his attackers be punished and exposing for all to see the violent world in which blacks in the South lived.

(continued)

Born on July 25, 1941, in Chicago, Illinois, Emmett Louis "Bobo" Till had no firsthand knowledge of the dangers that awaited him in Mississippi. Although Mamie Till had lived only the first two years of her life in Mississippi, her parents had grown up there. Her parents and other southern-born African Americans in Chicago talked openly about life in the deep South. As Mamie Till helped pack her son's luggage for a summer visit with his uncle in Money, Mississippi, she cautioned him to watch how he behaved with whites. There were important rules that blacks had to follow in the South. Many of these rules were "unofficial" and referred to under the term "racial etiquette." These unofficial rules were taught through socialization and sometimes by trial and error, but violations, however small or seemingly insignificant, could reap dangerous, if not fatal, consequences to the transgressor. The custom of averting eye contact, deferring to whites on a sidewalk, and calling whites "Sir" or "Ma'am," while at the same time being subjected to the derogatory terms "boy," "gal," or "nigger," were just some of the rules of racial etiquette.

On August 24, 1955, Emmett Till made the fatal flaw of committing what in that twisted society was considered one of the most serious crimes. What actually transpired is unclear. It is alleged that Till was responding to a dare by a friend at Bryant's Grocery and Meat Market when he either whistled at or called out "Bye baby" to a twenty-one-year-old white woman named Carolyn Bryant. She was the wife of the owner of the store, Roy Bryant.

Several days later, on August 28, Bryant and his half-brother, J.W. Milam (and possibly others), went to his uncle's house at 12:33 A.M. and awakened Till. The white men took Till to a shed on a plantation in Sunflower County and brutally beat him and then shot him and tried to dump his body in the Tallahatchie River.

NAACP activists, including Medgar Evers, a Mississippi field secretary, tried to find the whereabouts of the missing teenager, hoping against hope that he was still alive. When his body was found in the river, the brothers were arrested and put on trial. They were acquitted on September 23.

At Till's funeral, Mamie insisted that her son's casket remain open so all could see the viciousness of the crime against her son. She toured the nation to tell others about what had happened to Emmett Till and published an autobiography *Death of Innocence: The Story of the Hate Crime That Changed America* (2003).

In 2007, the Emmett Till Unsolved Civil Rights Crime Act was passed, sponsored by several senators, including Christopher Dodd and Barack Obama, and congressmen such as John Lewis, Maxine Waters, and John Conyers. This landmark act will try to help resolve hundreds of civil rights crimes that have been committed in the nation.

Lewis could have been a good preacher; he most certainly lived a saintly life. But he did not see that as an achievement: he felt that he mostly stayed out of trouble because there was nowhere for a teenager in Troy to go for fun and amusement. And he did not have a driver's license to go anywhere else. Lewis was in fact unwieldy behind the steering wheel and lost his courage to drive after he failed his first driving test. He would finally get his license in 1982, at forty-two years old.

But he excelled in other areas. In 1956 (the same year he failed the driver's test) Lewis preached his first sermon at Macedonia Baptist. The congregation was ecstatic. Shortly thereafter, a story, with photo, was published in the black section of the local newspaper to document his important day. But his happiness was shrouded by the news of the shocking murder of a distant relative in Columbus, Georgia, who was killed for his involvement in the NAACP. The man who shot him admitted his guilt, but the murder was ruled justifiable homicide.

His relative's death shocked and angered him. The young child who had complained about the system of sharecropping had become a teenager who was keenly aware of the depth of the racial injustice around him, the racial violence, and Jim Crow. The practice of Jim Crow law in his own community spurred him to take his first act of resistance.

Lewis walked into the Pike County Public Library and requested a library card. He knew he was going to be turned away because, thanks to Jim Crow laws, the library prohibited blacks from using its facilities and borrowing books. Lewis next approached his friends and neighbors and asked them to sign a petition requesting library service. Some could not think of including their names on such a radical document. Others were willing. But Lewis' brave attempt went for naught. The library ignored the petition.

Lewis' next move was to join the NAACP. This was, perhaps, Lewis' most brash action, given his relative's murder and the fact that the organization had been banned in some states, including Alabama. But for John, the latter fact was a singularly motivating force.

Going to college was another act of resistance. Historically, black slaves in America were deprived of education. Reading and writing—the most basic aspects of education—were strictly forbidden. In this way, whites maintained their positions of superiority and privilege. In post-slavery years, education continued to be a hotly contested issue. There were white liberals who supported it, but there were also plenty of racists who distrusted or were intimidated by educated African Americans. There were others who felt education was tolerable as long as black and white students were separated and blacks were not taught advanced subjects and were, generally, discouraged from pursuing higher education.

Ten out of Lewis' graduating class of thirty-seven blacks went to college. Initially, Lewis hoped to attend the same institutions as had his idol, Dr. King. King had gone to Morehouse College, a historically black institution for men in Atlanta, Crozer Theological Seminary in Pennsylvania, and Boston University in Massachusetts. But Lewis could not afford to go to Morehouse. And because he was not an exceptional student, he could not get admitted on his academic performance. So Lewis decided to go to American Baptist Theological Seminary (ABT) in Nashville, Tennessee, where students could pay for tuition, room, and board through a work-study program.

Tears trickled down his mother's face on the day that Lewis left home. It was not only that she would miss Lewis, who would be away from home for many months for the first time. She knew that he would face unseen dangers, for he was venturing into territory that could be hostile for young black men. His father said very little as the truck jostled along the rugged roads during the drive to the Greyhound bus station. At their parting, he shook his son's hand. The bus arrived. Because of Jim Crow law, blacks had to sit in the back of the bus or give up their seats for whites if no other seating was available. Lewis mounted the bus and walked to the rear.

AMERICAN BAPTIST THEOLOGICAL SEMINARY

At seventeen, Lewis had not yet outgrown his youthful, boyish appearance. He would, for most of his life, appear innocuous and dovelike. But his mild aspect belied a fearlessness and relentlessness that would astonish the world. His start into the world of activism began during his years at the American Baptist Theological Seminary.

It was not that ABT endorsed the civil rights struggle, at least not at first. Lewis' interest and subsequent activities were largely self-motivated. Lewis was taken aback to find out there was no NAACP organization on campus. ABT was tied financially to southerners who wanted to maintain the extant racial relations and customs. As a result, the institution could not publicly condone or encourage activism without losing significant financial support. When Lewis went (during his second year) to hear lectures by well-known activists such as Fred Shuttlesworth, Roy Wilkins, and Thurgood Marshall, he had to go on his own time and leave campus and travel to the historically black university, Fisk.

Some of Lewis' peers were confounded by him. One friend asked him why he was so preoccupied with Dr. Martin Luther King, Jr. A large number of African Americans shared Lewis' zeal for King. But many others preferred racial separatism or, like Lewis' parents, were wary of King, if not resentful of the havoc his demonstrations created. Indeed, King's campaigns subsequent to the Montgomery Bus Boycott were designed to force a violent reaction from whites. This was a necessary part of his strategy to engage the news media and force the federal government to act on their behalf.

King had mobilized a large segment of the black church community. But among college-aged individuals the civil rights struggle had not yet taken off. Lewis was a harbinger of the changes to come to Nashville. And he was not entirely alone. One of his professors, John Lewis Powell, lectured on radical themes such as protest and the eradication of segregation.

In other ways, Lewis fit in well with the student population. At ABT, students were not allowed to drink alcohol or dance. For fun, the students played games or listened to sermons on the radio. Lewis did not appear to object to the rigid rules of the seminary. He was accustomed to leading a clean and puritanical life. But he did find it frustrating that women were not attracted to him except in platonic, familial, or maternal ways. Lewis did not have a girlfriend in high school, and this trend continued at the seminary. But if there was anyone he would have dated, it would have been Helen Johnson. Lewis and Johnson went on many walks together along the nearby river.

When Lewis was not working in the campus cafeteria where he washed dishes (a job he found harder than sharecropping) to pay for his education, he was studying diligently and keeping up to date on the progress of the Civil Rights Movement. He kept an eye peeled for opportunities to participate.

Lewis met with the president of the seminary and asked if he could form an NAACP group on campus. The president said no, but Lewis understood. In 1957, Lewis deliberately applied to Troy State College, an all-white institution in his hometown. When, as expected, he was denied admission, he gathered the courage to write Dr. King, who had helped establish the Southern Christian Leadership Conference (SCLC) in that same year. Lewis thought his rejection could be used as a test. Lewis' heart pounded in his chest as he sealed the letter and mailed it off. When he received a response, Lewis wrote that he felt "overwhelmed" (Lewis, 67).

MEETING WITH MARTIN LUTHER KING, JR.

Lewis could hardly believe he was sitting in the same room as his idol. The importance of that moment weighed on him heavily. Ralph Abernathy, the SCLC's secretary-treasurer and King's closest associate, and Fred Gray, a black attorney, were also there. They spoke to him in quiet, gentle tones. King stared kindly and somberly at him and said, "I just want to meet the boy from Troy." Lewis was shocked speechless (Lewis, 68).

It took a while for him to warm up and give them a brief narrative of his life. They listened intently, then described the dangers he would face if he decided to challenge his rejection letter and sue Troy State. There would be harassment and, potentially, violence. Lewis was willing. But they told him that he had to make sure his parents were in agreement. If they were okay, the SCLC would proceed with the case.

Initially, Lewis' parents supported John, though they admitted they were concerned for his safety, as well as their own and that of their extended family and neighbors in their community. Before too long they changed their minds. The threat was too great. Lewis had to abort his plans.

NASHVILLE STUDENT MOVEMENT

In 1958, Lewis returned to ABT, but the climate was not the same. Everyone, he recalled, now appeared to be caught up in the movement. One of the most popular slogans of the year was "Free by '63," reflecting the belief Jim Crow would be eradicated in 1963. Lewis attended many lectures and special events, such as a mass rally where Coretta Scott King addressed a large crowd. Dr. King could not attend because he had been attacked by a deranged African American woman and was recuperating.

Lewis was in attendance one Sunday when one of the more popular ministers, Reverend Kelly Miller Smith, introduced a guest at his church. Lewis was spellbound. This man, James Lawson, was a member of the Fellowship of Reconciliation, an integrated pacifist organization, and was enrolled at the Divinity School of Vanderbilt University in Nashville, Tennessee. Lawson, working almost single-handedly, would go on to train black and white youths for an unprecedented assault on segregation.

Lawson conducted workshops in the basement of a Methodist church to prepare college students for nonviolent activism. Lewis likened these workshops to college lectures, and he felt that Lawson's teachings were beyond anything he had yet experienced. The workshops began with a study of the major world religions—**Judaism**, Christianity, Islam, **Buddhism**, and **Hinduism**. Lawson facilitated discussions on the philosophies of individuals like Henry David Thoreau and Reinhold Niebuhr. They talked about nonviolent resistance and love. For example, Lawson taught them a method to use when approaching a hostile person. He told them "to imagine that person—actually *visualize* him or her—as an infant, as a baby. If you can see this full-grown attacker who faces you as the pure, innocent child that he or she once was—that we *all* once were—it is not hard to find compassion in your heart" (Lewis, 77).

What Lawson strived to impart was not merely "a technique or a tactic or a strategy or a tool to be pulled out when needed" but a lifestyle (Lewis, 77). He stressed that nonviolence was not just an action (or inaction), it was something that demanded that the natural reaction to violence would no longer be to hit back in self-defense.

There were rules to resisting during an actual demonstration:

No aggression. No retaliation. No loud conversation, no talking of any kind with anyone other than ourselves. Dress nicely. Bring books, schoolwork, letter-writing materials. Be prepared to sit for hours. Study, read, write. Don't slouch. No napping. No getting up, except to go to the bathroom, and then be sure there is a backup to fill your seat while you're away. Be prepared for arrest. Be prepared to be taken to jail. (Lewis, 93)

Lawson's teaching involved other activities besides the workshops. A weekend trip to Highlander Folk School, an institution dedicated to developing grassroots organizing near Monteagle, Tennessee, was invigorating for Lewis. It was inspiring to go to a school dedicated primarily to social activism. Lewis was especially delighted because King had received training there.

Back in Nashville, Lawson's students engaged in intense role-playing sessions. Both blacks and whites positioned themselves as activists and aggressors. Lawson taught them how to prepare themselves for physical attack. One of the important things to do when attacked, he explained, was to hold the body in a way to protect the internal organs, and to keep the eyes locked, not aggressively, on the assailant's eyes. Lawson taught that an assailant is likely to be less violent if the victim does that.

In 1959, Lewis helped co-found the Nashville Student Movement, comprising the young adults undergoing Lawson's strenuous training program. Diane Nash, a black female activist who would play a visible role in the civil rights struggle, was elected its chairman. This was the start of something big, something thrilling. The group planned to wage a systematic sit-in campaign at various venues in Nashville. The first demonstration was held as a test case at a department store in downtown Nashville. Essential to this newfangled youth movement were the church leaders who permitted the use of the churches for headquarters, and the church members who provided transportation.

Lewis grappled briefly with some anxiety and did not feel brave enough to participate in the test demonstration. The direction his life was taking challenged some of the core values his parents had taught him. Lewis had never been in trouble with the law or arrested. All his life, he believed that only bad people, criminals, were arrested. On the other hand, he realized that to challenge Jim Crow being arrested was inevitable and that arrest, on those terms, was victory. Lewis' anxiety quickly vanished after participating in the test sit-ins.

Everything the demonstrators set out to do during the test sit-in on Saturday, November 28, 1959, had been planned before that day. The black and white activists entered the store and purchased an item, then went into the department-store lunch counter. The waitress told them, politely, that she could not serve them.

Diane Nash had been designated to speak to the manager. She was the only one that spoke during the demonstration. The manger answered all her questions, telling her that the whites could not be served, because they were with the black students. This was the store's policy. The activists left, returning to the church to process what had just occurred and to celebrate their first trial run.

The group staged another test demonstration the next week at a different department store. Lewis was selected to ask the manager if they could be

Diane Nash

Diane Nash's name is not as well-known as those of other women who participated in the Civil Rights Movement and is utterly overshadowed by the names of the men who dominated the struggle (this subject is explored in *Women in the Civil Rights Movement: Trailblazers and Torchbearers, 1941–1965* [1990]). However, during the famous March on Washington for Jobs and Freedom in 1963, her name was among those honored by Bayard Rustin. The others were Rosa Parks, who was the star plaintiff in the case that started the Montgomery Bus Boycott in Alabama, in 1955; Daisy Bates, the NAACP leader who played an instrumental role in providing protection and support for the first blacks, the "Little Rock Nine," to integrate the Little Rock Central High School in Arkansas; Gloria Richardson, leader of the Cambridge Nonviolent Action Committee in Maryland; and Mrs. Herbert Lee and Myrlie Evers, two widows whose husbands were murdered during the movement.

Diane Nash was born on May 15, 1938 in Chicago, Illinois. Influenced by the Catholic schools she attended, she once aspired to be a nun, but in college her life took a dramatic turn toward protest. While attending Fisk University in Nashville, Tennessee, Nash grew increasingly frustrated with Jim Crow laws, so much so that she decided to go to the civil disobedience workshops facilitated by Reverend James Lawson. Nash's intensity and dedication made her the natural leader of the group that was eventually formed, the Nashville Student Movement. In 1960, they launched a sit-in campaign that lasted from February to May. In May, all lunch counters in Nashville, Tennessee were desegregated.

After that success, Nash quit school and made a full-time commitment to activism. In 1960, she helped establish the Student Nonviolent Coordinating Committee (SNCC). In 1961, she helped coordinate the 1961 Freedom Rides and the "Right to Vote" campaign in Selma, Alabama. In that same year, she married James Bevel, another activist who started out with the Nashville Student Movement. In 1962, while four months pregnant, Nash was briefly imprisoned for teaching children nonviolent techniques in Jackson, Mississippi. Nash also worked with the Southern Christian Leadership Conference (SCLC) and in 1965 received the SCLC's most prestigious honor, the Rosa Parks Award. In 1968, Nash and Bevel divorced. They have two children. Since the Movement, Nash has returned to Chicago, where she lectures and maintains her advocacy of issues affecting African Americans.

served. When they were told no, the group rose from their seats and left the lunch counter.

On his way home for winter break, Lewis and his friend Bernard got on a Greyhound bus and sat directly behind the bus driver. When the bus driver told them to move to the rear of the bus where blacks were required to sit according to Jim Crow law, they refused to budge. The driver moved his seat as far back as possible, so that the two young men had to sit with their knees against their chests during the entire journey home.

When Lewis returned to campus after the holiday break, he found the Nashville Student Movement welcoming more members. Lewis and the others continued their training, while the new members went through the preliminary lectures and role-playing sessions.

The newspapers were soon ablaze with coverage of an event that occurred in Greensboro, North Carolina, on February 1, 1960. Four black students, Ezell A. Blair, Jr., David Richmond, Joseph McNeil, and Franklin McCain, from University of North Carolina Agricultural and Technical State University, had launched a sit-in at a lunch counter at a Woolworth's store.

Upon hearing about the sit-in in Greensboro and all the attention it garnered, the Nashville group became restless. But Lawson was adamant that everyone be thoroughly trained and prepared for the forthcoming demonstrations. Through careful and intensive preparation, Lawson hoped to increase the effectiveness of the group and help stave off serious injuries or worse.

The first actual sit-in was planned for February 13. But during a meeting at the First Baptist Church the day before the demonstration, some of the adults expressed their concerns: they were not sure the demonstration should move forward. The grim news of arrests and death threats in Greensboro made them urge the students to reconsider the demonstration. But the events in Greensboro had the opposite effect on the Nashville students (and students elsewhere), who felt compelled, white and black students alike, to mobilize and join what became known as the sit-in movement.

The first real sit-in staged by the Nashville Student Movement was launched the day before Valentine's Day. Nashville was flooded with swarms of quiet, well-dressed, and polite young adults—hardly the image of menacing radical troublemakers. Lewis recounted how it was observed that the impression of the Nashville Student Movement on the locals was akin to an alien invasion. People were shocked, confused, and alarmed. Lewis and the others hoped to educate the locals, to show them a dignified approach to protest. They also wanted to prove that whites and blacks alike were fed up with discriminatory laws and that whites and blacks could work together.

To cover the most ground, the demonstrators were split up into smaller groups. Lewis was the designated speaker for the group that headed toward a downtown lunch counter at Woolworth's. The manager closed the restaurant after Lewis asked to be served. The customers and the servers left the activists sitting at the counter in the dark. After several hours, some white men began to verbally harass them. The activists remained at the lunch counter until early evening and then left to discuss and analyze their experience and celebrate a successful first demonstration.

A maelstrom of activity ensued. Demonstrations continued throughout downtown Nashville. Membership swelled, and a boycott of the downtown stores was launched by local blacks. But the opposition increased, too. Lewis was physically assaulted and arrested. To his surprise, the experience was glorious. He described it as "holy, and noble, and good" (Lewis, 100).

Because of the sit-ins, the stores began to lose money. Customers did not want to be around when the activists streamed into the various restaurants, so in response to the activists the store managers usually closed their stores. The store owners and city leaders panicked. A moratorium was requested. The Nashville activists abided by it for a while, until it was apparent that the authorities were not going to concede to their demand to end segregation at the various locations. The activists saw the moratorium as a tactic for the city to buy more time.

In a move of desperation, authorities created anti-protest laws to avert demonstrations. But the plan backfired. The youths were charged with disorderly conduct and trespassing, but they smiled triumphantly and broke out into song as their wrists were bound and they were hauled off to the local jail. Then they refused to pay bail. The mayor was forced to intervene to set them free. The city had lost control.

The youths were unstoppable. Even when Lawson was dismissed from his position at the Divinity School of Vanderbilt University, activists continued to pour into downtown retail stores. Even when a black attorney's home and a local African American hospital were bombed, the youth did not desist.

The support the students received during these demonstrations emboldened them. Local blacks launched a boycott of the downtown retail stores. And Dr. King's SCLC sponsored a youth conference that ran from April 15 through 17 to encourage and possibly assist in the organization of the young activists in Nashville and elsewhere. The result of that conference was the formation of the Student Nonviolent Coordinating Committee, known as SNCC.

On April 19, 1960, 3,000 individuals marched from Tennessee State University to city hall, where Diane Nash and the mayor faced off before the crowd, to demand that the city integrate downtown stores. The next day, newspapers published an unprecedented headline: the mayor had agreed to desegregate Nashville lunch counters. On May 10, 1960, nearly three months after the first demonstration, the desegregation became official. The Nashville Student Movement produced a giant win for civil rights.

Lewis was now considered to be one of the student leaders of the movement. He and several others toured campuses throughout the nation to talk about what they had accomplished and how they had done it. They were looked upon as heroes. But at home, in the peaceful town of Troy, his parents were distraught. His mother pleaded with Lewis to stop protesting.

Everyone in the community was talking about him and his arrest. It was as if their good child had gone off to seminary school and become a wayward miscreant. His parents were embarrassed—and fearful that his activities would affect them or destroy his life. Lewis' involvement in the movement strained their relationship, a tension that would not be relieved for a long time. Going home during vacations, Lewis felt awkward and uncomfortable. He could hardly wait to get back to his life of protest.

FREEDOM RIDES

They called themselves Freedom Riders. And not just anybody could be one. An application was required, and individuals were selected after careful consideration. Lewis mailed off his application with a letter of recommendation from Lawson. When Lewis received his acceptance letter, he was overjoyed.

This Freedom Ride was the first of several that occurred in 1961. Lewis' group included thirteen members: six blacks and seven whites. They went through rigorous training, similar to Lawson's program, in Washington, D.C. The objective of the Freedom Rides was to challenge the laws that legalized segregation in interstate travel, including buses and facilities, such as the restrooms, drinking fountains, and restaurants at the terminals. The thirteen planned to depart from Washington, D.C. and travel through eight segregated southern states.

The mood was somber at the dinner that was held for the Freedom Riders on the eve of their departure. To put the times into perspective, Lewis had never eaten with whites before. But the extraordinariness of this experience was muted by the reality of what they faced the next day. Everyone knew that they might not ever return to their respective homes. They might never see their family, loved ones, and friends again. Violence was inevitable. Death was a possibility.

At first, nothing dramatic occurred. Not until the Freedom Riders reached Rock Hill, South Carolina, where Lewis walked toward the "white-only" restroom and was stopped by a group of white boys. They questioned him about where he was going. They did not like his answer, and one of them struck him on the side of his head. As he had been trained, he did not resist. He was repeatedly hit while a police officer stood nearby, watching. After some time, the police officer broke up the attack. Lewis did not press charges; this was a deliberate strategy. The irony was that if Lewis had charged the boys, they would, more than likely, have been given a light punishment or no punishment at all.

After this incident, Lewis left the Freedom Riders for a short time to go to Philadelphia, Pennsylvania, to take care of some personal business. He had applied for foreign service with the American Friends Service (AFS). In Philadelphia, the AFS committee awarded him a position in India.

Lewis was on his way back to meet up with the Freedom Riders when tragedy occurred in Anniston and Birmingham, Alabama. In Anniston, the bus of one group of riders was besieged. The tires were slashed, and the bus was firebombed. As the Freedom Riders escaped from the burning bus, whites beat them. Whites boarded another bus headed to Anniston and brutally beat the Freedom Riders. This group continued on to Birmingham, where a white mob waited for them. At the terminal, the group was beaten again. There were no police officers in sight. Police Chief Eugene "Bull" Connor said he had given his officers the day off for Mother's Day. The Congress of Racial Equality (CORE), who had sponsored most of the Freedom Rides, called off the campaign.

STUDENT NONVIOLENT COORDINATION COMMITTEE

The newly formed Student Nonviolent Coordinating Committee (SNCC) was determined to keep the Freedom Rides going. So were the members of the Nashville Student Movement. When SNCC sent out a request for ten volunteers, Lewis eagerly signed up. Thus began Lewis' often turbulent relationship with SNCC.

Lewis, at only twenty-one years, was considered a veteran of the Civil Rights Movement. He had the marks to prove it: arrest and battle scars.

On May 17, 1961, Birmingham police ordered the Freedom Riders, including Lewis, off their Greyhound bus. They were detained for two days, then, at midnight, removed from their cells and carried off down isolated country roads. No one knew where they were being taken. The specter of danger loomed large. The Ku Klux Klan was known to hold rallies or perform lynchings behind the shade of the dense pine woods. The tension was palpable; perhaps they were being led to an ambush.

When the unmarked police station wagon reached a nondescript destination and dumped them out, Lewis and the others were relieved to discover that no ambush awaited them. But they had no idea where they were or how they would get themselves out of this predicament. The Freedom Riders proceeded through the darkness until they came to a house that belonged to an elderly African American couple. The husband stared at them warily but the wife urged them inside and let them use their phone. Lewis called Danielle Nash. She promised to get them transportation. She also had good news for them: eleven more freedom riders had been recruited.

Southern locals and authorities were not the only ones who opposed the Freedom Rides. The federal government was anxious about them. To be sure, President John F. Kennedy, a charismatic and youthful leader, had lent a sympathetic ear to Dr. King and the other civil rights leaders. African Americans, in general, felt Kennedy was a beacon for positive change. But his approach, much to the frustration of Dr. King and the other civil rights leaders, was to ask for more time. Unfortunately, Kennedy would not live long enough to pass significant legislation.

The truth was that the civil rights demonstrations caused trouble for Kennedy politically. They also diminished the nation's credibility with countries abroad. American citizens, too, were appalled as news of the beatings and arrests filled the pages of the newspapers and were reported almost daily on television. When the Freedom Riders refused to back down from the demonstrations, Kennedy was compelled to authorize protection for them. At the same time, he looked into ways to legally put a stop to the rides.

The bus that Lewis and the other Freedom Riders rode was escorted by various police patrols and, at one point, an airplane. The sirens that blared dramatized the urgency and importance of the historical moment. Not only had the riders secured protection, but by their sacrifice, they had compelled the federal government to act on their behalf. No other form of protest— neither negotiation nor litigation—had produced such a compelling moment. When the bus arrived in Montgomery, Alabama, Lewis was the first to disembark in anticipation of speaking with the news media.

But in addition to the reporters, a mob made up of men, women, and children waited for the Freedom Riders. In the subsequent chaos, Lewis tried to get his group to safety. Baseball bats were swung and fists raged. A violent strike to the head left Lewis incapacitated. He was still on the ground in a daze, with blood flowing steadily from his head, when he heard gunshots. The authorities had arrived just in time. But the rescue of the Freedom Riders was bittersweet. The Alabama attorney general read a statement as the activists slowly recovered from the sudden attack, stating that the Freedom Rides had been stopped.

The Freedom Riders fought the injunction by going to court. In four days, the injunction was lifted, and the riders prepared to resume their ride to Mississippi. In Jackson, Lewis and the others were arrested. James Farmer, the national director of CORE, was also present. They were all sentenced to six weeks in prison. While imprisoned at Parchman State Penitentiary, Lewis wrote to the seminary and to the American Friends Service. Lewis was more certain than ever that his future would not be in preaching. He also had no interest in going to India at that time. His destiny was in the Civil Rights Movement.

CIVIL RIGHTS LEADERSHIP

Lewis emerged from prison on July 7, 1961 a different man. He was not only several pounds lighter, but he had the aura of someone who had aged beyond his years in a short period of time. He was speaking better and appeared more confident and at ease. He had the striking glow and

James Forman

James Forman was the executive secretary of the Student Nonviolent Coordinating Committee from 1961 to 1966. Forman was born on October 4, 1928 in Chicago, Illinois. After graduating from high school in 1946, he joined the U.S. Air Force and served in the Korean War.

In 1957, Forman received a B.A. from Roosevelt University in Chicago. Afterwards, he was employed by the *Chicago Defender*, a major black newspaper. Forman wrote several articles on the growing Civil Rights Movement in the South and was inspired by those experiences to quit his job in 1960. This was a critical year for the Civil Rights Movement, for it ushered in the Sit-in Movement, led by idealistic young adults, black and white, and the rise of prominent civil rights organizations such as the Congress of Racial Equality (CORE) and the Student Nonviolent Coordinating Committee (SNCC).

Forman first worked with CORE, providing aid to sharecroppers who had lost their jobs and their homes by attempting to register to vote in Tennessee, and then became an organizer for SNCC. In 1961, he participated in the Freedom Rides and was elected the executive secretary of SNCC. In his early thirties by that time, Forman was older than most of the members. But he was well-respected, though he projected a militant side that unnerved the mainstream civil rights leaders. He could be argumentative and preferred militant demands to the political nonviolence of leaders like Dr. Martin Luther King, Jr. of the Southern Christian Leadership Conference and Roy Wilkins of the NAACP. During the 1963 March on Washington for Jobs and Freedom he advocated for a much more militant version of the tempered and amicable demonstration.

In 1965, Forman lost his cool at a rally before an audience that included King and other middle-class ministers. In his speech he castigated Lyndon B. Johnson, although the president had just given a speech in support of a major voting rights bill, and threatened to physically strike back at Alabama governor George Wallace if he continued to thwart justice. He was not the only one who disliked Wallace, who was shot during an assassination attempt by a white man named Arthur Bremer, in 1972, and was left paralyzed.

With the emergence of the Black Power Movement, with its advocacy of militancy and separatism, Forman found a home. He was one of its staunch supporters. Although Forman resigned from his position in SNCC in 1966, he helped navigate the organization toward its new militant identity. Attempts to merge SNCC with the Black Panther Party in 1967 were unsuccessful.

In 1969, Forman interrupted services at the Riverside Church in New York City to demand reparations. He read from a document known as the Black Manifesto. Although his demands created a clamor, they were not heeded.

(continued)

In the 1970s, Forman attended graduate school at Cornell University in New York, where he majored in African and African American studies. In 1982, he received a Ph.D. from the Union of Experimental Colleges and Universities in Washington, D.C.

Forman married twice, and a third relationship produced two sons. Forman published several books, one of which was his autobiography, *The Making of Black Revolutionaries* (1985). He died in 2005 from colon cancer.

competence of a leader, characteristics that were only enhanced by his innate quietness and composure.

Much to his surprise, considering his humble origins, Lewis' name was being bandied about town, across the nation's college campuses, and in very prestigious circles. It did not take him long to reach greater heights.

The SCLC offered Lewis and the other Freedom Riders scholarships, making it possible for them to continue their college careers. Lewis chose to attend Fisk University to study philosophy. In the fall of his first year at Fisk, 1961, Nash moved to Jackson, Mississippi, and Lewis was elected chairman of the Nashville Student Movement in her stead. Eventually, the Nashville Student Movement became a branch of SNCC. In 1962, Lewis was elected to SNCC's Executive Committee. Dr. King nominated him to the SCLC Board. When, in 1963, SNCC elected him to be the organization's chairman, he quit school and moved to Atlanta, Georgia to be close to headquarters. James Forman became the executive secretary of the organization.

MARCH ON WASHINGTON FOR JOBS AND FREEDOM

In 1963, SNCC was only three years old. As such, it was the youngest of the major civil rights organizations, and like CORE, it comprised mainly college-aged youths. SNCC, CORE, and the SCLC were all engaged in dramatic demonstrations. The NAACP was by far the most conservative of these groups. The National Urban League was not originally a civil rights organization, but its leader, Whitney Young, broke fresh ground as he rose through the ranks of the prominent leaders of the era.

SNCC received an invitation to the planning meetings for the March on Washington for Jobs and Freedom, thus validating its status among the established ranks of civil rights organizations. But the invitation also ruffled many in SNCC, including Lewis, who were not keen on participating in a passive event.

Among the main speakers were the major heads of the civil rights organizations: Dr. Martin Luther King, Jr. of the SCLC; Floyd McKissick, who substituted for CORE's James Farmer; Whitney Young of the National Urban League; and Roy Wilkins of the NAACP. Although Dorothy Height, who was the president of the National Council of Negro Women, was the only woman admitted in the exclusive "club," she did not speak on that day. Nor did any other woman—except for those who gave musical performances—address the audience of some 250,000 participants.

Some believe it was a reflection of the times that women were omitted from speaking, a situation that was symptomatic of restrictive thinking that limited women to minor roles. Height did not quibble about the situation. She knew her worth and made grand contributions from within the sphere of women's organizations. But, as Lewis explained, Ella Baker, an activist who was employed by the NAACP and the SCLC at different times, was none too pleased with the absence of women in leadership roles within the Civil Rights Movement. Lewis wrote that "long before people began using the term 'male chauvinism,' Ella Baker was describing it and denouncing it in the civil rights movement, and she was right" (Lewis, 214).

Lewis was the youngest member to speak at the March. But his speech provoked controversy among the leaders, who pored over it just minutes before he was due to mount the podium. They hastily asked Lewis to make some corrections, because they thought some aspects of his speech were too militant. At first, Lewis stood his ground. But King and a frantic Randolph, who had conceived the march back in the 1940s, convinced him to change his mind. While the speakers' voices rose from the podium, Lewis sat down to edit the strong wording out of his speech. He eliminated statements such as describing "the President's [civil right's] bill as being 'too little and too late'" and "the word 'cheap'" to characterize some politicians (Lewis, 227). Lewis finished making the changes in time to take his turn at the podium.

The moment was titanic. The march had drawn people from almost every walk of life, including celebrities like Paul Newman, Marlon Brando, Dick Gregory, Sidney Poitier, Lena Horne, Ossie Davis, Charlton Heston, Sammy Davis, Jr., Harry Belafonte, and Diahann Carroll.

"As I laid my papers on the podium," he wrote "and looked out at that sea of faces, I felt a combination of great humility and incredible fear" (Lewis, 227). That day would go down as one of the most poignant moments in American history. President Kennedy had tried to talk A. Philip Randolph, one of the key organizers, out of going ahead with the march. He feared that violence would erupt. But in the end, Kennedy was so thrilled by the day that he invited the civil rights leaders to his office afterwards.

COUNCIL ON UNITED CIVIL RIGHTS LEADERSHIP

When Stephen Currier brought together the leaders of the civil rights groups to form the Council on United Civil Rights Leadership (CUCRL), Lewis and Forman alternated as SNCC's representative. The other members included Dr.

Martin Luther King, Jr., Roy Wilkins, James Farmer, Dorothy Height, and Whitney Young. The main objective of this group was to raise money to be split amongst the various organizations and to collaborate on programs.

Lewis was critical of these gatherings, stating that he "encountered the same tone of one-upmanship and infighting and political positioning that we'd witnessed during the planning for the march." He felt that because SNCC was "considered the kids, the upstarts ... we were given peanuts compared with what the others received" in terms of financial donations (Lewis, 236). However, these criticisms did not terminate SNCC's collaboration efforts with the others.

VOTER REGISTRATION

In 1963, segregation was only one of several problems that concerned African Americans. Disenfranchisement was another. After the March on Washington, SNCC targeted voter registration in the South.

Voting in the South was complicated by outmoded laws, irrelevant literacy tests, violence, and intimidation. Another problem was that the registrar kept erratic hours, conveniently closing at times of the day when African Americans were most likely to stop by.

SNCC went down to Selma, Alabama, where only one percent of the black population was registered to vote. Their representatives went into the community, gave orientations at churches and in people's homes about voting rights, and encouraged blacks to register. One of the Ruleville, Mississippi locals was a woman named Fannie Lou Hamer, who not only registered to vote but rose to the forefront of the civil rights struggle in her state.

Lewis played an important role in Selma. He made several trips there between his other commitments, such as a sit-in campaign in Atlanta restaurants. Lewis joined the demonstrations in front of the Selma courthouse, protesting the obstructions that made voting nearly impossible for blacks. Lewis and others were arrested. The police officers used cattle prods during the arrest and held the demonstrators in converted chicken coops.

FREEDOM SUMMER

Following the voter registration campaign in Selma, SNCC prepared for a bigger project for 1964: the Mississippi Freedom Summer. This was a program comprising a voter registration campaign, the establishment of Freedom Schools, and the support of the Mississippi Freedom Democratic Party.

During one meeting with civil rights leaders prior to the launching of the Mississippi Freedom Summer, Lewis found himself bristling in his seat. Roy Wilkins had asked for a moratorium on any civil rights demonstrations to please President Lyndon B. Johnson, who wanted to circumvent bad press during this critical period in time to better his chances for re-election. Lewis, as well as Farmer, objected. SNCC and CORE were based primarily on the principle of demonstrations. Lewis did not foresee anyone in his organization willing to abide by a moratorium, especially considering that the Mississippi Freedom Summer was just underway. They would not agree to stopping their demonstrations, even for a brief period.

The excitement gained momentum in the days preceding the Mississippi Freedom Summer. With the exception of a few dance parties, Lewis admitted that there was little time for or interest in recreation. In hindsight, he felt there should have been. The urge to act and a deep commitment to the struggle were shared by everyone. But most of these twenty-something activists had barely reached adulthood. Normally, they would have been just settling down into a full-time job, a marriage, or raising children. Lewis explained that he was married to the movement.

Lewis' "marriage" would be tested greatly during the ensuing months. The Mississippi Freedom Summer began on June 13, 1964. The troubles began shortly thereafter. While in training, three activists, Andrew Goodman, Mickey Schwerner, and James Chaney, were reported missing. Goodman and Schwerner were Jewish and hailed from New York (a number of Jews and whites were eager participants in the project). Chaney was black and a native of Mississippi. Everyone was worried about the three missing activists. Nonetheless, plans went forward as scheduled.

Behind the scenes, Farmer, Lewis, and others flew down to Mississippi to investigate the disappearance of the activists. Talking to authorities yielded no new information. Lewis and others went into the community, asking questions of those locals who were brave enough to provide information. In the meantime, President Johnson dispatched FBI agents to search for the missing activists. Though this appeared to be an extraordinary gesture given the times, Lewis was bothered by it. Numerous black activists had lost their lives or been beaten, and the FBI had not lifted a finger.

The fact was that by this time, Lewis had come to understand the enormity of the task ahead of them and the dangers of becoming overconfident because of their recent successes. On July 2, President Johnson had announced the Civil Rights Act of 1964. This was the strongest civil rights legislation of the century. The next day, Lewis had given a speech at a Ruleville church and reminded locals that they had to stay vigilant; that the civil rights struggle was not over yet.

On August 4, everyone's worst fears were realized when the bodies of the three activists were found. Chaney had been viciously beaten and shot three times. The others had been murdered by a single shot. This was not the only violent tragedy that summer. The Mississippi Summer was fraught with violence, including church burnings, bombings, and multiple beatings.

MISSISSIPPI FREEDOM DEMOCRATIC PARTY

The violence only served to spur on the activists. Later in the summer, SNCC assisted a newly formed political party to challenge the traditional all-white and ultra-conservative Mississippi Democratic Party. Fannie Lou Hamer was among the delegates representing the Mississippi Freedom Democratic Party (MFDP). Lewis toured several Mississippi towns and gave speeches to canvass support for them. When the delegates traveled to Atlantic City, New Jersey, for the National Democratic Convention, Lewis watched from the sidelines. He was proud; their optimism was catching. But when, at the end of the convention, the delegates were awarded only two seats in a back-room compromise, all their hopes contorted to anger and frustration.

The activists and their leaders were torn over how to respond. Some did not want to acquiesce to the compromise. Lewis believed that the Civil Rights Movement began to collapse at that point, as the event fed the polarization between the conservative integrationists on the one hand and the militants on the other. For example, SNCC was largely disillusioned by leaders such as King, who were in favor of the compromise.

The atmosphere at the culmination of the Freedom Summer was dismal. Despite the results of the campaign—seventeen thousand African Americans had successfully registered to vote and massive support was mobilized for the MFDP—the activists were burned out, frustrated by the non-stop violence, and disenchanted by the loss in Atlantic City.

AFRICA

Eleven SNCC activists, including John Lewis, went on a three-week trip to Guinea, in West Africa, in the fall of 1964. Lewis and a friend also visited, strictly as tourists, Liberia, Ghana, Zambia, Kenya, Ethiopia, and Egypt.

The trip to Guinea had a dual purpose: Harry Belafonte, a black musician and actor, had offered them a respite after the long and difficult summer. Furthermore, Belafonte's friend, Ahmed Sékou Touré, first president of Guinea after it received its independence from French rule in 1958, desired to facilitate an international dialogue between the African American civil rights activists and the young people of his country.

Lewis was impressed by the Guineans' shrewd knowledge of world politics, including the events occurring in America. He felt solidarity with them, largely because they were also activists. Throughout the continent, Africans waged struggles for liberation from foreign colonialism.

However, Lewis found that the African activists in Guinea and elsewhere on the continent were far more militant than the SNCC activists. These young men and women were, ideologically, nationalists and willing to literally fight for liberation. Among the barrage of questions directed to Lewis, a large number concerned Malcolm X, whom many of them venerated. Malcolm X was not only one of the most militant black activists in America, he was a Pan-Africanist, which meant that he was concerned not only for blacks in America but all descendents of Africa.

While Lewis was in a hotel in Nairobi, Kenya, he met Malcolm X for the first time. Each was surprised to see the other. Malcolm commented that he was pleased "to see SNCC reaching out like this to Africa, and how more black people in America needed to travel and see and learn what was happening with blacks outside our country, not just in Africa but all over the world" (Lewis, 297). Malcolm was in Kenya attending a conference of non-aligned nations in Cairo, where he spoke about his new Organization of Afro-American Unity.

Lewis was bewildered at the change in the man that sat before him, talking so amicably about racial unity. Malcolm X had been notorious for his intense anathema for whites and his scorching criticisms of racism in America, as well as of prominent civil rights organizations such as SNCC. But the former firebrand had undergone a dramatic transformation as a result of a trip to Mecca in 1964, where the sight of blacks and whites seemingly uncorrupted by racism opened his eyes to a new form of activism, one not based on fiery, angry speeches. When they departed ways, Malcolm X wished the SNCC activists well and encouraged them to press on.

Back in America, black SNCC activists were undergoing a metamorphosis toward the opposite end of the spectrum. This shift stemmed from their resentment over whites taking leadership positions in SNCC as well as the conservative leadership of the Civil Rights Movement in general. They reached their breaking point after repeated merciless beatings and killings by racist police officers and white mobs. The disappointing results of the summer's Mississippi Freedom Democratic Party challenge also figured into the general feeling of discontent. One of the loudest voices of opposition to SNCC's conservative position on integration and nonviolence was Stokely Carmichael. Even James Forman exhibited militant tendencies.

Everyone knew that Lewis was the antithesis of Carmichael and Forman. He was the mild-mannered one—the gentle one. When members took to calling leaders, such as his hero Dr. King, **Uncle Toms**, Lewis knew that his influence on the organization was slipping away.

BLOODY SUNDAY

Lewis remained supportive of King. In January 1965, he joined the great leader in a voter registration campaign in Selma, Alabama. On the eighteenth of the month, Lewis and King led four hundred locals to a courthouse. When they reached the steps of the courthouse, they found a sign affixed to the door that read "Out to Lunch." This was an old tactic. Selma's registrar office was open only two days a month. Restricting office hours was one way in which whites prevented blacks from registering to vote.

Later that day, King was attacked at a hotel. Lewis fended off the attacker and detained him until police arrived to arrest him. This incident portended dangers to come. But for now, the demonstrations proceeded smoothly. There were more marches to the courthouse, and there were arrests. The pressure caused by the demonstrations and arrests compelled the federal government to order the registrar to expand office hours.

During one of the demonstrations, Lewis confronted the local sheriff. This sheriff ordered Lewis and the demonstrators to leave the vicinity. Lewis stood up to him, even though the sheriff wielded a billy club.

Until that point, there had been no fatalities associated with their efforts. But on February 18, at a voter registration demonstration in Marion, Alabama, an army veteran was shot and killed. SCLC organized a march from Selma to Montgomery to publicize that murder.

Lewis and Hosea Williams, an SCLC civil rights leader who had been arrested 125 times during the Civil Rights Movement, set out on Sunday, March 7 with six hundred men, women, and children. The marchers were stopped by a barricade of Alabama state troopers as they prepared to cross the Edmund Pettus Bridge. Some troopers were on foot; others were mounted on horses.

Lewis and Williams instructed everyone to kneel and pray. Moments later, Lewis received the first blow. He staggered to the ground and braced himself for the next blow. The second hit, with a billy club, fractured Lewis' skull. The troopers unleashed an all-out attack on the marchers, who were dressed in their church clothes. Fortunately for the demonstrators in particular and the country as a whole, reporters were there and caught every terrible moment with their cameras. That day became known as Bloody Sunday.

A second march was planned, but Governor George Wallace would not allow it. On March 9, a white Unitarian minister, James Reeb, was beaten to death. Shortly thereafter, Lewis (still bandaged), King, and others gathered in the living room of a Selma resident. Their eyes were glued to the television set as President Johnson began one of the most memorable speeches in the history of the Civil Rights Movement, wherein he announced to the world his support for voting rights for all Americans.

On the next day, the demonstrators were permitted to proceed with the march. What had started out as a protest march became a victory march, encompassing more than twenty-five thousand people. The march culminated at the state capitol in Montgomery, where Lewis was honored. The Voting Rights Act was signed on August 6.

LIFE AFTER SNCC

By the end of Mississippi Freedom Summer, Lewis' authority within SNCC had dwindled to next to nothing. He had seen it coming, but the realization was painful, even traumatic. Stokely Carmichael was elected as chairman of SNCC in his place at the 1966 annual conference. Lewis lingered on for a rally in Mississippi in June. But the change had already taken effect, and this event was unlike any that had gone before. The rallying cry was for black consciousness, self-defense, and black power. As tough and brave as Lewis had proved himself to be, a militant he could never be. Everyone knew that about Lewis, including himself. He was devastated to see all that he struggled and sacrificed for unravel.

Full-Time Work, Marriage, and Family

Lewis looked for a job that would allow him to work on the issues as he had with SNCC, with the same objectives. He moved to New York and worked for the Field Foundation for a year. This organization helped fund civil rights and child-welfare programs. But Lewis liked the South better. He was glad to move to Atlanta, Georgia for his next job as a community organizer for the Southern Regional Council in 1967.

With more time on his hands, Lewis turned his attention to some academic and personal business. In 1967, he graduated from Fisk with a bachelor's degree in philosophy. At a party, he met Lillian Miles. He invited her to his twenty-seventh birthday party, and they began dating shortly thereafter. Lewis also began the slow and difficult process of reconnecting with his parents, who were still baffled and hurt by his participation in the Civil Rights Movement. They eventually reconciled.

Politics

In 1968, Lewis fostered a new, unexpected relationship with rising politician Robert Kennedy, the brother of former President John F. Kennedy. Lewis believed that Bobby was more empathetic and willing to endorse causes for African Americans after the assassination of his brother in 1963. Lewis became a volunteer on his campaign for the presidency. He took a leave of absence from his job at the Southern Regional Council to help galvanize black voters. But Lewis was blind-sided by two assassinations: Dr. King's on April 4, 1968, and Kennedy's on June 6, 1968.

Lewis, as well as much of the nation, was distraught. The questions on everyone's mind, especially within the black community, were: What happens now? Who will lead us? Who will fight for us now? There had always been other leaders, but King had seemed to eclipse them all with his charismatic speechmaking and his overwhelming popularity among blacks and whites. But the struggle continued. Ralph Abernathy took King's place as the leader of the SCLC, and the leaders of the other prominent civil rights organizations pressed forward.

When Lewis had recovered from these staggering blows, he redirected his energies toward politics. In August 1968, he was one of the Georgia delegates who challenged the Democratic Party at the Democratic National Convention in Chicago, Illinois. The results were better than during the 1964 Mississippi challenge. The two Georgia delegations split votes down the line.

When he returned to Atlanta, Lewis was hospitalized due to exhaustion. Miles stayed with him, and he asked her to marry him. They married on December 21, 1968. King's father, Reverend Martin Luther King, Sr., officiated over the ceremony.

The desire to better his community had been a driving force for Lewis throughout his adult life. As he entered his thirties, Lewis reaffirmed that commitment. In 1970, he headed the Southern Regional Council's Voter Education Project to oversee voter registration drives and rallies, to provide classes for the community, and to monitor the status and progress of blacks.

Lewis was at the top of his game when, in 1975, he was featured in *Time* magazine. The following year, he and his wife adopted a baby boy, whom they named John-Miles. Shortly thereafter, Lewis attended a SNCC reunion. There were no hard feelings on either side.

In the ensuing years, Lewis remained active in Georgia politics. After an unsuccessful run for the U.S. House of Representatives in 1977, President Jimmy Carter appointed him associate director of ACTION. This appeared to be an ideal job, since he could play a significant role in the coordination of several volunteer social action programs.

But the job made him restless. He no longer wanted to be involved in grass-roots work. He desired to be a part of the decision-making process. That, he felt, was where he could be the most useful at this juncture in his life.

U.S. House of Representatives

Lewis successfully ran for Atlanta City Council in 1981. Five years later, Lewis, as a member of the Democratic Party, became the second black to be elected to the U.S. House of Representatives, representing Georgia, since Reconstruction. The first was Andrew Young, a civil rights activist and close advisor to King, who served terms in 1972, 1974, and 1976.

Lewis remains a prominent figure in Congress, where he addresses issues that concern blacks as well as all Americans, and helps maintain the legacy of the Civil Rights Movement. In 1991, he was appointed Chief Deputy Whip of the House. He has served the longest of any senator or congressperson in Georgia.

Also in the 1990s, Lewis was among the high-profile protestors who challenged the design of the state flag of Georgia. Lewis argued that the design, featuring a Confederate Battle Flag, had been created in response to the 1956 Supreme Court ruling that desegregated public schools in the South. In 2001, Georgia designed a new flag.

This issue parallels the ongoing conflict concerning the **Confederate flag,** which is used to symbolize the entire region of the South. Those who find the flag offensive assert that it glorifies a culture and community that was based on the systematic oppression of human beings. To them, confederacy and slavery are inseparable, and thus neither ought to be venerated.

In 2000, when suspicions abounded that the voting process had been compromised, Lewis disputed the presidential election of George W. Bush. In 2001, after the terrorist attack on America, Lewis gave an inspiring speech to help unify and hearten Americans during a traumatic period.

Lewis has an intimate understanding of what it means to live through extremely distressing times. For him, the civil rights struggle was both exhilarating and deeply troubling. To stare hate in the face, to confront death and brutal attacks, and to battle seemingly impossible odds and enemies took courage, determination, and an ornery conviction of the rightness of one's goals and the certainty of triumph.

Each year, Lewis returns to the site of the Selma, Alabama march of 1965, where he and others were beaten on Bloody Sunday during their quest for equality and justice. Undoubtedly, the scene plays back through his mind, and the ghosts, not yet half a century old, are awakened as he marches over that old familiar bridge. He is perhaps comforted, if not invigorated, by the fact that that battle was won, and America was made the better for it.

See also Ella Baker; Stokely Carmichael; James Farmer; Fannie Lou Hamer; Dorothy Height; Martin Luther King, Jr.; Malcolm X; Thurgood Marshall; A. Philip Randolph; Roy Wilkins; and Whitney Young.

FURTHER RESOURCES

Arsenault, Raymond. *Freedom Riders: 1961 and the Struggle for Racial Justice.* New York: Oxford University Press, 2006.

Forman, James. *The Making of Black Revolutionaries.* Seattle: University of Washington Press, 1997.

Lewis, John. *Walking with the Wind: A Memoir of the Movement.* New York: Simon & Schuster, 1998.

"Reporting Civil Rights; 1941–1973." *The Library of America* (February 2008). See http://reportingcivilrights.loa.org.

"SNCC 1960–1966: Six Years of the Student Nonviolent Coordinating Committee." *SNCC Project Group* (February 2008). See http://www.ibiblio.org/sncc/index.html.

"U.S. Congressman John Lewis." *U.S. House of Representatives* (February 2008). See http://johnlewis.house.gov.

Malcolm X (1925–1965)

Malcolm X was a spokesperson for the Nation of Islam (NOI). He emerged as one of the most radical and militant leaders during the Civil Rights Movement. Toward the end of his life, Malcolm X went through a spiritual and ideological metamorphosis following a pilgrimage to Mecca, which led to his embracing traditional Islam and tempering his animosity toward whites.

Malcolm X was the epitome of extreme radicalness, though he did not project the emotional fervor of some. He was poised, deliberate, and steely-eyed beneath his brow-line glasses. When he gave speeches, he spoke with a measured, controlled rhythm.

But the content of those speeches was a scathing, incisive, and shrewd attack on whites and a declaration of the privations and oppression of blacks. He lambasted all whites, making little, if any, distinction between those who were and those who were not racists. Sometimes he added a touch of humor, generally at the expense of conservative, middle-class African Americans, or Uncle Toms as he contemptuously called them. All in all, his message reflected his own tragic experiences with racism and oppression. His father, a zealous Garveyite, had been murdered by racist whites. Poverty and the unraveling of his mother's sanity actuated the splitting up of his six siblings. The world Malcolm X knew was cruel and wretched, fueling his intense hatred for whites and the institutions dominated by them.

Malcolm X contended that it was a good thing that his time spent as a wayward and confused youth landed him in jail, for that was where he was introduced to the Nation of Islam (NOI). He attributed his nearly overnight transformation into a self-disciplined devotee to this event. A major reason why the Nation of Islam captivated him so was because it centered on the importance of blacks, and in doing so, nurtured the esteem of black men denigrated by society. In this way, the NOI was similar to the Garvey Movement, which was named after the spirited Marcus Garvey. Garvey founded and led the Universal Negro Improvement Association and African Communities League (UNIA-ACL) in the early twentieth century. The Garvey Movement's message of race uplift spread like wildfire throughout America's urban black communities. The NOI also encouraged the expression of racial pride and **black nationalism** but through the medium of religion. Malcolm X became an ardent student of the Nation of Islam. Furthermore, he took the message into the streets, speaking from soapboxes. He enthralled his audiences and soon gained a reputation as a speaker.

His swelling fame coincided with the burgeoning of the Civil Rights Movement, for which he did not have any use. Malcolm X regularly castigated the nonviolent methods advocated by the Movement's leaders, criticized organizational collaborations between blacks and whites, and disapproved of the pursuit of integration. Malcolm X volubly advocated armed self-defense and called for violent revolution and black separatism. He was, in essence, one of the chief antagonists of the Movement.

Soapbox

A soapbox is a wooden carton in which soap is packed, but it can refer to any object used as an improvised platform. The term is also used metaphorically to describe someone who is voicing their opinion on an issue, and usually, at length.

Soapbox orating is a practice that dates back to the American Revolution (and much earlier in countries such as England), when early Americans addressed the public in impromptu or prepared speeches on any given topic, usually political. What distinguishes soapbox orating from other speaking performances is that it is usually done by ordinary people and outdoors. New York is famous for its many soapbox orators. Certain streets in New York in the early twentieth century were a hotbed of activity for orators, including communists, socialists, and others deemed as radical freethinkers. Soapbox orating epitomized the American ideals of democracy and freedom of speech.

Among popular early twentieth-century African American soapbox orators were Hubert Henry Harrison, A. Philip Randolph, and Marcus Garvey. Spending time on the soapbox frequently preceded a more formal leadership role. Soapbox orating served as a way to hone one's speaking skills, to develop ideas and ways to express those ideas, and to cultivate a following and some notoriety. It was also the most direct way to disseminate an important message to the people. For example, before Randolph became the leader of the Brotherhood for Sleeping Car Porters, he was a young, passionate, and fiery radical mounted on a makeshift podium speaking against racism and classism. Before Marcus Garvey launched his eponymous movement, he too tested the waters on the soapbox and in other venues. Malcolm X, a young upstart in the Nation of Islam, became a household name while soapbox orating in Harlem, New York.

But however adamant he seemed, Malcolm X was not immune to change. Following a break with the Nation of Islam on March 8, 1964, he founded the Muslim Mosque, Inc. And after a pilgrimage to Mecca later that spring, he underwent a final metamorphosis. While in Saudi Arabia, Malcolm X was moved by the fact that Muslim adherents of all colors worshiped together. No one that he saw discriminated against anyone else, causing him to seriously reconsider and, ultimately renounce, his volatile and anti-white rhetoric. He wrote about this experience in his famous *The Autobiography of Malcolm X*, a comprehensive social study on his life and times. However, he did not live long enough to advance his new approach. Malcolm X was assassinated on February 21, 1965.

CHILDHOOD

Malcolm Little was born on May 19, 1925 in Omaha, Nebraska to Reverend Earl and Louise Little. He had eight siblings, three of whom, Ella, Earl, and Mary, were from his father's first marriage. Wilfred, Hilda, Philbert, Malcolm, Reginald, and Yvonne were the children of Reverend Little's second union.

Reverend Earl Little was an anomaly, to be sure, and was, undoubtedly, a forceful role model for the young Malcolm. A native of Georgia, Earl Little, unlike his surname, was a giant of a man, six feet four, booming, and fearless. It is fair to say that Garveyism was Little's true calling, but he was a Baptist preacher by trade and as a way to support his family. Many African Americans at that time would not dream of going about town trying to spread Garveyism. But this is what Little did, even though it caused him trouble with the local whites.

Malcolm knew by heart the story of the night the Ku Klux Klan rode down to their home, wielding their rifles, and ordered Earl Little out of the house. Mary Little, pregnant with Malcolm at the time, toddled to the porch and told those men that her husband was not home. Before riding away, they broke every window of their home. The men were practicing an old custom of violent intimidation against anyone who challenged the system of white supremacy. This was one way in which they diffused any form of black organizing and any talk of racial pride and empowerment.

This sort of intimidation and the threats to Reverend Little's life did not thwart him. He had seen plenty of white hatred and racial violence in his life. Four of his six brothers were murdered by whites. After his violent death, another brother would share the same fate. Only one of Malcolm's paternal uncles died of natural causes.

Mary Little played a different role in the family. She was overwhelmed with housekeeping, preparing meals, and the ordinary day-to-day struggles of maintaining a large household. Mary Little was born in the British West Indies and stood in a stark contrast to her husband. She looked white, whereas the Reverend Little had very dark skin. Malcolm X believed she had received a good education, whereas her husband had only gone on to the third or fourth grade. Both were martinets, but Mary Little was usually the enforcer of the frequent whippings her children received. Both, Malcolm observed, were inflicted with a common form of skin-color prejudice. Mary Little favored the darker-toned children; Reverend Little showed a preference for the ones with fairer complexions.

Malcolm X had the lightest skin of all his siblings. He felt that that was why he received special treatment from his father. Frequently, Reverend Little carried Malcolm to his Garvey meetings. Malcolm was dissatisfied with the impassioned black church service, but he was transfixed by the dignity and gravity that the Garveyites exuded, and by the empowering exclamations of racial pride and uplift. Etched in his memory were the solemn framed pictures of Garvey himself, the man who transported a race from hopelessness to optimism, self-determination, and self-reliance. Although Garvey died in 1940, his followers continued to stoke the flames of his memory and aspirations, but the movement would never attain its former grandeur.

The house that Malcolm Little recalled most was the one his father built with his own hands on the outskirts of Lansing, Michigan. This house was constructed because the previous one had been burned down in 1929 by two white men. Reverend Little shot at those men, but it was too late. The family clambered to safety, then stood with the police and fire department and watched the house burn down.

At the new home, the Littles lived in relative peace for some time. They raised chickens and kept a garden. Occasional fights erupted between the parents, at times culminating in domestic violence. Outside the home, Little continued to mobilize the locals to Garveyism and teach, sporadically, at various Baptist churches.

One day, following an argument, Reverend Little stormed out of the house. Mary Little ran after him, distressed by a sudden premonition of his impending death. But her husband only stopped to wave back at her when she called after him. She never saw her husband alive again, for that night he was attacked and stretched across the railroad tracks. His body was nearly cut in half.

Mary Little would never recover from that shock and the subsequent tumult that her family faced. One insurance company refused to release the money owed Mary Little, stating that her husband had committed suicide. This despite the fact that it was common knowledge that the Black Legion, an organization akin to the Ku Klux Klan, was to blame. The welfare checks and widow's pension sufficed for a while. But Mary Little could not hold down a job. Her employers would not keep her on after it was discovered that her husband was the radical Little. Mary's grief overwhelmed her, as did her inability to make any money. The household slowly came undone, and the children were left to try to maintain a sense of normalcy in the home.

The administrators of the welfare assistance made matters worse. Malcolm X wrote that "they acted as if they owned us, as if we were their private property" (Malcolm X, 13). They scrutinized everything about the Little family. Little became a Seventh Day Adventist, only to have the welfare workers call her crazy for turning down some pork someone offered her family (pork is prohibited in the Seventh Day Adventist religion). They later targeted Malcolm when he began stealing food. Malcolm and his brother Philbert started acting out at school, getting into fights with some of the white students.

After Mary Little was rejected by a potential suitor, the situation became irreparable. Mary began to talk to herself. Welfare stepped in and removed

Malcolm from the home. He went to live with the Gohannas, a local black family. Malcolm liked living with them, and was close friends with the child everyone called Big Boy. Together, they hunted and fished. Every now and then, Malcolm went on awkward visits back home, but seeing his mother in her worsening state made him uncomfortable.

In 1937, his mother was admitted into the state mental hospital in Kalama-zoo, where she remained for twenty-six years. Malcolm Little's siblings were split up, but they continued to maintain connection, largely through letter writing. In 1963, Mary was released and went to live with friends of the family.

Living with the Swerlins

When Malcolm was thirteen years old, he was sent to live in a detention home in Mason, Michigan with a white couple, Mr. and Mrs. Swerlin, for his unrelentingly unruly behavior. The Swerlin's opened their doors to many wayward youth. The Swerlin's and the other children who lived with them were all very kind to Malcolm. Mr. and Mrs. Swerlin treated him almost like one of their own. But when they talked about "niggers" in his presence, Malcolm was troubled.

Despite that, Malcolm flourished. Everyone at the predominately white school, Mason Junior High School, liked him and welcomed him in. He produced stellar grades and was asked to be a part of almost every extracur-ricular event. In the second semester of the seventh grade, he was elected class president.

When white spectators—or even his peers and teachers—called out racist names from the bleachers at basketball games he played in, he pretended not to notice. At school dances, he navigated through the awkward waters of being and yet not being one of them. He was not allowed to dance with the young white girls. So, he talked and laughed with his friends, and then quietly departed for home. Malcolm was too shy to ask out the local black girls.

There were other issues that Malcolm Little did not dismiss so easily. In history class, his teacher, Mr. Williams, would tell "nigger jokes." He also recalled how the sum total African American studies in the history book consisted of one paragraph. Within that paragraph there was a shocking statement about how African Americans "were usually lazy and dumb and shiftless" (Malcolm X, 29).

One of Malcolm's favorite things to do was to escape to the nearby black ghetto, just to watch the blacks going in and out of the bars and restaurants and to listen to the pulsating music vibrating from within was thrilling. Malcolm Little was drawn to this sort of life, so it was only natural that he used the money he made washing dishes at a restaurant to buy himself a green suit and shoes.

Malcolm realized after a summer trip to Boston to visit his vivacious and successful half-sister, Ella Little, that one of the reasons he was adored at the Swerlin's, at work, and at school was because of the way people perceived him. In his later analysis as an adult, Malcolm felt he was being treated like a mascot, and that he was accepted as he behaved in a way that was non-threatening. Malcolm X admitted that, while living with the Swerlins, he tried, in every way, to be white.

The Boston trip had changed Malcolm in a profound way. For the first time in his life he was immersed in a large community of African Americans. The Swerlins and their ilk did not understand why Malcolm became reticent and looked so irritated when anyone used the word "nigger." Upon his return, he felt suddenly out of place, self-conscious, and unhappy. He did not fit in that world.

Another incident that confirmed his unhappiness occurred in the classroom, between himself and his English teacher, Mr. Ostrowski. Upon being asked what he wanted to do when he grew up, Malcolm Little proudly asserted that he wanted to become a lawyer. Mr. Ostrowski then explained that he should be "realistic about being a nigger, and suggested that he pursue carpentry, instead" (Malcolm X, 36).

Malcolm felt that the Swerlins would not have understood why Mr. Ostrowski's comment was so destructive and so painful. The Swerlins were exasperated by the cloud that had come over his formerly sunny disposition. They did not know what else to do, so they had him moved from their home. Malcolm dropped out of school and moved to Boston to live with Ella.

STREET LIFE

In Boston, Little observed two black identities: the "Roxbury Negroes acting and living differently from any black people [he'd] ever dreamed of … and looked down their noses at the Negroes of the black ghetto, or so called 'town' section" (Malcolm X, 40). Malcolm gravitated toward the latter, although his half-sister was a member of the former. Ella did not like the change that took place in Malcolm following his arrival. His friend Shorty, a denizen of the town section, served as Malcolm's guide, translator, and advisor, overseeing his transmogrification into a street kid.

Shorty hailed from Lansing too, but that was the only commonality between the two boys, who met when Malcolm wandered into town one day. Shorty shot one look at Malcolm and knew he was not in tune with the latest trends. He didn't talk with the parlance of the city; use terms such as "stud," "cat," and "cool"; he did not dress in the fashionable zoot suits, or wear his hair in the processed style (called a conk). Because Malcolm had reddish hair, Shorty called him Red, and that became his street moniker.

Shorty also helped Malcolm Little get his first job in Boston. Malcolm knew Ella would not approve, because shining shoes at the Roseland State Ballroom was not high class. It was a job that was relegated to blacks. But the job demanded more than the ability to work the rag so as to make it pop (a sound that gave the impression that the shoe shiner was working harder than he actually was); Malcolm was also expected to hustle or provide other services or products, such as alcohol and reefers.

The shoe-shining job provided Malcolm with an up-close view of the happenings at Roseland State Ballroom, where the dances were segregated. The black dances were especially lively, featuring improvisational and dramatic moves that worked the crowds into a frenzy. The Lindy-hop was one of the dances that was all the rage. Malcolm would eventually become a popular fixture there.

Malcolm was grateful for the new job and for having met such a knowledgeable friend. As a result of this acquaintance, Malcolm started gambling, smoking cigarettes and reefers, and drinking alcohol. He also received his first conk (he would later describe this as his "first really big step toward self-degradation") and purchased his first zoot suit on credit (Malcolm X, 54). When Malcolm posed for his sister in his suit, she was dismayed. He wrote his brothers and sisters, intoxicated with his self-satisfaction over his stylish transformation.

Malcolm was not the only one drawn to this irresistible way of life. The woman Malcolm referred to in his autobiography as "Laura" was fascinated by it as well. Malcolm met Laura after he quit shoe shining, and while working as the soda fountain clerk at the Townsend Drug Store located in the Hill. Malcolm was miserable working with what he deemed to be self-absorbed snobs. But Laura, who lived in the Hill neighborhood, was different. She came often to the soda fountain to read. At first they said little to one another. Gradually, they started having conversations, and that sparked a date when Laura lit up at the mention of Lindy-hopping.

Laura was a fantastic dancer, one of the best. But during one dance, a white woman Malcolm called "Sophia" appeared, and once she and Malcolm locked eyes, there was no turning back. Malcolm snubbed Laura after that. He always believed it was his fault that Laura abandoned her college dreams and delved dangerously into street life. She was never the same after that.

Malcolm and Sophia became inseparable. They had an unspoken agreement: Sophia lavished gifts and money on Malcolm, and he in turn displayed Sophia on his arm. This gave him instant status in the ghetto and permitted her to go with him into the taboo black world, in which he knew it was a thrill for many whites to take part. Malcolm was sixteen years old.

Ella was relieved when Malcolm took a job with the New Haven Railroad, because, for African Americans, it was one of the best jobs around. It would also, she thought, steer him away from his relationship with Sophia and help to settle him down. Ella wanted Malcolm to meet a nice woman from the Hills, marry, and live a good, quiet life.

But Malcolm did not stop seeing Sophia. And for him, the job was primarily a way to see New York, the epitome of fascinating city delights.

Malcolm had no intention of slowing down—if anything, he accelerated his street activities at a dangerous, dizzying pace.

While working with the railroad, Malcolm worked several jobs: washing dishes, selling snacks, cleaning, and renting pillows. His customers were black and white. With the white customers, Malcolm learned to do what he called "Uncle Tomming," which meant kowtowing to whatever needs or wants they might have; in effect putting on a good show and being eager to please. Malcolm was good at this—when he wanted to be. Other times, he got into trouble for acting outside his expected subservient role—for being a recusant. He once nearly got into a fight with a white soldier. The complaints over Malcolm's cheekiness increased, and he was eventually fired from the New Haven. For a while, he worked on the Silver Meteor until he was let go over a confrontation with the assistant conductor.

In 1942, Malcolm ended his stint with the railroad and moved to New York, where he promptly descended into the city's iniquitous underworld, taking on the name Detroit Red. In Boston, Malcolm had been a neophyte; Shorty's artless underling. In New York, Malcolm would upstage his former mentor.

Malcolm was given the name "Detroit" to distinguish him from other red-haired black men. He took to telling people that he was from Detroit, Michigan, since most people did not know that Lansing, Michigan even existed. As Detroit Red, Malcolm would launch an outrageous career in the streets.

His first job in New York was as a waiter in a popular bar, where he began what he referred to as several hustles or illicit money-making schemes. One of them involved soliciting potential clients for his prostitute friends. When he was dismissed from his waiting job, he turned to selling marijuana, robbery, and playing the numbers.

In 1943, Malcolm Little received a draft letter, but he had no interest in becoming a soldier. He circumvented the draft by feigning mental instability. He described his physical preparation for that day by saying: "with my wild zoot suit I wore the yellow knob-toe shoes, and I frizzled my hair up into a reddish bush of conk.... I went in, skipping and tipping" (Malcolm X, 105). Talking in his wildest street vernacular, he went to the induction center, and when directed to see the psychiatrist, he told the befuddled white man that he could not wait to get inducted to, in his words, "Organize them nigger soldiers, you dig? Steal us some guns, and kill up **crackers**!" (Malcolm X, 106).

Malcolm spent most of his time hustling and doing drugs (along with a few nondestructive activities like going to movies and listening to music). He began abusing cocaine as well as marijuana. And he was still seeing Sophia, even though she had married a white man. When his brother, Reginald, left the merchant marines, Malcolm introduced him to the street world, where he had become a sophisticated and well-known presence. Reginald, however, did not delve as deeply into crime as his brother.

Malcolm later commented that he should have died many times leading such a fast life. A West Indian gangster named Archie who ran the numbers game pursued him over money that Malcolm did not remember owing him. Italian ruffians hunted him down over some crime for which they blamed him. There were other threats on his life, as well as the fact that Malcolm's drug use had him in a constant haze. And the law had been after him for a long time, since he had first been targeted as one of the infamous drug sellers in the city.

Sammy, a friend and partner in crime Malcolm made while in New York, contacted Shorty, who drove to New York to rescue Malcolm from his iniquitous and dangerous lifestyle. Back in Boston, however, Malcolm continued in his parlous life of crime. He recruited Shorty, who had become a musician, but was barely making enough money to make ends meet. Malcolm became the leader of a small group of thieves comprising Shorty, Sophia and her sister, and a biracial man named Rudy. They burglarized several white homes before they were apprehended. Following the trial in February, 1946, Malcolm and Shorty each received a sentence of ten years in prison. Rudy somehow escaped during the incident, and was never captured or tried. The women were sentenced to one to five. During the trial, Malcolm ascertained from all the questions regarding his and Shorty's relationship with Sophia and her sister that the "white women in league with Negroes was [the] main obsession," not necessarily their actual crimes (Malcolm X, 149). The fact that the average sentence for a first-time offense was two years illustrates how racism, again, was at play.

PRISON

Little served the first couple years of his sentence at Charleston State Prison. He continued to smoke, and to substitute his drug habit, he, like other prisoners, drank a concoction of nutmeg water. His penchant for making trouble caused him to be sent to solitary more than once. He was so raging, foul mouthed, and obstinate that the inmates began calling him Satan.

It was a black man named Bimbi who provided Little with his first glimpse of redemption through education. Bimbi was a favorite with everyone because he had an enormous amount of knowledge. Other inmates, including Little, and sometimes the guards, huddled around him, spellbound by his intellect. His sources were an eclectic mix, including various philosophers, like Henry David Thoreau. Thoreau was born in 1817 and was a famous contemplative thinker, naturalist, as well as abolitionist and advocate of nonviolent resistance to government. He would influence famous activists like Mahatma Gandhi and Dr. Martin Luther King, Jr.

Bimbi was also different from the others because he did not curse. Little, who appeared to have the baddest reputation at Charleston, was quietly intrigued by him. When Bimbi told Little that he ought to consider taking the correspondence course that was offered at the prison and spend some time at the library, Little, who had only eight years of formal education, listened.

Learning was tough going for Little. He felt that his years of degradation had eroded much of what he had learned in his school years. Malcolm X later explained how his writing had become atrocious, and that he had lost the ability to write a simple sentence. Little took a correspondence course for English as well as Latin.

In 1948, Little was moved to Concord Prison. While there, he discovered that all of his siblings had converted to the Nation of Islam and they wanted him to do he same. Little was not eager to comply. But Reginald knew how to approach him. In a letter, he urged Malcolm to stop eating pork and smoking and that he would "show him how to get out of prison" (Malcolm X, 155). To Malcolm, the letter was as puzzling as it was provocative. He did not yet understand how smoking and eating pork were related to his imprisonment, but it was a chance worth taking. He stopped smoking the very day he received the letter, and he did not eat another piece of pork while in prison.

Much of Little's learning about the Nation of Islam took place through correspondence with his siblings and the leader of the Nation of Islam, Elijah Muhammad, while he was imprisoned. He would later discover that, among other things, Black Muslims were not allowed to gamble, use drugs, or consume any drug, alcohol, or food (including pig) that would be harmful to the body, dance, or go to the movies. In other words, engage in the kind of behavior that characterized Little's life prior to his imprisonment. He was also obligated to pray to Allah. Praying was, perhaps, the hardest aspect of his conversion. He wrote that "picking a lock to rob someone's house was the only way my knees had ever been bent before" (Malcolm X, 169).

The Nation of Islam not only advocated a clean, healthy, and a spiritually regimented lifestyle, it raised the **racial consciousness** of African Americans. From his own experience, Little knew a certain amount about his race's history, about Africa, slavery, and the effect racism and ignorance had on the continued oppression of blacks in America. The only learning he had received in a history class was that blacks were lazy and shiftless. The discovery that Africa was not a savage, uncivilized country and that blacks indeed made numerous accomplishments empowered Little.

Elijah Muhammad also taught an erroneous tale that all whites were, literally, devils. Studying the history of the world and analyzing the long history of white oppression over other races, and seeing the effects of racism in his own life, made Little susceptible to Muhammad's interpretation. Elijah Muhammad blamed whites for his own predicament, asserting that "the black prisoner ... symbolized white society's crime of keeping black men oppressed and deprived and ignorant, and unable to get decent jobs, turning them into criminals" (Malcolm X, 169).

The transmogrification of Malcolm Little was nearly instantaneous. It helped that Norfolk, unlike most prisons, encouraged intellectual growth among the inmates and housed a capacious library, with an unending supply of books on religion and history. Little delved into this wide array of books, intently reading history and philosophy. Little milled about with the other prisoners in the hope of proselytizing them. He even took to participating in a number of prison debates. He went on a letter-writing campaign, so zealous was he for his new-found faith. He wrote to his friends from his former street life. He wrote the Massachusetts mayor and governor. He wrote reprimanding letters to President Harry Truman explaining "how the white man's society was responsible for the black man's condition in this wilderness of North America" (Malcolm X, 171). He did not receive a response.

Malcolm wrote Elijah Muhammad every day, and Muhammad frequently wrote Little back. Little's embarrassment over his poor penmanship and his inability to construct sentences fueled his pursuit of knowledge. One of the first actions he took to remedy this problem was to handwrite an entire dictionary. He also took many of the classes that were offered at the prison.

Though Malcolm was changing dramatically, his brother Reginald was regressing. During a series of visits, Malcolm watched as his brother showed increasing signs of trouble. He had been ousted from the Nation of Islam because of an illicit relationship with another member. Reginald did not hide his burgeoning scorn for the organization, or his physical decline. One of the trademarks of the Nation of Islam was physical cleanliness and orderliness in dress and appearance. Little observed that his brother began to dress in a slovenly manner. When Reginald told him, during one visit, that Malcolm's beard looked like writhing snakes, Malcolm attributed it as a punishment for having turned away from the Muslim faith. He later felt that Reginald's fall was aided by the rejection he and his siblings showed him because he was no longer a Muslim. Eventually, Reginald, like their mother, was put into a mental institution.

In 1952, Little was shuffled back to the Charleston State Prison. He was not the same man that had entered there in 1946. He wore his hair neat and bereft of straightening chemicals. Because of his voracious reading habit, he began wearing the brow-line glasses that became his trademark. He was composed and disciplined, and he would never utter another obscenity or raise his voice to rant and rage.

What did not change was his outspokenness and his readiness to challenge people with whom he disagreed. But now when he spoke it was to expose racism and racial stereotypes. During a bible class, Malcolm point-blank challenged the notion that Jesus was fair-skinned, blue-eyed, and blond, since he was a Hebrew. Although Little had always been a terrible fighter, he could spar effectively using his intellect and newfound knowledge, as well as his expanding vocabulary and his knack for using it. His direct, in-your-face style of intellectual combat was mesmerizing.

NATION OF ISLAM

On August 7, 1952, Malcolm Little was released from prison, after serving seven years. He felt as if it had been the equivalent of an advance degree in the Nation of Islam and self-development. His transition into life after prison was facilitated by several mundane jobs: at a furniture store, a factory, and with the Ford Motor company. His ongoing development in the Nation of Islam was facilitated by sharing a home with his brother Winfred and his family, who regularly prayed to the east (toward Mecca) as directed by the Prophet Muhammad, and maintained the dietary restrictions and other practices of the faith. Little went regularly to the temple to listen to Elijah Muhammad speak. Black Muslims gathered in buildings called temples.

Also during this time, Little officially changed his name. For Malcolm X, names served as benchmarks for critical periods in his life. While submerged in street culture, he was known as "Red" in Boston and "Detroit Red" in New York. During the first few years in prison, he was called "Satan." Upon his release, his new name, Malcolm X, symbolized not only his rejection of the surname (which belonged to slave masters) that had been imposed upon slaves in the New World, but the confirmation of his complete conversion to the Nation of Islam. It signified his own rebirth into a life of faith and purpose.

At the center of this new life was Malcolm's devotion to Allah, as well as his blinded idolization of the small-statured, smooth-faced, and coppery-complexioned Elijah Muhammad. Malcolm X digested every word that escaped from his mouth. Elijah Muhammad was not only a man filled with sagacious wisdom, he was humble (known to sweep the floor of a Muslim-operated store), gentle, patient, loving, and even sometimes reproving of others, including Malcolm X. He was the antithesis of Malcolm's own tempestuous father, who acquired obedience from the children through intimidation. Although Malcolm likened their relationship to that of Socrates or Aristotle to their students, Elijah Muhammad was also a surrogate father, someone he sought for guidance with spiritual, as well as personal, problems.

When, during a dinner with Elijah, Malcolm asked him what the best way was to build membership, he took his first step toward his ascent within the Nation. Elijah told him that the way to increase their numbers was to look among the young people.

Malcolm proved to be extraordinarily good at drawing in young men. In due course, Elijah fostered Malcolm's leadership potential by allowing him to speak before the Muslims. In 1953, Malcolm officially became a minister and was instructed to build more temples in critical locations. Malcolm traveled to Boston, Massachusetts, Philadelphia, Pennsylvania, and finally New York City to establish new temples.

Seriousness was a trait that characterized the Malcolm X of this period. His strict adherence to his fast-paced schedule denotes a man driven by purpose, not by frivolity. Sleepless at night, he traversed the city with his thoughts, agonizing over the oppression of African Americans and pondering ways to save the lives of those whose experiences were so similar to his own past degradation. He is usually stony-faced in his few extant photos from this period. In later pictures, taken after having received several death threats, he wields a rifle and stares furtively out a window. Photos of Malcolm X smiling broadly are a stunning contrast to the working Malcolm or the public Malcolm.

Malcolm arrived in New York in 1954 and set up residence, bedazzling the African American community in ways that had not been seen since the glamorous days of his father's beloved Marcus Garvey. He also turned his attention to the issue of making an appropriate marriage and starting a family.

Even in love and marriage, Malcolm X carried himself with gravity. Most of the eligible women were enthralled by him. Some were openly miffed that he would not pay them any attention. But Malcolm undertook the subject of marriage as if approaching a business deal.

Betty X, formerly Betty Sanders, had an education degree from Tuskegee Institute. She taught health and hygiene classes to the women at Temple Seven in New York. Malcolm X's portrait of Betty was terse and unembellished: "tall, brown-skinned—darker than I was. And she had brown eyes" (Malcolm X, 227). He also liked the fact that she was not loquacious. But this description belied the fact that he had noticed her in an "interested-kind-of-way" from the start. But he hid this fact, even from himself, for he demanded the same commitment from himself as he did from others, which was to focus on their work.

Malcolm X spent a great deal of time analyzing the idea of marriage and ultimately figured that "Sister Betty X, for instance, would just happen to be the right height for somebody my height, and also the right age" (Malcolm X, 229). Their courtship was brief. Although dating was not permitted among Muslims, there were group outings that Betty and Malcolm X went to, such as lectures or events at other mosques. Malcolm X mentioned only one outing alone with her, to the Museum of National History under the dubious guise that the outing would benefit her classes.

From Betty X's perspective, Malcolm was winsome, although grave. He got Betty to open up about her own experiences with racism. It was while driving from here and there that Betty X and Malcolm X "exchanged glances and smiles in the rear view mirror" (Jeffrey, 35). There was, evidently, a subtle and coy mutual attraction. But nothing could have prepared Betty for the unexpected call she received from Malcolm, asking for her hand in marriage.

Malcolm X saw Elijah Muhammad in person to request his guidance on the marriage question. After meeting Betty X, Elijah gave Malcolm his blessing. Fortunately, Betty had no reservations. She accepted his proposal, even though her parents were against it. Like a number of African Americans, they felt Malcolm X was too radical and his brand of protest too dangerous.

Angry Black Man

The website http://www.urbandictionary.com attributes the Angry Black Man complex to African American sports athletes, but the term was originally associated with men, like Malcolm X, who expressed their frustrations with the social, economic, and political status of African Americans and rampant racism in a hard-hitting and direct way.

The Angry Black Man image is certainly an urban construction. Since slavery, the stereotypical characteristics of a black man were docility, childlikeness, joyfulness, and stoic spiritualism. This image was reinforced in large part by Jim Crow laws, a sense of powerlessness, intimidation, and anti-black violence. In reality, feigning these characteristics was often used as a tactic on the part of blacks as a means of survival or to gain access to opportunities.

Following the migration of blacks from the South to the North, there emerged a phenomenon in which black men, in greater numbers, became openly discontented with racism and oppression and more apt to confront racism head on. The race riots in the North during the 1940s and 1960s are cases in point, wherein black men refused to accept racism or submit to white superiority. African Americans saw this expression of anger, defiance, and assertive resistance as a form of empowerment. They perceived hiding behind the mask of meekness as demoralizing and weak.

However, the "angry black man" image presents many dilemmas. Sometimes blacks criticize, or lampoon, the "angry black man" role that is frequently cast in contemporary movies. The criticism is that the angry black man reinforces another stereotype of a one-dimensional, perpetually angry character who is incapable of rational thinking skills or complex emotions. Famed writer James Baldwin criticized Richard Wright's portrayal of Bigger Thomas in *Native Son* (1940) as a stereotypical figure, whose inner turmoil and rage cause him to commit heinous crimes. But most applaud Wright's novel, because he dared to protest the system of racism through the medium of anger and demonstrated how poverty and racism triggered Bigger Thomas' violent acts.

The "angry black man" is problematic in more ways than one. For example, while W.E.B. Du Bois worked with the National Association for the Advancement of Colored People (NAACP), he had to contend with those who felt he viewed every issue in terms of race. This is a trait that is also associated with the angry black man, who is frequently deemed overly sensitive, and thus his protests fall on deaf ears.

They were married on January 14, 1958, with, ironically, a white man officiating and white witnesses. The ceremony took place in Lansing, Michigan, where they could get married without having to wait too long and without all the romantic fuss Malcolm wanted to avoid. Malcolm and Betty had six girls: Attilah (born 1958), Qubilah (1960), Ilyasah (1962), Gamilah-Lamumba (1964), and Malaak and Malikah (1965).

In the wake of Malcolm's marriage, several events contributed to the burgeoning visibility of the Nation of Islam in the black community and mainstream America. The first was a television documentary program called *The Hate That Hate Produced*, which presumed to tell the story of the Nation of Islam. This generated a great deal of attention, almost exclusively negative in nature. The documentary sensationalized the organization, and the public responded with near-hysteria, as they could not get beyond the idea that this group hated whites and advocated violence.

The mainstream media had a field day after the documentary aired, bombarding Malcolm X with phone calls (this routine would continue until his death) and distorting the image of the organization and Malcolm himself. The press branded the organization with labels such as "hate-teachers," "violence-seekers," "black racists," and "black fascists." Malcolm X became, he wrote, a "symbol of 'hatred'" (Malcolm X, 239, 381). To be sure, Malcolm contributed to the construction of that identity with his fiery, confrontational, and self-confessed angry speeches. But the rest of his message, which called racist whites to task for the economic, social, and political oppression of blacks, for obliterating black history and carrying out racial violence with impunity, was rarely addressed.

Malcolm X told one journalist that he was wrong "to accuse the Honorable Elijah Muhammad of teaching black supremacy and hate! All Mr. Muhammad is doing is trying to uplift the black man's mentality and the black man's social and economic condition in this country" (Malcolm X, 241).

A number of conservative, high-profile black integrationists echoed the sentiments of weary whites. At first, Malcolm X held back from criticizing them. Elijah Muhammad did not want to give in to what he perceived to be an attempt by whites to fuel dissension between blacks. But when he gave the signal, Malcolm X went full steam into attack mode, calling prominent leaders "Uncle Toms" and publicly haranguing them. The schism between the conservative integrationist and the radical rebel was exacerbated by religious differences. Most of the prominent leaders were Christian. Their historical differences complicated any possibility of a parley.

The media could not get enough of Malcolm X. He began to receive more and more requests to participate in sundry panels and debates. Eventually, Elijah Muhammad invited the white press to attend private Nation of Islam rallies, for media attention was a powerful tool for outreach and public exposure. Through Malcolm's controversial speeches, he drew increasing attention to himself, fast becoming one of the most vocal adversaries of the civil rights leaders and their struggle for integration. Eventually, Malcolm X would become the face of the Nation of Islam.

Among blacks, the Nation of Islam, as well as Malcolm X, was becoming increasingly popular. Nation of Islam news was circulated within the black community through printed media, helping to spread the message to more individuals than could ever be reached by a door to door campaign. Malcolm X wrote articles for the popular black newspaper, *Amsterdam News*, and later for the *Los Angeles Herald Dispatch*. Following a trip to Los Angeles to establish another Temple, in 1957, Malcolm X helped launch the Nation of Islam's organ, *Muhammad Speaks*.

One night in 1959, one of the members of Temple Seven called the Muslim-operated restaurant to inform them that Brother Johnson Hinton had been assaulted by two New York police officers. The story was that two Muslims had witnessed a fight that had broken out on the street. When officers arrived and told everyone to leave, the two Muslims stayed. One of them was rushed to the nearby precinct house—not a hospital—after receiving several blows to his head.

Malcolm X was one of some fifty Muslims who gathered to stand "in ranks-formation outside the police precinct house" to which the injured Muslim had been brought (Malcolm X, 233). Malcolm X, their spokesperson, confronted the lieutenant in charge, telling him that that injured man should be in a hospital. The lieutenant complied. The Muslims followed the ambulance to Harlem Hospital and stood, silent, poised, until it was confirmed that the Muslim was being treated. Also present that evening were crowds of restive blacks, suspiciously watching what was going on and taking in, with an air of awe and respect, the quiet demonstration staged by New York's Temple Seven and the coppery-haired man who led them.

The Nation of Islam Temple in New York proved to be very attractive to African Americans. For one thing, the temple was officiated by the charismatic, no-nonsense minister, Malcolm X, who was unusually approachable. He could literally speak their complicated language. He had been one of them and had no problem making that fact known. Most importantly, he provided an alternative to the cold, empty hopelessness of city life by promoting an agenda of clean-living, strong self-worth, dignity, and responsibility. The temple ran programs for drug addicts and alcoholics. It offered camaraderie and racial pride in a safe environment, where they could vent their frustration with racism. For young blacks, the Nation of Islam presented an alternative to the allure of dangerous street life. Malcolm X was the easy winner over the appeal of superficial, trendy fashion, ill-gotten gains, and false prestige.

As Malcolm X's profile rose, the government carried out an investigation of this baffling new phenomenon. Spies infiltrated the organization, but as Malcolm X explained, this tactic frequently backfired. A number of black spies converted, and either quit their jobs with the feds or worked as counterspies for the Nation of Islam, which was growing by leaps and bounds.

Plans were underway to build an Islamic Center; businesses were being launched, and Elijah Muhammad's gentle voice could frequently be heard on the radio airwaves. Muhammad revealed to Malcolm X that he wanted him to take an unprecedented step as a Black Muslim: to become a public personality. With this commission, Malcolm X was expected to devote more time to broadcasting the Nation of Islam's stance through the media.

As much as the white media were confounded and even fearful of Malcolm X's radicalism, they could not get enough of him. Students, white and black, at universities and colleges, were equally mesmerized. Malcolm X throve in this environment, just as he had when going into the streets proselytizing to blacks. Thanks to his varied experiences, Malcolm was able to hone his speech-making skills and intellectual agility.

As Malcolm X toured the nation in the early 1960s promoting the Nation of Islam, the Civil Rights Movement, one of his favorite topics, reached full force. When Malcolm X called the famous March on Washington for Jobs and Freedoms the "Farce on Washington," his biting commentary made headlines. Malcolm charged that that event did more to aggrandize the egos of the participants than to address the problems blacks faced.

Malcolm regularly attacked one of the fundamental goals of the civil rights struggle: **integrationism**. Instead he endorsed separatism, advocating that each African American "should be focusing his every effort toward building his *own* businesses, and decent homes for himself … patronize their own kind, hire their own kind, and start in those ways to build up the black race's ability to do for itself" (Malcolm X, 275).

Before the public, Malcolm X appeared to be unswerving, impenetrable, and hard-edged. But the truth was that beneath the public armor, he was dealing with a very personal and crushing matter. As early as 1961, Malcolm surmised from innuendos and backdoor rumor-mongering that there were some in the Nation who were jealous of him. Elijah Muhammad had predicted that that might happen. But the gossip was escalating. Some said he was hoarding money and trying to outdo Elijah Muhammad. Malcolm was mortified. He underscored in his autobiography that he and his family lived on the bare essentials, that he had a terrible argument with his wife because he did not make enough money to provide for them. Malcolm X declared repeatedly that he would die for Elijah Muhammad and that he was not the self-seeking person that some made him out to be. To reduce this negative attention, Malcolm X tried to play down his role, declining a number of high-profile interviews in magazines such as *Life* and *Newsweek*.

In the early spring of 1963, Elijah Muhammad showered Malcolm X with seemingly ingenuous praise at a rally, and followed this by making him the first National Minister of the Nation of Islam. However, in that same year, Malcolm X became aware of another rash of rumors—this time concerning Muhammad himself. Muslims alleged that Muhammad had fathered children outside of his marriage. Malcolm X spoke with the mothers of the children to find out the truth, even though they had been isolated from the Nation of Islam and his religion forbade him from seeing members who had been cast out for violating a NOI rule. What he discovered nearly shattered him. The three women he questioned confirmed the terrible truth: Elijah Muhammad had committed fornication. He also discovered that Muhammad himself feared that Malcolm would abandon him and the Nation of Islam. Malcolm X tried to do damage control, but the situation in the Nation's leadership continued to worsen.

That summer, Malcolm X sensed something sinister fermenting in the ghettos. Anyone who was aware of the insidious problems of ghetto life, or who simply took the time to see for themselves, would realize how despair was turning into frustration and anger, creating something that could burst at any moment. Overcrowding, hunger, and poverty were getting worse, as were the tensions between racist white cops and young black men. When Malcolm X greeted youths as he walked the streets to the New York temple each day, he saw something fierce and unmistakable in their eyes.

Few are aware that Malcolm X extended invitations, in July, to at least three of the major civil rights leaders: Dr. Martin Luther King, Jr., of the Southern Christian Leadership Conference; Whitney Young, of the Urban League; and James Farmer, of the Congress of Race Equality. In that letter, Malcolm X wrote, "The present racial crisis in this country carries within it powerful destructive ingredients that may soon erupt into an uncontrollable explosion. The seriousness of this situation demands that immediate steps must be taken to solve this crucial problem, by those who have genuine concern.... We are inviting several Negro leaders to give their analysis of the present race problem and also their solution." He promised to "moderate the meeting and guarantee order and courtesy for all speakers" ("Letter to Martin Luther King"). If the civil rights leaders had attended, it would have been deemed radical. James Farmer, however, at least agreed to speak publicly in media-covered debates. As a result of those interactions, Farmer and Malcolm X forged a respectful relationship behind the scenes.

Despite attempts by the Nation of Islam to address the sweltering tensions in the ghetto, riots broke out beginning the following summer, in New York (Harlem, Rochester, and Brooklyn), New Jersey (Paterson and Elizabeth), Illinois (Chicago), and Pennsylvania (Philadelphia). In 1967 alone, there were some fifty-nine riots.

Violence was seemingly everywhere. In the South, activists faced vicious attacks by white mobs. And on November 22, 1963, violence would strike where it was least expected when President John F. Kennedy was assassinated. Elijah Muhammad issued a warning that everyone must refrain from commenting on that tragedy. Malcolm X, however, sometimes made statements that he would later regret. This time his mistake would cost him.

Malcolm X did not trust the media. He frequently complained that they manipulated his words and questioned him in ways that required intellectual agility. During the question-and-answer period following his speech "God's Judgment of White America," a reporter pointedly asked what his thoughts were concerning the president's assassination. Malcolm X blurted unguardedly that "it was ... a case of the chickens coming home to roost." What was not included in subsequent articles was his expansion on that statement, which explained how "the hate in white men had not stopped with the killing of defenseless black people, but that hate, allowed to spread unchecked, finally had struck down this country's Chief of State" (Malcolm X, 301).

Publicly, Malcolm X accepted his error in judgment. He was penitent and self-effacing. In private, Malcolm X was disconcerted, not only because as punishment he was not permitted to speak publicly or in his temple for three months, but because word reached him of a possible threat to his life by members of the Nation of Islam. That meant, Malcolm believed, that his mentor, his idol, the man he credited with his own redemption, wanted him dead.

Malcolm X had faced public attacks before, and in his former life he had confronted threats to his life, but this was an entirely different situation. He went to his family doctor, who told him to take some time off. He and his wife and children went on their first family vacation ever, accepting the invitation of Cassius Clay, later and famously known as Muhammad Ali, while he was in Miami training. But Malcolm could not unwind, not completely. Part of him was captivated by Clay's charm and talent. But he was, for the most part, an emotional wreck.

Malik el-Shabazz

Malcolm changed his name to Malik el-Shabazz and announced his split with the Nation of Islam on March 8, 1964, causing quite a stir. But in a photo during a press conference, Malcolm reveals a gleaming smile. Perhaps he felt a sense of relief at leaving the organization. In addition to his troublous relationship with Elijah Muhammad, there were rumors that some within the organization were demanding money from members (for dues and newspaper sales) who could barely feed their families. And there was the fact that the police and FBI agents were infiltrating the Nation of Islam and causing turmoil within the organization. In the face of these troubling events, Malcolm X established a new organization on March 16, 1964, called Muslim Mosque, Inc. This organization, he promised, would be more actively involved in administering to the African American community.

On March 26, 1964, Malcolm X and Dr. Martin Luther King, Jr. came face to face at a press conference for the first time. The meeting only lasted for a matter of minutes, but the two men spoke and shook hands. They then smiled for the camera and went their separate ways. The moment was replete with meaning. Could it be that the two biggest rivals of the Civil Rights Movement would come together?

As Malcolm worked to build his new organization, he also made preparations for a spiritual journey to Mecca. In this he had the help of his sister,

Ella, who helped provide funds for the trip, and Dr. Mahmoud Youssef Sha-warbi, the director of the Federation of Islamic Associations in the United States.

Dr. Shawarbi was gracious when the two met. They discussed the fact that not everyone could go to Mecca; only true followers of Islam were permitted to engage in that once a-year-pilgrimage (or Hajj) to the holy land. Dr. Shawarbi provided Malcolm X with a letter of approval and gave him a book, *The Eternal Message of Muhammad,* written by Abd-al-Rahman Azzam. This book was originally published in Arabic, in 1933, under the title, *The Hero of Heroes or the Most Prominent Attribute of the Prophet Muhammad.*

Mecca

The trip to Mecca was extraordinarily humbling and life changing. In America, Malcolm X projected a cool confidence and a surly independence that unsettled some. In Saudi Arabia, Malcolm was reduced to an almost childlike dependence on the kindness of strangers. He did not understand the rituals, nor could he speak the language. But he found friendliness and acceptance at every turn. A large number of individuals recognized him and approached him curiously, asking questions about America and how blacks were treated there. And they were patient with him, instructing him tenderly on how to pray, what words to say, and other important parts of the Hajj.

Malcolm X was not only enlightened as to the aspects of orthodox Islam to the degree that he converted wholeheartedly to it, but his viewpoint on race was shattered. Before the trip, no one could have convinced him that race simply does not matter. But in Saudi Arabia, he worshiped side-by-side with dark- and light-skinned followers of Islam. He saw that all were treated equally and no one was shown preference. Others he met confirmed to him that his calling whites "devils" was not spiritually right.

Malcolm returned to America in May of 1964 a greatly changed man. Though he remained primarily concerned with black issues, and with the entire population of descendants of Africa (a view known as Pan-Africanism), for the first time ever he saw the possibilities of working with whites and with civil rights organizations. His new approach to life was mirrored by another name change. As a result of his going on the Hajj, he was able to add "El" to his name. He was now known as El-Hajj Malik el-Shabazz.

EL-HAJJ MALIK EL-SHABAZZ

On June 18, 1964, Malcolm X announced the formation of a group he called the Organization of Afro-American Unity. This organization would be the way in which Malcolm could expand and explore his new ideas, including coalitions with whites and civil rights leaders. However, he stressed that whites were not necessarily going to join his or any black organization, but rather to organize amongst themselves, so that their organizations could then collaborate, each bringing its own racial perspective.

Although Malcolm X was now an adherent of Islam and had expressed a new-found tolerance for whites, he was still an ardent proponent of self-defense. He sent King a telegram on June 30, 1964, while the latter was in St. Augustine, Florida on a civil rights campaign, asking him—almost begging him—for the chance to send some of his "brothers" down to provide protection to the demonstrators.

Indeed King faced one of his greatest challenges in his attempt to desegregate the small southern community of St. Augustine. Ku Klux Klan activity was strong there, as was resistance among top white officials. Despite several demonstrations and arrests, the campaign failed to produce the spectacular results that had followed so many of his other campaigns.

Meanwhile, the reception to Malcolm X's change of heart within the Nation of Islam was a cold one. In fact, Louis Farrakhan, the young minister in the Nation of Islam who took over Malcolm X's former leadership duties in the Harlem Mosque, published a series of scathing criticisms and denouncements of Malcolm X. To the Nation of Islam at that time, Malcolm X was a traitor.

Malcolm X received many death threats during this time. He kept a rifle in his home and remained ever-vigilant, but he continued to forge ahead with his program. In July, Malcolm attended the Organization of African Unity conference in Cairo, Egypt. He met with several African leaders, such as Jomo Kenyatta, president of Kenya, and Milton Obote, president of Uganda, to discuss the problems African Americans faced and the need for unity among all descendants of Africa.

During a discussion with a white ambassador from the United States while in Africa, Malcolm X marveled when the ambassador said "he never thought in terms of race, that he dealt with human beings, never noticing their color [when in Africa] ... only when he returned to America would he become aware of color differences" (Malcolm X, 371). Malcolm X came to realize from their conversation that whites were not evil—that it was society that cultivated racist thinking and behavior.

While in Cairo, Malcolm X bumped into John Lewis, then chairman of the Student Nonviolent Coordinating Committee (SNCC), and Don Harris, a close friend who was also a member of SNCC, in the hotel where they both stayed. This was Lewis' and Harris' first trip to Africa. Malcolm X joined them in their hotel room to talk. Lewis was stunned by

Malcolm X's transformation. In his autobiography, *Walking with the Wind* (1998), Lewis wrote that "the man who sat with us in that hotel room was enthusiastic and excited—not angry, not brooding … he got most enthusiastic about his idea of bringing the case of African Americans before the General Assembly of the United Nations and holding the United States in violation of the United Nations' Human Rights Charter" (Lewis, 296, 297).

BACK TO AMERICA

Malcolm X returned home on November 24, 1964. Shortly thereafter, he held a press conference to speak to the United Nations about his plans to address the issues facing blacks. The media could not help but notice the striking contrast between the Malcolm X they had once known and this Malik El Shabbazz, whose speech carried none of the fiery denunciations that had been so omnipresent prior to his trip to Mecca.

Indeed, Malcolm X, the 6 foot 3 inch, lean, and broadly smiling black leader, felt a fresh optimism as he set about his self-appointed tasks. Indeed, Malcolm X's interests now most resembled the work of his father's hero, Marcus Garvey. Garvey was a Christian, but he attempted to unite blacks, not by religious affiliation, but by their ancestral link to Africa. And he did not base his ideology on racial hatred.

Sadly, Malcolm X's work was hindered by increasing violent acts against him and his family. In December 1964, Louis Farrakhan wrote, in an issue of *Muhammad Speaks*, that "only those who wish to be led to hell, or to their doom, will follow Malcolm…. Such a man as Malcolm is worthy of death, and would have met death if it had not been for Muhammad's confidence in Allah for victory over his enemies" (Magida, 83). On February 14, 1965, someone tried to set his home in Queens, New York on fire. No one was hurt, but Malcolm X was outraged. Yet he did not stop.

On February 21, Malcolm agreed to deliver a speech in Harlem's Audubon Ballroom. His wife and children were present, as well as a crowd of some four hundred. During Malcolm X's presentation, a commotion broke out in the audience. Minutes later, men ran up toward Malcolm and gunned him down. He died that day at the age of thirty-nine.

Three members of the Nation of Islam were apprehended, tried, convicted, and sentenced to life in prison for the murder of Malcolm X: Norman 3X Butler, Thomas 15X Johnson, and Talmadge Hayer. However, Butler and Johnson maintain their innocence.

See also James Farmer; Louis Farrakhan; Marcus Garvey; Martin Luther King, Jr.; John Lewis; and Whitney Young.

Ossie Davis

Many civil rights leaders did not attend Malcolm X's funeral due to the extreme radicalism he demonstrated in life. Presumably, they did not want to be affiliated with him, even in his death, and jeopardize their roles and influence as the civil rights struggle went on. But Ossie Davis, an actor who was associated with civil rights activism and known for his venerable baritone voice, not only attended the funeral service but gave Malcolm X's eulogy.

Born on December 18, 1917 in Cogdell, Georgia, Davis attended Howard University and Columbia University School of General Studies, but he wanted to be an actor, so he quit school. There were few roles for African Americans in the first half of the twentieth century, and even fewer for those who desired to play positive characters outside the ordinary fare of maids, servants, and butlers. In 1950, however, he got his first break with a role in a Sidney Poitier film, *No Way Out.* The film itself was a major breakthrough because of its theme of racism, as well as the fact that Sidney Poitier played the protagonist (an African American doctor named Luther Brooks). Davis plays one of his brothers, John Brooks. His wife, Ruby Dee, whom he had married in 1948, was cast as his wife, Connie Brooks. The real-life union produced three children and countless contributions to African American protest and American movies.

Davis and Dee were a power couple. Both were actors in their own right, having built substantial careers in the movies, and both were heavily involved in activism during the Civil Rights Movement. Davis appeared in numerous movies, such as *Fourteen Hours* (1951), *A Man Called Adam* (1966), and *Slaves* (1969). He was a fixture in many Spike Lee films, including *School Daze* (1988), *Do the Right Thing* (1989), *Malcolm X* (1992), *Get on the Bus* (1996), and *4 Little Girls* (1997). He also was cast in movies with nonracial themes, such as *Gladiator* (1992) and *Grumpy Old Men* (1993). He directed a handful of films, most notably *Cotton Comes to Harlem* (1970), and appeared in made-for-television movies such as *Roots: The Next Generations* (1979) and *Deacons for Defense* (2003). The roles he chose, and the plays and books he published, such as *Escape to Freedom: The Story of Young Frederick Douglass* (1977), *Langston* (1982), and *We Shall Overcome: The History of the Civil Rights Movement as It Happened* (2004), are indicative of Davis' commitment to black achievement and protest.

During the 1960s, he and his wife provided support to the Civil Rights Movement, sometimes behind the scenes and sometimes visibly, as in the 1963 March on Washington. Davis spoke not only at Malcolm X's funeral, but Dr. Martin Luther King, Jr.'s as well, after he was assassinated on April 4, 1968. Davis and his wife also participated in anti-war rallies during the Vietnam War. On February 4, 2005, Davis died of natural causes.

FURTHER RESOURCES

Ali, Noaman. "Letter to Martin Luther King." *Malcolm-x.org* (April 2008). See http://www.malcolm-x.org/docs/let_mart.htm.

The Eternal Message of Muhammad (April 2008) See http://www.islamic-council.org/lib/rahman-azzam/Azzam_Main.htm.

Jeffrey, Laura S. *Betty Shabazz: Sharing the Vision of Malcolm X.* Berkeley Heights, NJ: Enslow Publishers, 2000.

Lewis, John. *Walking with the Wind: A Memoir of the Movement.* New York: Simon & Schuster, 1998.

Magida, Arthur J. *Prophet of Rage.* New York: HarperCollins, 1996.

Malcolm X. *The Autobiography of Malcolm X.* New York: Ballantine Books, 1964.

Myers, Walter Dean. *Malcolm X: By Any Means Necessary.* New York: Scholastic, 1993.

Perry, Bruce. *Malcolm: The Life of a Man Who Changed Black America.* Barrytown, NY: Station Hill Press, 1991.

Thurgood Marshall (1908–1993)

Thurgood Marshall was a civil rights attorney for the NAACP and was the first African American to serve on the U.S. Supreme Court (1967–1991). He is most widely known for his work on the famous *Brown v. Board of Education* case, which desegregated public schools in 1954.

Thurgood Marshall began his journey to success and fame when he replaced his mentor Charles Hamilton Houston as attorney for the National Association for the Advancement of Colored People (NAACP) in 1936. Marshall was only twenty-eight years old, full of zest, humor, and confidence. With his fair complexion, silky black hair, and manicured mustache, Marshall bore a resemblance to two other African Americans who attended the same university and rose to the top of their fields: Cab Calloway, the zoot-suited and bodacious musician who reigned supreme during the 1930s and 1940s; and the thought-provoking Langston Hughes, master poet and writer who made a living both celebrating black life and culture and showing its unglamorous side, as well as delving into the most controversial subject of the early twentieth century: racism.

Marshall was a master in his field, as well. He attained celebrity status thanks to a number of high-profile victories in court. He won twenty-nine out of thirty-two cases that he argued before the U.S. Supreme Court. There is a picture of him, taken in 1956, that personifies the man who was such an extraordinary champion of black justice and equality. The photo catches Marshall, at six feet tall, weighing over two hundred pounds and broad-shouldered, poised in mid-stride as he leaves the federal courthouse in Birmingham, Alabama. He wears a long khaki trench coat and has one hand in his pocket. To his left and right and behind him are a phalanx of black supporters. To his immediate right is plaintiff Autherine Lucy, at that time in the midst of her struggle to maintain her enrollment in the University of Alabama. They look as if they are marching, with the striking figure of Marshall, who is at least a head taller than everyone else, in the lead.

Lucy was in her mid-twenties when Marshall won his most famous case, *Brown v. Board of Education*, in 1954, the ruling that decimated the Jim Crow law that had segregated schools in the South for so long. In 1955, she approached him to help her obtain admittance to graduate school at the University of Alabama. The Supreme Court upheld her right to be admitted in the *Lucy v. Adams* ruling in the fall of 1955, and Lucy registered at the university shortly thereafter. But on the third day, a white mob formed and surrounded the building of one of her classes. Lucy was trapped inside. It took the intervention of the state police to rescue her from the building. But rather than punish the mob, the university suspended Lucy. Marshall went to court again and won. The university retaliated by expelling Lucy.

Marshall sized up the situation—and surrendered. He knew that the university was legally permitted to expel her (or anyone they wanted) and that to pursue the case further would be costly and, quite possibly, unproductive.

Obstacles like this one only served to motivate Marshall. He fought tirelessly for blacks, primarily in support of voting rights and against segregation. Marshall helped all classes of blacks and took on many cases in the South, where racism and white retaliatory violence and intimidation were most visible and pervasive—not to mention tolerated, if not instigated or supported, by local authorities. Marshall slept little and worked hard, but was always fresh, charismatic, and riveting in the courtroom. Out of the office, Marshall was genial and fun-loving. He liked to tell jokes. He also liked to smoke and to drink martinis.

When, in 1967, President Lyndon B. Johnson made Thurgood Marshall the first black U.S. Supreme Court Justice, it was the pinnacle of his career and a historic milestone in American history. Two years after his retirement from his long and luminous career in 1991, Marshall died. He was eighty-five years old.

CHILDHOOD

Thurgood Marshall was born in Baltimore, Maryland on July 2, 1908. His parents were William, a waiter, and Norma Marshall, a teacher. He had a brother, William Aubrey, who was three years older than himself. Sometime in his early childhood, Thoroughgood made up his mind to shorten his name to "Thurgood," because it was too long to write. His parents supported that decision.

The year that Marshall was born is the focus of a book written by Jim Rasenberger, entitled *America 1908* (2007). Rasenberger explores the glory of the industrial developments and America's growth, as well as the grim realities of tumultuous race relations. The year 1908 marked forty-five years of freedom for African Americans, forty-five years since President Abraham Lincoln issued the emancipation proclamation, declaring slavery illegal. At the end of the Civil War (1861–1865), slavery was officially a thing of the past. But in 1908, blacks were hardly in better shape than they had been during the difficult years following emancipation. Anti-black violence permeated the South. An epidemic of race riots perpetrated by whites against black communities occurred during the early twentieth century, the most notorious occurring in Atlanta, Georgia (1906), Springfield, Illinois (1908), East St. Louis, Illinois (1917), Elaine, Arkansas (1919), and Tulsa, Oklahoma (1921). In the year 1908 alone, it was reported that eighty-nine blacks had been lynched.

In 1908, despite the passage of forty years since the end of the Civil War, blacks were without basic civil rights. Although black men were legally allowed to vote, most did not due to unchecked intimidation, discriminatory tests, and, in some places, unaffordable poll taxes. Unwritten Jim Crow laws in the South mandated that in every aspect of life, blacks were to be excluded from mingling with whites. For example, there were separate black schools, parks, churches, restaurants, and other facilities. Blacks were not even allowed to use the same water fountain or restroom facilities as whites. Significantly, the facilities reserved for blacks were substandard and not well-maintained. When, in some situations, blacks and whites were allowed in the same space, such as on a public bus, blacks were restricted to seats in the back and expected to give up their seats for whites if no other place was available. At some restaurants, blacks had to go to the back entrance to pick up their orders.

Another notorious problem concerned the fact that blacks were discriminated against in the courtroom, where blacks received little justice and were not allowed to serve as jurors. When white persons committed a crime against blacks, they were generally not punished. When black persons committed a crime against whites, they were given harsher and longer sentences.

The early twentieth century was arguably one of the lowest periods for blacks in United States history. Poverty, lack of opportunities, as well as social, economic, and political oppression plagued most blacks. The first promise of change would come with the establishment of a formidable civil rights organization, the NAACP, in 1909, and a social service agency, the Urban League, in 1910.

The year of Marshall's birth heralded in a long-overdue era of radical destruction of discriminatory laws. In his youth, however, Marshall was for the most part oblivious to the all-consuming problems that affected blacks. Although he did attend segregated schools, he lived primarily in a sheltered, integrated community in Baltimore, Maryland. Between 1910 and 1914, the Marshalls lived in New York so that William could pursue work with a railroad company, but they returned to Baltimore after Thurgood's grandmother, who lived there, broke her leg.

Marshall's father, William, was so fair he could pass for white. He even had blue eyes. "Passing" was a phenomena in which some blacks capitalized on the lightness of their features and the straightness of their hair to penetrate white society. But William and his wife, Norma, were proud of being black, and they passed his pride on to their two children.

One of the many stories that impressed young Thoroughgood was the legend of a slave relative. According to Marshall, he had one grandparent who had been a slave. All the other grandparents were born free. This one radical slave, like the mischievous trickster figure in slave tales, was always causing trouble for his slave master. As the legend went, his master eventually freed Marshall's distant relative to be relieved of his antics.

Whether this story is true or not, it served to bolster the concept of defiance. Slaves expressed their fondness for this sort of mischief through the telling of the 'ventures of Brer Rabbit, who always outsmarted everyone, including Brer Fox and Ole Master. In these cunning tales, Brer Rabbit symbolized the black slaves, while Ole Master (naturally) represented their slave master.

But Marshall's father did more than subtly instruct his son on the value of defiance; he told him directly to, when necessary, fight back. When

Marshall was seven years old, a white person called him a nigger. William told his son that the next time that happened again, he could physically strike him.

One of Marshall's fondest memories of growing up was dinner with his family. Although the Marshalls were by no means wealthy, they had enough to get by and to live in modest comfort. The dinner table was always set with good food and stimulating conversation. At the evening meal times, William initiated a tradition in which the boys debated any given issue. William liked to stay on top of current news and made sure his boys did the same. Marshall treasured these moments. He liked to talk, and he enjoyed coming up with arguments and facts to support his arguments. He also was mesmerized by watching the trials at the local courthouse. That was something William did as a diversion: go to the courthouse and observe trials.

Marshall was as lively at school as he was at home, which often got him in trouble. He was a known "troublemaker" at school: not following his teacher's instructions; talking when he should be paying attention to the lesson; teasing and pulling pranks.

Marshall got his first job at an early age: he was seven years old when he went to work at a grocery store. Later, he was a delivery boy. He also worked at a hotel, toting luggage for guests. When Marshall entered high school, his work experiences would open his eyes to the realities of racism and segregation.

HIGH SCHOOL

Because of his good grades in grade school, Marshall skipped the eighth grade, so he was only thirteen when he started his first year at Colored High and Training School. As the name of the school implies, Colored High was segregated. Everyone knew that the white school was better in every way, but few, if any, protested. This was just one of the facts of life.

Marshall was one of the most popular students, though he could still be troublesome. He joined the debate team, where he excelled, thanks to the nightly debates with his father and his brother. The girls also took notice of him. They "were taken by Thurgood's lanky walk, the way he swung his long arms and longer legs" (Williams, 36). The other popular student at the school was the hip Cab Calloway, who was one grade behind Marshall. Calloway tended to skip classes to make money hustling on the streets. Hustling is a term used to describe the earning of money by illicit or unethical means, such as gambling. "A hustle" could refer to any means of making quick money. For example, Calloway worked a number of jobs, such as selling newspapers, waiting tables, and shining shoes. Calloway would go on to make a name for himself as a jazz singer and as someone who helped popularize the fashionable zoot suits in the 1930s. The zoot suit was the epitome of coolness. It consisted of baggy, tight-cuffed, high-waisted trousers and an oversized jacket with overly broad, padded shoulders and wide lapels. The suit was completed with accessories, such as suspenders and a long watch chain. The suits often came in bold, bright colors.

When Marshall got in trouble for pranks or other mischief-making, he was given a creative punishment by the school: he was sent to the basement and assigned a section of the U.S. Constitution to memorize. Marshall recalled that that was how he came to know the entire Constitution by heart.

One of Marshall jobs during high school was at Mr. Schoen's hat and dress shop. Mr. Schoen was Jewish, and he treated Marshall kindly. One day as he rode the trolley making a hat delivery, a white man called Marshall a nigger. Remembering his father's instructions, he immediately began throwing punches at the man. Marshall was arrested, but he was released with the help of Mr. Schoen, who empathized with his situation. He confirmed what his father said "and told him he had done the right thing" (Williams, 16).

But he soon realized that physical fighting would not get him very far if he planned to be a lawyer, which is what he decided he wanted to be during high school. He said "I got the idea of being a lawyer from arguing with my dad.... We'd argue about everything" (Williams, 36). Marshall graduated from high school in 1924. His next challenge was to figure out how to pay for a college education and become a lawyer.

LINCOLN UNIVERSITY

Marshall was accepted by Lincoln University, an all-black institution in Oxford, Pennsylvania in 1925. Known as the "Black Princeton," Lincoln was one of the premier schools for blacks in the day. Marshall studied liberal arts.

He took a job working on the B&O Railroad before starting at the university to help fund his education. Thanks to this experience, Marshall had to pocket his fists and learn how to accommodate to keep his job. One co-worker was fired after he suggested to other black workers that they should form a union. Labor unions were one way workers protected themselves from abusive treatment and low wages. During this period, blacks were not allowed to join the predominately white labor unions, and blacks rarely formed unions themselves due to the high cost of intimidation, violence, or loss of employment. Marshall did not want to risk losing his job. He needed the money to get through college.

Marshall's freshman year was unspectacular. He spent most of his days having fun and enjoying his newfound freedom away from home. He gained a lot of popularity as a member of the debate team. One of his most memorable experiences with the debate team was the trip to Boston, Massachusetts, where the Lincoln University debate team challenged several prestigious teams from Harvard University.

The next summer, William hired Marshall to wait on tables at the exclusive Gibson Island Club. But only whites were allowed to enjoy the myriad delights of the club, as a signpost attested: "No Niggers and Dogs Allowed." Marshall was caught off-guard when a white senator who frequented the club referred to him as "nigger" or "boy" and was obnoxious when ordering him to fetch meals and beverages. Yet every day the senator left Marshall a twenty-dollar tip. This was a lot of money in those days. Marshall endured the daily abuse until his father spotted him "running up to the [senator's] table, bowing and saying, 'Yes, sir!' " (Williams, 44). William fired Marshall on the spot.

Another experience marked a pivotal turning-point in how Marshall responded to racism. He and several other friends went into town to catch a silent cowboy movie. The attendant told them that they were not allowed to sit in the main part of the theater; they had to sit in the balcony reserved for blacks. The students demanded their money back and then protested by vandalizing the property. One of Marshall's friends recalled how after "the usher refused to give refunds … we had a disturbance … pulled down curtains, broke the front door … they didn't catch anybody" (Williams, 48).

In 1926, Langston Hughes arrived on campus. The Marshall of that year reflected greater maturity, growing his trademark mustache and joining the Alpha Phi Alpha fraternity (where he did indulge in occasional fraternity pranks). Hughes' appearance caused a stir on campus. He was already well-known for his intellectual and literary interest in race relations and black culture and for being well-traveled and well-published. He joined Marshall's rival fraternity, the Omegas. But he was a resource for Marshall when the latter began to reflect on serious topics concerning race.

During this period, Marshall read W.E.B. Du Bois, Carter G. Woodson, and Jerome Dowd. All three individuals spent their lifetimes engaged in the study and writing of African American history, racial problems, and social issues. Du Bois was one of the founding members of the NAACP and the famous editor of *The Crisis* 1910 and 1934.

In the spring of 1928, Marshall sustained a serious injury and did not return to the university until fall. As a result of his absence, he had to work double-time to catch up. In that same year he began dating Vivian Burey, who was a freshman at the University of Pennsylvania. Marshall called her "Buster." They married in 1929 at Philadelphia's First African Baptist Church. After the wedding, Vivian moved to Baltimore to live with his parents while he stayed to finish school. He graduated with honors in 1930, at the start of the Great Depression.

HOWARD UNIVERSITY

Marshall knew he wanted to go to law school. His heart was set on the University of Maryland School of Law, but there was no way they would admit a black man. But Howard University, located in Washington, D.C., turned out to be a fortuitous choice. His attendance there was greatly attributable to the sacrifices his family made to pay for his education. His mother pawned her wedding ring and her engagement ring to help out.

One of his law professors was Charles Hamilton Houston. Although he was a diminutive man, he packed a powerful punch as a professor and an attorney. And he was a model of black ability to transcend incredible odds and break through seemingly impregnable barriers. Houston had graduated from Amherst College in Amherst, Massachusetts in 1915. As a result of encounters with racism during his enlistment in World War I, he decided to make the struggle to end Jim Crow his life's mission. He enrolled at Harvard Law School and received his doctorate in 1923.

By the time Marshall arrived on campus in 1930, Houston was the vice dean of the law school and served as the legal counsel for the NAACP. Houston's martinet behavior inside the classroom was notorious. Students called him "Iron Pants" or "Cement Drawers." But the fact was that Houston was preparing his students to be better than the best. They had to be, since they would soon face a world dominated by whites who felt that blacks were inferior to them. Black attorneys were a rarity. Statistics showed that only 1,000 out of the 160,000 attorneys in the country were black.

During Marshall's third and final year (1933) at the law school, "Houston began to treat the few remaining students, especially the transformed Marshall, as if they were partners in an elite black law firm" (Williams, 57). Marshall was one of the students selected by Houston to join him on a case in Virginia concerning a black man accused of murdering two white women. Marshall helped prepare the case and learned a great deal more by simply watching Houston in action. Although the black man was pronounced guilty of his crime, Houston rescued him from the death penalty.

The trip to Virginia was Marshall's first exposure to the South. It moved him deeply to observe the harsh conditions there. Although he had experienced segregated school and racism, he had not known the enormity of the oppression that blacks in the South endured. The omnipresence of Jim Crow was like a smothering pressure over the chest. Overt racism was shocking and disturbing.

After graduating in 1933, Marshall took his bar exam and passed it on the first try. He quickly opened his own law practice back home in Baltimore. This was an audacious move, not only because he was a black practicing attorney, but because he had nerve enough to embark on a solo venture during the dismal years of the Great Depression. There would be no let-up from the harsh conditions until the start of the new decade.

ON HIS OWN

Marshall was an idealistic crusader from the get-go. He took on almost any case that came his way. He was moved, body and soul, by the desire to better conditions for blacks. He frequently worked for little or no money at all.

During this period, Marshall joined Houston on several trips to the South. Houston, doggedly carrying on his personal and professional mission to smite Jim Crow, was attacking segregated schools. The state of black schools was deplorable: "The schools usually were wooden structures, no more than shacks. They had no insulation, and it was common to be able to see the sky through the many holes in the roofs. The floors were sometimes dirt and ran thick with mud when rain fell" (Williams, 63). Wielding a heavy camera, Houston and his towering compeer tramped through thick woods, along paths trodden by children, and down long and meandering unpaved roads under steamy heat, capturing evidence of the gross inequities of the *Plessy v. Ferguson* (1896) separate-but-equal ruling.

Murray v. Maryland (1936)

Marshall's practice began to bear fruit. In 1934, Houston and another black attorney, William Gosnell, assisted Marshall with one of his earliest victories. Marshall's first major victory all on his own was the case of *Murray v. Maryland*. The plaintiff was Donald Murray, a black graduate, who had been turned away from the University of Maryland's law school. The trial began on June 17, 1934 and ended the next day in Marshall's favor. Marshall was ecstatic: "The victory made history, and it gave Marshall a rush of pleasure at having defeated the law school that had deemed itself too good for any black, including him" (Williams, 78).

In 1936, Marshall led the way to assist blacks in Baltimore to get a new high school, as the nearest black high school was ten miles away. Of course, there was no way officials would outright agree to building a new school. Marshall approached the case with the idea of suing the principal, the county superintendent, and the Baltimore County School Board. He thought that if he could get the plaintiff, thirteen-year-old Margaret Williams, into the local white high school, he might, in a roundabout way, force white officials to build a new school in the county rather than permit a black in the all-white school.

The trial was pure misery. Marshall was utterly dismayed by the overt racism exhibited by the judge and the board's lawyers: "This was the first time Marshall had seen lawyers argue that the essence of southern tradition was to keep blacks on the bottom of the social caste system" (Williams, 80). But Marshall kept his cool and remained as pleasant as possible. Nonetheless, Marshall's argument fell on deaf ears. The case was a failure—except for one thing: the NAACP was impressed with Marshall's performance.

In 1936, Marshall learned of an opening at the Howard University Law School. He thought a change of pace might do him good. Besides, his law office was failing. It would help tremendously to receive a steady paycheck. But Marshall was not destined to teach just then. Houston contacted him with another offer. He was no longer working at Howard, but was one of the paid members of a special legal counsel working for the NAACP. He wanted Marshall on his team. Houston offered him the job, and Marshall accepted. Houston envisioned that while he went on the road fundraising, Marshall would oversee the legal cases.

This happy note in Marshall's life belied a crisis in his family. His father was out of work, as his defiance against whites kept getting him into trouble. And losing jobs made William turn to alcohol. Tragically, Marshall's brother, William Aubrey, who had become a doctor, was dying from tuberculosis. Norma was the only one working. The Marshalls were distraught over the idea of Thurgood leaving his mother all alone. But Norma Marshall insisted that he go on. She and her husband had always pushed him to scale greater heights; she could not let him stop just as he was gathering momentum.

NATIONAL ASSOCIATION FOR THE ADVANCEMENT OF COLORED PEOPLE

Assistant Special Counsel

Marshall and his wife moved to Harlem, New York in the fall of 1936. Autumn days in New York can be breathtaking, with leaves glistening like gold on quivering branches against a bright blue sky. The air was brisk and invigorating. At night, the city was illuminated with the pulse of electric lights and the steady rhythm of the famous Harlem nightclubs.

The Harlem Renaissance was still in full-swing when the Marshalls arrived. Marshall even knew a number of the celebrities: Cab Calloway was a high school chum, and Marshall, Hughes, and Duke Ellington, a jazz genius, had all attended Lincoln University together. Marshall was surrounded by the icons of African American literature and the foot-stomping, skirt twirling music of the stars of the big band era.

But Marshall had little time for play. Between 1936 and 1938, he shuttled between his offices in New York and Baltimore. When his brother was transferred to a hospital in New York, where one lung was removed, Marshall visited him every week. Happily, Marshall's brother gradually recovered.

In Maryland, Marshall worked on two cases, targeting equal pay for black teachers. In the first case, Montgomery County agreed to settle out of court to avoid a scandal and began paying black teachers in their district the same pay as whites. In the second case, Marshall went to trial, and the judge ordered Anne Arundel County schools to begin paying black teachers the same as whites.

These wins were pivotal for Maryland. In the grand scheme of things, Marshall had a long way to go, for he wanted to eradicate Jim Crow in the South, and "the South," consisting of sixteen states, was a large region to cover. But Marshall's plan involved calculated patience. He knew that small wins over time added to bigger wins from which there would be no going back.

Marshall and his mentor Houston were of the same mind. They made a great team at the national offices of the National Association for the Advancement of Colored People (NAACP). Both were away working on separate campaigns most of the time, but they stayed in contact.

Before Marshall arrived, the NAACP was a dour environment. It was all business and little frivolity. But when Marshall entered a room, the entire office was soon alight with laughter. Walter White, executive secretary, delighted in Marshall's joviality and his impressive work. Roy Wilkins, the assistant secretary, enjoyed Marshall too. When time permitted, they enjoyed an evening together over cigarettes and a drink.

White gave Marshall the responsibility of taking the lead in the NAACP's anti-lynching campaign. Marshall traveled to Washington, D.C. and gave it his best shot. But the Senate killed the NAACP's anti-lynching bill. White also sent Marshall to the South.

There were nonstop cases to handle in the South. Marshall wrote back often with reports. As always, the South presented overwhelming challenges, and Marshall was not exempt from the physical dangers that threatened locals every day. If anything, he was a prime target because of the work he was doing and because of the threat he posed for whites determined to keep blacks "in their place." In the court rooms, white attorneys and judges hardly knew how to act with a black man standing before them, speaking as an equal, and defending blacks who had so long been without a crusader for their cause. Blacks beamed with pride. Before long they came to cherish two names above all others: "Thurgood Marshall" and the "N-double-A-C-P."

When he returned to New York, it was business as usual. Although Marshall was not paid as handsomely as his older mentor, he enjoyed his work and was driven by the knowledge that he toiled for a greater purpose. He found that he liked the structure that the New York office brought. The constant ringing of the telephone, the murmur of voices, and the smell of coffee provided a sense of normalcy, and sharing office space with Houston was not all that bad. Marshall reveled in the company.

But in 1938, Houston announced that he was leaving. He felt better suited to a less regimented environment. He wanted to run the family law firm. Marshall took the news surprisingly well considering that Houston had been his anchor, his safety net, his lamppost in the murky wilds of the court system. Whenever he got lost, Houston was always there to tell him where next to turn.

Chief Legal Officer

In the fall of 1938, Marshall faced the challenge of becoming the leader of the national legal office of the NAACP. He was excited and understandably nervous, but he maintained his rigorous schedule. If needed, Houston was only a phone call away.

One day, Marshall discovered a potential case while scouring a black newspaper. He called Houston immediately. Houston had also read the news and was equally intrigued by the story of the black president of a college in Texas, George Porter, who had faced discrimination when called for jury duty in Dallas. Because of discriminatory laws, the blacks who had been called were told they could leave. But the college president stayed. He demanded to see the judge, who informed him that he would not be able to serve on the current case. Porter refused to leave, going out to lunch and then returning to the jury room, where a white man dragged him out of the room and hurled him down the courthouse stairs. Battered and bruised, Porter climbed back up the stairs, forced his way through white men who attempted to stop him, and ran into the judge's courtroom. Nevertheless, the judge dismissed him and all the other jurists not chosen for the trial.

Marshall and Houston discussed the case for some time, and Marshall wanted to take it on. Word got out that the famed black attorney would soon be on his way to Dallas, Texas. Then Marshall learned, through the rumor mill, that if he went to Texas, his life would be in peril. Conservative white southerners did not particularly care for northerners, especially black ones who caused trouble, as Marshall was apt to do. Marshall was not above feeling fear, and this direct threat unnerved him.

Notwithstanding the overwhelming climate of racial hatred in the South, there were whites who exhibited kindness and demonstrated the pure ideals of freedom and justice for all. Marshall made friends easily, and sometimes even white racists could not help but respect the sophisticated and disarming lawyer. James Allred, the governor of Texas, was one such man who demonstrated integrity. He responded quickly to Marshall's call for assistance. Allred promised to provide him with protection, and he did. Marshall headed for Texas after all.

Still there were problems for Marshall. The Texas Ranger who was assigned to guard Marshall had an irritating habit of calling him "boy." "Boy" was a common term used by whites to refer to any black male no matter what his age. Marshall called Allred and explained his concerns. How was Marshall to know that the Texas Ranger was not in cahoots with the alleged threat on his life? The governor insisted that that ranger was the best he had. After a brief phone call with the Ranger to "straighten him out," Marshall did not have any further problems (Williams, 103). In fact, the Texas Ranger quite possibly saved Marshall's life when one afternoon the chief of police ran towards Marshall, wielding a gun. His intentions were frighteningly clear. However, "the ranger ... calmly pulled his gun and faced the chief. 'Fella, just stay right where you are'" (Williams, 104).

Marshall was disappointed that he was unable to prosecute anyone or change the law prohibiting blacks from participating in jury duty. But he did bring exposure to the incident, and that, he concluded (undoubtedly with a sly smile), was what caused the judge, a few weeks later, to admit one black to the jury for a subsequent trial.

Back in New York, things began to look up, beginning with the establishment of the NAACP's Legal Defense and Educational Fund (LDF), a tax-exempt agency, in 1940. In that same year, Marshall defended three black men accused of killing an elderly white man in the case known as *Chambers v. Florida*. There was no certainty that these black men were responsible for the death of that white man. In fact, forty total African American men had been arrested over the death. This was a common practice, otherwise known as **racial profiling**. The phenomenon occurs when white officers target any black man for a crime simply because of his race, with no discriminating or fact-based evidence. In the early twentieth century, innocent blacks were frequently arrested, charged, convicted, and punished. Jailed blacks were often beaten or intimidated to coerce a false statement of guilt. This is what had happened in the Chambers case, and Marshall was eloquently and forcefully able to persuade the Supreme Court justices to find in the defendants' favor. This was Marshall's first U.S. Supreme Court case.

Walter White, leader of the NAACP, was proud of Marshall's growing prestige as well as his effectiveness in court. He invited Marshall to private social events at his home. These were exclusive gatherings, with some of the biggest names in New York, white or black, in attendance. These important affairs served a dual purpose: they expanded Marshall's network of contacts and, as if Marshall were a débutante, served as a coming out for the NAACP's star attorney.

Wartime

White worried, after the bombing of Pearl Harbor in 1941 and America's entry into World War II, that Marshall would be drafted. However, Marshall did not serve in the war, although he did participate in several cases involving black soldiers. Indeed, there were so many black soldiers in need of legal assistance that Marshall hired more lawyers: Milton Konvitz, Edward Dudley, Robert Carter, and others.

In 1942, another civil rights organization was created. The group, comprising radical-thinking youths, called themselves the Congress of Racial Equality (CORE). CORE was one of the earliest organizations to implement Mahatma Gandhi's nonviolent tactics of direct-action demonstrations. The group challenged Jim Crow in various locations, but because there was little media coverage in the early years following its formation, CORE was not widely known during the war years. But it did represent one more contingent within the full-scale Civil Rights Movement, which was slowly gathering steam.

White carefully orchestrated his organization's plan of attack against discrimination and racism. As civil rights organizations go, the NAACP was generally deemed the most conservative of all. But it was also the most powerful and sophisticated. White had at his disposal numerous efficiently run chapters located across the nation. Behind-the-scenes skirmishes occurred between combatants dressed in business attire over dinners or in conference rooms, and victories were won through strategic networking and by forging relationships with people in political office and other decision-making positions. And thanks to Marshall's LDF and his new lawyers, the NAACP could tackle more legal issues than ever before.

White made sure that Marshall's work remained wide ranging. He was not only to manage legal cases, but to help address racism that manifested itself in every day situations. Through the first half of the new decade, he kept Marshall involved in campaigns to address the copious amounts of racist labels used in marketing goods. Racism was seemingly everywhere.

In the early twentieth century, racist epitaphs were used openly and daily, but old customs were about to change—whether speedily or otherwise—with the vigilant Marshall and the NAACP on duty. For example, a shrimp company sold a brand of shrimp called "Nigger Head Shrimp." One campaign that Marshall spearheaded was a protest over the brand name of Whitman's candy called "Pickaninny Peppermints." The company claimed that the term "pickaninny" was a term of endearment for a black child. Marshall wrote them back, stating that, according to blacks, the term was derogatory and insulting, just as any racist label would be for any racial group. Marshall contacted *Afro-American*, a prominent paper in New York, to have them run an article on the front page about it. The title of that piece was: IF YOU WANT TO BE CALLED A NAME, BUY WHITMAN'S. Whitman's scrapped the name altogether.

In 1941, Marshall attacked segregation in Texas politics head on, scoring a significant win. Southerners made no secret of the fact that they meant to keep blacks and whites living separate lives in separate worlds, period. Enforced by written and unwritten Jim Crow laws, the political structure of the South kept whites in power and blacks underfoot. Intimidation, poll taxes, and other methods kept blacks from registering to vote, and thus, from the opportunity to put in lawmakers who might change their situation. Whites knew this: for blacks to register to vote and then exercise the right to vote undermined their control. Southern states like Texas even implemented laws to prohibit blacks from voting in primaries. The problem with these laws was that they were in direct violation of the Fifteenth Amendment, which gave all citizens, regardless of race, the right to be involved in the voting process. This was what Marshall argued.

It was not until 1944 that Marshall and Bill Hastie, the new dean of the Howard University School of Law, presented their case to end the practice of all-white Texas primaries before the U.S. Supreme Court on behalf of plaintiff Lonni Smith, a black doctor who lived in Houston, Texas. Marshall and Hastie's big win was published in newspapers—black and white—throughout the nation and commented upon in editorials.

One of the earliest lessons Marshall had learned during his tenure as an attorney was that patience and the ability to assess a situation were essential skills in the struggle for civil rights. Victories did not come overnight. And the most far-reaching (and therefore important) wins occurred before the U.S. Supreme Court, which was the highest court of law, because these rulings generally affected all the lower courts.

In 1944, the illustrious W.E.B. Du Bois returned as editor of the NAACP's *Crisis*. He was the antithesis of Marshall. Marshall, at only thirty-six, was outgoing and jovial. At seventy-six, Du Bois appeared dour and introverted. He kept mostly to himself, with his face buried in the stacks of paper he scrutinized before sending them off to press. His surliness undoubtedly had a lot to do with his unhappiness at the office. He and Walter White lived in a constant state of contention. Du Bois felt stifled by White's heavy-handed management of the organization. White was distressed because Du Bois would not conform to the ideological stance of the organization. This feud had been sparked when Du Bois first left the organization in 1934 and remained unresolved. Du Bois would leave again four years later.

In the same year that Du Bois returned to the NAACP, Marshall worked on two high-profile cases, one involving black sailors in California and the other a criminal case in Oklahoma. Fifty black sailors were charged with mutiny for refusing orders from their white officers. Marshall learned the reason that the sailors had so behaved was related to an explosion that killed some 300 men (mostly black) at Port Chicago shortly before. The explosion was the result of the white officers who "placed bets on which group of black sailors was fastest at loading ammunition ... even instructing them to throw boxes of ammunition so they could win the bet" (Williams, 129). This "race" had resulted in the horrific explosion. Despite Marshall's presence, the sailors were found guilty in the California courts. The following year, Marshall argued the case in Washington, D.C., before the Navy's judge advocate general (JAG), and won.

The case in Hugo, Oklahoma resulted in a bitter and tragic loss. *Lyons v. Oklahoma* involved a black man named W.D. Lyons who was accused of killing a white family and setting the house on fire with the bodies still inside. The tragedy of this case was that two white men had originally confessed to the crime and a number of whites, including the father of the murdered woman, believed Lyons did not commit the crime. But Oklahoma Governor Leon Chase Phillips initiated a cover-up because, it was believed, the two white men were prison inmates who had committed the crime during one of their frequent visits to town. These visits were permitted by the prison, even though they were unlawful. Lyons, it was said, had been apprehended because officers found out he had been hunting rabbits near the vicinity of the murdered family.

What occurred in the wake of Lyons' arrest was abominable. The officers tortured him, starved him, and harassed him over the next few days. Still, he refused to break and confess to a crime he denied committing. Finally, one of the officers threw the bones of the victims into Lyons' lap. Lyon was "superstitious about human bones" (Williams, 114). When they led him to an electric chair to intimidate him, he signed a confession. The statement also absolved the officers of any wrong doing, as it asserted that he had not been coerced. Marshall was unable to convince the judges of Lyons' innocence. But he had strong suspicions of a "political cover-up" (Williams, 118). This was Marshall's first Supreme Court loss. Lyons received a life sentence.

Marshall's upbeat personality helped him maintain his fighting spirit through that and other difficult setbacks. And there were difficulties in his private life as well as the public. Marshall wanted children badly, especially a boy. But Buster continued to miscarry. The couple tried to maintain optimism, but there was an absence in their lives.

The second half of the decade brought with it an array of new obstacles, threats, and victories for LDF. In the fall of 1945, Marshall hired the first woman attorney on the team: Constance Baker Motley. Motley was forever grateful, because in that day and age few women were admitted into law firms or given opportunities to take on cases. But Marshall kept her busy. Following the end of the war, there was a high number of court-martial cases to attend to. Despite the expansion of the team of lawyers working for the LDF, office life remained much as it had been when Marshall had toiled single-handedly during the early years of his employment with the NAACP. There was never a dull moment. Despite the fact that blacks had made great contributions toward the allied victory in World War II, their status remained very low.

One of Marshall's most notable cases in the post-war period was *Morgan v. Virginia* (1946). The situation that sparked the case occurred in 1944 in one of the earliest (though not widely known) acts of defiance by a black who refused to give up her seat on a public bus. Irene Morgan, who was just twenty-seven years old at the time, was ill the day she mounted a Greyhound to go to see the doctor. When Morgan refused to give up her seat to a white person, she was arrested. Her trial went to the U.S. Supreme Court, where the justices ruled that segregation was unlawful on interstate buses.

This trial was especially important because it served as the inspiration for the Journey of Reconciliation demonstration, a predecessor to the Freedom

Constance Baker Motley

In 1946, Constance Baker Motley was the first African American woman to be hired by the National Association for the Advancement of Colored People's Legal Defense and Education Fund. She began as a law clerk and worked her way up to become the NAACP's lead trial attorney.

Constance Baker was born on September 14, 1921, in New Haven, Connecticut, to parents who had immigrated from Nevis, in the Caribbean. She was the ninth of twelve children. Both parents were domestics and poor, but her mother was wont to challenge the system of racism and discrimination within their northern community. In fact, she founded a local chapter of the NAACP.

Discrimination in the North was not as prevalent as it was in the South in those years. In New Haven, for example, Baker attended integrated schools. But she still periodically experienced racism, such as when she was barred from going to the beach or entering the local roller rink. These experiences, as well as her parents' poverty and the lecture she attended by George Crawford, an NAACP attorney, inspired her to pursue activism. Her resolve and poise moved Clarence Blakeslee, a white philanthropist, to finance her aspiration to go to college.

Baker attended Fisk University in Tennessee, going on to receive her bachelor's degree in economics from New York University in 1943. She then became the second African American woman to graduate from Columbia University Law School. In 1946, she married Joel Motley and was hired on by Thurgood Marshall to work for the NAACP-LDF, where she became the first African American woman to argue a case before the U.S. Supreme Court. She won nine out of her ten Supreme Court cases.

In later years, Motley continued to be "the first" to achieve other high positions. In 1964, she was elected to the New York State Senate, and in 1966, President Lyndon Johnson appointed her to be a federal court judge. Motley died on September 28, 2005, at the age of 84.

Rides of the 1960s. In 1947, sixteen young activists, black and white, set out to test that states were abiding by the Supreme Court's ruling. Despite the fact that these activists conducted several rides and faced multiple arrests and violence, their demonstration received little media attention and is much less well known than the Freedom Rides.

When, in November 1946, Marshall ran into serious trouble in Tennessee, even he, the famous and intrepid attorney, was visibly shaken. The problem arose while he was driving a car with two lawyers and a newspaper reporter as passengers. A white police officer stopped them and had Marshall get into his police car. The allegation was drunk driving, although it was evident that that was just an excuse. The tension was palpable. Marshall, because of his work, was a well-known "troublemaker," and his life had been threatened before while working in the South. Marshall's associates refused to leave him, sensing that he was in imminent danger. The police car drove toward a group of sinister-looking white men but then turned around, undoubtedly aware that they were being followed. The police took him instead to the local courthouse, where an elderly judge, with a keen sense of smell, possibly saved Marshall's life by releasing him, because he could tell that Marshall "hadn't had a drink in twenty-four hours" (Williams, 141). That was a close call.

In that same year, Marshall was awarded the NAACP's top award: the Spingarn Medal. This award, created in 1914, was named after Joel Spingarn, one of the NAACP's founding members, its second president, and chairman of the board of the NAACP. It is given annually to recognize extraordinary achievement.

The 1950s were a time of more change, joy, and intense sorrow. At the turn of the decade, Marshall grieved the loss of his friend and mentor, Charles Hamilton Houston. Shortly thereafter, Marshall embarked on the most well-known and celebrated case of his career. The plaintiff was Linda Brown, a third grader who had to walk twenty blocks to catch the bus to go to the segregated school she attended in Topeka, Kansas. This was the opportunity everyone in the NAACP had been waiting for, Marshall most of all.

When Marshall took the case before the U.S. Supreme Court Case in 1952, he faced the ominous task of disproving the *Plessy v. Ferguson* (1896) Supreme Court ruling that sanctioned segregation based on the doctrine "separate but equal." That ruling stated that it was lawful for states to uphold Jim Crow—as long as black facilities were equal to whites. But this was not the case. Most black facilities (e.g., school buildings) were shockingly substandard. In many places in the South, black teachers taught in one-room schools, while white students enjoyed brand-new and expansive modern facilities. Textbooks used in black schools were outdated and tattered, and there were never enough to go around the overcrowded classrooms.

The research that was conducted to bolster Marshall's argument was unparalleled; it addressed the psychological damage that racial separation caused. Critical to this issue was the pioneering work of Gunnar Myrdal in *An American Dilemma: The Negro Problem and Modern Democracy* (1944), as well as the doll experiments conducted by black psychologist Kenneth B. Clark and his wife Mamie Phipps Clark. In these experiments, young black children were asked questions regarding their preference of a black or a white doll. The children overwhelming picked the white doll over the black doll. Moreover, they attributed positive traits to the white doll and negative traits to the black doll. Marshall's expert witness during the trial was crucial to his victory.

Black Dolls

A black doll would appear to be an innocuous creation. After all, dolls are just toys. And yet, there was a time when all dolls in America were white, thus illustrating the magnitude of how blacks were considered of no value in society.

According to research on the history of black dolls by Dr. Sabrina Thomas, who is working on the forthcoming book, *Black Dolls as Racial Uplift 1900–1970*, W.E.B. Du Bois was among the first to protest against the blaring exclusion of black dolls. Du Bois argued that black dolls were important to the development of identity and esteem. When, in the early nineteenth century, The National Negro Doll Company began to manufacture black dolls, Du Bois published their advertisements in *The Crisis*, the organ of the National Association for the Advancement of Colored People.

When black mothers insisted that their black children have black dolls, this was a quiet form of resistance to white superiority and to the devastating and debilitating effects of oppression on self-esteem. Black dolls were among the earliest examples of black pride and Afrocentricism.

In the 1940s, black psychologist Mamie Phipps Clark conducted experiments using dolls to study black children's perception of race. In the 1950s, she and her husband Kenneth B. Clark testified as expert witnesses in the famous *Brown v. Board of Education* case. Their findings, that black children overwhelmingly preferred white dolls over black dolls, helped to prove that segregated schools were harmful and thus contributed to one of the most important Supreme Court rulings in history.

Others studies on dolls have since been conducted. Dr. Thomas, who teaches at North Carolina Central University, has learned that older black children choose black dolls over white dolls. In a 2007 film, *A Girl Like Me*, produced by Kiri Davis, a New York City high school student, results were the same as Clark's more than a half century earlier. Other tests suggest that blacks in predominately white schools choose white dolls, whereas in mostly black schools, black dolls are preferred.

A significant part of these studies are the questions that are posed to the black children: which doll is "good," and which doll is "bad," etc. Painfully, the many instances where the black doll is chosen as the "worst" illustrate the lingering effects of internalized racism.

Finally, in 1954, the ruling came down, and Marshall's victory was announced in newspapers throughout the nation. More than one future civil rights leader, such as John Lewis, who was an adolescent when he read the news from his home in Troy, Alabama, found that ruling to be the opening of a door into a life of activism.

It is true that this was one of the greatest Supreme Court rulings in civil rights history, but it is also true that it was not easily transferred to actual practice. Both whites and, to a lesser degree blacks, were resistant. There were threats, intimidation, and years of struggle for the first blacks who broke the color line in schools across the nation. One well-known cases involved the Little Rock Nine, who, in 1957, were thwarted from their first attempt to integrate the Little Rock Central High School by Governor Orval Faubus, who deployed the national guard to block the entrance of the school. Activists intervened and sought federal assistance to enforce the *Brown v. Board of Education* ruling and to afford protection to the black students. The students received an armed escort to and from school, but were vulnerable to taunting and heckling throughout the school year.

Some black parents, not wanting to put their children through the duress associated with those volatile years, preferred to keep them enrolled in black schools. Some blacks preferred black schools because they believed that the education their children would receive in the predominately white schools would not address black history and achievement. The process of integrating schools was slow and, frequently, very painful. Beginning in 1971, the federal government enforced mandatory busing to integrate predominately white schools.

Despite the knowledge that there was a hard row to hoe ahead, Marshall was euphoric—until he and his wife were faced with jolting news. The doctor told Vivian that she had only weeks to live. Marshall was distraught. He stayed home to care for his dear Buster. Only once before had he taken an extended leave from his duties, when he was sick with pneumonia and hospitalized. Vivian died on February 11, 1955.

On March 21, 1955, the NAACP office was hit with another tragedy. White died suddenly from heart failure. Wilkins took over the duties of executive secretary.

That December, Marshall married a woman named Cecilia Suyat, whom he knew from the office, as she was a secretary at the New York headquarters of the NAACP. The marriage created some controversy, not only because it occurred so quickly after his first wife's death, but because Cecilia had been born in Hawaii and was of Filipino descent.

But Marshall's friends and associates defended him. They felt that he had waited long enough and that because of his temperament, he could not bear to be alone. And he still wanted children. As far as the interracial nature of the marriage was concerned, the NAACP had had to face that issue before. White had caused a major scandal when he divorced his wife Gladys and married a white woman. But his marriage to Gladys in itself must have been somewhat unconventional, since White was a black man whose blue eyes, fair complexion, and straight hair showed his mixed racial heritage.

Montgomery Bus Boycott

December 1955 was a momentous month for other reasons, as well. On the first of that month, the Montgomery Bus Boycott was launched in Alabama. The leader of that demonstration was no other than a young newcomer to civil rights leadership, Dr. Martin Luther King, Jr. King was only twenty-six and had just received his Ph.D. from the Boston University School of Theology. He had been minister of the congregation at the Dexter Avenue Baptist Church in Montgomery for just a year and a half. The Bus Boycott was his first major demonstration, but it would catapult him into the vortex of the Civil Rights Movement.

The boycott was written up in nearly every major newspaper. It was big news. But Marshall watched warily as developments unfolded. Marshall was no supporter of direct action; he had made that known publicly during lectures whenever the topic was addressed by someone in his audience. The main reason was simple: demonstrations provoked violence. Marshall believed that the NAACP's approach was dangerous enough without the added complexity of direct action. But the new trend of direct action was gaining momentum through the massive appeal of Mahatma Gandhi. King would take Gandhi's techniques and popularize them even more, especially with black churchgoers. When the Southern Christian Leadership Conference (SCLC) was formed in 1957 with King as its president, it became the second major civil rights organization to advocate direct action, alongside CORE.

Marshall was not the only one keeping a close watch on these new civil rights organizations. J. Edgar Hoover, the director of the Federal Bureau of Investigation (FBI), was also extremely attentive. Both Marshall and Hoover were opposed to communism, but that was about all they had in common, though Marshall shared some of Hoover's misgivings about the demonstrations that occurred—for a while, anyway.

As the nascent Civil Right Movement began to take shape and gather steam, there were developments on the Marshall home front. Marshall's first son, Thurgood, was born in August 1956, and his second son, John, was born in July 1958.

Marshall went to Kenya in 1959 to visit with its first African leader, Tom Mboya. Kenya gaining independence from Great Britain was in keeping with Marshall's battle for the full of expression of freedom for blacks in America. While in Kenya, Marshall worked with Mboya to establish the country's first constitution. Before coming back to America, Marshall toured London.

The Unleashing of the Civil Rights Movement

It can be said that the Civil Rights Movement first gained momentum in the 1940s with CORE, or even before that with the pioneering work of A. Philip Randolph in the 1930s, or as long ago as the inception of the NAACP in

1910. But there is no arguing that, by the 1960s, the Civil Rights Movement was in full force. In 1960, college-aged activists launched the sit-in movement. In 1961, the Freedom Riders initiated the first of several bus rides into the South to test Jim Crow in interstate travel. The SCLC (lead by King) carried out many campaigns throughout the decade, as did CORE and the Student Nonviolent Coordinating Committee (SNCC). SNCC was the latest civil rights organization on the block, having been founded in 1960.

Marshall remained guarded about these developments. It was a challenging period for the NAACP, which, since its inception, had relied on litigation, lobbying, and the quieter, less radical forms of protest to achieve its goals. And because the organization had been around a lot longer than almost all the others, the effectiveness of its methods had been tried and found true. Nevertheless, when, in 1963, Stephen Currier, a rich white philanthropist, asked the heads of the major civil rights organizations to collaborate on fundraising projects and in intra-organizational dialogue, Wilkins agreed.

The working relationships among the organizations and their leaders were made difficult by their diverse ideologies and personalities. Wilkins, representing the NAACP, and Whitney Young, the leader of the National Urban League, were by far the most conservative (and it is not coincidental that these two organizations were the oldest). Nevertheless, significant progress was made. One of the most celebrated and well-known collaborative efforts was the March on Washington for Jobs and Freedom, which took place in 1963.

Eventually, Marshall's thinking would come around, and he would embrace the new movement. A series of discussions with young activists finally convinced Marshall that their cause was worth championing. But it was a stretch for Marshall, who could not at first grasp the notion of handling the cases of individuals who willingly disobeyed laws, even when the motivation of protest was scrupulous.

In 1961, Marshall handled the Supreme Court case known as *Garner v. Louisiana* on behalf of a group of young activists from Baton Rouge, Louisiana who were arrested and jailed for staging a sit-in in a local restaurant. On December 11, 1961, the Supreme Court overturned the students' conviction.

TO JUSTICE AND BEYOND

The 1960s was a decade of enormous transition and change. Blacks and whites joined forces in unprecedented numbers—defying the social constructs and laws that had tried for so long to keep them in separate worlds—to press for a new America with racial equality and civil rights for all races by means of sit-ins, marches, voter registration drives, and other activities. Some results were immediate. For example, when the Nashville Student Movement launched a comprehensive sit-in campaign, attacking Jim Crow restaurants, lunch counters in stores, movie theaters, and other locations in downtown Nashville, Tennessee, they brought forth direct results. In less than six months, the Nashville activists obtained a major victory when all lunch counters were desegregated.

Change was rampant in the political realm as well when, in 1960, America elected the youngest-ever and first Catholic president. His name was John F. Kennedy, a Harvard graduate, who advanced civil rights during his campaign. African Americans were enthusiastic about him from the first, but not everyone was thrilled with his performance. Marshall criticized Kennedy for his hesitancy in backing up his campaign rhetoric with tangible action. He felt that what progress had been gained was a result of the long, dogged work of the NAACP.

In 1961, Kennedy made a significant gesture by nominating Marshall to be a federal appeals court judge. The nomination was just a start, and Marshall had to endure an intensive questioning process by the Senate subcommittee. But in 1962 he was voted in. In November of the following year, President Kennedy was assassinated in Dallas, Texas, and his vice president, a Texan named Lyndon B. Johnson, took his place.

Johnson's persona paled in comparison to the fresh-faced Kennedy, but his accomplishments surpassed all expectation. It is argued that if Kennedy had not died, he would have finished what he had carefully started, for before his death he had taken steps toward a major civil rights bill. Perhaps, by his tragic death, Kennedy made what Johnson did possible. During Johnson's presidency, he not only signed the Civil Rights Act of 1964, he also put forth the Voting Rights Act of 1965. He also started several programs to alleviate poverty and to promote equal opportunity in the workforce.

Marshall's career soared during Johnson's tenure. In 1965, he became the solicitor general, and in 1967 he became the first African American justice of the U.S. Supreme Court. He was fifty-nine years old—mature, sagacious, and the happy father of two boys aged nine and eleven. Marshall was an active father. Whether playing football in the backyard or running the train set in the living room, the boys were a priority and a source of pure joy. But outside the home, the world again shape-shifted in something altogether new and unexpected.

The Black Power Movement exasperated Marshall. The new radicalism of the Civil Rights Movement was nothing compared to the militancy and raging violence that erupted in the ghettos. Marshall denounced the call for black separatism and self-defense. In time, black power waned. But in the 1980s, Marshall had to contend with a new challenge: Ronald Reagan.

A former star of a bygone Hollywood era, Reagan was elected president in 1980 and served two terms. During those years, Marshall was aghast at the numerous setbacks in substantial civil rights gains and poverty programs that Reagan oversaw. Programs to address poor blacks suffered, and the effects were felt everywhere, largely because funding was drastically cut. Marshall was also acutely aware of the effect of Reagan's conservatism as

Gavel

A gavel is a mallet used by a judge presiding over a trial to signal the start and end of a court session or to put a motion into effect. The gavel in the court of law is a symbol of ultimate authority.

Historically, blacks were denied access to this symbol of power. Indeed, inside the courtroom, justice eluded blacks in both the North and the South. As slaves, blacks were considered the property of white landowners and as such were denied freedoms, opportunities, and basic civil rights. Slaves could not sue or seek protection in the courtroom. In the North, free blacks faired better, with the help of liberal-minded whites. In general, when blacks were on trial for committing a crime, or a white was on trial for a crime against a black person, blacks, more often then not, did not receive justice. In addition, Blacks convicted of crimes received harsher punishments.

After the end of the Civil War (1861–1865) and the freeing of the black slaves, conservative whites instituted black codes that provided more freedoms and opportunities, but in a limited form. For example, blacks were allowed to marry, own property, and to sue in court. But they could not marry outside their race, carry weapons, or testify in court against a white person or serve on a jury. In effect, whites continued to maintain control. In 1866, the federal government intervened, establishing, for example, the Fourteenth Amendment to safeguard blacks' rights and freedoms. But these efforts did little to change the situation. Blacks faired better when cases were brought to the Supreme Court, where rulings were passed with greater impartiality than in local and state courtrooms.

A number of black leaders emerged to protest social injustices against blacks; some became activists and others attorneys. This helped to balance the scale of justice. However, it was not until blacks became judges in local and state courts, and finally in the U.S. Supreme Court itself, that the implications became colossal. Blacks who held the gavel could influence law, oversee justice, and rightfully share in the power that had once belonged solely to whites. This in itself was a symbol that white America's attitudes were improving.

he became surrounded by more and more conservative justices. Marshall became increasingly outnumbered and limited in his ability to make rulings that would benefit the lives of women, African Americans, and the poor.

It was health that eventually forced Marshall to bow out of his responsibilities as a justice of the Supreme Court. Indeed, Marshall struggled with health problems throughout much of his term on the Supreme Court. He retired in 1991, and, on January 24, 1993, he died. Marshall was eighty-four years old.

See also W.E.B. Du Bois; Martin Luther King, Jr.; John Lewis; A. Philip Randolph; Roy Wilkins; and Whitney Young.

FURTHER RESOURCES

Gatewood, Willard. *Aristocrats of Color: The Black Elite, 1880–1920*. Fayetteville: University of Arkansas Press, 2000.

Goldman, Roger. *Thurgood Marshall: Justice for All*. New York: Carroll & Graf Publishers, 1992.

NAACP Legal Defense and Educational Fund, Inc. (April 2008). See http://www.naacpldf.org.

Rasenberger, Jim. *America in 1908: The Dawn of Flight, the Race to the Pole, the Invention of the Model T and the Making of a Modern Nation*. New York: Scribner, 2007.

Supreme Court of the United States (April 2008). See http://www.supremecourtus.gov.

Williams, Juan. *Thurgood Marshall: American Revolutionary*. New York: Times Books, 1998.

Huey P. Newton (1942–1989)

Huey P. Newton was the co-founder of and minister of defense for the Black Panther Party for Self-Defense. To the bystanders in the red-light district of Oakland, California, in the winter of 1967, the group of black men patrolling the streets was like nothing they had seen before. They were uniformly garbed in black berets, leather jackets, powder-blue shirts, and black pants; moreover, they were armed with guns they made no effort to conceal. One African American man asked incredulously, "What kind of Negroes are these?" African Americans did not go about town flaunting weapons—especially not in front of the Oakland police, notorious for being made up of nefarious whites recently transplanted from the South. Like other urban communities, Oakland had a problem with police brutality and harassment.

While on that first patrol, Huey P. Newton and the other Black Panthers observed a cop ticketing an African American, who had assumed an all-too-familiar position—bent over the back of his car, waiting to be frisked or arrested. Newton and Bobby Seale, the founders of the Black Panther Party for Self-Defense, stepped forward from the ranks to introduce themselves and the organization to the baffled crowd. The locals expressed their approval, calling out like congregants at a church service. When the officer challenged Newton and Seale, Newton responded with legal expertise, declaring their right as citizens to observe and bear arms. A group of black youths arrived on the scene, breathless and gaping. Unlike the comic book crusaders or the fabled cowboys of the movies, these heroes were tangible, relevant—and cool.

"Anti-hero" best describes the five-foot ten-inch man with the chiseled good-looks who was the leader of one of the strongest black-power organizations of the time. But Newton was a complex figure—charming, daring, sensitive, as well as ruthless, reckless, and volatile. Newton reflected his environment: both the good and the bad. His friends and intimates, who both admired and feared him, suspected that he may have even had a manic-depressive disorder, complicated in later years by his alcohol and drug use. Though he exhibited strong mental facilities and developed his organization's ideology, played classical piano, and had a Ph.D., he also had learning disabilities and a low I.Q. In fact, he could barely sign his name if someone was watching him.

Although he was brought up within the embrace of his father's Baptist religion, Newton was no saint. He had an affinity for street life. After graduating from high school, Newton did a stint as a con artist and thief, and he would stay in trouble with the law throughout his life. And yet Newton achieved many good works for blacks in cities throughout the nation, protecting them from the tyranny of abusive and racist cops, providing free food and other services, and publicizing the hardships they faced.

Despite Newton's limitations and failings, the Black Panther Party for Self-Defense was, for some time, an extremely powerful and empowering resource for the African American community. It was not, particularly in the beginning, as the media portrayed it: a renegade gang out to terrorize, intimidate, and brutalize whites and engage in criminal activities. The organization was not based on an ideology of racism or thuggery. It originated out of the palpable need to help the black community.

But impediments complicated the effectiveness of Newton and his organization. In 1956, J. Edgar Hoover had launched an FBI Counter Intelligence Program (COINTELPRO) to investigate organizations of which it disapproved. This included civil rights groups as well as black power organizations like the Black Panthers. COINTELPRO was designed to probe and, if possible, to disrupt the workings of these organizations through infiltration, sabotage, arrests, and instigation. The US Organization (another militant group) and the Oakland underworld presented other dangerous challenges to the Panthers.

Newton also created problems for himself. The Black Panthers engaged in a scandalous dalliance with local criminals and engaged in criminal activities to fund some of their projects, to provide income for the armed Panthers, and to purchase weapons. Working with the local criminals marred the organization's image and provided ammunition to its critics. When Newton descended into drugs, he became his own worst enemy. The drugs made him unstable and dangerous. In the end, his addiction would cause his death. In 1989, at the age of forty-seven, Newton was shot and killed by a drug dealer.

CHILDHOOD

Growing up in Oakland, California, Huey P. Newton had a reputation as a tough kid who was known to wield an ice pick if accosted by anyone from school or his neighborhood. Huey was not the first member of his family to stand up for himself. Walter Newton, his father, also had a lot of nerve—but in a different way. The elder Newton was predisposed to radicalism and gravitated toward those who challenged the status quo. He idolized the governor of Louisiana, Huey Pierce Long, who talked brazenly about racial injustice and carried out programs to assist African Americans such as creating jobs and providing books for schools. That his hero was assassinated came as no shock to Walter Newton, because assertiveness was frequently punished in the South. When the youngest of their seven children was born on February 17, 1942, in Monroe, Louisiana, Walter and his wife, Armelia, proudly bestowed their hero's name upon him.

Walter Newton received the label "crazy" following an altercation with a white co-worker. When the man told Walter that he usually whipped an African American man for talking back to him, Walter warned him that he had better be a good fighter if he planned to try to beat him. Huey proudly recalled that his father lived up to the label, "for his refusal to let a white man call him 'nigger' or to play the Uncle Tom or allow whites to bother his family. 'Crazy' to them, he was a hero to us" (*Revolutionary Suicide*, 30–31). And when he, in turn, was called "crazy," it made him feel proud.

In 1945, the Newtons moved to Oakland, California, where Walter Newton hoped to find a good job thanks to the surplus of work created by the war. Walter was a hard worker who often held several jobs at once to enable his wife to stay at home with the children. Despite the numerous paychecks he brought home, he made little money. The family was very poor, like others in their diverse neighborhood.

Oakland was a rough environment. Huey quickly learned about racism, poverty, and the rules of survival. He also learned the importance of family, church, street life, and resistance. When Newton was very young, he had a soft and angelic face. He was also smaller than most children his age, and his appearance posed a problem. Even in kindergarten, the other children bullied and picked on Newton. He tried to get out of going to school by pretending to be sick, or tried to prolong the inevitable departure for school by feigning to have lost some item. Newton's mother eventually caught on, and assigned Walter Jr. the task of taking Huey to school. But Walter Jr. did more than that: he taught little Huey how to fight.

Newton explains in his autobiography that fighting was an essential skill in the disadvantaged community where he lived. Everyone had to know how to physically defend themselves. Moreover, through martial prowess, kids compensated for feelings of powerlessness. Newton was a quick study, thanks in large part to his brothers, Walter Jr. and Lee Edward. Both worked with Newton to help him perfect his brawling technique. Lee Edward told him "always to look an adversary straight in the eyes, and to keep moving forward. Even if you were hurled back three or four times ... eventually you would prevail" (*Revolutionary Suicide*, 24). Newton idolized Walter Jr., Lee Edward, as well as the popular boxers of the day: Sugar Ray Robinson and Joe Louis, brute, powerful fighters everyone held in awe. Huey was undoubtedly emulating these heroes as he beat up other boys in spontaneous tussles or organized boxing matches in the street or at the local Boys Club. By fighting, Newton earned respect and his own formidable reputation.

Newton also found ways to resist the racism he experienced in the public school system. To Huey and his black classmates, school was a form of oppression, a place where teachers sometimes called them "niggers" and were socialized to believe that whites were smart and blacks were unintelligent. In fact, it was perceived that all things good were associated with whiteness, and that all things bad were affiliated with blackness. In this environment, all the dreams that Huey and his friends nurtured, all the hopes for the future they had, were doused by feelings of ineptitude and hopelessness.

If Newton's learning disability was inborn, it was also exacerbated by the conditions in which he was educated, where racist belief systems predominated. Huey suffered academically. Once, a teacher told him to go to the blackboard and spell "business." Huey sensed the mockery in her voice and was aware that the purpose of this exercise was to embarrass him. He was humiliated, and so he froze, just as he did when someone hovered over him as he struggled to write his name. What Huey and other black students learned to do in the face of these demoralizing classroom situations was to fight back through disruptive behavior. This only served to magnify their problems and get them labeled "trouble kids."

Huey and his classmates found another way to weather their childhood troubles: they formed a gang. Huey and his friend David Hilliard belonged to a gang called "Brotherhood" when they attended the mostly white Wilson Junior High School. In the Brotherhood, everyone was called "brother" or "cousin." The members played together and sought solace through one another. They gambled with dice, and played taunting games known as "capping" and "the dozens." Huey admitted that he was not good at coming up with brilliant insults, so he relied heavily on his brawn to save face.

The Dozens

To an outsider, "the dozens" is nothing more than harsh teasing employed by schoolchildren on the playground. As cruel and vulgar as some of the teasing can be, it belies another phenomenon that has its origins in Africa. The name itself is believed to derive from a term used to describe undesirable slaves in America who were sold cheaply on the auction block and were grouped together and referred to as a "cheap dozen."

Seen in another way, "the dozens" is a game of word skill. Children exchange cutting and sometimes explicit jokes and insulting rhymes to put down one another. The winner of this teasing game is deemed to be the one who can come up with the cleverest statement, in the most elaborate and skillful way. Reward is bestowed by exclamations of applause, shouts, whoops, and laughter. This is one way in which black youths obtained status and esteem, although to the detriment of the one upon which he or she has heaped verbal attacks.

The dozens bears a similarity to games played by traditional African communities, which valued the creative use of language and its facile execution. In African culture, those who can speak well and best dramatize a story or an event are lauded and hold esteemed status in the community. Among the Igbos in Nigeria, small children and adolescents are known to play a game that is similar to the African American version of the dozens. This is explored thoroughly in "The Dozens: An African-Heritage Theory" in the 1976 publication of the *Journal of Black Studies*.

Besides his gang, Newton's family and church played a central role in surviving poverty, hopelessness, and racism. Huey's family was extremely close. Growing up, his siblings were his playmates. They always looked after one another. Their parents provided love, dignity, and, despite the poverty, a happy home. Huey recalled that his mother was gentle and had a sunny disposition.

Newton's brothers and his father were major influences in his life. Unlike many blacks, Newton's father did not back down from whites. Huey's brother, Lee Edward, was a shrewd navigator of Oakland's street life. Newton hung out with his big brother on street corners, and at pool halls, bars, and parties. From his other brother, Melvin, a serious student, Newton acquired a love of learning. Melvin eventually went to college, and he later taught sociology at Merritt College. Melvin tried to teach Huey how to read, but Newton did not really learn how to read until after graduation from high school, when, motivated by the desire to go to college, he taught himself. Melvin also introduced his brother to poetry and instilled in Newton an insatiable craving for books that would challenge his thinking and expand his critical-thinking skills. Huey had a sharp mind and an extraordinary memory. He could recite long passages of poems—and did so often to impress young women.

As a young child, Huey recognized the importance of the church and was greatly affected by his father's magnetism and influence over the men and women who listened to his Sunday morning sermons. Newton thought briefly of becoming a preacher himself. As a boy he was very active in the church, participating in the Baptist Young People's Union, the Young Deacons, and the junior choir. For a while, he was swept up by strong spiritual emotions, for the songs, the heartfelt prayers, and the warmth of the church family made Huey feel at peace with the world. At least until the next day when he had to face school and the city streets again. Later, Newton realized the power of the church, of belief, and of bonding with others of the same faith. He saw the church as being a "stable force;" a means of "escape" from the bitter circumstances of day-to-day life (*Revolutionary Suicide*, 38, 39).

Newton's favorite biblical champion was Samson, whose muscle power captivated him, underscoring as it did the message of survival of the fittest in Oakland. Samson's Herculean escapades were enthralling. He single-handedly slaughtered a lion, slayed one thousand of the despised Philistines with a jawbone, and later sent pillars crashing down upon his enemies in retribution for having been captured and blinded. In that final act, Samson lost his own life. Not surprisingly, power and martyrdom would occupy Newton's own thoughts when he became an adult.

Piano lessons were an unlikely instruction for a youth who was preoccupied with mastering the art of street fighting, but Newton's parents wanted him to learn how to play. Thus, he received seven years of instruction—and did not appear to mind. Throughout his life, people would marvel at his ability to play in the classical style. When Newton was an adult, a Black Panther happened to hear him play and was greatly surprised. Newton was constantly defying people's perception of him.

In high school, Huey discovered Fidel Castro. Initially, he liked Castro simply because he was someone that his teachers opposed. As Newton would later come to understand, Castro was a revolutionary, just as his childhood hero Samson had been. Angels had approached Samson's parents before his birth and told them that he had been promised to them by God to deliver the Israelites from the Philistines. Likewise Castro delivered Cubans from an oppressive leader, Fulgencia Batista.

At Newton's school, the teachers were, to the black students, their oppressors. In all his school years, Newton could recall only one teacher who was not antagonistic: a serene woman who taught his sixth grade class. None of the other children harassed her deliberately, because she did not provoke them.

In high school, Newton continued to build up his reputation as a trouble-maker. He vexed his teachers, and other students revered him. A defining moment in his life that became a local legend occurred when he hunted down some seven boys who had ganged up on him over a misunderstanding. When the cops arrived, Huey, a sophomore, was sent to juvenile detention for a month. After graduating from high school, he chose to go to college, even though not one of his teachers had encouraged him to do so.

HIGHER LEARNING AND THE BLACK POWER MOVEMENT

In 1959, Newton enrolled in Oakland City College. But he also attended Merritt College intermittently. He was interested in studying law and philosophy, as well as getting involved with the nascent Black Power groups on campus.

Newton's early years in college were filled with experimentation. When he came home one day with a beard like beatniks wore, his father was outraged and demanded that he shave. Newton moved out instead, preferring to live with a man named Richard Thorne, who had extremely nontraditional views on romantic relationships: he was a polygamist. Newton became one too.

The two men talked a lot about race, denouncing "the white man for everything; Huey explained that he was an angry young man at this time, drinking wine and fighting on the block, burglarizing [white] homes [and cars] in the Berkeley Hills." They also engaged in illicit money-making schemes (*Revolutionary Suicide*, 61). For Newton, stealing was not only done for money, it was a form of rebellion. He felt that the stolen goods and money equalized what he felt was the debt whites owed blacks for slavery and subsequent forms of oppression.

Newton spent a great deal of time on the street, hanging out with blacks and engaging them in discussions about what he was learning in college as well as his extracurricular reading. These discussions highlighted Newton's agitation over the system of racism, poverty, and oppression. He searched incessantly for an outlet—beyond stealing; beyond conversation—to find justice.

Newton became a member of several organizations, but he always found them wanting. He joined the Phi Beta Sigma, a fraternity, and the Afro-American Association. The latter was more radical than the former, but it was still all talk and little, if any, action.

Reading helped cool the fire that raged within him. He read scores of books on philosophy and the African American condition, books by activist and scholar W.E.B. Du Bois, literary writer Ralph Ellison, and accommoda-tionist Booker T. Washington. Other influences included Malcolm X, whom he heard lecture at a local high school. Malcolm and the Muslims fascinated Newton. He was intrigued by Malcolm X's program of militancy and self-defense, but he was not interested in following his religious teachings. New-ton's readings and personal interest in class disparities drew him to socialism, but after some consideration, he also rejected the Progressive Labor Party. Newton also looked into the organization called the Revolutionary Action Movement (RAM), but they were critical of him because he did not live in the poor communities where blacks lived. Later, they would tell his friend Bobby Seale that they did not trust him. He was, perhaps, too radical.

Both Newton and Seale were members of the Afro-American Association and attended Merritt College. Huey asserted that he and Seale did not always see eye-to-eye on issues. One of the draws to having Seale as a friend was that he had guns and taught Newton how to properly use them and let him borrow one from time to time.

One day, Huey got in serious trouble. A black man named Odell Lee, who had a scar, confronted Newton at a party in a way that he felt was aggressive. Newton knew that the code of the streets dictated that a scar on the body signified someone who was familiar with street fights. Newton interpreted Lee's scar to mean just that. During their brusque conversation, Newton felt Lee was challenging him. When Lee grabbed Newton's arm, he reacted instinctively, stabbing him repeatedly with a steak knife. Newton tried to say that in his world, this brief and violent encounter would have been construed as self-defense. However, the jury was not convinced. He was found guilty of a felony and sentenced to six months in the Alameda County Jail in Oakland in 1964.

ALAMEDA COUNTY JAIL

Huey was no stranger to the California jail system. Prior to his conviction for attacking Odell Lee, he had been put in jail for stealing on several occa-sions. Huey described this occasion as preparation for his prolonged sentences in 1967 and 1968, which catapulted Newton to national fame as a hero-victim.

Huey had no agenda when he entered Alameda County Jail. Early on, he was made a trustee, an unlikely position for a nonconformist. But when the inmates went on a food strike, protesting the bland and unwholesome meals, he joined them. He was the only trustee to do so. For punishment, Huey was sent to the room known to the inmates as the "soul breaker." Newton described the soul breaker in this way: "There was no bunk, no washbasin, no toilet, nothing but bare floors, bare walls, a solid steel door, and a round hole [for human waste] four inches in diameter and six inches deep in the middle of the floor" (*Revolutionary Suicide*, 100).

Newton survived the soul breaker longer than most. He accomplished this by devising a system based on techniques Gandhi had used during his demonstrations. Newton drank very little and ate even less, so he did not have to use the hole in the isolation room. He also did exercises and learned to control his thoughts by focusing on pleasant memories. Newton stayed for a month in the soul breaker. Most men begged to be released after only a few days.

Newton was transferred to two other locations before being returned back to Alameda. At the county farm at Santa Rita, where Newton was supposed to serve the rest of his sentence, he attacked an inmate who would not let him take extra servings of food in the mess hall. At Graystone, a maximum security prison, Newton was put directly into solitary confinement.

SOUL STUDENTS ADVISORY COUNCIL

Newton returned to campus after his release, still searching for a way to become involved in activism. Following Malcolm X's assassination on February 21, 1965, Seale quit the RAM. Malcolm X was among the high-profile militant black nationalists. His incendiary speeches calling for violent revolution inspired both Seale and Newton, even though they did not aspire to his Muslim faith. Seale had hoped that the RAM would be inspired to act in some meaningful way after Malcolm X's murder, but it did not.

Newton and Seale explored the Soul Students Advisory Council and liked what they saw. The organization initiated demands for a black history course at Oakland City College and protested police brutality. Newton, however, wanted to rev things up a bit. One day he recommended that they carry guns and go on patrols like other black self-defense groups, such as the Deacons for Defense and Justice, were doing. Seale concurred. But the group wanted nothing to do with guns, weapons, or armed patrols. Newton and Seale attended several more Soul Students meetings, challenging the group with piercing questions. But the organization could not be convinced.

THE BIRTH OF THE BLACK PANTHER PARTY FOR SELF-DEFENSE

Having exhausted all the black power organizations, Newton and Seale withdrew to Seale's home to discuss their future. They talked about the revolutionaries they admired such as Malcolm X, Robert Williams, Che Guevara, and Mao Tse-Tung. Robert Williams had established an armed guard to protect the black community in Monroe, North Carolina from racist attacks. Che Guevara, an Argentinean physician turned Marxist revolutionary, had a haunting appearance with his trademark black beret, from which streamed his jet black windblown hair, and an olive-drab military uniform. Though he would be executed in 1967, his legacy was indelible to those who had glorified his campaign of armed resistance. Guevara produced several works in which he discussed, in austere detail, his life, his ideology, and his experiences with guerrilla warfare. Mao Tse-Tung, a communist leader in China, had led his Revolutionary Army of Workers and Peasants to victory after more than twenty years of violent revolt.

Out of these informal conversations was born the idea of the Black Panther Party for Self-Defense. The ideology behind the organization was based on a compilation of all the revolutionary readings Huey had done. A ten-point program was created that would serve as the constitution of the organization. This included a call to end economic exploitation and police brutality against blacks and a demand for housing, jobs, food, decent education, and justice in the court rooms. The name of the organization,

Black Panther

The name and logo for the Black Panther Party for Self-Defense were inspired by a logo of a panther on a pamphlet belonging to the Lowndes County Freedom Organization in Alabama, an independent political organization founded by Stokely Carmichael. Newton liked the symbolism of the panther. He "suggested that ... the Black Panther [be their] symbol" and the name of their new organization, since "the Black Panther is a fierce animal, but he will not attack until he is backed into a corner; then he will strike out" (Hilliard, 29).

The symbolism of the panther not only conjured images of growing militancy in the latter half of the 1960s, but the color "black" denoted the fact that blacks were reclaiming the negative image of their skin color. No longer would black be equated with ugliness, ignorance, evil, and other negative words. Blackness would be celebrated as something beautiful, powerful, and strong.

However, the image came on too strong for many whites and conservative blacks, who were uncomfortable with black militancy. The symbolism contributed to widespread public perception that Black Panthers were ultra-aggressive and intent upon attacking whites for no reason at all.

Black Panthers, was derived from the panther symbol that emblazoned a voter registration pamphlet produced by a group called Lowndes County Freedom Organization. Newton explained that "The Black Panther is a fierce animal, but he will not attack until he is backed into a corner; then he will strike out" (Hilliard, 29). Their first member was a fifteen-year-old named Bobby Hutton, whom everyone called Lil Bobby.

Flores A. Forbes, who would become a member of the central committee and the special guard enlisted, among other things, to provide protection for Newton, explained to his father why he wanted to join the Black Panther Party when he was still a teen:

> I said, "Daddy, this is what I want to do. I want to be a Black Panther so that I can help my people. I see how things are in this country, and you always told me those stories about growing up in North Carolina and having to sit in the back of the bus. And then you and your brother refused to sit back there and you fought back and had that fight where you knocked the white boy out and stuff. You know what I mean? I'm tired of being pushed around and I want to fight back." (Forbes, 30)

Point Seven

Many adolescents were drawn to the Black Panther Party. Part of the draw was the allure of point seven of the ten-point program, which stated, in short, that "We believe we can end police brutality in our black community by organizing black self-defense groups that are dedicated to defending our black community from racist police oppression and brutality ... the Constitution of the United States gives a right to bear arms" (Hilliard, 33).

For the youth, as well as the adults, who joined the Black Panthers, there was the allure about belonging to a community, but there was something more: the opportunity to wield a gun. Guns are a universal symbol of power, but they have special import for African Americans. In slavery, African Americans were prohibited from owning or using a gun. Even in the free states, laws forbade gun ownership by blacks. In cities like Oakland, white cops dominated blacks not only with the institutional power they wielded, but also because they carried guns, which they could use maliciously. White cops were rarely indicted for crimes against blacks.

Black Panthers received extensive training on how to carry out their party duties, and on how to use guns. Panthers were taught how to clean guns and how not to point the barrel of the gun at any person (to do so was a crime). Panthers were required to memorize the ten-point program and to consume a healthy reading diet of philosophy, militancy, and the ideology of the organization. There were rules to abide by that emphasized respect for self and the community. For example, drugs and alcohol were forbidden while engaged in party work, and a Panther could not commit a crime against another member or any black person. It was important to Newton, who had learned about community from his family and at church, that the Panthers be tight-knit.

In the first phase of Panther activities, Newton launched the famous gun patrols. While on these patrols, Newton depended not only on armed self-defense but on the law. He would "stand there with his gun and his book, reciting the law, careful not to step outside the limits of the law, but rather, using the law and the gun as a means for legitimizing the rights for black citizens to protect themselves" (Hilliard, 38).

Newton believed it was important to educate the community about the law as well as about the organization. His objective was to empower African Americans, and to do this he had to get the word out about the Black

Clenched-Fist Salute

In the 1960s, almost everyone was raising their hand in the clenched-fist salute. Although it was used before then it was made popular in large part by several high-profile individuals in the Black Power Movement.

The clenched-fist salute is also known as the black power salute or the "Power to the People" salute. It is raised to express solidarity. Newton and the members of the Black Panther Party for Self-Defense made the salute frequently among themselves and in public. Newton, as well as other individuals associated with the Black Power Movement, made the salute upon release from stints in jail. Generally, the audience, in a call-and-response effect, made the salute back.

One of the most controversial moments in sports history occurred when the clenched-fist salute was raised during the 1968 Olympics in Mexico City. When two African Americans, Tommie Smith and John Carlos, entered the stadium to receive their medals, they wore no shoes to pay homage to impoverished blacks. Smith wore a black scarf to signify black pride, and Carlos wore a strand of beads to symbolize blacks who had been lynched or murdered by racists or by their oppressors. After mounting the podium, during the playing of the National Anthem, they raised their hands in the clenched-fist salute and bowed their heads. After dismounting the podium, the audience booed them. But the image made headlines all over the world. Back at home, the men received death threats and were heavily criticized. But their protest had the opposite effect on many blacks who venerated them for what they had done. A documentary on that incident, *Salute*, was scheduled to premiere at the Sydney Film Festival in 2008.

Since black power proponents began adopting the clenched-fist salute, others have followed suit, such as Native Americans and hippies during the Hippie Movement.

Panthers. His tactic worked, especially when his patrols, in party uniform, went into the communities themselves and disseminated their leaflets. Many of the new members included ex-convicts, prisoners, the unemployed, and the disenchanted.

White cops were generally enraged by the fact that the Panthers were watching them. During the patrols, the Panthers had strict orders to stand a certain distance from a cop. They were instructed not to interfere. However, when an officer engaged Newton, he did not back down. The patrols were hugely successful, staving off violent acts and resulting in a marked decrease in incidences of police brutality and killing.

Not all of Newton's ideas were so noble. One was outright scandalous. Huey wanted to exact financial support for panther programs from individuals outside the law, such as the drug dealers and panderers. In exchange, he planned to establish a defense fund to provide bail and legal representation. Most individuals did not warm to this idea, and were put off by Newton's interference in their personal matters. To some, this plan was nothing more than barefaced extortion.

ELDRIDGE CLEAVER: MINISTER OF INFORMATION

It took Eldridge Cleaver a while to become convinced that the Black Panther organization was for him. From the first, Newton tried to coax Cleaver into joining his organization. He believed Cleaver would be an asset in many ways. He was a professional writer and a charismatic speaker. That he had been to jail made him someone who could relate to the plight of black men in disadvantaged communities. Cleaver listened, without uttering a word, as Newton explained what his organization was all about. He initially declined to join because he wanted to help restart Malcolm X's Organization of Afro-American Unity, not realizing that Newton and Seale had the same intent.

Eventually, Cleaver changed his mind and asked Newton if he could join the Black Panthers. He did this for reasons that would eventually create havoc for the Black Panther Party. At a meeting in February 1967 to help coordinate a memorial to mark the fourth anniversary of Malcolm X's assassination, Cleaver was transfixed. He was awestruck by the demonstration of glinting weapons, urbane uniforms, and the imperturbable don't-mess-with-me posturing. It was then that Cleaver knew he wanted to be a part of the Panthers. At the memorial, as Huey and the Panthers served as guards for Malcolm X's widow Betty Shabazz, Cleaver witnessed one of numerous standoffs between Huey and a police officer.

The conflict started when a cameraman roughly brushed Newton's hand away as he tried to shield Shabazz from being photographed. Newton "asked a nearby officer to arrest the other man for assault" (Hilliard, 118).

Newton was ignored. Newton took matters into his own hands: when the cameraman tried to prevent him from covering up his camera, he "slammed him up against the brick wall of the building" and punched him (Hilliard, 118). Panicked, Seale tried to get Newton to run from the scene, but he would not. Instead, he outfaced a cop, dared him to use his gun, and called him a "big, fat, racist, pig" (Hilliard, 119). The cop backed down. Cleaver was awestruck.

Cleaver was drawn by the power, mesmerized by the excitement of precarious confrontation. However, he did not have the same communal spirit that Newton had, and he was averse to becoming a mentor and role model to the members.

DENZIL DOWELL CAMPAIGN AND BLACK PANTHER ARRESTS

When word spread that an unarmed twenty-year-old named Denzil Dowell had been shot and killed on April 1, 1967 by a police officer in North Richmond, a community near Oakland, Newton saw an opportunity for community outreach and a way to broaden the Panthers' influence. Newton and other Panthers met with the Dowell family and promised to lead an investigation into the tragedy. Newton organized rallies to inform the community of what had occurred. The Panthers pressed for police investigation and disciplinary action against the offending officer, but the officials at the police department were uncooperative.

The Black Panther newspaper grew out of the need to dispense information regarding the Dowell case and others like it. On the front page of the first issue, a summary of evidence resulting from the Panthers' investigation of the Denzil Dowell case was presented. There was also an advertisement for an upcoming rally, a description of the Black Panther Party's objectives, and a call for the community to get involved.

The magazine was only one way in which Newton hoped to get exposure for various causes and the party itself. Newton went on radio talk shows to educate the community about the goals of the Panthers, and to speak on pertinent issues such as the Dowell case. Early on, the black community was unsure about the Panthers. Their radicalism made many uncomfortable, and some feared the party's existence might attract more problems. In time, they realized the Panthers was having the opposite effect, and that racist cops were less likely to act out against blacks.

Whites, however, remained at odds with the Panthers. Donald Mulford was one of the Panthers' most powerful enemies. Mulford was a conservative state assemblyman. During one radio talk show event with Newton, he called in and threatened to endorse a bill to make it unlawful for Panthers to carry guns.

Newton planned a demonstration at the Sacramento, California legislature on May 2, 1967 (the day the bill was to be discussed) to protest the

Mulford bill. Since he was still on probation, Seale went in his place, but Newton crafted a message for him to read that elucidated the need for the Panthers and other blacks to arm themselves against racist attacks by malevolent individuals, organizations (like the Ku Klux Klan), and police officers.

Thirty armed Black Panthers flocked to California's capitol. Cameras flashed upon Seale as he repeatedly read the message. Newton, at his parents' home, watched the spectacle on television and was delighted by the coverage.

Seale and the other Panthers were arrested after leaving the capitol. According to David Hilliard, chief of staff of the Black Panthers, the cops fabricated charges against them. Newton used radio appearances and fundraisers to collect money for bail. In a deal that called for Seale to return to jail, the remaining Panthers were freed.

The exposure vaulted the Panthers to greater notoriety, but this came at a price. Yes, the Black Panthers garnered a lot of attention, which increased their numbers and improved their finances. But many powerful whites were incensed by this display of growing power.

A MURDER, AN ASSAULT, AND A KIDNAPPING

October 27, 1967 was planned to be a busy day of fundraising for Huey P. Newton. But though the day started with a speaking engagement at San Francisco State College where he raised $500, it ended in tragedy.

Newton did not like public speaking. He was more comfortable behind-the-scenes, thinking and guiding the development of his organization. But as part of the program to raise bail for Seale, he was willing to make the attempt. His speech at San Francisco State College was controversial because the black youths in the audience expected Newton to condone the spontaneous rebellions advocated by other black power proponents like H. Rap Brown. And they did not like that did he disapproved of racial separatism.

Newton once stated that he was not "anti-white. I don't hate a person because of his skin…. Because I wouldn't stoop to the level of the Ku Klux Klan, to hate a person because of the color of his skin" (Hilliard, 71). The Black Panthers were one of few organizations that endorsed and actively formed coalitions with whites and other marginalized people, like Native Americans, Latinos, and the disabled.

After giving his speech, Newton stopped by a fundraising party taking place at David Hilliard's house. The event was unconventional, at best: it was a gambling party where Newton and Hilliard also planned to sell marijuana. At some point in the evening, Newton borrowed a girlfriend's car to go out with friends and celebrate his last day of probation.

Newton and Gene McKinney, who was with him, were stopped by Officer Gene Frey. Officer Frey was eventually joined by Officer Herbert

Hearnes. Newton showed him his license and the registration papers, got out of the car, and was promptly searched. Officer Frey, like most if not all Oakland cops, knew or had heard of Huey P. Newton, the leader of the Black Panther Party. Frey ordered Newton to the back of his car, roughly pushing him along. He hit Newton, who stumbled backwards. According to Newton, Frey shot him in the stomach. What he remembered next was vague. He heard the sound of shots being fired and recalled struggling with the emergency room nurse to get admitted to the hospital.

Hilliard provided more details. He recalled how Newton burst into his home, while the party was still going on, and crumbled onto the floor, blood streaming from his wound. Hilliard took him to Kaiser Hospital. The cops appeared shortly thereafter.

Newton recalled how cops handcuffed him to his bed and beat him while a doctor looked on. Later, as he lay recuperating in a hospital room, cops continued to harass, beat, and intimidate him. Newton soon learned that they believed that he was responsible for the murder of their fellow officer, Frey, and for an assault on Hearnes. Newton would face three counts against him: murder, assault, and the kidnapping of a man named Dell Ross who accused him and McKinney of carjacking.

FREE HUEY CAMPAIGN

Subsequent events raised Newton into even wider fame. The Black Panthers launched a Free Huey Campaign, gaining sympathy and mass support from individuals who had never heard of him or had a negative opinion of the organization. The constant media attention did more to spread the news about the organization and to cultivate new members than anything they could have done themselves. And media attention was crucial to the promulgation of the Black Panther Party.

The Free Huey Campaign involved a number of other black power leaders such as Stokely Carmichael and James Forman. Angela Davis also joined the demonstrations and helped dispense information for the campaign. When Bobby Seale was released from jail, he and Eldridge Cleaver made crucial contributions as speakers. Cleaver staged a mass rally. The frenzy that was created by the rallies and demonstrations not only helped Newton but promulgated the plight of poor African Americans. The first day of the trial was attended by 5,000 demonstrators and 450 Black Panthers.

From jail, Newton created tapes and wrote letters to his organization. Newton used the trial itself as a platform from which to address the nation. He spoke about the history and objectives of the Black Panther Party; he exposed the police brutality and harassment that was rampant in his community. The trial itself endeared Newton to his audience and to his organization. That he endured solitary for a total of eleven months until the conclusion of his trial gave him superhero status.

The verdict was a huge disappointment. Although Newton was found not guilty of kidnapping and assault, he was found guilty of voluntary manslaughter and sentenced to two to fifteen years in prison. In a statement to the press, Newton asserted that he believed "the verdict reflected the racism that exists here in America, and that all Black people are subjected to. I am very sure that we will get a new trial not because of the kindness the appellate courts will show us, but because of the political pressure that we have applied to the establishment, and asked that the community refrain from reacting in violence" (Hilliard, 107).

CALIFORNIA PENAL COLONY (1968–1970)

Shifting Gears

Huey P. Newton spent most of his time in solitary at the California Men's Colony, East Facility, in San Luis Obispo, California, otherwise known as the California Penal Colony. But he saw a benefit to his seclusion. Throughout most of his life, Newton had been constantly bombarded by people and responsibilities. In jail, and especially in solitary, Newton had time to reflect on life, his organization, and his ideology. Solitary also afforded him the time and space to read without interruption. Malcolm X experienced a religious and intellectual transformation while in prison. Al Sharpton, the twenty-first-century civil rights activist, was reinvigorated by reading the writings of prominent activists while he served time in jail.

During his time in jail, Newton began to feel strongly that his organization needed to change direction. He did not like how the media depicted them (in Hilliard's words) as, "trigger-happy, gun-toting thugs who were more interested in gunplay than substantive social change" (Hilliard, 127). Newton came up with a plan to provide food and other resources to the community. He foresaw one potential problem: Cleaver, who made no secret of the fact that he preferred guns over community outreach.

Opposition

Cleaver was not Newton's only problem. In November 1968, the FBI, under Director J. Edgar Hoover, began a long and brutal campaign to dismantle the Black Panthers, along with many other black power organizations. The name of this notorious campaign was COINTELPRO, otherwise known as the Counter Intelligence Program. The FBI's methods included infiltration of the organization by agents provocateurs; schemes to frame leaders on trumped-up charges; and a campaign to print false, malicious, and damaging news in the media.

Before long, Black Panthers were regularly monitored and followed by the FBI. Bugging devices were planted in homes and offices. Homes and offices were routinely vandalized and searched, with documents and personal items stolen. Beatings were common. By 1969, twenty-eight Panthers had been killed by police and agents provocateurs.

David Horowitz, who had known Newton and had been one of the Panthers' supporters, became the organization's most voluble critic, but the more time he spent with the organization, the more uncomfortable he became. He painted a contradictory picture of the Panthers, by demonstrating, through numbers, the criminal activities of the organization: "348 arrests for murder, armed robbery, rape, and burglary in 1969 alone" (Collier and Horowitz, 151). Those statistics illustrated his belief that the Panthers were largely targeted by the FBI because of increased criminal activity.

But the Panthers saw COINTELPRO as an immediate threat to themselves and their organization. Panther chapters scoured through their membership and purged anyone suspected of being an agent provocateur, often at the price of ousting the innocent. In a notorious 1969 case, a group of Black Panthers tortured and murdered Alex Rackley, whom they suspected of being an informant. Bobby Seale and Ericka Huggins were arrested and charged with ordering the murder.

DEATH OF THE FIRST BLACK PANTHER

On April 6, 1968, while Newton was in jail, a confrontation between the Black Panthers and Oakland police ended in the death of Lil Bobby, who had been the first member of the organization. Bobby Hutton, Eldridge Cleaver, David Hilliard, and Wendell Wade were transporting food for a community barbecue planned for the next day. Before the incident that sent Newton to jail, he had organized the get-together to gain support for the newly created Black Panther Campaign Fund. Under the Peace and Freedom Party, Eldridge was running for president, Huey P. planned to run for Congress, and Bobby Seale and Kathleen Cleaver were running for assembly seats. According to Hilliard, Newton wanted to use the barbecue as a forum to help prevent riots in the black community in light of Dr. King's assassination. Violent riots had erupted elsewhere, and Newton wanted to prevent this from happening in Oakland. Cleaver, meanwhile, was brooding over an idea to fuel a violent backlash.

The cops, aware of the barbecue, were out in full force, and the city put restrictions on the event, preventing the Panthers from using a sound system. As the Panthers drove to the event, the cops arrived and chased after the Panthers. Cleaver and Lil Bobby fled to a nearby house. They were surrounded by cops who pelted the house with tear-gas and fire bombs. Lil Bobby and Cleaver were eventually forced out of the house. When an officer told both men to run toward a car, Cleaver could not, because he had been shot in his leg. But Lil Bobby ran, with his arms held high over his head. He was shot down in clear view of onlookers from the community.

Cleaver was charged with attempted murder for shooting at the cops who pursued him. Instead of facing trial, he escaped to Cuba and then to Algeria. Other Panthers were apprehended and charged with the same crime as a result of the confrontation with the police. No one was prosecuted for the murder of Bobby Hutton.

To fuel dissension among the Panthers, especially between Newton and Cleaver, COINTELPRO manufactured fake letters, written in both their names, to instigate trouble between them. Neither realized they were being set up. When the private conflict became public, Newton called up Cleaver, then in exile in Algeria, to confront him. Cleaver was ultimately expelled from the Black Panthers in 1971. He formed a rival organization in Algiers called the Revolutionary People's Communication Network (known as "The Network").

Expulsion was just one punishment for wayward or disobedient Panthers. Disciplinary measures were severe. One could be bullwhipped or mud-holed. Black Panthers on the receiving end of this antiquated treatment had to remove their tops and were lashed with a whip. Mud-holing was even more extreme, with some of the biggest, fiercest Panthers stomping on the offending member. The sad irony was that being bullwhipped had been a common punishment for slaves.

HUEY'S FREEDOM

On August 5, 1970, Newton was released from prison after serving twenty-two months and (thanks to his supporters) posted a $50,000 bail. The appellate court had overturned his conviction over technicalities in the instructions the judge gave the jury. But, as he had predicted, the court did permit Newton another trial. In the winter of 1970, the judge dismissed his case. This is what Newton recalled about that day:

> It was a bright, blue-sky day, just the kind of day I had wanted. Looking ahead, I could see thousands of beautiful people and a sea of hands, all of them waving. When I gave them the power sign, the hands shot up in reply and everyone started to cheer. God, it was good. I felt this tremendous sense of release, of liberation, like taking off your shirt on a hot day and feeling free, unbound by anything. (*Revolutionary Suicide*, 289)

Newton kept himself busy after his release. Though he went to China for ten days in September 1971, he ignored most of the other invitations he received requesting media appearances, interviews, and speaking engagements. Huey had enough to contend with inside his organization, and he wanted to implement the plans he had formed while in prison.

One of his first tasks was to initiate what he dubbed "survival programs," such as medical clinics, sickle cell anemia testing, a free-food program, a free-breakfast program, and a shoe program. Newton envisioned the Black

Panthers providing more services to the community, and he worked to set up these programs through chapters in other cities. He also spent a lot of time getting to know the other chapters, traveling the country to visit new chapters and new recruits.

These were perilous times for Black Panthers. Leaders such as Bobby Seale and Ericka Huggins were in jail facing various charges. A number of Panthers had fallen, either as a result of fatal confrontations with the police or with rival organizations. The Panthers worried that Newton was the next target.

To ensure Newton's safety, wealthy white friends, among them some Hollywood A-listers, helped secure him a new home: a lush, high-rise apartment away from the community the Panthers served. This new home was referred to as the Throne, aptly named since Newton was often referred to as a "prince" by his members. Newton was reasonably safe there, but not entirely. His home was once ransacked, and he was under constant surveillance.

PERSONA

Not everyone appreciated Newton's motivation for living in the Throne. Many African Americans were vehemently against the affluent white establishment and anything that hinted at acceptance of the white power structure, elitism, or privilege. The feeling was that Newton was getting out of touch with the organization. This was worsened by the fact that Newton stayed away from the Panther office. Most of his work was done from the Throne, and he rarely if ever went to the Panther office.

Those who met Newton for the first time or saw him speak were sometimes perplexed, because his true personality contradicted their expectations of him. As one attendant at a college lecture stated: "People saw him as the baddest in the world. Then you have this guy come up with this intellectual discussion" (Hilliard, 176). New Panther recruits who met Newton for the first time had the same experience. Instead of getting a fierce warrior, they encountered an intellectual with a high-pitched voice who delivered ideology, not tough, forceful oration. A number of black students were crushed to learn that Newton was not a black separatist.

But Newton could indeed be fierce. Robert Trivers, a professor and someone who spent a great deal of time with Newton, saw this side of him, and was unnerved by it. He wrote that "[Newton] was like a king, and therefore if you were a friend of his and in his presence, you were like a prince. On the other hand, he could be one of the more frightening creatures you would ever run into" (Hilliard, 257). Forbes, one of Newton's top guards, detailed how he and others regularly pistol-whipped individuals who challenged them, particularly those in the underworld who would not subject themselves to Newton. Newton's erratic and explosive temper was infamous. Accusations that Panthers committed murder or that Newton ordered those murders were rampant, tarnishing his hero image. Horowitz called him "Capone in blackface" (Collier and Horowitz, 156).

The new apartment was both a sanctuary and a torment. This was evident to anyone whom he invited to the Throne when he was alone and troubled. The quiet, introspective side of Newton was witnessed by those he trusted the most. Newton benefited from the quiet time to think and to reinvigorate himself. He was not an extrovert like Seale or Cleaver. But sometimes the quiet was confining, and he needed someone to talk to.

Newton was a man increasingly encumbered by his weighty responsibilities. He was constantly working on ways to improve his organization, trying to meet the needs of his members and the community, or brooding over some conflict that needed to be resolved. Sometimes, he expressed second thoughts about his position: "I'm not an idealist anymore," he told one confidant, "what am I supposed to do?" (Hilliard, 199).

Shortly after his release from jail, Newton was introduced to Gwen Fountaine, a new recruit to the organization, having joined in 1969. Doe-eyed and diminutive, Fountaine was a quiet constant in his life. She had two children, Ronnie and Jessica, from a previous marriage, and they became like Newton's own. Many of Newton's confidantes were women. But any woman who became close to Newton had to endure his unpredictable temper, his frantic schedule, and his decadent lifestyle. They also had to understand that the organization came first.

BLACK PANTHER SCHOOL

In 1970, Newton established the Children's House, later called the Intercommunal Youth Institute and the Oakland Community School. The children who attended this school wore uniforms. Both boys and girls wore berets, and the young girls wore dark skirts that hung above their knees. The school was a sensation. Celebrities came to visit, and local black schoolteachers fed up with the traditional public school system were eager to work there.

Newton, like everyone else in the community, knew the hazards of the public school system. He created an atmosphere where children could be taught racial pride and receive a good education without the humiliation he himself had experienced. The school was funded by the Educational Opportunities Corporation using federal and local grants. Some alleged that the school was eventually funded by criminal activities, such as extortion and illegal drug sales.

PANTHER WAR ON DRUGS

It did not matter to Newton that he himself used drugs out of the public eye; he was determined to keep drugs out of the black community. A campaign was created to educate the community on the hazards of drug use. Slogans such as "Capitalism Plus Dope Equals Genocide" were used. Newton declared that he wanted to sustain a healthy community. At the same time, Hilliard claimed that the FBI spearheaded a scheme "to 'criminalize' our revolution by … pinning a narcotics rap on the Black Panther Party" (Hilliard, 204).

In 1974, Newton was charged with pistol-whipping a black man and with the murder of a seventeen-year-old prostitute. There were some who thought the indestructible Newton had finally been caught. They were wrong.

Disguised as a woman, Newton escaped with Gwen Fountaine to Cuba. Horowitz asserted that the Panthers tried to explain away Newton's sudden flight by presenting an audiotape that exposed a plot on Newton's life. Presumably, the criminal world in Oakland had marked Newton because they did not like how he tried to dominate them. Newton gave the real reason in his autobiography that he knew he had no chance in court. Exile was the only option.

The escape was harrowing. They departed from Oakland by plane, then drove from Los Angeles to Mexico. In Yelapa, he and Fountaine spent weeks swimming, relaxing, and riding horses. From Yelapa, they took a boat and crossed turbulent waves onto Cuban shores. Newton changed his name to Peter Simon. At first, "it was nice to be anonymous and unbothered by people." Later he wanted to be Huey again (Hilliard, 216).

CUBA

Newton and Fountaine (later joined by her two children) were married after they arrived in Cuba, and they lived there for almost three years. For Newton, this new life was a dramatic change. For one thing, he was married. For another, he went to work at a cement factory, where he repaired trucks, and taught a social-movement course at the University of Havana. In the evenings, he and his family had quiet dinners. On the weekends, they sometimes went on outings, to the beach and elsewhere, with Newton's co-workers. In his spare time, he read.

This relatively normal existence seemed to presage a stabilizing of Newton's life, but that proved to be unrealistic. He was not planning to spend the rest of his days in Cuba. While in exile, he kept in daily contact with Elaine Brown, whom he made the first woman leader of the Black Panther Party in his absence. Brown was intensely loyal to Newton, partly because he was someone she respected and partly because, like many women, she was infatuated with him. Under her leadership, the organization was catapulted to even greater success. She carried on his Survival Programs and oversaw the daily functions of the organization and the Black Panther School. She initiated Panther involvement in local politics. Horowitz summarized her accomplishments in a chapter entitled "Baddest" in his book *Destructive Generation*. While Brown was at the helm, "the organization was instrumental in the campaigns of Lionel Wilson, first black mayor of the city ... and John George, first black supervisor of the county." Brown later (1976) served as a delegate at a Democratic convention (Horowitz, 158, 159).

RETURN TO THE UNITED STATES

Newton flew back to the United States on July 3, 1977, drawing a huge crowd of fifteen hundred to greet him. Huey was confident that, since the Republicans were no longer in control of Oakland politics and an African American man had been elected a superior court judge, he stood a chance to get a fair trial in the face of the charges against him.

Newton gave a speech at the airport. He expressed his commitment to the struggle, saying he would "continue my fight against a system that denies decent housing, clothing, and medical care to people to fight against the evil of heroin sales in our community, despite the contract put on my life by heroin dealers with the knowledge of law enforcement.... Now I am going to jail. I believe I will be acquitted" (Hilliard, 244, 245).

Newton was right. He was acquitted of all charges. But according to Horowitz, Newton was guilty of the crimes. He said that Newton, while high on drugs, shot a prostitute after she called him "Baby." Newton had been tormented as a youth by kids who called him "Baby Huey," a cartoon character. Horowitz said Newton assaulted the black man, a tailor, when he made the same error as the prostitute. The murder charge resulted in a hung jury. He was cleared of the assault charge by allegedly paying off the tailor. Newton claimed that the tailor could not or would not identify him as the perpetrator.

HIGHER EDUCATION REVISITED AND BOBBY SEALE'S DEPARTURE

Education remained important to Newton. He received an associate's degree in social science in 1966. In 1974, he received his bachelor's degree from the University of California, Santa Cruz. This was the year Bobby Seale was expelled from the Panthers.

In the years preceding his forced departure, Seale and Newton drifted apart. When they started the Panthers organization they had been close friends, seeming, in numerous pictures, inseparable; bound like blood brothers. But Newton talked behind Seale's back, bitterly complaining that he was not keeping up with him with regard to the ideological development of the organization. When Newton moved to the Throne, Seale was rarely invited. When Seale did finally visit Newton on a day in 1974, Newton was in a mood. An argument ensued, and Seale was promptly ousted.

After Newton's return to America and his acquittal of criminal charges, he decided to go back to the University of California, Santa Cruz. It was a love-hate relationship. Sometimes Newton attended classes dressed like a seventies star from a black exploitation film. And he was always flanked by his guards. He also made the other professors nervous. Newton continued to lead the Black Panthers during his time at Santa Cruz. In short, he was a celebrity, and at times disrupted classes, especially when he gave a public lecture on his dissertation. In 1978, Newton earned his Ph.D. His dissertation was titled "War against the Panthers: A Study of Repression in America."

DRUGS, CRIME, AND MARRIAGE

Despite his academic achievements, Newton served additional jail time for various crimes, including possession of a handgun and narcotics paraphernalia. Newton's descent from power was propelled by heavy drug use, which eventually contributed to the demise of his marriage. Newton caused an accident while driving under the influence. His stepchildren were in the car at the time and nearly died. Gwen left him.

Newton tried to start a new life with his marriage to Fredericka Slaughter in 1984. He joined her church and attempted to turn over a new leaf. In that same year, a crack epidemic began to sweep across the major cities of America, lasting through 1990. Oakland was one of the locations hit hard by the new drug, and Newton would eventually become one of its casualties.

Newton remained in trouble with the law. He faced another jail sentence for embezzling state and federal funds from some of the Panther programs. For periods at a time, Newton was sober. But those periods did not last for long, and personal setbacks or the curse of addiction itself plummeted him back into drugs for days or weeks at a time. Despite a few good times, Newton was in a downward spiral.

The Panther Party was floundering; Newton and his wife lost their home, and Newton was devastated when his deal for a Hollywood film biography did not go through. On August 22, 1989, Newton got into an argument with a young drug dealer. Ironically, this young man had been a recipient of his free-breakfast program when he was a child. Newton was shot three times in the head. He was forty-seven years old. In 1993, Fredericka Newton, Elaine Brown, and David Hilliard established the Huey P. Newton Foundation. It serves as a repository for Black Panther Party history and information.

See also Elaine Brown; Stokely Carmichael; Angela Davis; W.E.B. Du Bois; Martin Luther King, Jr.; Malcolm X; Al Sharpton; and Robert F. Williams.

FURTHER RESOURCES

Collier, Peter, and David Horowitz. *Destructive Generation: Second Thoughts about the Sixties*. New York: Simon & Schuster, 1996.

Forbes, Flores A. *Will You Die with Me? My Life and the Black Panther Party*. New York: Atria Books, 2006.

Hilliard, David. *Huey: Spirit of the Panther*. New York: Thunder's Mouth Press, 2006.

Horowitz, David. *Hating Whitey and Other Progressive Causes*. Dallas: Spence Publishing Company, 1999.

A Huey P. Newton Story. Directed by Spike Lee. 40 Acres & A Mule Filmworks, 2004.

"It's about Time." *Black Panther Party Legacy & Alumni* (March 2008). See http://www.itsabouttimebpp.com/index.html.

Newton, Huey P. *The Huey P. Newton Reader*. New York: Seven Stories Press, 2002.

Newton, Huey P. *Revolutionary Suicide*. New York: Writers & Readers Publishing, 1995.

Newton, Huey P. "War against the Panthers: A Study of Repression in America." *Mindfully.Org* (March 2008). See http://www.mindfully.org/Reform/War-Against-Panthers-Newton1jun80.htm.

Seale, Bobby. *Seize the Time: The Story of the Black Panther Party and Huey P. Newton*. New York: Random House, 1970.

Rosa Parks (1913–2005)

Rosa Parks was a domestic worker, seamstress, and activist. She is most known—and indeed celebrated—for a single and spontaneous act of protest, when, on December 1, 1955, she refused to give up her seat to a white passenger on a public bus in Montgomery, Alabama.

Parks was an unlikely and unassuming hero. She was only forty-two when she was arrested for violating Alabama state law, but she appeared almost grandmotherly, with her trademark hair pinned neatly back and a pensive, strained expression on her bespectacled face. Even to those who knew her, Parks was quiet, reserved, soft-spoken, and timid. To the white community, she was invisible amongst the droves of African American women plodding back and forth from home—the black side of town—to a long day of cleaning, laundering, and other menial work for white employers in the white section of town. No, Parks was neither a notorious troublemaker nor a charismatic rebel leader. And yet beneath her mild-mannered demeanor there lurked a revolutionary. Parks was a secretary of the local chapter of the National Association for the Advancement of Colored People (NAACP), a devoted member of the African American Methodist Church, and the wife of an activist.

That day when Parks refused to give up her seat to a white passenger and told the white bus driver "no" when he ordered her to do so, though she risked violence or worse, was not her first act of protest against racism. Even as a fragile and sickly child Rosa had fought back—sometimes verbally and other times physically—against racial attacks. That day did not even mark her first incident on a racially segregated bus. What was different this time was that her act of resistance on that day in December would launch her from obscurity to instant fame as a protest icon and give impetus to a massive bus boycott led by a young Baptist minister by the name of Dr. Martin Luther King, Jr. This would jumpstart the remarkable era known as the Civil Rights Movement, and Rosa Parks, though she had no children of her own, would come to be known as its "mother."

CHILDHOOD

Rosa McCauley was born on February 4, 1913, in Tuskegee, Alabama near the famous Tuskegee Institute founded by Booker T. Washington, one of the leaders of the African American community at the time. Washington and his philosophy of accommodationism was quite popular with both blacks and whites, and the practice was accepted as the norm in the South. Those who challenged the complicated rules of racial etiquette and discriminatory laws were marked for intimidation, violence, or death. In those days, African Americans had few rights, and were considered to be in every way imaginable inferior to whites.

Rosa's father, James, and mother, Leona, struggled to create a good life in that hostile world. James, a handsome carpenter of mixed African

American, white, and Native American ancestry, was a restless wanderer constantly in search of money-making opportunities. Leona, whose heritage was Scotch-Irish, African American, and white, was intelligent and driven. She had received a teacher's certificate (a high-status profession for African Americans) from Payne University in Selma, Alabama, but had stopped teaching while in Tuskegee to care for Rosa, her husband, and her brother-in-law, who took classes at the nearby Institute. Leona was lonely much of the time, for James was always working, and she made no friends and had no family in the African American community of Tuskegee. Despite this, she hoped her husband would eventually take a job at the Institute, for among the benefits of being a faculty member was a home, a good education for Rosa, and stability (Parks, 8). But teaching did not provide enough income for the restless James, so he moved the family to his hometown of Abbeville, Alabama.

Leona's dreams for the family dissolved after the move to Abbeville. She did not like living with her husband's relatives, so while James again left the family for a job in the North, Leona, pregnant with their second child, packed her and Rosa's belongings and moved back home, living with her parents in the rural town of Pine Level, Alabama. James lived off and on with his wife and children for several years, until, when Rosa was five years old, he permanently left them. Thus, Rosa spent the bulk of her childhood in Pine Level, where her education was vastly inferior to what she might have received at the Institute. She was raised mostly by her grandparents, for her mom lived and taught in a somewhat distant town during the work week.

In Parks' autobiography, *My Story*, she recounts many childhood memories of her life in Pine Level, a small segregated town. The African Americans were mostly sharecroppers, while whites owned the businesses and stores. Rosa's grandparents were the only African Americans who owned land and were able to subsist on the family farm. They raised chickens and cows on their eighteen acres, and grew fruit and nut trees as well as a garden. For additional supplies or income, Rosa's grandfather traveled on his wagon to the local stores to sell or trade. Another source of income came from cotton picking. Rosa was a field hand as a young child. Picking cotton was a laborious job made all the more unendurable under the scorching Alabama sun.

The education of little Rosa began long before she made her formal entrance into the one-room school house designated for Pine Level's black children. Integral to her education was learning her role as an African American in a white-dominated society. Her earliest memory of Pine Level gives a glimpse of a young child who had the potential to be a fine example of a "good Negro," which was someone who went along with the laws and rules that whites set without complaining or protesting. On this particular occasion, her grandfather had taken Rosa to the doctor, a white man. She was only two and was suffering miserably from a severe sore throat caused by chronic tonsillitis. Because of Rosa's weak heart, surgery was not an option. Rosa recalled proudly in her autobiography "that everything the doctor asked me to do, I just obeyed very nicely," and those around her, including her grandparents and mother, were delighted "with my being so small and being so little trouble" (Parks, *My Story*, 11). As a child, Rosa relished being a "good girl," exactly what society demanded she be.

Rosa learned her early lessons in race relations through stories about life in slavery, firsthand experience with radicals who challenged the system of racism in her everyday life, and lectures on the importance of accommodating whites. Rosa heard many stories about the horrific realities of slavery from her mother, as well as her grandparents, who had been born into slavery. These stories taught her that slavery was a great evil. In them she heard about the dramatic measures slaves took to submit under the tacit (as well as explicit) rules of bondage, such as pretending to be happy with their lot to appease whites and to avoid hostility. Servility was a means of survival—or at least a method to ensure a peaceable existence. For the most part, African Americans in the South in the early twentieth century continued to conform to laws (explicit or not) that were just as humiliating and oppressive as the slave laws.

For young Rosa, protest was exemplified by her cantankerous and mischief-loving grandfather, Sylvester, and a local denizen named Gus Vaughn. Sylvester's early years had been traumatic and had embittered him toward whites. After the death of his mother, a house slave, and his father, a white plantation owner, Sylvester had been daily abused by an overseer who beat him and starved him. As an adult, Sylvester, like the trickster of traditional African American folktales, enjoyed playing tricks on whites, always "doing or saying something that would embarrass or agitate the white people" (thus challenging the rules of racial etiquette), such as shaking the hands of unsuspecting strangers or introducing himself to them as "Edwards," or "call[ing] white men by their first names, or their whole names, and not say 'Mister' " (Parks, *My Story*, 16). He had high expectations for his children, hoping that they would get an education. For some reason, Rosa's grandfather was never harassed for this behavior or his beliefs (or for the fact that he owned land). The custom in the South was that individuals who challenged the system were frequent targets of racist organizations such as the Ku Klux Klan.

Rosa's grandfather was not easily frightened by local whites or by the Ku Klux Klan riders who frequently thundered past their property in the middle of the night. Rosa recalled those tense nights, when she, still dressed in her clothes in case she had to escape from an attack, lay at her grandfather's feet, while he sat in his rocking chair with his double-barreled shotgun at his side. On those nights, Rosa was wide-eyed, not from fear, but because she wanted to see her grandfather use his gun. He never did have that opportunity, for the Ku Klux Klan never molested him or his family.

Trickster

A trickster is an archetypal figure in folklore who outwits a seemingly unconquerable foe. The symbol and antics of the trickster were important coping mechanisms in slavery, and also demonstrated a form of resistance employed by blacks in slavery and post emancipation. Trickster myths were part of the folklore of African communities.

In America, black slaves continued the rich traditions of storytelling, giving birth to an Americanized form of the African trickster figure, which gave life to animals endowed with human characteristics. Brer Rabbit was one of the most popular characters. His nemeses included Brer Fox and an array of colorful characters. Brer Rabbit was not strong, but he was sassy and smart and able to outwit, outdistance, outmaneuver, and transcend anyone or anything through subtle or overt maneuverings. His tales are classic underdog-overcomes-all narratives. But more than that, the characters and situations in the Brer Rabbit stories represented slaves and their own impossible predicaments. Sometimes, the antagonist was "Ole Massa" himself.

This vibrant imaginary world formed a backdrop for the real-life antics of individuals who outwitted the white oppressor. The stories vindicated blacks who daily endured oppression and indignities. It also slyly encouraged black slaves to find ways to undermine whites. For example, blacks who stole their white master's choicest pigs and fruits without getting caught were heroes. Blacks, during the Jim Crow years of the late nineteenth century to mid-twentieth century, found ways to challenge the white system through subtle mockery or in-your-face challenges. Unfortunately, the repercussions of playing the role of a trickster could be dangerous, and sometimes fatal.

Gus Vaughn was another African American in Rosa's community who dared to challenge whites. While his family picked cotton, Rosa recalled how "Mr. Gus Vaughn didn't do anything but walk around on his stick. He didn't work for anybody. He didn't do anything but walk around with his stick and talk big talk," such as the day when a white man seethed, "Gus, I don't like you" to which Vaughn replied, "There is no love lost," implying that he didn't like the white man either (Parks, *My Story*, 36). Rosa did not mention anything ever happening to Vaughn for what she referred to as "sassing" or talking back. He and her grandfather were two of the very few African American men who got away with putting themselves on equal terms with whites and challenging racism.

Notwithstanding the humilities that Rosa and her family suffered, her childhood comprised some happy memories: fishing trips with her grandparents, frolicking with her little brother Sylvester (named after their grandfather) on the family property, reading, and going to school. Rosa, unlike her grandfather who forbade her and her brother from playing with the local white children, felt no animosity towards whites, insisting in her autobiography that not all white people "were hostile to us black people" (Parks, *My Story*, 38). For example, there was a white Union soldier who patted a two-year old Rosa "on the head and said [she] was such a cute little girl," causing his southern father-in-law to "turn red as a coal of fire" and the kindly elderly white woman who frequently visited Rosa's grandparents and took her fishing (Parks, *My Story*, 3).

Despite her lack of hostility, Rosa was frustratingly aware of the disparity between whites and blacks in Pine Level. While white schoolchildren rode buses, the black children walked to school, often forced to trudge through the fields rather than the road to avoid being harassed by the children lumbering past on the school bus. The white children enjoyed a new school made of brick, "built with public money, including taxes paid by both whites and blacks," and went to school for nine months. The black children attended school for just five months a year, because they were needed to work in the fields. When the black school was closed, Rosa and her brother walked eight miles to and from school at Spring Hill, where their mother taught.

Unfazed by the social constrictions imposed on her race (and her gender), as well as her own sickliness and small size, Rosa, at age ten, single-handedly engaged in her first battle against racism. When a white boy "balled his fist up as if to give [Rosa] a sock," Rosa "picked up a brick and dared him to hit [her]. He thought better of the idea and went away" (Parks, *My Story*, 22). She alluded to the explanation of her reaction to the white boy's unprovoked threat when she wrote that the notion "that you don't put up with bad treatment from anybody" was "passed down almost in our genes," that "the habit of protecting [her] little brother helped [her] learn to protect" herself and that she "had a very strong sense of what was fair" (Parks, *My Story*, 15, 22). Her grandfather undoubtedly set a strong example for Rosa, but the women in her family did not applaud her efforts in challenging whites. Rosa was reprimanded by her grandmother for threatening the white boy with a brick. She told her that she was "too high-strung, and that if [she] wasn't careful, [she] would probably by lynched before [she] was twenty years old" (Parks, *My Story*, 23). Rosa wrote that she "got very upset" by her grandmother's words, mostly because she felt she had her "rights to try to defend" herself, and she thought that her grandmother had taken "his side" (Parks, *My Story*, 23).

Since the schools for blacks went only to the sixth grade in Pine Level, Rosa's mother sent her daughter to the big city of Montgomery, Alabama to further her education. Rosa attended the Montgomery Industrial School, where, significantly, the teachers were all white women from the North. Rosa learned "English, science, and geography, cooking, sewing, and the care of the sick." More importantly, the teachers reinforced what her family had taught her: that she "was a person with dignity and self-respect," and that she "should not set [her] sights lower than anybody else just because

[she] was black" (Parks, *My Story*, 49). This aspect of the curriculum made the teachers very unpopular with the locals.

Parks recalled that the downside to living in Montgomery was the stringent rules of segregation. Glaring reminders of white superiority and black inferiority were more prevalent in the big city than in little Pine Level. Signs regulating black and white life were everywhere. In particular, the "black-only" and "white-only" signs on the water fountains initially puzzled Rosa, because she could not "understand that there was no difference in the water. [Both water fountains] had the same color and taste" (Parks, *My Story*, 46). Rosa encountered an increasing number of racial incidents in Montgomery, and her habit (to her mother's angst) was to challenge them at every turn. Once, a young white boy on roller skates attempted to "push [Rosa] off the sidewalk" but found himself pushed instead (Parks, *My Story*, 48). When his mother, who stood nearby, protested, Rosa countered by stating that she "didn't want to be pushed, seeing that I wasn't bothering him at all" (Parks, *My Story*, 48). At another time, Rosa and a cousin were picking berries when a little boy shouted at them, "You niggers better leave them berries alone" (Parks, *My Story*, 51). But they countered back with a threat that they would harm him if he tried anything. They told their aunt who, like Rosa's grandmother several years prior, scolded them and told them that they ought to keep their "mouths shut. If he'd gone and told somebody, they would have had y'all lynched" (Parks, *My Story*, 51). Rosa, however, would not be silenced. She later told a band of white teenagers after they had "threatened to throw her brother in the creek," that "you won't be putting nobody in the water unless all of us go in together" (Parks, *My Story*, 52).

Rosa luckily survived these trying incidences, as well as the removal of her tonsils, but in the end she had to abandon her education. Following her stint at the Industrial School, Rosa attended Booker T. Washington Junior High and Alabama Normal School, but she had to drop out in her eleventh year to care for her grandmother. Her grandmother died shortly thereafter, but Rosa then had to care for her mother. To help provide for her family, Rosa worked as a domestic for whites. She also worked in a shirt factory and helped out on the family farm. This turn in Rosa's life would have no doubt disappointed her grandfather, had he been alive, for the proud Sylvester had held grander hopes for his family. But opportunities for African American women were hardly any better for Rosa's generation than her mother's, and they were all the more limited for Rosa since she had not finished high school.

COURTSHIP AND MARRIAGE

When Rosa first met Raymond Parks, she did not like that his skin was so fair. He had a light complexion, like her grandfather, and was "in his late twenties and working as a barber in a black barbershop in downtown Montgomery." Rosa was in her "late teens" and "very shy" (Parks, *My*

Story, 55, 56). Coming often to her mother's house, Raymond eventually gained Rosa's trust and would take her for rides in his car. Rosa explained in her autobiography that owning a car was a big deal at that time. However, Rosa became interested in Raymond for another reason:

> [Raymond Parks] was the first man of our race, aside from my grandfather, with whom I actually discussed anything about the racial conditions. And he was the first, aside from my grandfather and Mr. Gus Vaughn, who was never actually afraid of white people. So many African Americans felt that you just had to be under Mr. Charlie's heel—that's what we called the white man, Mr. Charlie—and couldn't do anything to cross him. In other words Parks believed in being a man and expected to be treated as a man. I was very impressed by the fact that he didn't seem to have that meek attitude—what was called an "Uncle Tom" attitude—towards white people. (Parks, *My Story,* 59)

Raymond was a member of the NAACP when Rosa met him and a regular reader and subscriber of radical African American newspapers, like the *Pittsburgh Courier, Amsterdam News,* and *Chicago Defender.* Many of his clients at the barbershop read them too. During their time together, Parks often spoke about the organization and its current undertaking: raising money to help save the young boys of the infamous Scottsboro trial. The NAACP, deemed a radical organization at the time, had to work under the radar. The local chapter, of which Raymond was a member, functioned as an underground organization, meeting late at night. A lookout was positioned to watch for the police or any other signs of trouble, and the members carried guns. Parks was often cryptic when he talked to Rosa about the Montgomery Chapter. He did not want to expose Rosa to the dangers of what he was doing. This was not mere overprotectiveness on his part, for at least two of the men associated with Raymond's activism had been murdered.

In August 1932, the smitten Parks brought up the idea that he and Rosa "ought to get married" (Parks, *My Story,* 64). That December they exchanged vows in a quiet ceremony and reception at Rosa's mother's home. Theirs was a supportive marriage. Although Parks feared for her husband's life, she did not attempt to deter him from his activism. And her husband encouraged Parks to work toward getting her high school diploma, which she received in 1933. Despite this achievement, she continued to take menial jobs. In 1941, Parks worked on an Army Air Force base, where jobs had been integrated as a result of Franklin D. Roosevelt's issuance of Executive Order 8802. But off the base, segregation was still in full force.

EARLY ACTIVISM

The National Association for the Advancement of Colored People (NAACP)

As has been shown, though Rosa Parks had a history of speaking out and fighting back when confronted with racism, she was often discouraged from doing so. She was also discouraged from joining the NAACP. In the early years of her marriage, Rosa did not express any interest in joining an organization for the purposes of resistance, but even if she had, her husband had made it clear that the NAACP was too dangerous. Parks speculated that this was the reason why many women may not have joined. It was not until more than ten years into her marriage, in 1943, that she challenged this status quo and joined the NAACP.

Even then, Parks had not exactly intended to join the NAACP. She decided to go to a meeting to reconnect with an old school friend, a woman named Johnnie Carr, who, ironically, did not attend the gathering. But by the end of that meeting, Parks was not only a member but an officer, and her career as an activist had officially begun. Parks recalled that she "was the only woman there, and they said they needed a secretary, and I was too timid to say no" (Parks, *My Story*, 81). Some time later that year, Parks was not "too timid" when she tried to register to vote and, not for the last time, stood up to a bus driver who ordered her to get off his bus.

Voting Rights

Parks was unable to secure her voting rights after that first attempt in 1943, but her ongoing involvement and interest in the issue is shown by the fact that the Voters' League frequently held meetings in the Parks' home. Voting rights was also a major issue for the Montgomery chapter of the NAACP. Voting was recognized as a powerful tool, with which African Americans could affect the laws and elect the people who made those laws. Knowing this, whites, since emancipation, had made it as difficult as possible for African Americans to vote. In Montgomery, African Americans either had to be vouched by a white person or had to pass a tough literacy test. Initiating the steps to take the test was an ordeal in itself. Edgar Daniel Nixon, who was president of the Montgomery chapter of the Brotherhood of Sleeping Car Porters and of the NAACP, and Arthur A. Madison, an African American attorney based in New York, were instrumental in helping to endorse black voting power. Madison was arrested and jailed for his work, illustrating the continuing perils of trying to change the system. Embittered by his experience, the lawyer returned to the North upon his release.

First Bus Protest

Parks revealed in her autobiography that "the second time I tried to register to vote, I was put off a Montgomery city bus for the first time. I didn't follow the rules" (Parks, *My Story*, 76). The laws and established customs for riding segregated public buses varied from town to town (and bus to bus, in some cases) in the segregated South. In Montgomery, whites sat in the first ten seats, and African Americans filled the back ten seats. All the other seats in the middle were to be filled at the bus driver's discretion. The gun-toting bus drivers wielded a great deal of power, enforcing the laws at their whim and fancy, and, as Parks described it, frequently mistreating African Americans in the process. One day in 1943 Parks entered the bus from the front rather than the back, because it was packed with people. After the driver ordered her to reenter the bus from the back door, she and the driver engaged in the following sharp exchange:

> I told him I was already on the bus and didn't see the need of getting off and getting back on when people were standing on the stepwell, and how was I going to squeeze on anyway? So he told me if I couldn't go through the back door that I would have to get off the bus—"my bus," he called it. I stood where I was. He came back and he took my coat sleeve; not my arm, just my coat sleeve.
>
> He didn't take his gun out ... I just didn't get off and go around like he told me. So after he took my coat sleeve, I went up to the front, and I dropped my purse. Rather than stop or bend over to get it, I sat right down in the front seat and from a sitting position I picked up my purse.
>
> He was standing over me and he said, "get off my bus." I said, "I will get off." He looked like he was ready to hit me. I said, "I know one thing. You better not hit me." He didn't strike me. I got off, and I heard someone mumble from the back, "how come she don't go around get in the back?" (Parks, *My Story*, 78–79)

This same Parks, who could be outright bold and outrageously defiant in some situations, appeared docile and submissive in others. As a secretary, Parks filled a subordinate (albeit important) role in the NAACP. She was not a decision maker, but a duteous supporter to the men who were. She followed instructions well and without complaint. She had many responsibilities (including taking minutes and other administrative duties), none of which brought her a stipend, but she was happy with what she was doing. She would have liked to do more, but as a co-worker had told her, her mother and husband were protective of her. Among her many jobs was to record "cases of discrimination or unfair treatment or acts of violence against black people" (Parks, *My Story*, 84). It was a distressing task, considering how often African Americans were denied justice.

In 1945, Parks won a personal victory when she finally passed the literacy test. If she had not passed the third time, Parks had planned to sue the voter registration board, because she believed she had answered the questions correctly. As proof of foul play, she copied down by hand the test questions and her answers. She described her first time voting as anticlimactic, considering the hurdles she had personally overcome in specific and the historic struggle for black suffrage in general.

Following this brief triumph, it was business as usual for Parks, who volunteered even more of her time to activism, eventually attaining a significant place in the NAACP. In 1946, Parks traveled to Jacksonville, Florida for an NAACP leadership training seminar, where she was introduced to

Ella Baker, the national director of the NAACP. The two women fast became friends. Baker mentored Parks. A year later, Parks served on a committee that elected Edgar Nixon as president of the Alabama NAACP. She even presented a speech before convention goers in Mobile. The audience was "surprised" and impressed by the diminutive Parks as she "passionately" "quoted the Bible and Booker T. Washington, decried the mistreatment of African American women across the black belt, and chided those dandies who used the annual convention as an occasion for southern boosterism" (Brinkley, 69). On that same day, she was appointed secretary of the statewide NAACP conference. New endeavors followed in the ensuing years. Parks, as advisor to the NAACP Youth Council, helped high school students in their efforts to check out books from the white public library. During this time, she worked a number of house-keeping and seamstress jobs for whites and was an active member at St. Paul AME, preparing communion and teaching Sunday school.

Between 1949 and 1952, Parks took a break from the NAACP to care for her mother, who frequently suffered from bouts of illness, but eventually continued her efforts, joining in the celebration of the monumental Supreme Court decision *Brown v. Board of Education* in 1954. During this time, she was befriended by (and did some sewing for) a white woman named Virginia Durr. Durr and her attorney husband were two of the few south-ern-born whites who assisted in the struggle of African Americans. A true iconoclast, Durr challenged racial etiquette by requesting that Parks call her by her first name (though Parks declined her request), engaged her in long friendly conversations in her home, and formed an integrated women's prayer group (in which Parks participated). Virginia Durr contributed hugely to Parks' development as an activist. She gave Parks books to read to supplement her education in, for example, politics, and insisted that she attend a workshop on "Racial Desegregation: Implementing the Supreme Court Decision" at the Highlander Folk School in Monteagle, Tennessee. With the help of Durr and a scholarship, Parks was able to attend the ten-day workshop in the summer of 1955.

Parks enjoyed herself immensely at Highlander, a school for aspiring acti-vists. Although it was surrounded by a community of all whites—and racists at that—within the walls of the school there existed an unprecedented multiracial utopia, an illuminating experience for Parks. In this environment, Parks took part in discussions on race, speaking openly and unguardedly "without any repercussions or antagonistic attitudes from other people" (Parks, *My Story*, 107). Recreation included swimming, playing volleyball, and square dancing, in which Parks did not participate. Among the memorable aspects of the work-shop was the forging of a friendship with Septima Clark, an African American woman activist and teacher at the Highlander School, where she taught "adults to read and write and learn about basic citizenship so they could become teach-ers of others, so they could register to vote," and the fact that whites, not blacks, did the cooking every day (Parks, *My Story*, 104, 105).

Septima Poinsette Clark

Septima Poinsette Clark was an educator and activist. She was born in Charleston, South Carolina, on May 3, 1898, to Peter Poinsette, who had been born a slave, and Victoria Warren Anderson, who had been raised in Haiti but returned to her place of birth, Charleston, after the Civil War (1861–1865).

After graduating from high school in 1916, Poinsette wanted to go on to college, but she could not afford it. Instead she found a job as a schoolteacher in John's Island, South Carolina. Poinsette became an advocate for equal pay for black and white teachers when she realized that she and the other black teacher in the same school of one hundred thirty-two students received $35 and $25 a week, respectively. The white principle and teacher at the all-white school with only three students in the same town received $85 a week.

In 1919, Poinsette began teaching the sixth grade at the Avery Normal Institute in Charleston, South Carolina. She soon began to attend meetings of the National Association for the Advancement of Colored People (NAACP). She and her students often went door-to-door for the NAACP, canvassing for support for various causes.

A year later, Poinsette married Nerie Clark. They had a son, Nerie Clark, Jr., and moved to Dayton, Ohio. However, in 1925, her husband died. It was hard going as a single mom. She sent her son to live with his paternal grandparents in Hickory, North Carolina. While she taught, she took classes at Columbia University in New York and Atlanta University in Georgia. Further education at Benedict College, Columbia University, and Hampton Institute produced bachelor's and master's degrees. She returned to Charleston and continued to teach at various schools, including the famed activist institution, Highlander Folk School in Tennessee, where she facilitated an adult literacy program and taught students how to fill out voter registration forms. She also served as director of workshops for a time. In 1961, Clark became the Southern Christian Leadership Conference's director of education and teaching. She died on December 15, 1987.

There was tension in the air when Parks returned home to Alabama. The usually sleepy (with regards to African American protest) city of Mobile was abuzz with discontentment, particularly over segregated seating and abuse suffered on the public buses. This had long been a sore subject for the African American community, who, with only a few exceptions, endured the humiliation in silence. These exceptions included Nixon, storming down to the bus company to make futile demands, and Jo An Robinson, leader of the Women's Political Council, whose protest resulted in the expansion of bus service into black neighborhoods and nothing else of major consequence. While the bigwigs in the NAACP, led by Nixon, contemplated a plan of legal action, Parks had her own thoughts. She believed that the church should be at the forefront of whatever activism took place, and that a bus boycott was the solution to getting their demands met by the bus company. The problem with the bus boycott, as she found out after questioning some folks in town, was that the likelihood of mobilizing support was virtually nil. Though "a group of activists took a petition to the bus company official and city officials" making such requests as "courteous treatment" and the elimination of the signs that designated the black and white sections on the bus, Parks was not among them. She stated that she "would not go anywhere with a piece of paper in [her] hand asking white folks for any favors" (Parks, *My Story*, 112).

Parks was witness to, and may have participated in, the intense discussions regarding whether or not to take legal action, a popular means of protest for the NAACP, against the bus companies. The odds for leading a successful legal attack were deemed to be weighted heavily against them. The conditions would have to be just right: the bus passenger would have to be charged with violating the laws of segregation, and, at the same time, to be "above reproach" so as to win over the religious African American community and withstand attacks by the opposition (Parks, *My Story*, 111). Only then would it be feasible for the NAACP attorneys to have their day in court before the Supreme Court with the possibility of victory. Justice for African Americans in the South, with its abundance of racist judges and all-white hanging juries, was inconceivable. Potential cases with two young women had come and gone, but had not proved viable, because one woman was pregnant out of wedlock and the other did not want to protest. None of the activist leaders dreamed that the responsibility would fall upon the slender shoulders of the impeccable Parks, who made an unpremeditated act of defiance on December 1, 1955.

PRELUDE TO THE MONTGOMERY BUS BOYCOTT

Thursday, December 1, 1955

On what seemed an ordinary evening following a day of work at Montgomery Fair, a department store in town, Parks ascended bus number 2857. She was possibly irritated when she noticed, after paying her fare, that the bus driver, one James Blake, was the same man she had had a run-in with in 1943 when he had ordered her off his bus when, following a spat, she did not enter the bus from the back. Since that confrontation, Parks had made a point of avoiding him. But it was too late to get off the bus now. She continued on, picking her way down the aisle and sitting down in the front row of the "black-only" section. Beside her were two women and one man.

When a group of whites later entered the bus, the driver demanded that the four blacks (Parks included) give up their seats to a white man. The three other passengers hesitated, but when the driver commanded, "Y'all better make it light on yourselves and let me have those seats," the three relinquished their places (Parks, *My Story*, 115). Parks stood up to let the black men sidle past her and sat down again, sliding over to the window seat. The bus was intensely quiet, watching to see what Parks would do. Parks did not move.

Parks' resistance—by not yielding her seat to the white man—was not because her feet were sore, as people would later say, and not because she foresaw the opportunity to induce an incident that could be used by the NAACP as a test case to fight segregation. Parks had a long history of stubbornly resisting racism. As she sat in her seat, her thoughts turned to memories of her radical grandfather, who stood up to racism with bold "sassiness" and readiness to defend himself and his family with his shotgun, and her bitter frustration over having to always bow down to white supremacy. This act of defiance was personal.

The ensuing scenes played out without pandemonium. There was no explosive exchange or violent confrontation between the driver and Parks; the other passengers were not involved. The dialogue between the driver and Parks was brief: he asked her if she was going to give up her seat; she told him, "No." When he said, "I'm going to have you arrested," she cheekily replied, "You may do that" (Parks, *My Story*, 116).

Neither the driver nor the two police officers who arrived on the scene physically assaulted Parks, which in that period would have been permitted. The first question one of the officers asked her was why she did not stand up. Parks responded with a question of her own: "Why do you all push us around?" (Parks, *My Story*, 117) By questioning the officer, Parks demonstrated that she was not obligated to answer to anyone. By making known her dissatisfaction with white oppression, she risked physical harm or death. But her question seemed to befuddle the officer, who replied, "I don't know, but the law is the law and you're under arrest," and then the two officers, in a gesture that could be interpreted as courteous, carried her bags to the police car (Parks, *My Story*, 117). While en route to jail, she was asked again why she did not comply with the bus driver. This time Parks said nothing.

No major incidents occurred at the jail, with the exception that Parks was ignored when she asked to make a phone call. Parks was stoic while in jail. In the cell she shared with two other African American women, she was more concerned with one woman's narrative of domestic abuse and how she had landed in jail because she had attempted to defend herself than she was with her own situation. When she was finally allowed to make a phone call, she called home. Her mother was relieved that her daughter had not been beaten. Her husband promised that he would be there soon.

Word quickly spread within the African American community about Parks' arrest. Nixon and the Durrs were on hand to greet Parks when she was released (a white friend of Parks' husband supplied the bail money).

Virginia Durr greeted Parks with a tearful embrace. Parks, suddenly letting her defenses down, recalled that she "didn't realize how much being in jail had upset me until I got out" (Parks, *My Story*, 123). Raymond Parks "gave his wife a bear hug that swept her off her feet" (Brinkley, 114). Nixon soon broached the topic of taking her demonstration to greater heights, asking Parks if she would be willing to be the test case. Parks, with her "sterling character," was the ideal plaintiff (Brinkley, 117). But Rosa Parks, who had not even considered allowing her personal moment of protest to go beyond what it was, had no immediate answer for Nixon.

Parks went home that evening to discuss what to do with her husband and her mother. Both Leona and Raymond were wary of sacrificing Rosa's future for the sake of challenging segregation on Montgomery buses. Besides, Raymond thought that there was no possible way to gain support from the community. No situation or experience had ever shown him that that was a possibility.

The three of them deliberated for some time, finally deciding that Rosa should agree to work with the NAACP. That very night, Fred Gray, a black attorney, contacted Jo Ann Robinson, who agreed to ask for support from the Women's Political Council for a bus boycott scheduled for the same day as Parks' trial (Monday, December 5). Through Robinson's efforts, more than "35,000 handbills (handbills, leaflets, brochures)" were produced to spread the word about the boycott (Parks, *My Story*, 126). Little did any of them know that that the heroic struggle toward civil rights had begun.

Friday, December 2, 1955

The next day, Parks went to work as usual, though she took a taxi owned by an African American company, vowing that she "was not going to ride the bus anymore" (Parks, *My Story*, 128). She stunned her boss, who had neither heard the news nor read it in the morning's paper. Meanwhile, Nixon began orchestrating the two-pronged battle: in court, with Parks as plaintiff, and in the community, via the bus boycott. Essential to this strategy was his utilization of the press and the African American church. Nixon's behind-the-scenes masterminding was crucial to the success to come.

Another significant move on Nixon's part was to involve the African American church. Most African Americans in Montgomery and across the nation were churchgoers. Their deep-seated faith stemmed from the religious traditions of Africa, their ancestral homeland, and had survived the grueling **Middle Passage** and the period of slavery. Nixon made a call to a prominent local Baptist preacher, Ralph Abernathy, who in turn brought on a young newcomer named Dr. Martin Luther King, Jr. The two men were among the eighteen other ministers designated to lead the boycott. Nixon also coordinated a meeting that night to discuss the planned boycott. Significantly, the press was invited.

During the lunch hour, Parks went to Fred Gray's office to help answer phone calls and provide any other administrative assistance. That evening, she went to the meeting at Dr. King's Dexter Avenue Baptist Church, where she talked about her ordeal. As a result of the first meeting, some ministers "agreed to talk about the protest in their Sunday sermons," and another pamphlet was created to appear "on the front page of the Montgomery Advertiser" (Parks, *My Story*, 129, 130). No strong consensus was reached regarding the duration of the boycott, and an additional meeting was scheduled (for the first night of the boycott).

MONTGOMERY BUS BOYCOTT

Monday was an important day: the Montgomery Improvement Association (MIA) was forged, with Dr. King at its helm; Parks had her day in court; and the first day of the Montgomery bus boycott was launched with full participation from African Americans (with the exception of a few riders who had not known about the boycott). Notwithstanding the history-making significance of the day, Parks woke that morning without anxiety. She stated, "I did not spend a lot of time planning what to wear." Nevertheless, she remembered precisely what she wore: "a straight, long-sleeved black dress with a white collar and cuffs, a small black velvet hat with pearls across the top, and a charcoal gray coat." She carried "a black purse and wore white gloves" (Parks, *My Story*, 132). Such were the modest, non-flashy, and conservative battle clothes befitting of the demure Parks. As Parks strode up the steps of the courthouse later that morning, a woman called out behind her, "Oh, she's so sweet. They've met with the wrong one now" (Parks, *My Story*, 133).

During the trial, Parks—unlike so many icons of African American protest who engaged in extensive public speaking and elaborate denunciation—said nothing. Her mere presence was all that was necessary, while the attorneys, Charles Langford and Fred Gray, spoke on her behalf. As the protest leaders had hoped, Parks was "found guilty of violating the segregation laws" and was charged a fine of $14.00 (including court costs) (Parks, *My Story*, 134). After the trial, Parks went to Gray's office. Keeping her identity incognito, she answered the non-stop phone inquiries on the results of the trial and this unknown woman named Rosa Parks.

That evening there was a "pep rally" for the boycotters, at the Holt Street Baptist Church. As became the custom for such meetings, prayers and rousing speeches were given, religious songs were sung, and scriptures were read.

At that time in African American history, the church was both a symbol and a tool for activism. Political speech making and the singing of protest songs stemmed from African American sermons and spirituals. At the head of this movement were the spiritual leaders of the African American Community: the preachers. Women held conventional and limited roles.

Parks, though she was the one who had sparked the massive demonstration, was not exempt. When she asked if she should "say anything" at the church on Holt Street, she was told that she had "said enough and you don't have to speak" (Parks, *My Story*, 139). Parks seemed content with the explanation, explaining that she was not compelled to say anything anyway. Her introduction alone seemed to satisfy the enthusiastic crowd that flowed out the front door and spilled out onto the front lawn. The program featured Dr. King, who was received with thunderous applause and the reading of "the list of demands that the Montgomery Improvement Association was going to present to the bus company and the city's white leaders," which included "courteous treatment on the buses"; "first-come, first-served seating, with whites in front and blacks in back"; and "hiring of black drivers for the black bus routes" (Parks, *My Story*, 140).

The boycott proved to be a long and harrowing affair; no one had expected it to last 381 days. Parks was the only woman to share center stage with Dr. King, whose popularity increased tremendously during the boycott. Parks was the quiet one; King was the charismatic orator. Both embarked on speaking campaigns. Parks, however, had to keep a full-time job to provide for her family. The monies she made from speaking engagements went to support the boycott. Parks also went to work behind-the-scenes for the MIA, which coordinated an elaborate transportation system utilizing black cab companies and church-owned vans. Others affected by the boycott opted to simply walk.

Parks' determination was severely tested during the boycott. Not only did the bus company and city officials (including the mayor) make every effort to oppose the demands of the boycotters, white racists made ruthless attempts to intimidate her and the leaders of the MIA. Both she and her husband lost their jobs. Rosa was fired, while Raymond quit when a supervisor threatened to fire anyone who mentioned his wife's name. Rosa, along with other MIA members, was regularly threatened. Hate calls streamed in daily to the Parks' home. But she and her family were never attacked—unlike some of the leaders, like King, whose home was bombed. Nonetheless, the daily bullying put a strain on the Parks.

That February, eighty-nine indictments were handed down to ministers, MIA leaders (including King), and Rosa Parks, justified by "an old law that prohibited boycotts" (Parks, *My Story*, 148). King was the only one to be tried and sentenced, but his case was later appealed. The photograph of Parks getting fingerprinted was published on the front cover of the *New York Times*. Parks was becoming a household name.

The attention was sometimes unsettling. One of the only times that Parks broke down publicly was when she was interviewed by an aggressive reporter out of San Francisco who told her he "was going 'to take me apart and see what made me tick,'" and the interview made Parks so nervous that she recalled how the cup in her hand "was rattling, I was shaking so"

(Parks, *My Story*, 153). "The man was being obnoxious, and I was being as polite and nice as I possibly could," she said, "suddenly I just couldn't stand him any longer, I went into hysterics" (Parks, *My Story*, 153). Roy Wilkins, President of the NAACP, who was present at the interview, comforted her.

The heroic struggle to boycott Montgomery buses took its toll on everyone. What got them through was the strength of their numbers, their unified commitment to protest, and extraordinary leaders like King. Bi-weekly meetings at the churches affirmed their purpose; songs were sung to strengthen their hearts, and brilliant legal work and media coverage documented the struggle in print and on TV for all the world to see. Above all was the unifying symbol of an ordinary woman like Parks. On November 13, 1956, the boycotters received joyous news: the Supreme Court had ruled that segregation on Montgomery buses was unconstitutional.

Back to Highlander

In December, Parks, along with her mother and Nixon, traveled to Highlander on an invitation to encourage six black students from Clinton, Tennessee, who were growing disheartened in the struggle they faced being the first blacks to integrate their high school and were considering dropping out of school. The black students were taunted, harassed, and received no protection. Parks was able to convince the youths to return to school. The visit was a good one for both mother and daughter. Indeed, Parks was invited to join the faculty at Highlander, but she had to reluctantly decline. Her mother did not want to stay.

End of the Boycott

Following the Supreme Court decision in November, King had warned the activists to keep boycotting until the ruling was made official. Thus, the boycott did not officially end until December 20, 1956. It was a joyful occasion.

There were celebrations and a sense of accomplishment; pictures were staged on buses (Parks included), and similar demonstrations were launched in other parts of the South. However, the ensuing years were hard and dangerous. There were more bombings and threats, and whites even shot at buses.

In the meantime, Parks became increasingly uncomfortable in encounters within her own circle. A Baptist preacher "teased" her one day, "exclaiming, 'Well! If it isn't the superstar!'" (Brinkley, 175). Nixon had "turned a cold shoulder toward her, telling Arkansas NAACP activist Daisy Bates that Parks was a lovely, 'stupid woman' the media had built up into an icon'" (Brinkley, 175). Abernathy "refused to take Parks seriously as a civil rights leader, dismissing her as a mere 'tool' of the MIA" (Brinkley, 176). The threat of violence, compounded by her inability to find work and possibly

Highlander Folk School

The Highlander Folk School, now known as the Highlander Research and Education Center, was a popular landmark during the Civil Rights Movement. Most activists attended workshops in social activism for training and development. Among some of the famous activists who have been associated with Highlander were Dr. Martin Luther King, Jr., Rosa Parks, and John Lewis.

Highlander was founded in 1932 by Myles Horton, Don West, and James A. Dombrowski. It was originally situated in Monteagle, Tennessee. After Rosa Parks refused her seat on a Jim Crow bus in Montgomery, Alabama, in 1955, racist whites did everything imaginable to thwart the subsequent boycott. So intense was the reaction against Parks that in 1961 the state of Tennessee closed Highlander. Parks had attended Highlander for a workshop prior to her demonstration. It reopened later that year in Knoxville, Tennessee and became known as the Highlander Research and Education Center. In 1971, it changed locations for a third time to New Market, Tennessee.

Highlander was attended mostly by white students. Indeed it kept its doors open to all races, with a goal of developing and supporting activists and demonstrations locally, nationally, and internationally. Highlander was, in its time, an unconventional institute, since few schools in the South were integrated. In addition to workshops, Highlander offered a variety of recreational diversions. In this camp-like atmosphere, blacks and whites bonded while holding discussions on race, activism, and other important issues. *Highlander: No Ordinary School* (1996) provides an in-depth glimpse into this extraordinary institution.

by the discomfort of being a status symbol in her own hometown, induced Parks to move to the North. Her friends and co-fighters (Nixon among them) were sad to see her go. However, they bid her farewell with a party and a parting gift of $800.

CIVIL RIGHTS MOVEMENT

Rosa Parks' move to Detroit in 1957, where her brother and his family lived, coincided with the burgeoning of one of the most important periods of African American protest: the Civil Rights Movement. This movement was concentrated in the South and led primarily by men, with King as its most popular leader. Though her role remained constrained—not by her departure from the center of agitation in the South, but because of her own temperament, the social traditions, and the expected gender roles of the time—Rosa Parks was an important player in the movement.

Parks' day-to-day existence during these years was a juggling act between making a living, caring for her mother and husband when they fell sick, and her activism. Parks found work as a seamstress at the Stockton Sewing Company (beginning in 1959). While there, she befriended Elaine Eason Steele.

Unlike other leaders who were paid to engage in full-time activist work, Parks volunteered as often as she was able or when she was requested to appear at a function or demonstration. She was involved in the Detroit chapter of the NAACP and maintained a steady lecturing schedule. From time to time she attended conferences of the King-led Southern Christian Leadership Council (SCLC).

King was revered by many. A permanent fixture of most African American homes was the big family Bible, accompanied by framed drawings of the biblical Jesus and Dr. Martin Luther King, Jr. Hand fans imprinted with King's face were used in African American churches across the nation. Parks herself, who read his books and regularly played his speeches on her record player in her home, was one of his biggest admirers.

Whether in person or secondhand, Parks closely followed the goings-on of the Movement. When she was told that King was stabbed at a book signing in Harlem in 1958, she was beside herself. She was present at the unprecedented March on Washington in 1963. It was a sign of the times that women were not allowed to participate as speakers on the program, with the exception of the introduction of the prominent women activists (including Rosa Parks) during the "Tribute to Women" portion of the program. Parks was "more hurt than angered by the slight" (Brinkley, 185). "Nowadays," she wrote in her autobiography, "women wouldn't stand for being kept so much in the background, but back then women's rights hadn't become a popular cause yet" (Parks, *My Story*, 166).

Growing Tide of Militancy and Racial Consciousness

A new movement was developing within the urban African American communities of the North, right in Parks' own backyard. While the Civil Rights Movement was making huge strides in the South, African American separatists and militants were gaining a foothold in impoverished African American neighborhoods in the North. This countermovement aimed to replace the call for nonviolence with self-defense and revolution, integration with black separatism and autonomy, and to address the frustration increasingly experienced by city youths over the poverty, despair, and lack of opportunities in their communities.

The signing of the Civil Rights Act of 1964 was a major victory. It was felt most profoundly by middle-class African Americans living in the segregated South. In the integrated (by law, if not always by practice) North, segregation was not a major issue, but drugs, crime, alienation, racism, and unemployment were. Malcolm X was one of the most prominent militant leaders. His activism was launched on soapboxes on street corners. When he gave a speech in Detroit, he caught the attention of an unlikely person—Rosa Parks.

Parks wrote that she "didn't disagree with [Malcolm X] altogether," and indeed some of Malcolm X's ideas resonated with Parks (Parks, *My Story*, 178). She liked "his stance on alcohol and drugs" and "black self-sufficiency" (Brinkley, 192). She also agreed with the radically perceived concept of self-defense—up to a point. Although she saw the effectiveness of nonviolence as a strategy as King utilized it in massive demonstrations, she believed that individually, self-defense was at times necessary. What she did not subscribe to was "hatred for whites" and violence as a means to an end (Brinkley, 192). Parks heard Malcolm X speak (following his life-changing pilgrimage to Mecca that caused him to rethink his stance on integration) shortly before he was assassinated on February 21, 1965.

Into the World of Politics and Religion

In 1965, Parks was appointed deaconess of her home congregation, St. Matthew's AME, and accepted a full-time position on the staff of a young civil rights activist turned politician named John Conyers. As a deaconess, her "duties expanded to include fostering and promoting the general interests of the church, soliciting the friendship and sympathy of the general public, cheering the downcast, feeding the hungry, clothing the naked, sheltering the homeless, and saving the lost by visiting them in mental hospitals and prisons" (Brinkley, 190). Parks' work at Representative Conyers' office was similar to responsibilities she held when she volunteered for civil rights organizations. In this way, Parks was finally getting paid to do the work that she loved, with the added bonus that she was allowed to take time off to go to a speaking event or demonstration, such as King's Selma to Montgomery March in March 1965.

Selma to Montgomery March

Parks did not participate the first time demonstrators tried to march from Selma to the Montgomery capitol. Before they could cross the Edmund Pettus Bridge, police officers attacked them with tear gas, billy clubs, and electric cattle prods. That day became known as "Bloody Sunday." Parks saw the horrific violence on television. King led a second march, but this one was brief and more symbolic than anything else so as not to provoke a repeat of the first tragedy or to challenge a restraining order to prevent a full march. When that order was lifted and Parks was asked to participate in a third and successful march to the capitol, Parks, without hesitation, said yes.

In attendance were King and a host of celebrity activists such as comedian Dick Gregory, singer Harry Belafonte, and gospel singer Odetta. Parks, however, was given a rocky reception, for she was put out on several occasions (by younger participants who did not recognize who she was) only to be invited back in by those who saw her standing on the sidelines. At the end of the march, she was escorted to the front of the line at the Montgomery capitol building, where an angry gathering of whites was "jeering and shouting" at them (Parks, *My Story*, 171). Several months later, Parks was a witness to the signing of the Voting Rights Act of 1965. This monumental civil rights legislation was largely made possible due to the heroism demonstrated during the Selma to Montgomery marches.

Black Power Movement and Racial Consciousness

By 1966, the Black Power Movement was in full force. Among the most visible leaders were Stokely Carmichael, former integrationist, who coined the term Black Power in that same year, H. Rap Brown, Huey Newton, and Bobby Seale. This movement dominated in the urban settings of the North.

Parks was caught up to a small degree in the racial consciousness that spread throughout the nation. She "began wearing colorful African-inspired garb on occasion, attending performances at the concept east theater, the first African American theater company in the urban North, and listening to WCHB, the nation's first major black-owned-and-operated radio station," and she also "started making appearances at rallies sponsored by Detroit's Freedom Now Party" (Brinkley, 202). What Parks could not empathize with or endorse was the rioting that erupted in the North beginning in 1965. King's response to the crisis (and the conditions triggering the riots) in the North was to implement a program and a series of marches to address unemployment and poverty. His activism in the North met with little success.

When rioting made its way to Detroit in 1967, Parks was outraged. She called the rioters "thieves," and referred to the riots as "pure hooliganism" (Brinkley, 203). She told *Ebony* that "it harmed the cause when looting and burning were passed off as being 'in the name of civil rights'" (Brinkley, 204).

When King was assassinated on April 4, 1968, the world mourned. Parks and her mother, who heard the devastating news on a radio broadcast, "wept quietly together" in their home, and 168 riots erupted in cities across the nation (Parks, *My Story*, 179).

THE YEARS FOLLOWING THE CIVIL RIGHTS MOVEMENT

That Parks' life was affected by King's death, as well as by the emergence of new civil rights leaders, the Black Power Movement, and personal circumstances, was obvious. Parks' popularity and activism were closely linked to King and the SCLC (which "drifted into irrelevance" after King's passing) and to a generation that was gradually being replaced by a new leadership that did not know and had never worked personally with Parks (Brinkley, 207). Ill health in her family—her brother, mother, and husband experienced bouts of illness, as did Parks herself—kept Parks closer to home and less and less out of the battlefield. All three of her family members succumbed to cancer during the 1970s. These circumstances made her realize that she was becoming more "symbolic and less activist"; more isolated from leaders in the thick of activity. Her interviews and appearances were reduced to focus on that of a single act of protest that occurred on December 1, 1955.

With the coming of the new decade, Parks' life was as busy as ever, but less overwhelming and less lonely thanks to Elaine Eason Steele, the friend she had met at the Stockton Sewing Company. Steele stepped in at a time when Parks was badly in need of friendship and helped her manage her overwhelming commitments. Eason was indispensable, helping Parks through a car accident in 1987, heart surgery, and the start-up of Parks' own project: the Rosa and Raymond Parks Institute for Self-Development in 1987, which reached out to several thousand of the nation's youth. In 1988, she retired from working with Representative John Conyers to focus on the Institute.

In the 1990s, Rosa Parks took on the mantle of one of the oldest living activists from the Civil Rights Movement and as such was celebrated throughout the world. Her popularity far exceeded that of the male leaders who had dominated the Movement. In 1990, she met Nelson Mandela, an anti-apartheid activist; Mandela had always wanted to meet Parks. The encounter was an emotional one for both:

> Tears filled his eyes as he walked up to the small old woman with her hair in two silver braids crossed atop her head. And in a low, melodious tone, Nelson Mandela began to chant, "Ro-sa Parks. Ro-sa Parks. Ro-sa Parks," until his voice crescendoed into a rapturous shout: "Ro-sa Parks!" ... then the two brave old souls, their lives so distant yet their dreams so close, fell into each other's arms, rocking back and forth in a long, joyful embrace. (Brinkley, 230–231)

In the spring of 1994, Parks traveled to Tokyo to visit Dr. Daisaku Ikeda, President of Soka University, whom she had met in 1992 and "discussed new strategies for building a global grassroots movement to spread the philosophy of nonviolence" (Brinkley, 221). During her visit, Japanese students sang "We Shall Overcome" in English. That summer, Parks—an international star—survived a shocking attack. A teenager beat and robbed her of $103 in her own home. Shortly thereafter, Parks was moved to "the riverfront towers, a twenty-four hour gated and guarded modern high-rise complex overlooking the Detroit river," where Parks surrounded herself with "precious souvenirs" and honors and mementos (Brinkley, 217, 218).

Parks' final years were spent reading books about activists and gazing out of the window overlooking "the majestic span of the Ambassador Bridge to

Canada," the refuge for a number of slaves and African Americans after emancipation (Brinkley, 218). There were still engagements to attend and appearances to make, but Parks was content. At age ninety-two, on October 24, 2005, Parks, the unlikely heroine and living legend, died.

See also Ella Baker; Stokely Carmichael; Malcolm X; Martin Luther King, Jr.; Huey P. Newton; and Roy Wilkins.

FURTHER RESOURCES

Brinkley, Douglas. *Rosa Parks*. New York: Viking, 2000.

Dove, Rita. *On the Bus with Rosa Parks: Poems*. New York: Norton, 1999.

Kohl, Herbert R. *She Would Not Be Moved: How We Tell the Story of Rosa Parks and the Montgomery Bus Boycott*. New York: New Press, 2005.

Montgomery Boycott.com. *Montgomery Advertiser* (June 2007). See http://www.montgomeryboycott.com.

Parks, Rosa. *Dear Mrs. Parks: A Dialogue with Today's Youth*. New York: Lee & Low Books, 1996.

Parks, Rosa. *I Am Rosa Parks*. New York: Dial Books for Young Readers, 1997.

Parks, Rosa, with Jim Haskins. *Rosa Parks: My Story*. New York: Dial Books, 1992.

Parks, Rosa, with Gregory J. Reed. *Quiet Strength: The Faith, the Hope, and the Heart of a Woman Who Changed a Nation*. Grand Rapids, MI: Zondervan Publishing House, 1994.

RosaParks.org. Rosa and Raymond Parks Institute for Self-Development (June 2007). See http://www.rosaparks.com.

The Rosa Parks Story. Directed by Julie Dash. Santa Monica, CA: Xenon Pictures, 2002.

A. Philip Randolph (1889–1979)

Asa Philip Randolph was the founder of the Brotherhood of Sleeping Car Porters. Randolph was a leader in both the labor movement for African American workers and in the struggle to eliminate segregation in the war industry and armed forces, and a pioneer in the Civil Rights Movement. Randolph's entry into activism during the second decade of the twentieth century occurred during the heyday of prominent African American leaders such as Booker T. Washington, W.E.B. Du Bois, and Marcus Garvey. Randolph was most influenced by Du Bois, though he eventually grew to oppose the immensely popular leader's conservative ideology. Randolph came to believe that socialism was the solution to the deplorable conditions facing blacks in America.

Protesting **racism** and inequality while espousing socialism was a precarious and radical position in early twentieth-century America. In his early adult years, Randolph was, in fact, the quintessential radical—a firebrand even—and deemed one of "the most dangerous Negroes in the United States" (Anderson, 83). Later, Randolph's radicalism, which was tempered with diplomacy, dogged patience, and extraordinary dignity, and his activism, through negotiations and multiple demonstrations, was instrumental in making great strides in ablating barriers that obstructed African American progress and inclusion into mainstream American life and to laying the groundwork for emerging black leaders. For his contributions to the pursuit of civil rights, he was considered an honored and respected activist by the pre-eminent African American organizations of the day and by the very government he had once opposed.

EARLY YEARS

Asa Philip was born on April 15, 1889 to James and Elizabeth Randolph in Baldwin, Florida. He had one brother, James, who was two years older. Their father, a reverend in the African Methodist Episcopal (AME) church, named Asa after a king in the Old Testament. According to I Kings 15, King Asa negotiated with a Syrian king to rescue the people of Judah from Israel. This name proved to be prophetic in Philip's later years, when he emerged as a leader driven to liberate African Americans from the bonds of segregation and injustice. The man Asa was to become was profoundly influenced by his parents (especially his father), his upbringing, and his experiences as a young adult.

Although Asa was born in Baldwin, most of his upbringing occurred in Jacksonville, Florida, where his father accepted a preaching position at a small congregation. Asa's parents were hardworking, religious people. Money, however, was a constant issue. The reverend and his wife found creative ways to supplement James' modest income from his preaching. They both "repaired, dyed, cleaned, and pressed clothes" (38). Elizabeth sewed the family's clothes, and food was raised in the backyard. The Reverend

Nat Turner

Nat Turner (1800–1831) was an African American who led one of the largest slave rebellions in the American South. His life illustrates one of the earliest examples of militant resistance to slavery.

Turner was a slave on a plantation owned by Samuel Turner in Southampton County, Virginia. Unlike most slaves, he could read and write. Whites prohibited the education of slaves to maintain control over them and to prevent escape and resistance.

Turner's ability to read and write along with his religious leadership raised his status among blacks in Southampton County. Turner preached sermons and was known to experience visions. Other slaves called him "The Prophet." Through his visionary experiences and his interpretation of unusual natural events (such as two eclipses), Turner came to believe he was called by God to lead a slave rebellion. He devised a plan, which he divulged to four slaves he trusted—Henry, Hark, Nelson, and Sam. They planned to kill as many whites as possible and free the slaves.

On August 21, 1831, the five slaves launched their revolt, attacking whites with hatchets and knives. It took two days to quell the rebellion. Turner and his rebels, who had swelled to fifty or more other slaves and free blacks, killed some fifty-seven white men, women, and children.

Turner was found hiding in a cave. He was tried, convicted, and sentenced to death. He was hung on November 11, 1831, and his body was flayed, beheaded, and quartered. All the blacks involved in the rebellion were executed. A white mob killed nearly another two hundred blacks, many of them innocent.

Turner's rebellion was not the first of its kind. Slave rebellions were reported to have occurred as early as the eighteenth century aboard slave ships during the passage from Africa. At least 250 slave revolts are known to have occurred in the South, although none were as notorious as the one launched by Nat Turner.

In the aftermath of most rebellions, whites imposed tougher laws and restrictions on the slaves. This, and the onslaught of white-induced violence against innocent blacks, helped to quell future uprisings. Most blacks in the South learned that accommodation rather than resistance was the only way to protect self and community.

Randolph tried his hand at selling meat and wood on separate occasions, but these and other ventures were unprofitable. Although Elizabeth and the Reverend Randolph may have been poor in terms of material possessions, they were rich in terms of the education of their children. The Randolph home was imbued with love, discipline, and character-building instruction that was instrumental in setting the foundation for Asa's activism and philosophy.

Young Asa was familiar with the concept of African American protest. His parents belonged to a segment of African Americans that radically defied the preconceptions of the times, such as the notion that African Americans were a stigma, inferior to whites, and passive in response to white oppression and racism. The Reverend Randolph and his wife supplemented their children's education with their own brand of militant instruction and example. First and foremost, the Randolph family belonged to the AME Church, which Asa's father proudly acclaimed "was the first black militant institution in America" (26). The AME Church, which had separated from the Methodist Episcopal Church to form a predominately black church and engaged in anti-slavery protests, played a large role in forming the Reverend Randolph's own radical views and intense racial pride.

As a part of his children's informal education, the elder Randolph required daily reading. Among the books in the diverse family library were radical African American newspapers and books on African history. He taught his sons about extraordinary African American leaders like Nat Turner, Frederick Douglass, and Henry McNeil Turner. His parents were "constantly reiterating that the boys were 'not supposed to bow and take a back seat for anybody,' but rather stand up for their rights" (Pfeffer, 7). Elizabeth's insistence that her children fight back when challenged by their peers served to foster courage in her children. Though Randolph was a reluctant fighter in his childhood and a lifelong advocate of nonviolence, his agitation required a certain pugilistic spirit in facing off with the opposition.

The Reverend Randolph and Elizabeth were in their own uncelebrated ways extraordinary activists. When Asa was ten years old, his father joined a group of armed men to prevent the lynching of an African American man. In his father's absence, his mother, "a deadly shot," stood guard on the family porch with a shotgun (Anderson, 42). From this experience, Asa learned the lesson of self-defense and the importance of collective action. He also felt pride for his mother, who was stoically and unflinchingly prepared to defend their home. However, Randolph was not, as an adult, an advocate of self-defense. When Jim Crow laws came to Florida, Asa's father "forbade his sons to read their books in the segregated reading room of the Jacksonville public library. Nor, he ordered, should they ride the Jim Crow streetcars. They should do as he did: walk to wherever they wanted to go in the city" (Anderson, 42).

Asa's parents worked to instill in him and his brother a confident bearing and a strong sense of self-esteem. This youthful training was the basis for Asa's legendary eloquence and poise that were manifested in both his everyday life and his oratory style. Asa's father emphasized the importance of articulation, as a result of which, both boys were naturally enamored with words and their pronunciation (and the spirited Asa enjoyed mimicking his father's sonorous voice). The father, who "walked graceful[ly], just as straight as you can get," also "taught the boys to walk like him. If he caught one of them slouching, he would call out, 'come on, now shoulders back'" (Anderson, 37). The father inspired his sons to always display exemplary conduct and deportment, which they certainly achieved. Self-esteem, which was wanting in a society that classified African Americans as inferior, was strong in the Randolph boys. The father constantly pointed out positive African American role models to his children and introduced his sons as "two of the finest boys in the world" (Anderson, 40). The parents were, however, unable to instill in their children religious beliefs.

Asa attended high school at the Cookman Institute. He and his brother were popular with the other students and had spotless reputations. Asa excelled academically, mostly due to the encouragement of two African American teachers, Lillie M. Whitney and Mary Neff, and in athletics. Asa "displayed gifts which marked him the school's best student in literature, public speaking, and drama" (Anderson, 45–46).

This was a pivotal period in Asa's young life. At home, Asa and his brother delighted in discussing the hot topics of the day that concerned African Americans with their father. The boys had big dreams "of leading the fight for human rights as congressmen, or working as educators, scientists, doctors and writers" (Reef, 28). At graduation, Asa, the class valedictorian, gave his first public speech, entitled "The Man of the Hour." He was, in that moment, on top of the world, and his future appeared destined to be a gleaming success.

The five years following Asa's optimistic send-off at his high school graduation in 1907 were anticlimactic. Because his parents were unable to afford college, Asa went the way of the majority of African Americans in the South: he collected insurance premiums from African Americans, "clerked in a grocery store, drove a delivery wagon for a drug company, stacked logs in a lumberyard, pushed wheelbarrows in a fertilizer factory, and carried water and shoveled dirt for an outfit laying railroad crossties" (Anderson, 47). What was most important to him were his extracurricular pursuits: reading "literature, history, and contemporary affairs," "giving public readings of the Bible, Shakespeare, and the poetry of Paul Laurence Dunbar at black churches and theaters," and joining a barbershop quarter (Anderson, 47). The Reverend Randolph wanted Asa to become a preacher, but his son had other intentions: Asa wanted to become an actor.

Asa's life took a significant turn after he read Du Bois' *The Souls of Black Folk*. The book ignited his desire to "fight for social equality," and it became "clear to him that the climate for whatever interests he wanted to pursue—be they on the stage or in politics—would be more favorable in the North" (Anderson, 52). Asa had been to New York once to visit his cousin, and the city had filled him with wonder and exhilaration. Thus it was that, at the age of twenty-two, Asa set his sights northward.

BECOMING A RADICAL SOCIALIST

In 1911, Asa Randolph, with Du Bois' book still fresh in his mind, set out to make a life for himself in New York. He was one of numerous African Americans swept along by the current of migration to the cities of the North in search of freedom and opportunity. After renting a room in Harlem with a friend who had joined him in his journey to New York, Randolph explored his new neighborhood, "sightseeing and taking in the stage shows" (Anderson, 55). He visited several local churches and miscellaneous organizations, perchance to find an outlet for the expression of his newfound ideas and thoughts inspired by *The Souls of Black Folk* and enrolled at the City College.

Randolph's search for radically minded individuals turned up short. Expecting a more receptive and eager audience in the North, Randolph was disappointed. When Randolph met with the Epworth League, a group of young people who met to discuss the Bible and, to a certain extent, current issues, he found only a few individuals open to his radical views. Where Randolph advocated immediate change, most of the other members of the League espoused a slower, gradual approach. Nevertheless, the persuasive Randolph was able to recruit a few individuals to his philosophy.

College life was much more rewarding for Randolph. Initially, Randolph studied public speaking to improve his oral delivery for acting but switched to taking up courses in socialism. A major reason for this was his parent's moral objection to acting. Another reason was his introduction to socialism in one of his classes.

Randolph was immediately taken by socialism. For Randolph, socialism provided a way to understand the plight of African Americans in America. He came to believe that capitalism caused conflict among people, "thus intensifying the competitive struggle between black and white workers, exacerbating racism, and politicizing hate," and individuals tended to look at "the stereotypes and myths of race and people instead of looking at the human being or the economic situation" (Anderson, 63). Randolph felt that both the Democrats and the Republicans neglected African Americans; thus, socialism was the only recourse.

Randolph was not the only one on campus or in his community to embrace socialism. Students were forming radical organizations and actively fundraising and coordinating rallies in support of striking laborers in America. Men like Hubert Harrison, "a pioneer radical intellectual in Harlem" and "member of the Socialist party" gave speeches from soapboxes on street corners (Anderson, 61). These examples of protest undoubtedly added fuel to Randolph's intense inner yearnings and provided ideas on how to execute his activism through organizing, politics, and speechmaking.

One of Randolph's first solo acts was to form the Independent Political Council, which comprised a few of the former members of the Epworth League. He unsuccessfully assisted in the campaign for the Board of

Aldermen by an African American running as an Independent. He then engaged in several protests at work (Randolph roved from job to job, holding traditional blue-collar jobs restricted to African Americans). Randolph, now known as a "troublemaker" by the Epworth League, was "stirring up trouble and sowing seeds of discontent among [his] co-workers" (Anderson, 65). As a porter for the Consolidated Gas Company, Randolph tried to rouse the other employees to push for advancement: "'Look around you,' he told them, 'is it only white men who can be bookkeepers and supervisors? Why can't negroes do those jobs? Are we only good for sweeping floors and washing windows?'" (Anderson, 66). Randolph quit that job when no one took up his call for protest. On another occasion, Randolph was fired (as was frequently the case), when he tried to "organize the waiters and kitchen help against conditions in [their small, crammed, foul-smelling quarters]" (Anderson, 66). Randolph used his group, the Independent Political Council, to dispense his radical views to the community. In 1914, Ernest T. Welcome, a member of the Epworth League, hired Randolph to work for his Brotherhood of Labor agency to help educate African Americans migrating from the South to the North "in the political and social conditions of life in New York City" (Anderson, 69).

Randolph always said that in his early years in New York he was a carefree spirit with no thought of settling down to either steady employment or marriage. But his auspicious encounter with a beautiful, thirty-one-year-old widow named Lucille Green made possible a full-time commitment to activism. Lucille was an intelligent and enterprising woman who owned a prosperous hair salon. She was a socialite, mingling with the up-and-coming elite professionals and attending St. Philip's Episcopal Church, "the wealthiest and most prestigious black congregation in the world" (Anderson, 72). Randolph, of course, did not care for the world of the elite because of his socialist beliefs, nor was he religious. Nevertheless, the two had in common an interest in socialism, community involvement, and the theater. They were married in November 1914—despite Randolph's protest—in her church.

Lucille Randolph was extremely supportive, in more ways than one. She provided the family income, supporting Randolph and his close friend, Chandler Owen, whom he met shortly after his marriage, so they could spend their days learning more about socialism and pursuing their radical activism. Randolph was able to quit his job with the Brotherhood, and the two inseparable friends came to be known as Lenin and Trotsky.

SOCIALIST ACTIVISM: 1916–1925

Soapbox Oration and the Hotel Messenger

In 1916, Randolph and Owen formally became socialists. Shortly thereafter, Randolph quit school and, along with Owen, mounted his soapbox to spread socialism. The two joined the ranks of men like the aforementioned Hubert H. Harrison, who was one of the most popular soapbox activists in Harlem. The eloquently spoken word was an effective means of getting the message across to the people, especially when the church was inaccessible to "radicals." Randolph, who had a rich baritone voice and a diction that made people think he was educated at Yale or Harvard, enchanted his audiences. He and Owen "quickly became the most notorious street-corner radicals in Harlem, exceeding even Harrison in the boldness of their assault upon political and racial conditions in the country" (Anderson, 77).

In 1917, Randolph used the power of the pen as an editor of the *Hotel Messenger*, a magazine aimed primarily at waiters at the invitation of William White, who was president of the Headwaiters and Sidewaiters Society of Greater New York. Through the *Hotel Messenger*, Randolph and Owen were able to further spread their message of protest.

Randolph was coming into his own as a mature activist, no longer a meandering radical protesting impetuously, but a man with focus who took his responsibilities at the magazine seriously. Symbolizing his growth, Randolph began to refer to himself as A. Philip Randolph. When America entered World War I in 1917, Randolph and Owen protested the participation of African Americans.

However, Randolph and Owen soon learned that freedom of speech often came with a price. They were fired after publishing an article contending that the sidewaiters were being cheated by the headwaiters. Since the headwaiters were a large reason why William White was president, he let them go in the same year they started editing for the society's organ.

The Messenger

Due to the "'steady and numerous requests'" of their "'intelligent, radical, forward-looking and clear-eyed patrons,'" Randolph and Owen started their own magazine called the *Messenger* that same year (Anderson, 81–82). Here, at last, Randolph had a medium that he could control, wherein he could publish his views without censure. This magazine was declared by the Justice Department to be "by long odds the most dangerous of all the Negro publications" (Anderson, 82).

One of the major issues the *Messenger* covered was the war. Although African Americans moved in remarkable numbers to join the war effort, they faced racism and segregation in the armed forces and inequality and violence at home. Lynching and race riots were at their worst in the early twentieth century in both the North and the South. Prominent African American leaders such as Du Bois denounced the horrible conditions faced by African Americans, but Randolph and Owen went further in their protests by advocating that African Americans not participate in the war. This was a radical position that illustrated Randolph's break from W.E.B. Du Bois and the extent of his defiance despite the great risks involved. Du Bois, who in Randolph's and Owen's eyes was too conservative, was criticized frequently in their magazine.

The *Messenger's* radical articles were considered a menace by many in the African American community, as well as by the U.S. Government. Shortly after the onset of the War, "Congress had passed the Espionage Act, empowering the government to censor newspapers or ban them from the mails, and to punish, by fines of up to $10,000 and imprisonment of twenty years, anyone found guilty of obstructing conscription" (Anderson, 104–105). In 1918, the government declared that "even the attempt at obstruction" was a felony (Anderson, 105). As an antiwar and socialist-promoting paper, the *Messenger* was a target. On more than one occasion, "agents of the Justice Department, broke into the *Messenger's* office and vandalized their property and confiscated back issues" (Anderson, 104). In the same year, Randolph and Owen faced trial. They were charged with violating the Espionage Act. The judge let them go, doubting that the two African American men could be "old enough" or "smart enough" to have authored the "red-hot stuff in the *Messenger*" (Anderson, 107). When the men insisted that they were responsible for the magazine, the judge warned them to get out of town. Randolph and Owen willingly complied, but only to engage in more agitation. Shortly thereafter, near the end of the war, Owen was drafted and served for 120 days. Randolph avoided this fate, for the war ended before he could be drafted.

Politics

Randolph engaged in several political adventures. In 1917, he and Owen worked for the campaign of Morris Hillquit, a socialist with aspirations to be mayor of New York City. Randolph and Owen organized "the first Socialist club in the area—the 21st A.D. Club," which "fanned out through the community, canvassing in Hillquit's behalf and heckling the public meetings of the regular-party candidates" (Anderson, 94). Although he lost, Hillquit did win a substantial number of votes.

In 1918, Randolph was hand-picked by Garvey's Universal Negro Improvement Association to be one of the African American delegates to speak on issues facing African Americans at the peace conference in Versailles, France. Randolph, because of his controversial reputation, was refused a passport. Du Bois, whom Randolph called one of the "good Socialists," was allowed to go (Anderson, 124).

Randolph and Owen were later among Marcus Garvey's most strident critics and denounced him frequently in the *Messenger*. They were against his "doctrines of black capitalism" and imperialism, and believed that his advocacy of "black nationalism" and a return to Africa were "palliatives rather than solutions" (Anderson, 90). Randolph, like Du Bois and other conservative leaders, was in support of bettering conditions for African Americans in America, not elsewhere, and ultimately helping to create a world not of racial separateness but of total inclusion. Nevertheless, Randolph readily admitted that Garvey was able to rouse more African Americans than any other leader of his time. In 1920, Randolph lost in both campaigns for state comptroller and secretary of state.

Organizations

Randolph founded several organizations through which he hoped to advance socialism and labor unionism, as well as promote racial uplift. But this period of organizational leadership, beginning in 1917, was unfruitful, primarily because the African American community at large was conservative and therefore not receptive to either socialism or unionizing and steered clear of notorious radicals such as Randolph. The 21st A.D. Socialist Club and the Independent Political Council, which Randolph formed shortly after his arrival in New York, were obsolete. Another early venture, the United Brotherhood of Elevator and Switchboard Operators, was "was taken over by the Elevator and Starters Union" only a year after Randolph established it, and in 1919, his National Association for the Promotion of Labor Unionism "failed to materialize" (Anderson, 149). He founded the National Brotherhood Workers of America in the same year, but it failed two years later. Other organizations such as the Tenants and Consumers League and a Harlem branch of the Journeymen Bakers and Confectioners Union suffered the same fate.

But Randolph was impervious. In 1920, Randolph founded another organization, the Friends of Negro Freedom. This organization had a short lifespan—only because it was established for one purpose: to oust Marcus Garvey from his "political leadership or from the United States" (Anderson, 130). This singular aim banded Randolph with unlikely protest leaders (such as his philosophical archrival Du Bois) whose efforts of speechmaking and letter (and article) writing coalesced to form the "Garvey Must Go" campaign. African American opposition to Garvey was based on an array of protestations—over his philosophy of black nationalism and racial separatism, his controversial shipping line, and his acceptance of the Ku Klux Klan's agenda of separatism. Once Garvey was indicted for mail fraud in 1923 and later deported back to Jamaica, the Friends of Negro Freedom no longer functioned in any significant way.

Opposition to Randolph's Social Activism

Between 1916 and 1925, opposition to Randolph's agitation was immense. His views provoked contention between himself and other African American organizations, tragically preventing the formation of a united front that could better the lives of African Americans in the early twentieth century. The masses he strove to entice into socialism and labor unionism were largely unresponsive. Among the many reasons for this was the fact that African Americans were as a whole conservative and doubtful that socialism—a class-focused doctrine—was a solution to racism. Moreover, labor unions were segregated, and nothing in their history had shown them that blacks united could effect change against powerful white-owned and historically racist corporations and businesses. Indeed, many African Americans were beginning to renounce socialism, because it did not adequately address race. The class structure in the United States was in itself a problem, and being black added an additional layer of challenges and dangers.

Opposition to Randolph intensified in 1922, when he began receiving death threats. On one occasion, he was mailed a severed hand with an ominous letter signed "KKK." Though the KKK had every reason to go after him, Randolph believed Garvey was behind the letter. Garvey retorted that Randolph had himself devised the incident as a publicity stunt.

Randolph was beginning to grow weary of his opposition, his many failures to launch his programs, and by the death of his father. Then, in 1923, his closest friend, Owen, moved to Chicago after the death of his brother. Randolph replaced his former partner with George Schuyler. Schuyler was a black journalist who was, at one time, interested in Garveyism but then turned to socialism. But he was not a gung-ho socialist, like Randolph. After a few years, he lost interest when he perceived that socialists did not appear concerned about black issues. More change was in the wind, as evidenced by Randolph's own growing disillusionment with the Socialist Party.

By 1925, Randolph "had withdrawn from Socialist activism and lost interest, if not in socialism, in the party" and asserted that "the Socialist party had no effective policy towards Negroes, and didn't spend enough time organizing them'" (Anderson, 149). All that remained of Randolph's activism was the *Messenger,* though its readership had declined severely, and its sharp edge had dulled. It seemed that Randolph was in his final days as a voice of African American protest when he received a call for help from an unexpected source that would change the course of his life forever.

CIVIL RIGHTS ACTIVISM: 1925–1935

The Labor Movement

In 1925, Ashley L. Totten, a Pullman sleeping car porter and noted "firebrand" within the porter community, invited Randolph to speak to the Pullman Porters Athletic Association (Anderson, 153). He wanted Randolph to address his fellow porters on a topic that he knew had long been Randolph's passion—labor unionizing. In fact, he wanted Randolph to be the one to lead them in their fight against the Pullman Company.

Since 1900, African American porters had tried to organize a labor union. African American porters were required to work extraordinarily long hours, for meager pay, while submitting to abusive, debasing, and racist treatment by their superiors as well as by white passengers. There was no protection, no defense for the African American porter. At the same time, the position was considered one of the most prestigious opportunities for African American men. In 1920, the Plan of Employee Representation was established to offer assistance to African American porters, but this organization was a ruse by means of which the Pullman Company could maintain its power over the porters. In another attempt to better wages and hours for porters, African American delegates, Totten among them, were picked by the porters themselves to negotiate with decision makers of the Pullman Company. This conference took place in 1924. However, the Pullman Company paid off all but a few of the African American representatives. Following this dismal attempt, Totten sought Randolph as his last hope for the African American porters.

Given Randolph's history of promoting unionizing, he surprisingly declined Totten's request, stating "that, flattered though he was by the request, he was sorry; he had no further interest in organizing anything. He told them of all his previous unsuccessful efforts, and that he was now satisfied to consider himself merely a propagandist for the idea of unionism" (Anderson, 155). Randolph went on to say that "the *Messenger* was now his whole life, and he was fully occupied in the struggle to keep the magazine going. Moreover, he added, he couldn't see himself jumping into a fight with a company like Pullman, 'one of the most powerful Brahmins of American Business'" (Anderson, 155).

Despite this rebuff, Randolph found that he could not fully turn his back on such a critical situation. He wrote two articles in support of the Pullman porters. Totten again approached Randolph, requesting his help. This time, the formidable leader overcame his doubts and agreed to head up the labor movement of the African American porters.

The Brotherhood of Sleeping Car Porters was established on August 25, 1925, with Randolph as its leader. This was indeed a historic moment, as this organization was one of a very few of its kind created for African Americans by African Americans. Although Randolph did accept money from "white Socialists and liberals in New York" for the initial set-up of the organization, he insisted that African Americans themselves provide the ongoing financial support and leadership. Randolph had no racist feelings towards whites; he simply felt that African Americans who had long been dependent on whites should rise to the occasion by being self-supportive, self-sustaining, and self-governing.

Randolph and the Brotherhood of Sleeping Car Porters would need that support and more to obtain their goals. Their position, like the biblical David who confronted the terrible and seemingly unconquerable Goliath, was fraught with long odds and impossibilities. The Pullman Company's economic power far exceeded that of Randolph and the Brotherhood. Historically, few African Americans had challenged whites and won. In fact, African Americans were frequently targeted and subjected to intimidation, violence, and even death whenever they challenged whites. In addition, the false belief in white superiority and black inferiority affected some African Americans, such as one porter who admitted that he "'never knew the Negro had a right to enjoy freedom like everyone else'" (Anderson, 177). As if that were not enough, many African Americans perceived unionizing as radical, a notion that was accepted and promoted by black newspapers, as well as black churches, who frequently condemned Randolph and his radical ideas.

Randolph was not immediately embraced by all the members of the Brotherhood, and he realized that he had to win over the porters. The eloquence and distinguished demeanor that were his best assets put off many of the African American porters who, seasoned and roughened by the nature of their profession, did not think he could be capable of leading them. Milton Price Webster was one such doubter, but he eventually warmed up to Randolph and in fact became one of the many Randolph-admirers and second in command in the Brotherhood. The two men worked well as a team, depending on one another's strengths during negotiations and speechmaking. At the organization's peak, the Brotherhood had offices in "New York, Chicago, St. Louis, Kansas City, Seattle, Minneapolis-St. Paul, Omaha, Wichita, Oakland, Los Angeles, Denver, Portland, Washington, D.C., Boston, Detroit, and Buffalo" (Anderson, 177). By 1928, they had almost 7,000 members.

The Brotherhood's most fierce and relentless opposition was the Pullman Company. Some of the tactics utilized by the Pullman Company to subvert the Brotherhood were nefarious at best. They paid off African American porters to act as spies; they slandered Randolph; and they ran a campaign to fire, threaten, and harass African American porters who were believed or found out to be members of the Brotherhood. In St. Louis, A.V. Burr, a superintendent "who boasted that he whipped niggers," fired members of the Brotherhood, including E.J. Bradley, who was in charge of the office there and, as a result, was unable to make payments for the rental of his office so he eventually "started running the office out of the trunk of his automobile" (Anderson, 175).

The Brotherhood engaged in various countermeasures. To circumvent spying, Randolph and others were frequently forced to conduct business in secrecy. At the first gathering of the Brotherhood, Randolph conducted the entire meeting himself so as not to incriminate any of the porters or allow Pullman spies to identify them. In Jacksonville, Randolph ordered Benjamin Smith, who was willing to sacrifice his life, to leave Jacksonville to avert being lynched. Randolph also outwitted Pullman spies by employing Brotherhood spies.

Randolph's first step as the leader of the Brotherhood was to seek political intervention. Although Congressman Emmanuel Celler of New York had responded to Randolph's request to seek a "congressional investigation of Pullman's labor policies," the resolution he introduced "died in the Rules Committee" (Anderson, 186). However, the "Watson-Parker bill—supported by the big railroad unions and all railroad managements—was passed as the Railway Labor Act of 1927" (Anderson, 186). This was a big win for the porters, for it legally gave them the power to pursue a "joint conference" with the Pullman Company "to 'make and maintain agreements' on rates of pay, rules, and working conditions" (Anderson, 187). With this newfound power to force negotiation, Randolph wrote the Pullman Company.

The Pullman president did not respond. In accordance with the rules of the Railway Labor Act, Randolph wrote again. When he again was ignored, Randolph sought the assistance of the Mediation Board.

This process was financially draining, for the Brotherhood was responsible for paying their lawyers and other fees. The mediation got them nowhere, for the Pullman Company insisted that the African American porters already had a company union representing their interests. In response, "Randolph collected some 900 affidavits" proving that the porters who supported the company union had been coerced to do so (Anderson, 190). This small, albeit significant, victory was followed by a deadlock. The Pullman Company refused to cooperate further in the mediation process. And it was within their legal right to do so.

By not cooperating, the Pullman Company dealt a staggering blow to Randolph and his organization. A number of individuals left the Brotherhood, as it appeared that there was no chance for victory. Randolph and his fellow union leaders found it even more difficult to raise money from the remaining members. Randolph himself also suffered financially. His wife, whose salon business had gone under as a result of Randolph's radical socialist beliefs, was no longer able to support them. Compounding the miserable financial situation was the fact that he had to frequently go without his modest $10 a week salary from the Brotherhood. His clothes, which had once been stylish and immaculate, became worn and tattered. Without money or members, there could be no Brotherhood. Exacerbating this critical situation were the death of Randolph's brother; the collapse of his paper, the *Messenger*, in 1928; and the ensuing Great Depression.

Randolph's response to these circumstances was energetic and self-sacrificing. He used his charismatic speechmaking skills to motivate the Brotherhood to continue the struggle, win back former members, and to raise money. In his first radical move, Randolph managed to convince the porters to execute a strike, knowing that if he could create an emergency situation, he could force Pullman to continue mediation. He sent word of the threatened strike to the Mediation Board, which promptly ruled that no emergency existed since the Pullman Company did not perceive it as such. The strike was called off. In 1929, he joined the American Federation of Labor (AFL). This was a controversial step in that some member organizations of the AFL excluded African Americans and Randolph himself had, in his earlier days, denounced the AFL for that reason. However, the survival of the Brotherhood depended upon its link to a solid labor union. Throughout this difficult period, Randolph remained committed to the Brotherhood, turning down a job offer "with the city government, at a salary of $7,000 a year," and maintained his optimism, believing that the Brotherhood would accomplish what it set out to do (Anderson, 214–215).

The pressure of the situation was finally relieved in 1932 during the presidency of Franklin D. Roosevelt, who instituted several important programs to alleviate the effects of the Depression. One of these programs, created with the assistance of a group of "labor executives," bestowed the right of labor workers to form their own unions and "banned company unions" (Anderson, 217).

At first, this legislation did not include porters, but Randolph quickly set about correcting this. He then set out to rebuild the Brotherhood and to make contact with the president of the Pullman Company. Meanwhile, the Pullman Company had "hand-picked a few loyal porters and authorized them to form their own 'independent' union, the Pullman Porters Protective Association" (Anderson, 219). To settle the question over which organization—the Brotherhood or the Protective Association—was the rightful representative of the African American porters, the Board of Mediation "ordered a secret ballot," which Randolph proudly wrote was "the first time that Negro workers have had the opportunity to vote as a national group in an election, under federal supervision, for their economic rights" (Anderson, 220).

The election took place in 1935. The votes were 8,316 in favor of the Brotherhood to 1,422 for the Pullman Porters Protective Association. Randolph's historic negotiation with the Pullman Company took place that same year. After two years of grueling struggle, the Brotherhood, through Randolph, had achieved the impossible and negotiated wage increases and fewer hours.

The Private Life of the Popular Protest Leader

Because of Randolph's victory over the Pullman Company, he was considered in the ensuing decades to be one of the most universally respected African American leaders in America. Despite his high public profile, little was known about his private life. Perhaps not much of a private life existed, considering the long hours he daily put into his work. Either way, Randolph was an intensely private man. He had no children. He did not discuss his inner life; he gave his time wholeheartedly to activism, sacrificing whatever leisure activities and hobbies, such as acting, he had at one time treasured. Though their marriage appeared to be strong and enduring, he spent long periods of time away from his wife. And when Lucille took ill, Randolph attended to her needs and brooded over her as much as he could. As for Randolph's health, his activism took its toll on several occasions. But ill health was usually a temporary inconvenience for the unstoppable A. Philip Randolph.

Although Randolph was frequently attacked by his critics, his impeccable reputation allowed him to weather these attacks. He took great pains to lead a disciplined life and warned others to take no part in disreputable habits or weakness that would hinder their work. Randolph could not be bribed. Neither did he allow himself to be entangled in illicit affairs with women. As a result, he was known by his closest associates to be a man of high reputation and morals. Lacking more substantive ammunition, his attackers were often forced to target Randolph's early radical socialist activism. In the face of such attacks, Randolph confessed that he had a "thick skin," a useful weapon against the jabs and barbs of life in the limelight and in activism.

Civil Rights Activism (1935–1979)

National Negro Conference

The National Negro Conference (NNC) was an organization that had been formed in 1935 to merge the efforts of various individuals, groups, and factions established to better conditions for African Americans in the United States. Randolph was made president of the NNC in 1936. Randolph's greatest concern—and what proved to be the organization's ultimate undoing—was maintaining the purity of the NNC's primary tenet, which was to refrain from being dominated by any one political entity, thought, or belief—even his own. He also believed that the organization should remain in the control of blacks.

Randolph hoped that the NNC would be able to build up the esteem of African Americans who had long been told that they could not be leaders. He worked to avoid being taken over by white communists who had intentions of infiltrating black organizations such as the NNC. But his attention was divided between the Brotherhood and the NNC. So he was caught off guard when communists worked their way into the NNC by way of generous monetary support. Randolph tried to fight the influence of the communists, but in 1940 he felt he had no other choice but to resign and carry on his activism elsewhere.

Protesting Segregation in the Armed Forces and Defense Industry

Following his resignation from the NNC, Randolph and the Brotherhood of Sleeping Car Porters mustered their resources to lead the fight to desegregate the defense industry and the armed forces (the Army, Navy, and Air Corps). Randolph's approach to this enormous task encompassed all the traditional and widely accepted forms of black protest, starting with negotiation with the U.S. president. Although President Franklin Roosevelt had created the New Deal, an ambitious social program to relieve the effects of the Great Depression, his work had done little to directly help African Americans.

Eleanor Roosevelt

Born on October 11, 1884, in New York City, Eleanor Roosevelt entered into public life as the wife of President Franklin D. Roosevelt in 1933. Her interest in issues affecting African Americans began during her husband's presidency, when she became aware of the disproportionate number of blacks who were not receiving assistance from the New Deal programs her husband had established to remedy the rampant economic hardships brought on by the Great Depression. She remained an advocate for African Americans until her death in 1962.

Roosevelt displayed an extraordinary empathy towards blacks and was actively involved in addressing the many problems they faced, including poverty, discrimination, segregation, and racism. Roosevelt sometimes worked behind the scenes but was not at all afraid of using her high public profile to advocate for African Americans. She expressed her support of integration and racial equality in numerous speeches and articles, including her "My Day" column. In 1934, she pressed her husband to endorse the NAACP's anti-lynching bill, to no avail. Despite her husband's ongoing unresponsiveness, she forged ahead, forming friendships with blacks and making meaningful contributions to their lives in a day and age of severe racial hostilities. One of her most prominent relationships was with the distinguished Mary McLeod Bethune, the prominent black educator and founder and president of the National Council of Negro Women.

Roosevelt is famously known for having resigned from the Daughters of the American Revolution (DAR) when, in 1939, they refused to permit Marion Anderson, a black contralto, to perform in Constitution Hall. President Roosevelt, Walter White, and others arranged for Anderson to perform on the steps of the Lincoln Memorial. In 1945, Roosevelt joined the board of the NAACP and the Congress of Racial Equality. She also participated in a workshop on civil rights at the Highlander Folk School, an institution for aspiring social activists, in Tennessee.

As a result of Roosevelt's support and activism, she endeared herself to a generation of blacks. The black press extolled her in their newspapers, and African Americans regularly wrote to her, telling her of their dire situations. If she could not help, she always got in touch with someone who could, though her success was often limited due to deeply entrenched racial barriers and anti-black attitudes. Roosevelt's position was unpopular with much of the electorate, and her fiercest critics could be found in Washington, D.C. But Roosevelt refused to be "politically correct" and remained an independent-minded woman who was committed to making a difference for her entire life.

Eleanor Roosevelt, the president's wife, played an instrumental role in the early discussions with Randolph and his delegation, which included Walter White, of the National Association for the Advancement of Colored People (NAACP), and T. Arnold Hill, of the National Urban League (NUL). Eleanor Roosevelt appeared empathetic to the cause, but to many in the federal government (including subsequent presidents), any civil rights gains needed to come about slowly and be handled delicately. And conservative leaders of such organizations as the NAACP and NUL were not disposed to pressuring government and political leaders, engaging in "radical" public demonstrations, or going against the law to achieve their aims. But Randolph, although he was extremely politic during these grave negotiations, still had a radical edge which, at fifty-one, made him restive with painstakingly slow and ineffectual negotiations.

When negotiations with the president failed to produce tangible maneuvers toward desegregation in the defense industry and armed forces, it became clear to Randolph that "such modes of protest—public statements, strongly worded telegrams to Washington, and conferences with White House officials"—were not working (Anderson, 246). He was not satisfied with the government's suggested solutions to the problem, such as establishing "training in aviation to Negroes," which was still segregation (Anderson, 246). Something was needed to get the government's attention, and Randolph decided that a massive demonstration was the answer.

Although black protest had previously included occasional demonstrations, such as sit-ins and marches, they were often done on a small scale. Randolph, however, planned a grand scheme of active protest to be carried out by the March on Washington Committee (formed in 1941). He envisioned a massive march on Washington consisting of 10,000 demonstrators. He and other Brotherhood leaders traveled the nation soliciting African Americans for support.

The NAACP and NUL were not so eager to embrace Randolph's idea of direct action, though both organizations still managed to lend their support in inconspicuous ways. The sharp claws of racism and oppression quelled much of the support for Randolph's efforts in the South. Communists, who were against American involvement in World War II, were also busy attacking Randolph, with the hope of preventing the march. The reaction at the White House was as expected: Eleanor, speaking for her husband, attempted to dissuade Randolph and the others from going ahead with the march. Randolph, as was his custom, remained true to his conviction, although he did state that if the president created an executive order to officially desegregate the armed forces and industry, he would call the march off. When Eleanor warned that violence could erupt at such a march, Randolph "replied that there would be no violence unless her husband ordered the police to crack black heads" (Anderson, 255). Following this exchange, the president agreed to meet with Randolph and the other delegates.

Randolph was in top form on the day he met with President Roosevelt. In his polite, patient, and refined way, he reaffirmed his position that the march would not be called off unless the president authorized a formal stance against segregation. When the president asked how many people would be participating, Randolph, without knowing the official number, answered, "one hundred thousand, Mr. President" (Anderson, 257). President Roosevelt was stunned. "Somebody might get killed," he said. Randolph, who had already sent invitations to the Roosevelts, suggested that the event would go well, "especially if the President himself came out and addressed the gathering" (Anderson, 258). Although the president insisted that the march be called off, Randolph still declined. It was this adamant refusal to yield under pressure that eventually lead to success.

The president had no choice but to submit to Randolph's demands or face the consequences of a massive protest at his front doorstep, though he only agreed to desegregate the government and defense industries, not the armed forces. His promise was made official with the issuance of Executive Order 8802 on June 25, 1941. This was a mere "six days before the march was scheduled to take place" (Anderson, 259). On July 10, he established the Fair Employment Practices Committee, which still exists today.

Because only one of their demands had been met, the younger members of the March on Washington Committee were outraged. They wanted the march, which Randolph had canceled (at least for the time being), to go ahead. While "the young militants accused [Randolph] of selling out to Roosevelt, the majority of Randolph's following ... applauded his handling of the march strategy" (Anderson, 259–260). And the triumph alone (even if in part) increased Randolph's popularity and strengthened his role as a leader in the African American community.

March on Washington Movement

Randolph learned an essential lesson during his negotiations with President Roosevelt—words were more effective when backed with action, and the march tactic was obviously one of his best ideas. If the threat of a march could force a president to accede to their demands, how much more could be gained with an actual march? The problem with this idea was that America had entered World War II in 1942. Objection to Randolph's march idea was loud and unanimous: protest during a time of national crisis "would damage the national interest" (Anderson, 264). Randolph's recourse was to find another means of agitation, utilizing (if not the march itself) the March on Washington Committee.

Through the March on Washington Committee, Randolph waged a series of demonstrations for civil rights. Among the Committee's objectives was the goal "[to] serve as a watchdog over the enforcement of the [Executive Order 8802], to carry on a campaign for a permanent Fair Employment

Practices Commission, to represent the temper of the masses at the time, and to engage in other protest activities," including "pressing a desegregation campaign," utilizing the tactic made famous by Gandhi—"nonviolent civil disobedience and non-cooperation" (Anderson, 262–263, 274). For a brief period during the early 1940s, his March on Washington Committee organized a dazzling succession of demonstrations and rallies that "Joel A. Rogers, the veteran Harlem historian and journalist, had not seen … 'since the days of Marcus Garvey'" (Anderson, 265). Literature, such as a radical pamphlet entitled "The War's Greatest Scandal: The Story of Jim Crow in Uniform," was also produced and dispensed to the communities.

The March on Washington Committee (as well as Randolph, who was its national director) was, needless to say, subjected to a flood of criticism by the NAACP, African American women vying for a voice in the movement, and his own compatriots in the Brotherhood. Critics within the NAACP (whose activities centered on lobbying, negotiating, and litigating) held that Randolph's committee was too radical and (predictably) dug up his controversial past as a radical socialist activist to prove their point. Other naysayers asserted that Randolph was doing the work that should have been carried out by the NAACP. Closer to home, Randolph came under fire from disgruntled members of the Brotherhood, such as Milton Webster, who argued that the organization had to contend with too many questions concerning its role as a leader on the civil rights front and was frustrated by the emergence of women leaders in the movement. The women leaders were, in turn, unhappy that they were unable to participate in a more meaningful way in the development of the Committee. Others in the Brotherhood complained that Randolph was devoting too much time to other projects and shirking his primary—if not sole—responsibility: "to negotiate and sign contracts, not to run around like a West Indian Communist agitator and dreamer" (Anderson, 267). And in the South, Randolph still could not penetrate the barriers of racism and oppression. Another challenge to Randolph and his Committee emanated from conservative political resistance, causing the eventual demise of the March on Washington Committee in 1950.

League for Nonviolent Civil Disobedience against Military Segregation

In 1947, Randolph and "Grant Reynolds, Commissioner of Correction for New York State, founded the Committee Against Jim Crow in Military Service and Training—which expanded, early in 1948, into the League for Nonviolent Civil Disobedience Against Military Segregation" (Anderson, 274). The executive secretary of this organization was Bayard Rustin, a former member of the Fellowship of Reconciliation, "one of the young militants who had denounced Randolph for calling off the 1941 march," and a ubiquitous activist within multiple civil rights organizations (Anderson, 274).

The League was established to resurrect the fight against segregation in the armed forces. Harry Truman, America's new president, had just issued a draft bill, "proposing universal military training" that "contained no provision for a ban against segregation" (Anderson, 274). What Randolph wanted was "nothing less than an executive order against military segregation," and he was prepared to use tactics of civil disobedience and direct action to make that happen (Anderson, 276).

Randolph, accompanied by Walter White, Mary McLeod Bethune, Lester Granger, and Charles Houston, went to Washington, D.C. to speak with the president. In the wake of that unsuccessful meeting, Randolph spoke at the hearings on the universal military training bill, where he announced that he "personally will advise Negroes to refuse to fight as slaves for a democracy they cannot possess and cannot enjoy," and that he would utilize "the thousands of white youth in schools and colleges who are today vigorously shedding the **prejudices** of their parents and professors. I shall urge them to demonstrate their solidarity with Negro youth by ignoring the entire registration and induction machinery" (Anderson, 276–277).

Randolph followed this appearance in Washington, D.C. with "a civil disobedience campaign against the draft" (Anderson, 280). In Harlem, "he launched a series of public meetings, at the corner of Seventh Avenue and 125th Street, in which he counseled young men to refuse induction in a segregated army. In giving such counsel, he said, he was fully aware he was violating the Selective Service Act" (Anderson, 278). In Philadelphia, "scores of blacks, led by Randolph" picketed the National Convention in Philadelphia, while Hubert Humphrey waged a separate fight "to obtain a strong civil rights plank" in government (Anderson, 280).

The response to Randolph's campaign was divided. Many African Americans were ready for his radical brand of protest, with 71 percent of young black men in Harlem voting in favor of Randolph's campaign. But the usual opponents such as the National Urban League "warned that Randolph's campaign 'would weaken the foundations of law on which our democratic processes rest'" (Anderson, 279).

On July 26, 1948, President Truman issued Executive Order 9981, "calling for an end to military discrimination 'as rapidly as possible'" (Anderson, 280). This victory was credited to Hubert Humphrey's civil rights campaign at the Democratic National Convention in Philadelphia, as well as to Randolph and his campaign of civil disobedience. However, the young militants within the League were upset with Randolph for "calling off the campaign" and "disbanding the League for Nonviolent Civil Disobedience" (Anderson, 280). Randolph's personal approach to protest did not call for "civil disobedience for its own sake, but merely as a drastic last resort," and he told them so (Anderson, 281). The militants went ahead with plans to keep the League going, but it ceased operating in November 1948.

AFL-CIO

Segregation had been the primary target of Randolph's agitation since the earliest days of his activism, and its elimination was his mission when he and the Brotherhood joined the AFL in 1935. Although the AFL did not endorse segregation, it did not seek to interfere with how its members ran their unions.

The fight against segregation in the AFL proved to be a long battle, but Randolph, with his patience of steel, was an endurance fighter. It did not faze him that he was one against many or that he was one of very few African American leaders within the predominately white AFL. He waged the battle against segregation on a number of fronts: as a speaker, a member of the esteemed Executive Council of the AFL-CIO, and a leader in a newly established Negro American Labor Council. In Randolph's favor was the fact that the newly elected president, George Meany, was sympathetic to Randolph's fight and respected the valiant leader. The merger of the AFL and CIO in 1955, and its increasingly progressive role in civil rights issues, was a big step in the right direction.

Although Randolph encountered many impediments on the road to his goal of desegregating all company unions within the AFL-CIO, his influence resulted in substantial progress. The biggest obstacles were Meany's hesitancy to bring about change as fast as Randolph wanted and his defense of the right of AFL-CIO members to self-governance. Although the AFL-CIO "was unable or unwilling [to engage in the] campaign against discrimination in its unions," Randolph's influence was undoubtedly reflected in the AFL-CIO's emerging role as "one of the strongest lobbyists for civil rights legislation in Washington," "the Supreme Court's decision outlawing school segregation" in 1954, and "President Kennedy's and President Johnson's civil rights programs" (Anderson, 310–312).

Randolph made significant contributions to the Civil Rights Movement—coordinating collaborative demonstrations with leaders such as Dr. Martin Luther King, Jr. in the Prayer Pilgrimage to Washington, D.C. in 1957 and the Youth March for Integrated Schools in 1958 and 1959. He also had some disappointments, including his involvement with the Negro American Labor Council (NALC). The NALC, which was founded in 1960, was designed as an alternative vehicle of protest within the AFL-CIO. As a result of the radical role he played in the NALC, the Executive Council censured Randolph in 1961. In 1964, Randolph resigned as president of the NALC as a result of the growing number of militant and separatist African Americans within the organization.

The March on Washington, August 28, 1963

The March on Washington on August 28, 1963 was one of the most memorable and powerful moments of the Civil Rights Movement. It assembled some 250,000 individuals (largely African American) on the steps of the nation's capital and pulled together, if only for a day, representatives of the nation's most prodigious civil rights organizations, such as Dr. Martin Luther King, Jr. of the Southern Christian Leadership Conference, Roy Wilkins of the NAACP, John Lewis of SNCC, Whitney Young of the National Urban League, and Floyd McKissick, who stood in for James Farmer of CORE while Farmer was in jail following his arrest during a demonstration in Louisiana. The march culminated with the singing of "We Shall Overcome."

The march reflected Randolph's influence and strategic genius and the culmination of a long-held desire (since 1941) to coordinate a massive march on Washington. However, it was Rustin who led multiple projects in the civil rights struggle, such as Randolph's Committee Against Discrimination in the Armed Forces, and served as an advisor to King and other leaders, who conceived of the March on Washington in 1963 for the purposes of "calling for jobs, a higher minimum wage, and a guaranteed income" for African Americans (Anderson, 324). Randolph was impressed with the idea and immediately set about to coordinate the event with Rustin as the organizer.

To President John F. Kennedy's surprise, the march was not violent. Indeed, Kennedy was deeply moved by the power of the event. To Randolph, that day, August 28, 1963, was "the most beautiful and glorious" of his life (Anderson, 331). Historically, the March on Washington remains the archetype for peaceful demonstration. In addition to the numerous speeches, there were musical performances by such artists as Mahalia Jackson, Joan Baez, Bob Dylan, and others. Although women did not participate in the speechmaking, several were given tribute, such as Rosa Parks, Daisy Bates, and Diane Nash. Parks was the woman who sparked the famous Montgomery Bus **Boycott**, in 1955, when she refused to give up her seat to a white person on a Jim Crow bus; Bates played a prominent role during integration of public schools in Little Rock, Arkansas in 1957; and Nash played a key role in the Nashville, Tennessee sit-ins and SNCC.

Although Randolph headed the coordination of this march, his popularity and prestige at this point of his career had dimmed considerably from his glory years. Younger critics "felt the time had come for Randolph to withdraw to the wings" (Anderson, 320). Others called him an "Uncle Tom."

In the wake of the March on Washington, the hope that a massive commitment to civil rights would arise and all African Americans would reap positive benefits disintegrated. Although the Civil Rights Act of 1964 and the Voting Rights Act of 1965 were extraordinary gains for African Americans, little else could be celebrated. Organizations remained fragmented; President Kennedy and Dr. King were assassinated in 1963 and 1968, respectively; the nation was preoccupied with the Vietnam War; and radical

Lincoln Memorial

The Lincoln Memorial is a colossal statue built in the likeness of America's sixteenth president, Abraham Lincoln (1809–1865). It is located on the National Mall in Washington, D.C., the nation's capitol. The memorial has a special meaning to African Americans, because it was Lincoln who created the Emancipation Proclamation, announcing the freedom of slaves. He also led America into the Civil War (1861–1865), where the Union victory secured the destruction of the slave system in the South.

The construction of the Lincoln Memorial began in 1914, and it was opened to the public in 1922. Henry Bacon designed it, and a team of only two men, the Piccirilli brothers, carved it over four years. The memorial is 190 feet long, 119 feet wide, 100 feet high, and weighs 175 tons. It portrays Lincoln sitting in a chair, his hands straddling the arms of the chair, his eyes starring pensively forward.

The March on Washington for Jobs and Freedom in 1963 culminated in the shadow of the Lincoln Memorial. It was there that the major civil rights leaders, including A. Philip Randolph, gave speeches. Dr. Martin Luther King, Jr.'s "I Have a Dream" was the most popular speech on that day. Many other protests have also taken place at the Lincoln Memorial.

In 1995, Louis Farrakhan, the Honorable Minister of the Nation of Islam, chose the U.S. capitol in sight of the Lincoln Memorial as the location for his Million Man March. Although his event was not considered a protest demonstration, the symbolism was unmistakable. One of Farrakhan's aims was to mobilize black men to register to vote. In the aftermath of the Civil War, blacks received several ephemeral civil rights, one of which was suffrage for freed black males. However, at the end of Reconstruction (1862–1877) the civil rights gains blacks had enjoyed for the first time in the nation's history were done away with as conservative whites regained power over the South.

militants who endorsed the violence breaking out in black urban communities rose to prominence. Randolph, not unlike other civil rights leaders, disapproved of radical militancy and violence but understood that that was a by-product of youthful fury and desperation over oppression, racism, and dire conditions within their communities.

The Randolph Institute

In 1964, Randolph established the Randolph Institute to help address persistent problems within impoverished African American communities and to "strengthen the ties between the labor movement, civil rights groups, and other progressive organizations" (Pfeffer, 282). Randolph, at age seventy-five, did not play an active role in the organization, but he hoped that the Institute would "carry on his ideas and methods" (Pfeffer, 281).

The Randolph Institute collaborated with several organizations, such as the AFL-CIO, the NAACP, and Jewish groups. Among the numerous programs it sponsored were those "to organize black trade unionists around the country to conduct voter registration drives ... to recruit, tutor, and place blacks and Puerto Ricans in the predominately white building trades apprenticeship training schemes," and to help combat poverty (Anderson, 314–315). In 1965, President Lyndon B. Johnson awarded Randolph the Presidential Medal of Freedom and appointed him to the national advisory council representing the public in the operation of his antipoverty program. In 1966, Johnson made Randolph honorary chairman of a conference on civil rights, where he made "his first public announcement of the [Freedom Budget] program he projected as the cornerstone of the institute's activity" (Pfeffer, 286). This was a comprehensive program to promote employment and combat poverty in African American communities and its problems of crime, drug abuse, and violence. But Randolph was prevented from implementing this program due to budget cuts.

FINAL YEARS

Randolph's "last public involvement" was his support for "thirteen teachers— twelve [Jewish] and one black" in the United Federation of Teachers strike in 1968 (Anderson, 312). Randolph's opposition was met with vociferous criticism from within the African American community, because it was blacks who wanted to maintain their control of the school district. In his defense, Randolph said, "I could not very well refuse to support the teachers' right to due process and job security since it is not only a basic part of our democratic life, but is indispensable for the ability of workers to hold jobs" (Anderson, 314).

Although no longer in the spotlight, Randolph remained a venerated hero for his lifelong activism. In 1969, he celebrated his eightieth birthday "at a black-tie dinner in the Grand Ballroom of the Waldorf Astoria" (Anderson, 347). In attendance were 1,200 people, including Bayard Rustin, Coretta Scott King, George Meany, and Roy Wilkins. In his last years, Randolph, who suffered from heart problems, lived alone (his wife Lucille had died in 1963). His days were spent "most of the time at home, resting, receiving visitors, or reading" and taking occasional walks. He also made occasional "trips out of town, to AFL-CIO conventions and executive council meetings, political affairs in his honor, or college campuses, to accept honorary degrees" (Anderson, 350–351).

On May 16, 1979, Asa Philip Randolph died. In life, Asa, like his biblical namesake, had been a leader of his people, tirelessly performing valiant acts that paved the way for a better future. He was ninety years old.

See also W.E.B Du Bois; James Farmer; Marcus Garvey; Martin Luther King, Jr.; John Lewis; Rosa Parks; Roy Wilkins; and Whitney Young.

FURTHER RESOURCES

A. Philip Randolph: For Jobs and Freedom. Directed by Dante J. James. San Francisco: Newsreel, 1995.

Anderson, Jervis. *A. Philip Randolph: A Biographical Portrait.* Berkeley: University of California Press, 1986.

APRI.org. A. Philip Randolph Institute (July 2007). See http://www.apri.org/ht/d/Home/pid/212.

Harris, William Hamilton. *Keeping the Faith: A Philip Randolph, Milton P. Webster, and the Brotherhood of Sleeping Car Porters, 1925–37.* Urbana: University of Illinois Press, 1977.

Kersten, Andrew E. *A. Philip Randolph: A Life in the Vanguard.* Lanham, MD: Rowman & Littlefield Publishers, 2007.

Pfeffer, Paula F. *A Philip Randolph: Pioneer of the Civil Rights Movement.* Baton Rouge: Louisiana State University Press, 1990.

Reef, Catherine. *A. Philip Randolph: Union Leader and Civil Rights Crusader.* Berkeley Heights, NJ: Enslow Publishers, 2001.

Taylor, Cynthia. *A Philip Randolph: The Religious Journey of an African American Labor Leader.* New York: New York University Press, 2006.

10,000 Black Men Named George. Directed by Robert Townsend. Hollywood: Paramount, 2002.

Transcript, A. Philip Randolph Oral History Interview I, October 29, 1969, by Thomas H. Baker, Internet Copy, LBJ Library. See http://www.lbjlib.utexas.edu/johnson/archives.hom/oralhistory.hom/RandolpA/randolp.asp.

Wintz, Cary D., ed. *African American Political Thought, 1890–1930: Washington, Du Bois, Garvey, and Randolph.* Armonk, NY: M.E. Sharpe, 1996.

Wright, Sarah E. *A. Philip Randolph: Integration in the Workplace.* Englewood Cliffs, NJ: Silver Burdett Press, 1990.

Al Sharpton (1954–)

Al Sharpton is a civil rights activist and has the distinction of being one of the most visible African American leaders of the twenty-first century. Al Sharpton, most often referred to as "the Reverend Al Sharpton," was a religious prodigy at the age of four and an activist in his teens during the Civil Rights Movement. Nowadays, when Sharpton appears on television, in print, on the Internet, or on the radio, one can almost hear the collective exasperated sigh of millions. Right-wing blogs and editorials are ablaze with fury and criticism over something Sharpton has said or some cause he has taken up. Blacks have mixed emotions about Sharpton. Some entertain a love-hate relationship with him; others think poorly of him. Many recognize that Sharpton is still relevant and will continue to be so as long as justice eludes African Americans. This last is how Sharpton himself explains the importance of his role. The fact is that when trouble does arise for African Americans, Sharpton and his long-standing friend Jesse Jackson are the two high-profile leaders who can be counted on to present the African American viewpoint and effectively rally media attention to the situation.

Problems may not occur on the same scale as a century ago, but modern-day crises keep Sharpton busy, even if all of his crusades do not end in success or showcase him in a flattering light. In the last three years alone, Sharpton has led the attack on a number of controversial issues. In 2006, he reprimanded Michael Richards, one of the stars of the hit television show, *Seinfeld*, for using the N-word during a tense moment in a stand-up routine. Sharpton addressed the heavy use of racist and sexist epithets by the hip-hop community as well. He played a visible role in the 2006 Duke University lacrosse scandal, wherein a black stripper accused three white members of the lacrosse team of rape. In 2007, the critics howled when Al Sharpton chose to defend several black men charged with raping and brutalizing a black woman and physically assaulting her son in their home in the Dunbar Village projects. In the same year, Sharpton lashed out at radio personality Don Imus when he set off a highly public scandal by calling the members of the Rutgers' women's basketball team "nappy-headed hos." In 2008, he was at the forefront of the attack on Kelly Tilghman, a broadcaster for the Golf Channel, when she commented that someone should "lynch [golfer Tiger Woods] in a back alley." It was the term "lynch" that sparked Sharpton to action. Most recently, Sharpton figured as the spokesperson for the family and fiancée of Sean Bell, who was gunned down by officers after leaving his bachelor party.

CHILDHOOD

On October 3, 1954, Alfred Charles Sharpton, Jr. was born. Sharpton has three siblings, Ernestine, Thomas, and Cheryl. Sharpton's southern-born and -raised parents, Ada Richards Sharpton and Alfred Charles Sharpton, Sr., were extraordinary people. Ada Sharpton taught the children to be confident and to excel at whatever they desired to do, which explains why Sharpton felt that he could do anything. Alfred Sharpton, Sr. was living proof that the impossible was possible. An ambitious and shrewd man, he owned multiple buildings and businesses, including a store and a newsstand located not too far from their home.

Sharpton's childhood started well. He spent his early years in a brick row house his father owned in Brooklyn, New York. He and his sister played in their parent's store. On special occasions, their father took them to Harlem to the Apollo Theater, the famous theater that stands today. When the Apollo was established in 1913, only whites were admitted. In 1934, during the dazzling era known as Harlem Renaissance, it became one of the most popular venues for new singing groups. Its Amateur Night catapulted numerous stars, such as Ella Fitzgerald, Diana Ross and the Supremes, the Jackson 5, and Stevie Wonder, to fame. James Brown was one of Sharpton's favorite performers.

On Sundays, the entire family went to a Pentecostal church named the Washington Temple Church. Sharpton was three years old when the family placed membership. Bishop Frederick Douglass Washington, who had begun preaching at the age of four, was an inspiration to young Sharpton.

Sharpton liked to pretend to be a preacher at home. In fact, he preferred that to playing games with the other children in his neighborhood. He preached to his sisters' dolls and built church buildings out of his toy blocks. When the church was preparing for its special anniversary service, Sharpton told Mrs. Hazel Griffin, who was in charge of coordinating the children's participation, that he wanted to preach the sermon. He wore a gold robe that day, July 9, 1959, and the congregation enveloped him in warm, loving shouts of encouragement and approval. He was only four.

BOY PREACHER

Sharpton had several mentors in his life, who played crucial roles in his development as a person, a spiritual leader, and an activist. Nothing could tear Sharpton away from his first mentor, the Bishop Washington. After school, while most children played or did homework, Sharpton went to Bishop Washington's office, where he mimicked everything Bishop Washington did. Once a month, he gave sermons at his church or traveled, first in New York, later to other states.

Sharpton was a novelty. The people he met called him "Wonderboy" or "Boy Preacher." Under the circumstances, it was not surprising that Sharpton had a hard time separating the boy preacher from schoolboy. When he was instructed to write his name on the chalkboard in the first grade, he wrote Reverend Alfred Sharpton.

As Sharpton's spiritual life prospered, so did his father's economic life. In 1960, the family moved to a new, sprawling home in Queens, New York. This house had a lawn on which Al and Cheryl could play, ten rooms, and a basement where Sharpton practiced his sermons. Sharpton was more fortunate than most black children, who grew up in the dire poverty of the South or the squalid ghettos of the cities of the North.

The young Sharpton did get a small inkling of what life was like for blacks in the South when, during a trip to Florida, where his father was brought up, a white man at a restaurant refused to serve his father. Sharpton did not understand why his father, a well-muscled former boxer, acquiesced. He did not understand the fatal consequences of black resistance until later.

For Sharpton, and for most of America, the years from 1963 to 1965 were complicated. One of the most important events for African Americans was the signing of the Civil Rights Act by President Lyndon B. Johnson. This act destroyed Jim Crow but left blacks and whites floundering to navigate in this utterly new world of integration. Reactions were varied. Many blacks were overjoyed but were uncertain of how to contend with begrudging whites who felt the government had forced them to open up their world to blacks. Other blacks worried about what integration would bring. Would it destroy their culture? Would it devastate the black community?

Meanwhile, Sharpton faced uncertainties in his own life when, in 1963, Alfred Sharpton, Sr. left his wife. They ultimately divorced. The divorce was difficult for everyone. The children were split up. Ada Sharpton kept Al and one of his sisters, and the three of them lived in the prodigious house until they could no longer pay for it. For a long time, they had to do without electricity and heat. Neighborhood children who knew about this teased Sharpton relentlessly, just as they taunted him about being a preacher. One day, a judge wanted to see Sharpton. He had heard that he was preaching and worried that he was being forced to do so to earn money for the family. He ordered Al to stop until he was convinced that it was his own conviction and desire, and not coercion, which motivated him to preach.

But there was no doubt about Al Sharpton's conviction. He became an ordained minister in the Pentecostal Church in 1964. He was ten years old, a portly child, with his hair shaved close to his head. He exuded confidence beyond his years. At the New York World's Fair in 1965, Mahalia Jackson, the famous African American gospel singer, invited Sharpton to preach during her performance.

Eventually, Ada Sharpton and the children moved to the projects and went on welfare. Ada Sharpton, unable to deal with the sudden crisis, stayed in a hospital for a while. The usually sunny Sharpton had his own adverse reaction, uncharacteristically missing class and becoming melancholy. Sharpton was helped during this time by the kindness of two teachers who showed him special attention. Another person who played a pivotal role in his life at this time was his new friend, Reverend Walter Banks.

AWAKENING

Many leaders of African American protest experienced an event or were influenced by individuals who served as a catalyst to awaken their social and **racial consciousness**. For Malcolm X, it took a long stint in prison and his introduction to the Nation of Islam. For W.E.B. Du Bois, the early twentieth-century scholar and activist who grew up in an austere New England town, it was his first exposure to a black community and his undergraduate years at Fisk University. For Sharpton, it was his parent's divorce, and undoubtedly, his brief exposure to life in the projects.

Sharpton had not known poverty—ever—until his mother had been forced to forge a life for him and his sister without the assistance of her ex-husband's vast resources. The abrupt change from comfort to poverty must have been startling and bewildering. But Sharpton's calamity had a sobering effect on him. Thanks to regular visits with Reverend Banks he came through this trial with an ultra-sensitive awareness of the world in which he lived.

Reverend Banks introduced Sharpton to Brentano's, a bookstore on New York's ritzy Fifth Avenue. He let Sharpton peruse the stacks of books and purchase anything he wanted. During one trip, Sharpton discovered a book about Adam Clayton Powell, Jr. Powell was a charismatic black minister and politician, and he was one of two blacks in Congress. He used his influential position to work diligently on behalf of blacks. He helped pass legislation and bills to desegregate schools, to make lynching a federal crime, and to eliminate the poll tax that blacks were required to pay to vote, and he campaigned to prohibit the use of the N-word during sessions in Congress. This he accomplished during a time when the climate toward blacks in the federal government was hostile at worst, or indifferent. But Powell was in many ways unconventional. He was flamboyant and cared very little what others thought or said about him.

In addition to following Powell's career with great admiration, Sharpton read heavily about other black leaders, like Marcus Garvey, the flamboyant personality who launched a brief but spectacular movement of black nationalism in America and abroad, and Dr. Martin Luther King, Jr., the face of the Civil Rights Movement.

CALL ME ADAM

Sharpton attended Somers Junior High School in Brooklyn, New York. Life was looking up. His mother had moved them to a new apartment, out of the projects, and had found employment as a domestic in Greenwich Village. He made two good friends at school: a black named Dennis Neal and a white named Richard Farkas. Like Sharpton, his two friends were interested in the Civil Rights Movement. They took to calling each other by the names of their favorite leaders. Dennis' alter ego was Stokely Carmichael, the young, lean leader of the Student Nonviolent Coordinating Committee (SNCC). Richard became U.S. Attorney General Bobby Kennedy, the brother of President John F. Kennedy. Al took on the persona of his hero, Adam Clayton Powell, Jr.

Adam Clayton Powell, Jr.

Adam Clayton Powell, Jr. (1908–1972) was the first black U.S. Congressman to represent New York. His political contributions and social activism made him a pioneer of the Civil Rights Movement.

Powell was born in New Haven, Connecticut. When he was still a baby, his parents moved to Harlem, New York, where his father, Adam Clayton Powell, Sr., became the minister of the Abyssinian Baptist Church.

After receiving his M.A. degree in religious education from Colgate University, a predominately white institution, Powell conducted several ground-breaking demonstrations in the 1930s. These demonstrations were to demand jobs for blacks at the Harlem Hospital and at other local businesses. During the Great Depression, he established food banks to assist the large black population in Harlem.

In 1937, Powell took over his father's church. But he continued to be a leader in local social activism. He coordinated several boycotts and picketing demonstrations, opening the way for blacks to find employment in all-white businesses and companies.

In 1944, he was elected as a Democrat to the House of Congress, though he continued to preach at Abyssinian. In his new position, he was often a lone advocate for civil rights. After the election of President John F. Kennedy in 1960, he served as the chair of the House Education and Labor Committee. He was instrumental in increasing the minimum wage and developing social programs such as Head Start. He also played a role in the establishment of the Office of Economic Opportunity, which would help tremendously in the twentieth century.

When Sharpton wanted something, he would not let up until he got it. It was this temerity that caused his mother to give in and let her son have his way when he wanted to meet Adam Clayton Powell. She did not want to go into Harlem. She thought it was too dangerous. But Harlem was where Powell's church, Abyssinian Baptist Church, was located. It took several visits before Powell appeared, but when he did, Sharpton marched right to his office and requested a meeting with him.

Powell, who had already heard of Sharpton, the "Boy Preacher," agreed to meet him and took him for a soda. Powell and Sharpton spent a great deal of time together during that time, and Sharpton learned much from him. One of the more important lessons learned was that "you cannot be a true leader if you care about what people think or say about you" (Sharpton, 186). Powell had a lot of experience ignoring what people thought about him. During an appearance on the *David Frost Show*, the host pointed out that Powell had been "a member of Congress for over twenty years, and … pastor [of] one of the largest congregations in the world, yet you have been married four times; you drink liquor publicly; you have girlfriends; you have been indicted for tax evasion and sued" (Sharpton, 186). Powell was unrattled.

ACTIVISM

Operation Breadbasket

In the mid 1960s, the Southern Christian Leadership Conference (SCLC) established an Operation Breadbasket office in Brooklyn, New York. Operation Breadbasket had as its objective to help address problems for blacks in the North such as unemployment and de facto segregation. This was significant because it represented a major civil rights organization's attempt to tackle problems facing blacks outside of the South. That it was a success was a relief to Martin Luther King, Jr. and the rest of the leadership of the SCLC. Problems in the North were more complicated than he had originally thought. The struggle in the South was harrowing enough, but the tactics used there (nonviolent marches and demonstrations) did not seem to work in the North. For one thing, blacks in the North were eager to fight back, and for another, racist whites were sometimes more vicious than those encountered in the South.

Sharpton attended several Operation Breadbasket meetings, but he eventually stopped going, because it "seemed kind of boring" (Mallin, 40). What Sharpton needed was another epiphany, which would come shortly after the assassination of Dr. King.

It was common knowledge that King faced the possibility of death on a daily basis. Like other activists, he constantly received death threats. But when he was shot at the Lorraine Motel in Memphis, Tennessee on April 4, 1968, it took the African American community by surprise. Grief shook the nation, including Sharpton's own mother. Her pain stunned him until she explained that the loss was intensely personal. Sharpton had not experienced Jim Crow law and custom. But Ada, who had grown up in Alabama, had. The Civil Rights Movement, King's gallant crusade, and the major victories such as the Civil Rights Act of 1964 and the Voting Rights Act of 1965 had been life-altering events for her.

While watching a movie on King's life and death several months later, Sharpton was struck by the words in a song that seemed pointed directly at him, "What will happen, now that the King of Love is dead?" Sharpton returned to the Operation Breadbasket and attended meetings regularly.

In 1967, a new leader, Jesse Jackson, was put in charge of Operation Breadbasket. Jackson was not like other ministers; he was hip and youthful with swagger and good looks. And he was a little unorthodox. Unlike the staid preachers of the old vanguard, he grimaced sometimes when he gave

Dashiki

A dashiki is a colorful, loose-fitting garment that is traditionally worn in West Africa. It became a powerful symbol for black culturalists and militants during the Black Power Movement of the 1960s.

The dashiki held meaning for blacks for several reasons. One, it was an expression of black pride and black power. Although most African Americans cannot trace their heritage to a specific location or tribe in Africa, due to the fact that white slave traders and plantation owners did not keep records, it is known that the majority of slaves were procured in the region of West Africa. During slavery, Africans were largely assimilated into their new environment—but not completely. Although their languages, religions, and most customs were lost, a number of Africanisms or African traits and traditions remained. However, many blacks (during and after slavery), in an effort to fit into mainstream culture as well as to yield to societal pressures and stereotypes that depicted blackness as inferior and negative, distanced themselves from anything associated with their African and slave past. For example, many blacks straightened their natural, coarse hair with pressing combs and chemicals and stopped wearing rags on their head (a surviving custom of African women) or any other clothing that might set them apart from mainstream society. They avoided eating traditional black southern foods (or soul food). Some blacks even tried to lighten the complexion of their skin with special creams and lotions.

The emergence of the dashiki in America in the 1960s thus represented a return to black roots and served as a physical expression of resistance. By wearing the dashiki, black men and women affirmed their unique culture and protested the notion of cultural assimilation. It was also a statement against the negative stereotyping of Africa and blackness. For many, the dashiki served to punctuate their desire to separate from white culture and life. Many whites were intimidated by blacks who dressed in traditional African clothing, although this was not necessarily the intention of the black culturalists, who believed that differences were to be celebrated, not feared.

Whites who participated in the American Hippie Movement, which gained momentum during the Vietnam War in the 1960s, sometimes wore dashikis as part of the counterculture.

speeches. He wore dashikis and medallions and sported an afro and side-burns. When he was arrested, photographs showed him and others with him giving the clenched-fist salute. He looked and acted more like a Black Power Movement adherent than anything else. But he was not.

When Sharpton met Jackson, he was starstruck. Because of him, Sharpton started wearing a medallion and grew sideburns and an afro. In 1969, Jackson made Sharpton, at fourteen years old, youth director of Operation Breadbasket. Sharpton became as fiercely passionate an activist as he was a preacher. He helped recruit individuals to assist with demonstrations. A large number of these participants came from the churches of the ministers who participated in Operation Breadbasket. Sharpton mobilized five hundred individuals.

Robert Hall Boycott

Sharpton's first demonstration involved the boycott of Robert Hall, a clothing store in New York. Among the items on their list of demands were "contracts for African American businesses, summer jobs for inner-city kids, and training programs so workers could move up in the company" (Mallin, 43). Robert Hall submitted quickly to the demands. Future campaigns would not be so easy.

Tilden High School

In the 1960s, the spirit of protest was infectious. College students formed activist groups and staged protests on campus' throughout the nation and the world. Sharpton was one of the main instigators at his Tilden High School. In fact, before he even started high school he led a march to support black leaders who wanted the school to be managed by local school boards. He later staged protests, seemingly without much discretion. Once, he led a strike for better cafeteria food.

Sharpton assumed a leadership position at Tilden, as well as in his community. He was heavily involved in extracurricular activities such as the debate team, the Afro-American Club, and the school newspaper. He was the leader of the Martin Luther King Memorial Committee. Not until 1986 would Dr. King be memorialized with a national holiday. But because of Sharpton's efforts, Tilden was the first school to display a picture of King and a plaque detailing information about him.

A&P Campaign

In 1971, Sharpton faced off with one of America's oldest chain stores in a campaign that proved to be one of the highest-profile demonstrations coordinated by Operation Breadbasket. The A&P (officially the Great Atlantic and Pacific Tea Company), was founded in 1859 in New York City. According to revenue reports for 2005 and 2006, the A&P chain, which consisted of five hundred grocery stores, ranked 35th and 21st, respectively, in the top seventy-five retailers in North America. In 1971, when Sharpton staged a demonstration, the A&P had four thousand stores.

It made sense that Operation Breadbasket should target A&P, since though many blacks frequented the stores, few blacks were allowed to work in them—particularly in management positions. Furthermore, the stores in black communities were not on a par with those in white neighborhoods (a problem that continues to pester black residents in inner cities to this day). Other issues included fewer stores in black neighborhoods and higher prices than in stores in white neighborhoods.

The A&P campaign was challenging. Sharpton and the other demonstrators picketed several stores in New York. At first, they tried to educate A&P shoppers with the hope that they would choose not to patronize the chain. The shoppers either ignored the activists or were indignant, like one woman who pushed a shopping cart into Sharpton. A&P executives refused to sit down with Jesse Jackson or Ralph Abernathy, who had replaced Dr. King as the leader of the SCLC.

Reverend Jones decided to take the demonstration to the national headquarters in Manhattan, New York. Sharpton was the youngest of thirty ministers who participated in this demonstration. When the men entered the headquarters, they did not ask to see the A&P president, a middle-aged man named William J. Kane. They simply walked into his empty office, sat down, and began to sing protest songs. During the **sit-in** in Kane's office, a white guard, impressed with his demeanor, gave Sharpton something to eat while they waited.

Late in the evening, Sharpton called Kane, using the phone on his desk. But Kane was unwilling to respond to their demands. Police officers arrested everyone but Sharpton. The security guard who had been impressed by the young Sharpton asked the police not to arrest him. Even so, Sharpton slept that night at the jail where the ministers were being held. His mother did not stop him. Early that next morning, Jackson called Sharpton to find out what happened and instructed him to mobilize activists for a rally he wanted to stage for the next day at the national A&P office.

When the arrest of the adult activists were aired on the news, the executives of A&P were forced to remedy the situation. The reputation of the franchise depended on it. This tactic—of forcing media attention on an issue via a nonviolent demonstration—was carried out repeatedly in the South by all the major civil rights organizations. Even the conservatively minded NAACP participated in **picketing**, from time to time. It had proven to be extremely persuasive.

Following negotiations, the A&P agreed to most of the demands submitted by Operation Breadbasket. More blacks were hired. A&P stores purchased the services of black-owned businesses and stocked their shelves with merchandise produced by black-owned manufacturing companies. They agreed to subsequent visits by representatives of Operation Breadbasket to check up on the compliance of the stores.

National Youth Movement

Sharpton was not yet eighteen when, in 1971, he formed the National Youth Movement to help impoverished youth. Jackson had decided to leave Operation Breadbasket and to mount his People United to Serve Humanity program, known as PUSH, or Operation Push, out of Chicago. PUSH resembled, in many ways, Operation Breadbasket, in that it waged demonstrations and boycotts against companies that did not hire minorities or support minority-owned businesses. PUSH also launched campaigns to support education and inner-city schools. One program, PUSH/EXCEL, sponsored extracurricular activities for youth and encouraged the development of public speaking skills. Through an application process, high-school seniors were selected for substantial scholarships to four-year universities.

Starting up an organization is an enormous undertaking for anyone, let alone an eighteen-year-old. Sharpton recruited friends from high school and Operation Breadbasket with uncanny ease, but he needed advice from experienced professional activists. The National Youth Movement was made possible because of the support of many blacks who lent their expertise and influence. Bayard Rustin, the tall and lanky civil rights legend, consulted with Sharpton and gave him $500. Rustin had been a little older than Sharpton when his interest in activism had been piqued. He was in his twenties when he went through activism training and participated in the world-famous Scottsboro trial, where nine young African American men were accused of raping two white women. Rustin was a ubiquitous figure in a number of organizations and civil rights activities. He participated in the Journey of Reconciliation to demand that nominal interstate travel laws that prohibited Jim Crow practices be enforced. He helped found the Congress of Racial Equality. He traveled to India to learn about Gandhian techniques. He was also an advisor for the Montgomery Bus Boycott, a major coordinator of the March on Washington for Jobs and Freedom, and many others.

Other activists responded to Sharpton's call. Shirley Chisholm was the keynote speaker at one of Sharpton's fundraising events. Chisholm, the first African American woman elected to the U.S. Congress, was a native of New York. She had a reputation for a sharp intellect, a no-nonsense attitude, and a distinctive appearance: oversized glasses, bouffant hair, and a winning smile. Since Sharpton was too young to incorporate on his own, the organization also needed a good lawyer. David Dinkins, who would become mayor of New York City between 1990 and 1993, provided the legal knowledge that ensured the smooth running of the operation.

Sharpton received the Tilden High School Community Service Award at his graduation ceremony. His mother watched from the audience, beaming proudly. Her son was the first one in the family to graduate from high school and to go to college. This was a proud moment for the Sharptons. However, Sharpton's father was nowhere in sight.

If he felt the sting of that absence, he did not let it fester. Sharpton was too busy furthering his education and his career. He was on his way to college and a new relationship with a singer named James Brown.

Brooklyn College

Established in 1930, Brooklyn College was well-known for its stately beauty as well as its solid curriculum. The motto at Brooklyn College was "Nothing without great effort." This held special meaning for an experienced activist like Sharpton, and could easily have been his personal mantra, given his dogged pursuit of justice. Unfortunately, in terms of his academic career, this worthy motto did not apply.

Sharpton was not impressed by his courses in contemporary politics and soon began to feel that he was wasting his time. A number of activists, notably King and his role model Jackson, had a great deal of education under their belts. But Jackson left school before he received his Ph.D. to work with King, who promised him experiences and opportunities that a classroom could not provide. Sharpton had confidence in himself, observing that his knowledge and experiences bested the experience of his professors and knowledge in the required textbook readings. Jackson tried to talk him into staying in college. Sharpton hung on for two years, joining the Black Student Union and the debate team, but then dropped out. He later regretted that decision.

James Brown

Sharpton was still enrolled at Brooklyn College when, in 1973, he met the sensational soul singer James Brown. During the climactic years of the civil rights struggle, Brown performed such hits as "Papa's Got a Brand New Bag," and "I Got You (I Feel Good)." He was widely known for his gritty sound, shouts, and frenetic dance moves. Some of his songs reflected the spirit of the times during the Black Power Movement, such as his "Say It Loud—I'm Black and I'm Proud" (1968).

Brown sought Sharpton out because he wanted to make a contribution to his National Youth Movement and soon became one of the most influential people in his life. In fact, Sharpton wrote that Brown "had more impact on my life than any civil rights leader—maybe even more than my own mother. What I learned from him makes it possible for me to do the things I do today" (Sharpton, 204). Brown not only imparted his personal style (for

Brown was the source of Sharpton's famous processed hairstyle) but "taught [him] about self-respect, dignity, and self-definition" (Sharpton, 205).

Brown and Sharpton connected instantly, and their relationship was mutually beneficial. After performing a concert to raise money for Sharpton's organization, Brown took him on tour with him. When his son died in a car accident, Sharpton became a surrogate son. Brown, like Sharpton's father, knew a lot about business. So when his business manager died, he groomed Sharpton to take on that responsibility. Throughout the 1980s, Sharpton worked in the music industry, the National Youth Movement, and preached regularly in churches. To this day, Sharpton continues to preach.

While working as Brown's manager, Sharpton met a backup singer named Kathy Jordan whom he would later marry. The had two children.

Over the course of his long relationship with Brown, Sharpton observed how the popular singer defied public ridicule and adversity while maintaining his dedication to social matters. Brown was someone who was often harshly criticized in the media. But, like Powell, he remained oblivious, bolstering himself with his a strong and confident sense of self. He was unfazed by those who ridiculed his style or anything else he said or did. Imitating his friend, Sharpton learned how to weather cruel remarks and barbs.

During an early 1980s trip to celebrate Martin Luther King Day in Washington, D.C., Sharpton witnessed how Brown broached the topic of the troublous social conditions in America with then-Vice President George Bush, Sr. Brown then opened the dialogue so that Sharpton could share some of his thoughts on America's problems and how to solve them. In the late 1980s, Brown served three years in prison for offenses such as carrying an unlicensed gun and driving violations. When he visited his friend, Sharpton was amazed to find that Brown did not sulk over his predicament but instead eagerly prepared for his comeback upon his release.

THE SHARPTON PERSONA

People—black and white—make fun of Al Sharpton. This has as much to do with his appearance as it does his politics. Sharpton referenced a 1988 article that asked why many whites found him so easy to hold in contempt. The answer, according to the article? "He's fat; he has show-business hair, a gold medal, a jumpsuit, and Reeboks. He's a perfect stereotype of a pork chop preacher" (Sharpton, 203). Sharpton began to cultivate his trademark look in the 1970s after forming a close bond with Brown, who wore a long, processed hairdo. He knew well enough that it would help him to get noticed; to stand out from the crowd. But it was his penchant for putting on a good show for reporters and cameras, for shouting out his take on racial incidents, and for delivering clever one-liners that made him famous.

EARLY NEW YORK PROTEST

Sharpton began the early 1980s with his fists poised and swinging. Like a costumed superhero, he was by day a Pentecostal minister, and by night a full-time defender of the oppressed. Sharpton kept extremely busy for more than three decades, fighting racists and pursuing justice, and most of his crusades concerned situations that transpired in the North, particularly in New York.

Sharpton was involved in two local campaigns in 1984. For one, he coordinated protests at Grand Central Station to demand that blacks be included on the board and hired for management positions with the Metropolitan Transit Authority. Mario Cuomo, the governor of New York at that time, responded favorably. The other situation produced lackluster results. In 1984, a white man named Bernhard Goetz shot four African American youths who asked for $5, paralyzing one of the young men.

Race and public interest complicated the situation. Many in New York applauded Goetz for defending himself against youths engaged in a crime against him. Sharpton and a number of blacks interpreted the situation differently. Historically, whites had gotten away with a number of crimes against African Americans. African Americans had been largely defenseless in the court system, and if found guilty of a crime, were given longer sentences than whites. During investigations of crimes, blacks also suffered at the hands of racist officials and a system biased to believe that blacks were automatically at fault. Sharpton was concerned that this situation would repeat the old racist pattern. In addition, there was suspicion that Goetz had "overreacted" when he shot the men (Mallin, 64). Sharpton organized a press conference at New York's City Hall, prayer vigils, and demonstrations at Goetz' apartment and the courthouse. Goetz was acquitted, but sentenced to 250 days in prison for illegal ownership of the gun.

HOWARD BEACH (1986)

Sharpton did not need to search for cases. Most of Sharpton's campaigns began with a phone call. They usually came in the middle of the night with a frantic voice on the other end of the line imploring him to action. That was how Sharpton's involvement in the Howard Beach incident started: a call from one of the members of the National Youth Movement who told him that one of his friends had been killed.

There were two aspects to the ensuing campaign. First, Sharpton asserted that this was his first major demonstration. Second, "it was the first case that began to project nationally our [effective] use of direct-action strategies in the North" (Sharpton, 225). Sharpton knew that King had made direct-action techniques popular in demonstrations in the South during the Civil Rights

Movement. He also knew that when those same tactics were transposed to the North, they were ineffectual. Sharpton's two-pronged approach—marches and court battles—made for a powerful punch.

The details of what happened at Howard Beach shocked the nation. In New York, there are still neighborhoods known for their antipathy for other races. In Howard Beach, a community in Queens, a group of whites acted out their hatred of African Americans on three blacks whose car had broken down there. The three men got out to look for a phone to call for help and were besieged by a group of whites. Following a fight, whites chased after the men with, one recalled, knives, rocks, and sticks. One of the three men ran onto an expressway and was killed when he was hit by a car.

Ed Koch, the mayor of New York City, called the killing of the young man on the expressway "a racial lynching" (Mallin, 67). Although lynching had been a common practice on the American frontier, it held a distinctive meaning between the late nineteenth century and early twentieth century, when lynching was almost exclusively racially motivated.

Despite this statement, Sharpton was not convinced that Koch was an ally. He launched his own campaign, consisting of a speech at the site of the pizzeria where the three men had been confronted by the whites. Sharpton purchased pizza for all the participants. A week later, while leading a march, Sharpton and the other marchers were met by incensed whites shouting vituperations. The media caught it all on camera. Sharpton held several more marches and demonstrations, while the legal team fought in the courts. One of Sharpton's ideas to help with the case was for the surviving victims to not provide any information to the investigation. This was a risky, questionable tactic.

A year and a day after the incident in Howard Beach, Sharpton dramatized the court case by holding a "Day of Outrage." He and other demonstrators stood on the tracks of a subway, calling out, "No justice, no peace!" This demonstration interfered with subway and car traffic headed toward the Brooklyn Bridge. Sharpton and the demonstrators were arrested, but others took their place on the tracks. In total, seventy-three people were put in jail. While in jail, Sharpton was informed that three of the four members of the Howard Beach mob had been found guilty of manslaughter and assault.

TAWANA BRAWLEY (1987)

Of all the campaigns Sharpton was involved in after the Howard Beach case, the high-profile case of a fifteen year old named Tawana Brawley was the most well-known. But this time Sharpton found himself vilified by the press.

Brawley was found wrapped in a trash bag in Wappingers Falls, New York in 1987. Feces covered her body, which was marked with racist epithets scrawled in charcoal. Brawley alleged that white men, police officers among them, had held her captive for several days and sexually assaulted her.

Sharpton coordinated a series of dramatic demonstrations for this case. He appeared on the popular TV talk show, *Phil Donahue*, and at the church to which Brawley's mother, Glenda, had retreated for protection. There were suspicions of a cover-up by the cops. Brawley and her mother refused to answer questions, which further damaged their case.

As time passed, the press began to report that evidence of the actual attack was insubstantial. Some suspected foul play, that Brawley's story was concocted, and that Sharpton was an accomplice. Sharpton denied that, and to this day contends that he believed Brawley's account. The case did not come to trial.

When Stephen Pagones, Assistant District Attorney, was named as one of the attackers, he sued Sharpton and Brawley's legal team. Sharpton had to pay him $65,000. Sharpton opines that the bad publicity he received over this case was unjust and did not take account of all the good work he has done.

BENSONHURST (1989)

Sharpton received a call one summer morning in 1989 from the father of a recent murder victim. Yusef K. Hawkins was only sixteen years old when he and other black youths went to Bensonhurst looking to buy a used car. Bensonhurst is a neighborhood in Brooklyn, New York, and some of its residents were known to be hostile toward blacks. Hawkins and his friends were attacked. During the melee, Hawkins was shot and killed.

But it was almost two years before Sharpton could turn his attention to the racially motivated crime, for he had to attend to other serious business. In 1990, Sharpton was charged with tax evasion and embezzling money from the National Youth Movement. He was not surprised by the charges, for Brown tipped him off after he was questioned by authorities. Sharpton dramatized the case in vintage style: He did not hide from the cameras. Rather he used the media attention, shouting out "They did this to King! They did this to Powell! They did this to Garvey! This is my inauguration! I have arrived!" (Mallin, 79).

Indeed, by this time Sharpton was a celebrity of sorts. But authorities and city officials were not crazy about him. To many, he was a nuisance: starting racial fires and exposing issues they would rather have attended to privately or not at all. He was resented, and he was vulnerable to attack.

When it came time to plead before the judge, Sharpton quipped, "I plead the attorney general insane!" The prosecution called eighty witnesses. Sharpton called no one. At the end of two long months, he and his attorney believed that the prosecution's own witnesses strongly supported Sharpton's case, and indeed Sharpton was acquitted of the embezzlement charges. All that was required of him was to pay a fine for tax evasion.

With the charges behind him, Sharpton planned a march to bring attention to the murder of Hawkins. The march was held on the weekend prior to King's birthday, two years after the murder had occurred. At the march, Sharpton was stabbed. The perpetrator was apprehended, and Sharpton was hurried off to the hospital.

Sharpton was not the only activist to become the victim of violence. While in Harlem in 1958, King was stabbed in the chest by a deranged black woman during an innocuous book signing for the recently published *Strive toward Freedom*. And his assassination was one of many that occurred during the struggle for civil rights and the Black Power Movement. Sharpton faced the possibility of death with a stoicism common among activists. He told Jackson, who visited him at the hospital, "I think I'll be all right" (Sharpton, 196).

The stabbing bore unexpected fruit. First, Sharpton had to make a public statement to quell the riot that was on the brink of erupting as a result of the attack. Next, Jackson called Sharpton to see how he was doing. This was unexpected because Jackson and Sharpton were not as close as they once were. In fact, a rift had appeared between them when Sharpton aligned himself with proponents of black nationalism in the 1980s. Jackson had reprimanded Sharpton for taking this position. The nationalists opposed men like Jackson because he was a part of the legacy of "Dr. King's vision of integration" and they called him a "sellout" because of it (Sharpton, 193). When Jackson ran for U.S. president in 1984, Sharpton did not support him. But the stabbing created a space for reconciliation and new beginnings for the two men. It also initiated a new relationship with Sharpton's father, who also called him during his recovery. It was the first time they had spoken in twenty years.

After the stabbing, Sharpton rethought his association with the nationalists. Militancy had never been a part of Sharpton's agenda. And after having become a victim of violence and racial hatred, he wanted to distance himself from any appearance of that brand of radical activism. The nationalists saw the change in Sharpton's thinking and called him to task for it. They demanded that he end his relationships and affiliations with their rivals, but Sharpton did not submit to their demands.

NATIONAL ACTION NETWORK

The idea for a new organization came to Sharpton while in the hospital. He called it National Action Network. Through this organization, he planned to carry out full-time civil rights work and to launch a political career. For Sharpton, the 1990s unfolded with new challenges, more protest, and grand political strivings. His relationship with Jackson took another hit, as Sharpton was highly critical of Jackson's fraternization with President Bill Clinton. Sharpton believed that relationships with presidents would compromise his activism. Sharpton wrote that "you can't be Dr. King and Whitney

Young at the same time. You need both, but you can't be both" (Sharpton, 197, 198). Whitney Young was the successful leader of the National Urban League. Despite Sharpton's characterization of Young, he was among the first to attempt to wear two hats: as a leader in an organization that was not conceived as a civil rights organization and as a participant in the leadership of the major civil rights groups.

The Sharpton–Jackson relationship was green fodder for a voracious media. For example: Sharpton waged a boycott against Burger King for withdrawing from plans to build more franchises that would create jobs and bring money into the black communities. Jackson's criticisms of the boycott made the news, and so did the subsequent bickering between the two men. But their bond was never dissolved completely. In fact, in the early years of the new millennium they were united in many campaigns, sometimes coordinating their efforts, and sometimes working in parallel.

CROWN HEIGHTS (1991)

Sharpton and Jackson were not the only ones to experience bouts of contention. New York had an infamous Jewish–African American racial problem for years. Black leaders like Louis Farrakhan, the Nation of Islam minister who started and headed his own organization in 1977, was accused of being anti-Semitic because of controversial statements he made about Jews. Sharpton has also been lambasted for the same reason. In his book *Al on America,* he diverts attention away from himself by exposing the anti-Semitism of high-profile white leaders.

The genesis of this notorious issue is complicated. Some scholars spout that racism and religious differences are to blame. Cornell West, an African American scholar, joined another intellectual, a Jewish man named Michael Lerner, to duke out their differences and understanding of problematic relations between Jews and blacks. They present their strategies to improve the situation in *Jews and Blacks: A Dialogue on Race, Religion, and Culture in America* (1996). For example, they cite how both Jews and blacks have historically been oppressed and marginalized. In addition, a substantial number of Jews made contributions to the Civil Rights Movement. Some gave their lives. Nevertheless, tensions play out on the streets of New York City. In some black neighborhoods, Jews are not welcome, while in some Jewish neighborhoods, blacks are not welcome.

In 1991, a Hasidic Jew lost control of his car, hitting and killing a seven-year-old African American named Gavin Cato and injuring his cousin Angela. The racial makeup of the individuals involved played a role in the eruption that followed. Blacks attacked the driver of the car. Riots broke out. Tragically, Yankel Rosenbaum, a young Jewish man preparing to become a rabbi, was cornered and killed by a black mob. When Sharpton emerged on the scene at the behest of the parents of the slaughtered child and led a march, people blamed him for the violence.

In subsequent trials, both the Jewish driver and the black man accused of murdering Rosenbaum were acquitted. The Jewish community's reaction was to stage demonstrations. Nevertheless, the stalemate quite possibly staved off an even more explosive racial confrontation.

POLITICS: U.S. SENATE CAMPAIGN

By 1992, Sharpton was angling for greater influence and he had a new look to show for it. Sharpton's physical image projected a kindler, gentler version of his former self. For one thing he had slimmed down. For another, his hair, though still straight, is gray at the temples, neatly trimmed, and combed back and away from his face. He wears suits and ties almost exclusively, and the medallion he used to wear is nowhere to be seen. On camera he is dignified and, though still the master of the political quip, magnanimous. His speech is careful, even-handed, and polite.

His goal was to play a role that no African American in New York had ever played: he campaigned for U.S. Senate as a Democrat. Initially, "Many people thought his candidacy was a joke" (Mallin, 90). But his professionalism and the speech he gave at a convention made his critics, some of whom dwelt within the Democratic Party itself, do a double-take.

The campaign was conducted in a grassroots style, with not a lot of funds but lots of good old-fashioned mingling with ordinary people—mostly blacks—at housing projects and churches. Unlike traditional candidates, Sharpton did not have a graduate degree or a litany of political credentials. But he was well known and, especially among blacks, he was a hero. His campaign highlighted core issues such as inequities in the criminal justice system, unemployment, and housing. Sharpton did not win, but he did receive fifteen percent of the total vote and twenty-one percent of the vote in New York City alone. Sharpton ran again in 1994, but lost.

FREDDY'S FASHION MART (1995)

Sarpton's moment of political favor was overshadowed by controversy in 1995. Sharpton called for a boycott on Freddy's Fashion Mart in the fall after hearing several complaints. Sikhulu Shange, a South African, subleased a Record Shack from Freddy Harari, the owner of the Fashion Mart. Shange felt Harari was trying to push him out of his store, which had been situated near the Apollo Theater for some twenty years. Harari's employees reported to Sharpton that they were getting paid below minimum wage and that they worked in unsafe conditions. Sharpton was heavily criticized for using the term "white interloper" while discussing the situation. He later backpedaled on his erroneous use of the phrase, acknowledging that he had quite possibly brought adverse attention to himself because of it.

Sadly, a deranged black man, unaffiliated with Sharpton in any way, shot several Freddy employees, then started a fire that killed himself and seven others. Some accused Sharpton of having provoked that tragedy. Sharpton contended that "what that man did was an act brought on by his own mind" (Sharpton, 216).

ABNER LOUIMA (1997)

One of Sharpton's best-known campaigns on behalf of victims of police brutality was the case of a Haitian man named Abner Louima. Louima was thirty years old and had a wife and child at the time of his terrifying assault. Louima was one of several men who attempted to break up a fight between two women at a Brooklyn night club. The police were called and Louima was apprehended, charged with allegedly hitting an officer. The horrific night began when the cops preceded to beat Louima during his transportation to the police station. At the station, Louima was violently assaulted with a plunger in the bathroom by an officer. The resulting injuries required several operations and a two-month hospital stay.

At first, Justin Volpe, the officer who brutalized Louima in the men's restroom, denied what he had done, even though Louima's injuries were irrefutable. In 1999, Volpe was sentenced to 30 years in prison without parole.

In the aftermath of the case, Louima joined Sharpton in his activism against police brutality. He set up community centers in Haiti and America to provide resources for Haitians in both countries. Louima turned tragedy into an opportunity to help others and to protect citizens from police tyranny.

AMADOU DIALLO (1999)

Sharpton responded to a call for help from a man who told him he was the leader of the Guinean National Association. He came to Sharpton's office on behalf of twenty-three-year-old Amadou Diallo, whom, he explained, had been shot at forty times by four police officers, resulting in Diallo's death. At first Sharpton was skeptical, but eventually he ordered an investigation at the man's persistence.

After some fact-finding, Sharpton uncovered the shocking truth: Diallo was indeed an innocent victim. Many blacks claimed racial profiling was partly to blame for this incident, for when plainclothes officers approached Diallo they thought he fit the description of a serial rapist. But they were wrong. Diallo was a hard-working college student who sold an assortment of items on the street by day and studied biochemistry in the evenings. During a tense moment, Diallo reached into his pocket to retrieve his wallet. But the officers thought he was retrieving a gun, and he was pelted with gunfire.

Sharpton unleashed a storm of protest in New York City. Jesse Jackson and actress Susan Sarandon, supported by various politicians, rabbis, and clergy, joined in the chorus. The negative press prompted the trial to be transferred to another city. All four officers were acquitted, but the parents who survived Diallo received one of the largest settlements ever paid out by the City of New York for their son's wrongful death.

VIEQUES (2001)

A large contingent of Puerto Ricans had rallied behind Sharpton during the Diallo Case. In 2001, Sharpton felt compelled to support Puerto Ricans who were outraged because the United States. was testing bombs on Vieques Island. Sharpton constructed a plan similar to the one he had used to protest Diallo's killing. He wrote that this protest strategy—maintaining a steady flow of demonstrators despite arrests—was a good one.

When it came to arrests, Sharpton was by this time a veteran. But he did not anticipate that his incarceration for trespassing on the island would last so long. His sentence was for ninety days. For forty of those days, Sharpton fasted. A forty-day fast is symbolic, for the Biblical Jesus Christ did the same when he went into the wilderness to be tempted by the devil. Once Christ overcame the devil, he entered his ministry, calling sinners to repent and be baptized.

Fasting is practiced by individuals of many religious faiths and denominations. It is considered a time for contemplation, meditation, and preparation, especially for seasons of extreme duress. Sharpton usually fasted whenever he went to jail. He said "it helps me to focus and strengthens my resolve and my faith" (Sharpton, 161). The fasting that he underwent this time had another purpose: it was a hunger strike.

The ninety days was a grueling experience for Sharpton, who was isolated from the world, his friends, his work, and even from other prisoners. Sharpton was subdued and indrawn. This was, he later recalled, a poignant and life-changing experience. He meditated deeply on the books he read, such as Nelson Mandela's *Long Walk to Freedom* and the autobiography of Dr. Martin Luther King, Jr. After he completed his ninety-day sentence, he emerged "a more focused, more disciplined person—like a soldier going through boot camp. It was a test, a test to see how much I could take…. And I passed" (Sharpton, xiv, xv).

He emerged ready to get back to work. A week after his release, on August 17, 2001, he endorsed the New York mayoral candidate, Freddy Ferrer. Sharpton himself had run for mayor unsuccessfully in 1997, and contemplated another run before participating in the Vieques campaign. Instead, he campaigned for Ferrer. In fact, Sharpton explained, all four candidates sought his support, underscoring the fact that he carried some serious weight in the community.

On September 11, 2001, a world-shaking event occurred in New York, Washington, D.C., and Pennsylvania. Two planes flew into the World Trade Center in New York, causing them to crash in a plume of smoke to the ground. An investigation discovered that Al-Qaeda terrorists had hijacked a total of four planes. The third plane crashed into the Pentagon. The crew and passengers of the fourth plane, alerted to the gravity of the situation, attacked the cockpit, and the plane subsequently crashed into an empty field in Somerset County, Pennsylvania. Nearly 3,000 people died that day.

Sharpton placed a temporary hold on the mayoral campaign and turned his attention to assisting any way he could in the nation's hour of shock, terror, and mourning. One of his contributions was to start a counseling program to help surviving victims and loved ones pick up the pieces of their lives.

The mayoral campaign took a drastic turn: Ferrer had to step out, and Mark Green took the lead. Sharpton was under a lot of pressure to endorse Green, but he refused to do so, because Green had previously publicly denied that he had asked for Sharpton's endorsement. Sharpton charged him with race-baiting. In the end, Michael Bloomberg won the race that year. Sharpton was disappointed by the fact that blacks in New York City experienced very little progress in the ensuing years.

The Ousmane Zongo case in 2002 was a case in point. Zongo, a Burkinabe immigrant, was shot and killed during a raid at a storage facility that had nothing to do with him. He had kept an artist's studio at the facility, which was under police surveillance as a CD and DVD pirating operation. Prosecutors believed that when Zongo ran, he was frightened and did not realize that the man who chased after him was an undercover cop. He was shot twice in the back during the pursuit. Sharpton launched several protests and helped Zongo's family win monetary remuneration. The officer responsible for killing Zongo lost his job but did not serve any jail time.

POLITICS: RUN FOR THE U.S. PRESIDENCY (2004)

When Sharpton sat down to write *Al on America* (2002), his focus was on explaining his life's work, defending himself from his harsh critics, and making a strong case for his run for U.S. president. Sharpton did not win, but he presented himself to the nation as one who had been made over.

During the campaign, Sharpton appeared more conservative than before. His look had been a work in progress since the 1990s. But in the new millennium Sharpton projected a sense of sophistication. But criticism of his life and work remained as biting as ever. Indeed, thanks to the emergence of the Internet, where individuals are able to post blogs and comments and responses to articles at will and ad nauseum, the criticism actually increased. Sharpton has been a favorite target.

In an article by Jeff Jacoby titled "Al Sharpton: The Democrat's David Duke," Sharpton is depicted as a liberal version of Duke, a white nationalist and former politician and Grand Wizard of the infamous Ku Klux Klan. Jacoby peered back to Sharpton's past exploits to point out actions he considered racist.

However, the general public took Sharpton seriously during his 2004 run for president. His speeches impressed, although he was not elected. Following the election, Sharpton announced that he and his wife were separating. For some years, they had been growing apart but agreed to stay together until their children had grown.

In 2006, Sharpton and Jackson provided highly visible support for a black stripper who alleged that three white members of the Duke University lacrosse team raped her. In 2007, the charges were dropped against the three accused Duke students due to lack of substantial evidence and several inconsistencies, and the white district attorney who had brought the charges was fired and disbarred. Dennis Prager wrote in a Townhall.com article that "any time Al Sharpton and Jesse Jackson get in front of cameras on a race matter, assume that they are there to inflame, not heal" (Prager).

THE N-WORD

To Sharpton the N-word is never okay, whether a white or a black uses it. A torrent of debate surrounds the racist term "nigger." It appears that the same number of blacks support its use as those who vehemently oppose it. Black leaders have been polarized over this issue. Dick Gregory, a comedian and civil rights activist, contends that as long as an individual does not allow himself to be defined by the term then its intended effect is stripped of its power. Others argue that when blacks use the word, or call each other *nigga* rather than *nigger*, its meaning is innocuous and can even be interpreted in some conversations to be a term of endearment.

Sharpton does not agree. He has made it a point to attack the hip-hop community for glamorizing the word and a series of epithets that demean women. In 2006, he castigated comedian and actor Michael Richards when his comedy routine took a sudden and shocking racial turn when he used the word "nigger" when confronting black hecklers in the audience. Sharpton worried that the fact that Richards used the N-word indicated deeper, scarier racial issues.

In the same year, the Cartoon Network declined an apology when Sharpton asked for one after an episode of "The Boondocks" showed an animated Martin Luther King, Jr. using the N-word. Sharpton thought that was an extremely undignified way to portray King.

According to black journalist Earl Ofari Hutchinson, Sharpton's crusades are valid. He writes: "Sharpton is a breathing, walking, reminder that race still matters and matters a lot in America. He is a slap in the face to the

Sharp Talk with Al Sharpton

Sharp Talk with Al Sharpton is a half-hour television series that appears on TV One, a cable television station that features African American programs and films. Sharpton's talk show debuted on October 28, 2005, and includes an all-black cast, with Al Sharpton, as host, and several guests. What makes this talk show different is that the discussions are held inside a barbershop, specifically Levels Barbershop in Brooklyn, New York. Sharpton and his guests sit in barber chairs, and in the background barbers are attending to clients.

The significance of this setting is that, historically, black barbershops were one of the few safe places available for black men to openly discuss a range of issues concerning politics, economics, and culture as well to exchange local gossip. In this space, male friendships were developed and frustrations over shared social experiences expressed. Many of these conversations would be considered scandalous or treacherous in a public setting. Topics related to racism or problematic race relations in ordinary life might never have been discussed in the presence of whites or in the context of mainstream life.

The movie *Barbershop* (2002), directed by Tim Story and produced by State Street pictures, illustrates this situation all too well. Al Sharpton and Jesse Jackson were outraged over one scene, in which, following an argument over Rosa Parks' relevancy, a derogatory remark is made about Jackson. Sharpton and Jackson led a boycott and then demanded that the scene be cut, to no avail.

In the spirit of the traditional black barbershop gathering, Sharpton has created a groundbreaking series. He brings in black leaders from across the nation, who represent a broad range of fields and professions, as well as prominent activists and celebrities. The discussions focus on issues relevant to African Americans. As host, Sharpton is generally generous, polite, and tolerant of his guests' myriad perspectives.

legions that duck, dodge, deflect, and flat out deny that there's still a lot of racial hurt inflicted on blacks" (Hutchinson).

The first decade of the twenty-first century has been a minefield of public racial slurs. In 2007, Don Imus referred to members of a girl's basketball team as "nappy-headed hos." Historically, the term "nappy" bears negative connotations for blacks: it is a term to describe the coarse texture of black hair. "Ho," a slang term for "whore," has permeated pop culture due to hip-hop lyrics.

Sharpton was not the only one to criticize Imus or Kelly Tilghman when, in 2008, she commented in a joking way that fellow players should lynch Tiger Woods, the biracial golf star, as the only way to stop him from winning. That Imus was fired and Tilghman was suspended ruffled the feathers of conservative whites, who either downplayed the statements that were made, justified them, or vilified Sharpton.

Blacks have always tended to be Sharpton's most loyal fans, but upon occasion they have objected to his campaigns. In the 2007 Dunbar Village scandal, wherein a horrific crime was carried out against a black resident of the Dunbar Village projects and her son, blacks were at the forefront of those attacking Sharpton for defending the perpetrators.

In 2008, the tide turned again for Sharpton, who took a stand for justice after the death of Sean Bell, shot by officers of the New York City Police Force as he was leaving a strip club where he been celebrating his bachelor party. The officers had been at the club investigating a possible prostitution ring. The three officers were cleared of wrongdoing. Blacks who witnessed the verdict shouted out in anger and disbelief. Sharpton, who represented the Bell family, declared that he wanted a federal investigation. Other civil rights leaders told reporters that there would be marches through the streets of New York in protest. Sharpton was again seen as an invaluable defender of the downtrodden.

On October 3, 2008, Sharpton turned fifty-four years old. He remains a tireless advocate for justice and keeps in-tune with the times with his radio Talk Show, *Keepin' It Real,* and his television show, *Sharp Talk with Al Sharpton*, which premiered on the black television network TV One in 2005. Sharpton is still in high demand on mainstream talk shows and on the news. His presence, whether negative or positive, illuminates the challenges that continue to beset African Americans in the new millennium.

See also Stokely Carmichael; Louis Farrakhan; Marcus Garvey; Jesse Jackson; Martin Luther King, Jr.; Malcolm X; and Whitney Young.

FURTHER RESOURCES

Hutchinson, Earl Ofari. "Why Al Sharpton Is the Man Millions Love to Hate." *The Huffington Post* (January 2008). See http://www.huffingtonpost.com/earl-ofari-hutchinson/why-al-sharpton-is-the-ma_b_73715.html.

Jacoby, Jeff. "Al Sharpton: The Democrat's David Duke." *Capitalism Magazine* (January 2008). See http://www.capmag.com/articlePrint.asp?ID=2411.

Mallin, Jay. *Al Sharpton: Community Activist.* New York: Franklin Watts, 2007.

National Action Network (January 2008). See http://www.nationalactionnetwork.net.

Prager, Dennis. "Duke Lacrosse Scandal: Eight Lessons." *Townhall.com* (January 2008). See http://www.realclearpolitics.com/articles/2007/04/duke_lacrosse_scandal_eight_le.html.

Sharpton, Al. *Al on America.* New York: Kensington Publishing, 2002.

Ida B. Wells-Barnett (1862–1931)

Ida B. Wells-Barnett lived an extraordinary life of protest against segregation, discrimination, racism, and racial violence against African Americans. Her claim to fame was her leading the way in the fight against lynching. She was a journalist, lecturer, suffragist, and social reformer, as well as wife and mother to four children. Both her life of activism and her personal life were revolutionary in that Wells-Barnett frequently challenged societal norms and the expectations of other activists, the ramifications of which provoked a torrent of criticism.

Wells-Barnett's activism was especially valiant considering she was an African American and a woman in a world that granted few privileges, rights, or freedoms to her race or gender and the fact that she often fought alone without the support or involvement of her colleagues, community, or the thriving organizations of the period. Late in Wells-Barnett's life, her achievements were minimized, overlooked, and, ultimately, shrouded by a conservative and male-dominated organizational leadership. Those who sang their loudest praise on Wells-Barnett's behalf, particularly in the years leading to her death in 1931, were African American women of the women's club movement. Subsequent recognition was lacking, and the memory of Wells-Barnett was fast becoming obsolete until her life and heroism began to be lionized in a number of publications and articles. Contemporary scholars such as John Hope Franklin, Henry Louis Gates, Jr., and Cornel West were among those whose works restored Wells-Barnett to her rightful position as a twentieth-century icon of African American protest.

EARLY LIFE

Ida Bell Wells, the oldest of eight children, was born a slave on July 16, 1862, in Holly Springs, Mississippi. This was just two years before the end of the Civil War and the subsequent liberation of millions of African American slaves in the American South. Wells' father was Jim Wells, who was apparently the only child of a white plantation owner in Tippah County, Mississippi and his slave, Peggy. As was sometimes the custom during slavery, Jim's father, the "master" of the plantation, spared him, to a great extent, the harsh cruelties and indignities of slavery and permitted him privileges denied the majority of African Americans. When Jim turned eighteen, his father apprenticed him to a Mr. Bolling, a carpenter in Holly Springs. Some slave masters even sent their mulatto children to colleges and universities in the North.

Wells' mother, Elizabeth Warrenton, was born in Virginia but was separated from her family when she was sold into slavery. Like many slaves, Wells' mother did not know much about her ancestry, except that her father was of mixed heritage: Indian and African. Once in America, African tribal identification was all but obliterated. Whites not only forbade slaves from speaking their native languages and practicing their diverse religions and traditions but rarely kept record of family lineage.

Elizabeth, undoubtedly, met her future husband while serving as a cook for Mr. Bolling. Elizabeth was a well-renowned cook, and Wells was proud of that fact. But her mother would not live a long life. She died before she was forty years old. She made a lasting impression on Wells, who recollected how her mother was very religious and provided a good home for herself and her siblings. She was disciplined, strict, and like most slave parents, she encouraged the education of her children. Elizabeth even went to school with the children at what was known as Shaw University, later called Rust College. In those days, the "university" was a school for recently manumitted African Americans of all ages, taught primarily by white teachers who stressed reading and moral conduct.

Wells was brought up in a house built and owned by her father, who was an expert carpenter. The vast majority of African Americans in this period were severely impoverished, but prosperous African Americans were not altogether a novelty. Small pockets of African Americans with money, property, education, and standing existed in both the North and South during and after slavery. A number of African Americans helped construct and develop vibrant all-black towns in the West following emancipation. However, Wells was not completely sheltered from the oppression that afflicted the majority of African Americans during this period.

Wells learned through her parents the horrors of slavery and the consequences of overstepping the color line. Ida B. Wells described her father as a man active in the political affairs of their small town. She became aware of the dangers associated with such activism early on, recalling that "mother walked the floor at night when [her] father was out to a political meeting" for fear of white retaliation (Wells, 9). Many whites and African Americans lost their lives advocating rights for freed slaves. As a child, Wells admitted she had "heard the words Ku Klux Klan long before [she] knew what they meant" (Wells, 9). And the very words conjured fear. Wells herself would learn about racial violence in the not-too-distant future.

In 1878, yellow fever devastated a large segment of the population in Memphis, Tennessee. The epidemic spread to Wells' hometown while she was away visiting her grandmother in the country. When she learned that her parents and youngest brother, Stanley, not even a year old, had died from the disease, the young Wells returned to Holly Springs to go to the aid of her surviving siblings in spite of the threat to her own life. The Masons (friends of her father, who had been a master Mason), decided that the surviving children should be split up and sent to different homes.

Wells could not bear to see the family torn apart, and so at only sixteen years of age, she protested "that [the Masons] were not going to put any of the children anywhere" and "that it would make [her] father and mother turn over in their graves to know their children had been scattered like that," and she went on to say "that [they] owned the house and if the Masons would help [her] find work, [she] would take care of them" (Wells, 9). There was no yielding with Wells. Eventually, they agreed, and Wells' family stayed together.

The Masons suggested she become a teacher. Teaching was one of the few avenues available for African American women (being a domestic was another). Although Wells had no particular aspiration to be a teacher, she entered the profession for the sake of her family, thus relinquishing plans to further her own education. Wells never did receive a formal academic degree, but she devoted all her spare time to learning.

Wells took a teaching job six miles away from their home. Her monthly salary was $25. At first, Wells and her family were assisted by their grandmother until she suffered a stroke and was forced to return home. Wells received some support from the community, but it did not completely lighten her load. Wells led a rigorous life of teaching every weekday and "washing and ironing and cooking for the children" every weekend (Wells, 17). At the end of the first term, Wells' Aunt Belle (her mother's sister) asked her to move to Memphis, Tennessee. She offered to take Eugenia, the paralyzed sister, and to allow the two brothers to work on her farm. Wells accepted this invitation and happily left the one-room school in the country. She took a teaching job located in Memphis, Tennessee.

New South Memphis presented an exciting new world for African Americans. Henry W. Grady, editor of the *Atlanta Constitution*, coined the term "New South" to refer to the new and improved social and economic developments of the South since the Civil War (1861–1865) dismantled its formerly slave-based economy. The city, in particular, provided more and better opportunities than the country for progressive, optimistic young professionals. Wells looked forward to the change of scenery, the faster pace of life, and the significant increase in pay that came with her new job. However, her optimism was soon to be tested.

Refusing a Seat on a Segregated Train

Shortly after Ida B. Wells arrived in Memphis in 1884, she engaged in her first public fight against segregation. Ironically, Wells literally fought for her rightful equal status with whites while traveling on a train. In the following excerpt from "Hard Beginnings," the second chapter of Wells' autobiography, she recounts what happened when she refused to sit in a segregated car:

> [The conductor] tried to drag me out of the seat, but the moment he caught hold of my arm I fastened my teeth in the back of his hand. I had braced my feet against the seat in front and was holding to the back, and as he had already been badly bitten he didn't try it again by himself. He went forward and got the baggageman and another man to help him and of course they succeeded in dragging me out. (Wells, 19)

Wells went on to say that the white women and men on the train applauded the men who tried to violently force her back to the "black-only" section. Rather than succumb, Wells opted to get off the train. Segregation on trains was just the first of a series of deliberate legal actions used to undo the civil rights of African Americans following emancipation and to usher in the era of Jim Crow.

Wells was quick to seek justice. She obtained an attorney, who helped her to win $500 for damages inflicted upon her during the ordeal. Wells pointed out that "none of [her] people seemed to feel that it was a race matter and that they should help [her] fight" (Wells, 21). Although Wells' case was eventually reversed, and she was ordered to pay court costs, she proved that she was willing to fight against any entity, no matter how powerful, for the cause of justice. And she would do it alone, if necessary.

Wells' action against the railroad garnered a great deal of attention—and a divided response—from the community and the nation. The *Memphis Daily Appeal*, mirroring the prevalent racist sentiment of the time, referred to Wells as a "Darky Damsel" in a headline of its December 25, 1884 edition. Other southern whites were indignant. Although Wells stood alone in this fight, many African Americans lauded her protest against the railroad. In Wells' words, this was "the first case in which a colored plaintiff in the South had appealed to a state court since the repeal of the Civil Rights Bill by the United States Supreme Court," and her "success … would have set a precedent which others would doubtless have followed" (Wells, 20).

Preparing for Activism

Despite losing her case to the railroad, Wells' experience in Tennessee was a turning point in the development of her lifelong activism, as well as in her personal life. Wells' social life flourished in Tennessee. Although she did not like teaching, it did facilitate her entrance into the elite world of the black society. Wells wrote fondly in her diary and autobiography of "socials, picnics, church fairs, receptions, surprise parties, moonlight walks, and 'entertainment for young ladies'" (Decosta-Willis, 6). She had a great interest in the theater, fiction, poetry, writing, shopping, and being in the company of potential suitors and male friends, and continued her education with elocution lessons and other studies. Wells also contended with the day-to-day struggles commonly faced by single young women of her class, whether African American or white. Wells frequently wrote of having financial troubles—paying the rent, providing money for her siblings, and managing her expensive shopping habit and various social activities—and her romantic struggles and disappointments.

Wells, until her death, subscribed to the ideals of polite behavior, virtuous qualities, and religious teaching. But though she appeared similar to most "genteel" women of her era, she broke away from the track of becoming wife and mother to explore areas traditionally closed to women. She challenged the traditional concept of womanhood, despite the repercussions of this "rebelliousness." Beginning in early adulthood, Wells often battled with herself to suppress her anger and outspokenness—two characteristics society deemed inappropriate for women but which proved essential to her radical activism.

Another dilemma Wells had to deal with was her single status. While most women her age were planning their weddings, Wells remained unmarried. Her diary and autobiography reflect several reasons for this. On the one hand, she simply enjoyed spending time with men and the occasional courtship. But she had no desire to settle down. On the other, she did not seem to have found anyone to compel her to accept the marriage proposals she received. Nor did she feel that she had the right attributes for marriage. So she pursued a career instead. Choosing to be single was in itself unconventional for women at that time.

Wells was not entirely alone in this area. Other women were making historical strides in traditional male occupations such as literature, journalism, medicine, and activism and turning down marriage. Nevertheless, men dominated most occupations and positions of leadership, while the majority of women continued to pursue marriage and motherhood. On the eve of the twentieth century, women who abnegated their expected roles or took male-dominated jobs stirred controversy. This was as true for African Americans as it was for whites. However, Wells was eagerly welcomed into the relatively uncharted world of African American male journalists. Her transition was facilitated in part by Wells' independent, adventurous, and fearless spirit, her ease in associating with men who had been throughout her young adult life her companions and mentors, and her passion for writing.

Wells fell into journalism while attending Lyceum meetings. In the 1870s and 1880s, middle- and upper-class whites and African Americans popularized the club and society movement. Both men and women started up clubs and societies for the purposes of discussing literature, music, culture, and religion, or social issues. The Lyceum was made up of mostly teachers who spent their time in meetings, reading books, debating, discussing local and world news, and listening to music. The Lyceum published the *Evening Star*. When the editor of the Lyceum magazine moved away, Wells was elected to take his place, and her success attracted the attention of others. Reverend R.N. Countee, a Baptist preacher, also published a weekly called the *Living Way*. He requested that Wells make contributions to his publication. Wells accepted his offer and a number of ensuing invitations that came her way. Her career as a journalist was established.

Although she had no formal training in writing and humbly noted that she had "no literary gifts and graces," Wells was regularly praised for her articles (Wells, 23). Wells did recognize that she had keen observational and critical-thinking skills and an innate sense for the importance of the written word in terms of empowering African Americans of all walks of life, particularly those who had no education. She wanted her articles to be accessible to people with little or no education, so she purposely "wrote in a plain, common-sense way on the things which concerned our people" (Wells, 24). She used the pen name, "Iola," for these articles.

Journalism helped to expand Wells' understanding of the world and to sharpen her commentary on the social situation of African Americans as well as the philosophy of activism she maintained for most of her life. As in her private life, Wells was unguarded and straightforward in her articulation of her thoughts. In the article, "Functions of Leadership," published in the *Living Way* in 1885, Wells criticized well-known African American leaders for their failure to respond to the needs of African Americans without money, prestige, and opportunity. She asserted that it was the responsibility of the African American leader to, "to some extent, devote his time, talent, and wealth to the alleviation of poverty and misery, and elevation of his people" (Decosta-Willis, 179). Wells consistently acted upon this belief, and as a result, she rarely took a break from some form of activism until the day she died.

In the summer of 1886, when Wells was twenty-four years old, she was briefly pulled in a direction that threatened to stifle her socially, emotionally, and professionally. Wells' aunt moved to Visalia, California and persuaded Wells to join her. Wells arrived, writing articles about her trip to the West along the way. She took a teaching job in an all-black classroom, noting in her autobiography her disappointment that African Americans insisted upon segregated schooling. Wells was unhappy on the western frontier, mostly because she was isolated from a substantial African American community and the lively pulse of city life. After moving to Kansas City, Missouri for a brief teaching stint, Wells, along with one of her four siblings, returned to Tennessee in the fall of 1886.

Wells returned to teaching upon her return to Memphis. Her antipathy towards the profession grew daily, but newspaper writing brought her much joy. During this same time, Wells accepted an invitation from a Reverend William J. Simmons, D.D., to be a paid correspondent to his Negro Press Association. She attended several press conventions, where great leaders of the day such as Frederick Douglass, Bishop Henry McNeil Turner, and Senator Blanche Kelso Bruce were in attendance. All three remain legends of American history.

Frederick Douglass became famous after the publication of his autobiography, *Narrative of the Life of Frederick Douglass, an American Slave* (1845). Douglass escaped slavery with the help of white abolitionists when he was twenty years old, quickly rising to become a prominent abolitionist and orator. Born free, Henry McNeil Turner was the first African American chaplain in the Union Army during the Civil War (1861–1865). In 1880, he was elected a bishop in the African Methodist Episcopal Church. He was elected to the Georgia Legislature in 1868. However, shortly thereafter, conservative whites passed a bill prohibiting blacks from holding political offices. Turner was a radical to the fullest, blasting criticisms of racist whites, as well as proclaiming to his congregation that God was black and advocating that African Americans return to Africa. Blanche Kelso Bruce, a former slave, served the U.S. Senate from 1875 to 1881. He was the first African American to serve a full term in the Senate.

In 1889, Wells was elected secretary to the National Press Association and invited to write for a large number of African American publications. Her success and popularity as a writer was noted by several leading African American publishers, editors, and leaders.

In the same year, Wells became writer, editor, and one third owner of the *Free Speech and Headlight*. Wells continued to teach until she published a controversial article about conditions in African American schools in Memphis. Wells described this article as "a protest against the few and utterly inadequate buildings for colored children," and the "poor teachers given us, whose mental and moral character was not the best" (Wells, 36). As a result of this article, she was fired. This was in 1891. Wells was not surprised. Nevertheless, she was disappointed, particularly because the parents did not show her any support and felt Wells should have refrained from her protests to keep her job. The tenacious Wells had no regrets.

Losing her teaching job was not a great disappointment to Wells. She taught primarily to make a living, while she pursued writing—her true passion—in her spare time. When her teaching career was taken away from her, Wells was compelled to try her hand at writing full-time. She traveled the South and happily immersed herself in writing and in garnering money and support for the *Free Speech*. She received an enormous amount of support from African American communities, organizations, churches, and associations. She was often "treated like a queen," not only because she was the editor of a successful paper, a fellow Mississippian, and the daughter of a reputable master Mason, but because being a woman who was also a journalist was considered a "novelty," not a handicap (Wells, 41, 42). Wells envisioned a comfortable and satisfying writing career. She could not foresee the horrific descent into racial violence that would jolt Memphis, Tennessee during her absence, a descent that would propel Wells into a life of activism.

ANTI-LYNCHING CRUSADE

In 1892, a fight broke out between African American and white youths during a game of marbles in Memphis, Tennessee. This incident triggered what Wells described as an opportunity for the owners of a local white-owned store to make an attack against the owners of its competition, an African American–owned store called the People's Grocery Company. The owners of the black store were Thomas Moss, Calvin McDowell, and Henry Stewart. Moss was a close friend of Wells, who was godmother to his daughter. The owners of the People's Grocery consulted an attorney who affirmed their right to arm themselves in self-defense. Several African American men guarded the store on the night of the rumored attack. When whites fired shots, the armed men shot back, wounding three of the white men. In the aftermath, Moss, McDowell, and Stewart were jailed. A number of African Americans guarded the jail to thwart off any attempts to harm the imprisoned men, but they went home when it was believed the threat had passed. On March 9, 1892, a white mob broke into the jail, carried out Moss, McDowell, and Stewart, and shot them despite their pleas for mercy.

The lynching (a term used to refer to any form of execution without due process of law) of Moss, McDowell, and Stewart was the antecedent to Wells' illustrious anti-lynching campaign, which coincided with the beginning of the Progressive Era. Wells heard the news while she was away canvassing for the *Free Speech*. When she returned to Tennessee, she immediately purchased a gun, "because [she] expected retaliation from the lynchers" and "felt that one had better die fighting against injustice than to die like a dog or a rat in a trap" (Wells, 62). She then wrote an article in her paper lambasting the lynchers for using violence to suppress African American advancement. She also launched an investigation into lynching and uncovered the fact that the majority of the allegations that the African American men lynched had committed a crime against a white woman were false. Such allegations were concocted for various reasons—in the case of Moss, McDowell, and Stewart, to impose white supremacy and thwart black economic progress. In one of her editorials, Wells bravely reported that "nobody in this section believes the old thread-bare lie that Negro men assault white women. If Southern white men are not careful they will over-reach themselves and a conclusion will be reached which will be very damaging to the moral reputation of their women" (Wells, 65, 66). Wells later pointed out that white men had long abused African American women with impunity, and that it was common knowledge that some white women pursued African American men. When African Americans refused their advances, ended the relationship, or a pregnancy occurred, white women accused their lovers of rape. The notion that white women and African American men could be in consensual sexual relationships was unimaginable to southern white men. It blotted the image of pure and chaste southern womanhood.

Wells did more than write scorching editorials on lynching; she wrote in support of the economic boycott and migration of local African Americans (which occurred in response to the lynching). A group of white men came to her to ask her to discourage both boycott and migration, but she refused to do so. Wells followed up this meeting with an article praising African Americans for their work and insisting that they keep it up. Wells also traveled to Oklahoma, one of the principle locations of the migration, and wrote several articles on the conditions there in an effort to quash embellished stories

Lynching Epidemic

The lynching epidemic refers to the overwhelming number of African Americans murdered, through hanging or other insidious means, during the late nineteenth and early twentieth centuries.

After the South lost to the Union in the Civil War (1861–1865) and black slaves were freed, white southerners resorted to violence, intimidation, and terror tactics to maintain order and supremacy over blacks. Between 1885 and 1942, in Texas alone, it is claimed that 339 blacks were murdered by lynching. Other victims included seventy-seven whites, fifty-three Hispanics, and one Native American. Most black victims were male. Between 1882 and 1930, there were 462 lynchings in Mississippi, 423 in Georgia, and 283 in Louisiana.

Although racism was at the heart of the majority of these killings, whites often claimed that they were carried out because of the "rape" of white women. During this period, the idea of romantic relations between white women and black men was a source of deep paranoia in the Southern white community. By accusing a black man of rape, whites were able to compel others in the community to form a mob and launch a terror campaign against the targeted person. Other blacks were targeted for violating Jim Crow customs and laws, as well as for exhibiting material success.

A lynching incident was often conducted like a sensational social event. Often times, the media reported on an upcoming lynching as if advertising a carnival. Hundreds, including white men, women, and children, might attend a single lynching. Families came from miles around to attend one. During a lynching, the victim could be hung or burned alive. Many times trophies—dismembered parts of the victim—were distributed among the crowd or displayed in town. Other lynchings were spontaneous, often occurring at the hands of a white mob or an organization like the Ku Klux Klan.

Because law officials often took part in the lynching, there was no one blacks could turn to for help. Ida B. Wells-Barnett was a pioneer of the anti-lynching campaign. Her work was followed by several organizations, most notably the National Association for the Advancement of Colored People. Efforts to stop lynching did not produce dramatic results as liberal politicians refused for years to pass federal anti-lynching laws. However, the campaigns helped to expose the atrocities, whereas previously, lynchings had proceeded unchecked. The lynchings waned at the start of the 1940s.

published by white newspapers to discourage black migration. During this time, the owners of the *Free Speech* decided that they would not keep the paper in Memphis, forcing Wells to consider where she should go.

In May 1892, Wells went to the A.M.E. General conference in Philadelphia at the urging of Frances Watkins Harper and the fiery Bishop Henry McNeil Turner. She then went to New York at the invitation of Thomas Fortune. While in New York, Wells discovered that a white mob had destroyed the offices of the *Free Speech* and threatened to kill her if she ever returned to Memphis. The destruction of the *Free Speech* came shortly after the *Commercial Appeal* reprinted the article in which Wells alluded to the questionable "moral reputation" of the white women who white men claimed were the victims of rape and then "called on the chivalrous white men of Memphis to do something to avenge this insult to the honor of their women" (Wells, 66).

But this attack did not silence Wells. She accepted Fortune's offer and became part owner and regular paid contributor to the *New York Age*. Wells frequently credited Fortune, as well as Jerome B. Peterson, who owned and edited this widely read paper, with giving her a platform upon which to speak. She asserted that "had it not been for the courage and vision of these two men, I could never have made such headway in emblazoning the story to the world" (Wells, 63). Thus, Wells continued her bold, uncensored, and shrewd attack on lynching. She regularly reported statistics on the multiple lynchings that occurred throughout the nation. She was the first journalist—African American or white—to protest lynching.

Wells, unlike the reporters for the southern papers who in many instances instigated or sustained the culture of lynching with their sensationalism and racist bent, relied upon facts for her articles. She changed her pen name from "Iola," to "Exiled"—a name that signified Wells' forced departure from her home in Memphis, Tennessee. Wells' work caught the attention of thousands in the South, including famed African American abolitionist Frederick Douglass. Throughout the few remaining years of his life, Douglass was a mentor, friend, and staunch supporter of Wells.

Wells' work also captured the interest of two African American socialites, Victoria Earle Matthews and Maritcha Lyons, who were responsible for coordinating Wells' first speaking engagement. This occurred in New York before a hall filled with African American women on October 5, 1892. The lecture was a success, though Wells admitted in her autobiography that she was so nervous that she read her speech, instead of improvising the events that led her to leave Memphis. She was mortified that she let her guard down and cried during her presentation. The tears were the result of her recollecting the pain of leaving her friends and loved ones. But her audience was mesmerized and all-the-more sympathetic to her cause because of it. Wells was adamant that she not give in to the emotion of her experience

ever again, and she never did. Future critics responded favorably to her im-
passive and poised locution.

Progressive Era

The Progressive Era is the period of reform that occurred from the 1890s to
1920s. The individuals who led this movement consisted mainly of middle-
class whites who lived in the nation's cities. One of the main criticisms of the
Progressive Era was that African Americans were largely neglected.

The Progressive Era spanned one of the most difficult times for blacks in
America. Rayford Logan, a black scholar, coined the term "nadir" to describe
these harrowing years. The nadir spanned from 1877 to 1901, but life for
blacks did not improve much in the early years of the twentieth century. The
nadir was marked by extreme poverty and anti-black violence in the form of
race riots and lynchings, disfranchisement, and discriminatory laws known as
Jim Crow. While whites tackled alcohol use, workers' rights, corruption in
business and politics, and prostitution, black issues remained invisible.

It took the African Americans themselves to make the move toward uplifting their community and to address the larger issues of Jim Crow and disfranchisement. Blacks who made critical contributions or at least valiant
attempts to alleviate the overwhelming social, economic, and political problems of blacks included women's organizations (like the National Association
of Colored Women in 1896) and a score of individuals (like Ida B. Wells-Barnett). Two major organizations were formed during these years, the National
Association for the Advancement of Colored People (NAACP) in 1909, and
the National Urban League (NUL) in 1911. The NAACP addressed broad
issues, working to expose lynchings in the South and launching legal campaigns to undo discriminatory laws. The NUL worked to employ blacks living
in urban centers. This was no small feat, as racism in the North frequently
closed the door on opportunities for blacks. For example, a number of
department stores and other companies simply did not hire blacks until the
NUL got involved. The NUL made sweeping strides in that respect.

The outcome of Wells' first presentation was profound. Not only was she
awarded a pen-shaped gold brooch and $500 to go toward a new newspa-
per to replace the one she lost at the hands of a mob, the women were
inspired to form African American women's clubs in their hometowns. Immediately following this success, Wells was invited to speak in Pennsylvania,
Delaware, Washington, D.C., Massachusetts, and elsewhere. Wells' lecturing
career blossomed from that point on. This gave her an opportunity to meet
numerous leaders within the African American and white communities. In
this way she had a fortuitous encounter with Catherine Impey at a speaking
engagement in New York. Impey played an instrumental role in the next

phase of Wells' war on lynching when she and Isabelle Fyvie Mayo of Scotland invited Wells to England—the same country where Douglass had rallied mass support to help abolish slavery in the American South. Douglass gave Wells his blessing and endorsed her campaign to enlist America's powerful and influential allies' support in ending lynch law and segregation.

ANTI-LYNCHING CRUSADE ABROAD

Wells engaged in two European lecturing campaigns, in 1893 (for three months) and 1894 (for six months). Her accomplishments during both trips were far reaching. Although she did not receive payment for her work, her needs were met by benefactors and hosts. She was well-treated—sometimes to Wells' astonishment. After all, in her own country, to show herself equal or superior to a white person could provoke violence or death.

Wells maintained a busy schedule, traveling to various locations throughout Scotland and England. She kept a diary through most of her travels and, during her second trip, published articles describing her experiences in the *Inter-Ocean*. Wells appeared before diverse audiences and organizations in an assortment of venues including wealthy homes, churches, and meeting rooms. She spoke "of condiitions in the South since the Civil War, Jim Crow laws, ballot-box intimidation, and laws against intermarriage," as well as her primary subject regarding the unrestrained violence against African Americans and other atrocities and injustices (Wells, 90–91). Her speeches shocked her audiences, who had thought African Americans had transitioned smoothly into post-slavery life and that racism was obliterated along with the end of slavery. Her listeners were moved to pass resolutions asserting their stance against lynching and racial discrimination. Wells' success was covered in the newspapers following each lecture, with journalists using such words as "quiet," "effective," "educated," and "forceful" to describe Wells' presentations. Other results of Wells' European tours were the formation of the Anti-Lynching Committee in London and a brief mention of Wells' international campaign in the American book, *Afro-American Women and Their Progress*.

There were times, however, when Wells' progress was jeopardized by individuals who opposed interfering in the affairs of a foreign nation. Some individuals thought England should not intervene in America's affairs, and others could not imagine the conditions in America were not resisted by Christians, popular reformers, and northerners, or traveling Americans themselves. Traveling Americans sometimes voiced their objections to Wells' crusade.

During Wells' first trip, controversy nearly ended her campaign when she supported Impey who disclosed her interest to an Indian man. Although Mayo was a progressive reformer, she frowned upon interracial relationships. Incensed, Mayo terminated her relationship with Impey and insisted Wells do the same. Mayo believed that Impey had compromised the great work to which they had committed themselves. When Wells sided with Impey, believing she had done nothing wrong in falling in love with a man of a different race, Mayo distanced herself from Wells as well. This was a blow for Wells since much of her success had been dependent upon Mayo's influence and support.

FIGHTING FOR RECOGNITION AT THE WORLD'S FAIR

Wells' protest at the World's Fair took place in 1893 in the interim between her two European campaigns. The World's Columbian Exposition and Fair was launched to celebrate the nation's four hundredth birthday. It featured forty-six countries, newly constructed buildings for the occasion, and splendid displays of cultural, artistic, and technical exhibits. Haiti was among the participants invited to the fair. Haitian officials chose Douglass (who served as a U.S. ambassador there from 1889 to 1891) to represent the country at the Haitian building. Glaringly absent from the program were African Americans. Outraged, Wells, in collaboration with Douglass and Frederick J. Loudin, a singer and musical director of the Jubilee Singers, set out to write and publish a book entitled *The Reason Why the Colored American Is Not in the World's Exposition*.

Financing for the book was troublesome. African American newspapers refused to offer support. Wells went to African American women, and with their help, coordinated meetings at various churches. With the money donated at the churches, plus personal contributions made by Wells, Douglass, and Loudin, the eighty-one-paged pamphlet was published and distributed.

The protest of Wells, Douglass, and Loudin was a success. Wells believed that it was Douglass' popularity and iconic status that drew large crowds to the Haitian building. Whatever the reason, she took full advantage to get the publication into as many hands as possible and went daily to the fair to disseminate it. Wells felt that exposing the truth to as many people as possible, especially during such an important event, was an indispensable part of rectifying the predicaments faced by African Americans.

These efforts, either indirectly or directly, resulted in the officials of the Fair declaring a "Negro Day." Every nation participating in the Fair was asked to make a presentation before all the attendees. Wells and some others rejected this invitation. They were vexed by the fact that they were asked to participate after having been snubbed originally. Douglass, on the other hand, coordinated the event himself and gave a masterful oration. The young poet Paul Dunbar recited some of his poems and the Jubilee singers gave a riveting performance.

BEGINNING OF THE WOMEN'S CLUB MOVEMENT IN ILLINOIS

Wells' launch into her role as an activist was greatly assisted by the help of African American women. Women were the first to respond proactively to

Wells' cries of protest after the lynching of the three businessmen in Memphis, and their support was integral to Wells' success as a lecturer. African American women came to her aid when she needed help to procure funds to publish the book to censure the absence of African American's in the World Fair program. Shortly after the World's Fair, Wells played a major role in the creation of the first African American women's club in Illinois, known as the Chicago Women's Club, later renamed the Ida B. Wells Club. W.T. Stead, editor of the *Review of Reviews*, inspired great interest in the club when he gave a rousing speech in which he insisted that the African American community needed "a solid organization to fight race prejudice" to be managed by an elite (Wells, 123).

ANTI-LYNCHING CRUSADE IN THE UNITED STATES

On July 24, 1894, Wells was greeted with fanfare upon her return to America following her second European tour. She dedicated the next year to an anti-lynching crusade in the States. Although resolutions were passed in many white churches (though not always as easily as in England), and anti-lynching committees were formed, Wells experienced various setbacks. African Americans, as a whole, continued to withhold their moral and financial support. On one occasion, some African Americans asked Wells to minimize her accusations against white women. Wells, of course, refused to do so, for her aim was to present the facts. The major reason for black resistance to Wells' work was fear of white backlash and of the belief that she was making matters worse (not better) for African Americans.

Wells' American anti-lynching campaign gave her access to other influential activists such as Susan B. Anthony, in whom Wells found a friend and who treated Wells with respect, kindness, and dignity. Wells continued to work with Douglass until his death on February 20, 1895. At the close of that year, Wells, at the age of thirty-two, and exhausted from her labor, decided it was time to attend to more personal matters.

SOCIAL ACTIVISM AFTER MARRIAGE AND CHILDREN

Ida B. Wells became Ida B. Wells-Barnett on June 27, 1895. The hyphenated last name embodied the roles she struggled to reconcile: activist and wife and eventually, mother. Wells-Barnett was able to retain much of the independence she demonstrated in her single life. Her husband, Ferdinand L. Barnett, an attorney, was himself an accomplished man. Their union was a good match. He encouraged her activism and did not protest when she carried the children with her on campaigns and braved multiple solo ventures. On many occasions, he gave money to her causes, or they worked as a team. She in turn helped to garner support for his career.

Despite the skeptics who did not approve of Wells-Barnett's decision to marry, she entered into matrimony with every intention of carrying on with her work. The loudest objections came from African Americans who felt she had abandoned them and their cause. Even Wells-Barnett's' friend and supporter, Susan B. Anthony, voiced her displeasure. It was expected that female activists give up marriage and children. But Wells-Barnett did not cease her work. She bought the newspaper, *The Conservator*, which belonged to her husband and others, was president of the Ida B. Wells-Barnett Women's Club, and continued her lectures.

Wells-Barnett faced another challenge in terms of keeping on with her work when her first son, Charles Aked (named after an English adherent) was born on March 25, 1896. Wells-Barnett dealt with this situation by becoming the self-proclaimed "only woman in the United States who ever traveled throughout the country with a nursing baby to make political speeches" (Wells, 244). Wells-Barnett seemed to have achieved the impossible: balance between motherhood and social protest. But after the birth of her second son, Wells-Barnett decided that being a wife and mother was a full-time job in itself and deserving of her full and undivided attention.

Motherhood turned out to be a poignant experience for Wells-Barnett. She had not believed she possessed the same desire as other women to bear children, both because of the grueling years as mother to her siblings and the fact that she had committed herself to an independent life and a career in journalism and activism. But motherhood caused Wells-Barnett to "wonder if women who shirk their duties in that respect truly realize that they have not only deprived humanity of their contribution to perpetuity, but they have robbed themselves of one of the most glorious advantages in the development of their own womanhood" (Wells, 251).

Despite this revelation, Wells-Barnett's' hiatus from public work was brief. Lynching across the nation had continued unabated. In 1898, the lynching of an African American federal officer brought her back to public life. Wells-Barnett, five-month-old baby in tow, was among the delegation that went to Washington, D.C. to urge President McKinley to take a stand against lynching. McKinley appeared attentive, telling the delegates that secret agents were looking into the matter. Following this meeting, Wells-Barnett turned her attention to raising money for the widow and surviving children of the victim. During this time, the Spanish American War began. Wells-Barnett was compelled to postpone her fundraising endeavors and return home. To her great disappointment, she was forced to abort further efforts in Washington, D.C. due to lack of organizational support, money, and interest.

ORGANIZATIONAL ACHIEVEMENTS, CHALLENGES, AND PROTESTS

Ida B. Wells-Barnett firmly believed that African Americans could make a greater impact in America through formal organizations. She envisioned a national organization that would be "numerically and financially strong enough to do the work which was so badly needed for making an organized fight upon" the persistent issues of racism, discrimination, segregation, and the emerging violence of the new century: riots (Wells, 267). On a side note, though Wells-Barnett was an active church member all her life and repeatedly sought out white and black churches during her activism, the church (though one of the leading agents in the antislavery movement) was an organization whose support was frequently sporadic.

Although Wells-Barnett worked primarily with African American organizations, she periodically enlisted white supporters. Her European friends were proof of that, as were those whites, for example, who formed a committee in response to Wells-Barnett's plea to put a stop to plans published in Chicago newspapers to abolish integrated schools. Her alliances with organizations brought some successes, but these liaisons were fraught with shortcomings, conflict, and opposition. Despite Wells-Barnett's assertiveness and impact, she was overshadowed by other leaders who dominated the public stage.

Afro-American League

The Afro-American League was re-established in 1899 to protest the issues that concerned Wells-Barnett. Wells-Barnett believed that the organization's progress was hindered by a lack of money and the accommodationism of men like Booker T. Washington. Accommodationism, a philosophy that advocates compliance to the status quo, was not only popular with a sizable number of African Americans but to an even greater degree with white America. Washington and other likeminded men were appointed to high political positions and advised white leaders. The influence of these men, particularly Washington, more than once, obstructed the work of the Afro-American League. By 1906, the Afro-American League had ceased to exist.

National Association for the Advancement of Colored People

The National Association for the Advancement of Colored People (NAACP), established in 1909 to tackle prominent issues facing African Americans such as racial violence, disfranchisement, and segregation, was another organization that initially evoked Wells-Barnett's optimism. Wells-Barnett was among those whose concerns helped shape this organization in its developmental stage. She was a member of the subcommittee charged with electing forty persons for the National Negro Committee, which would be responsible for the planning and development of the forthcoming NAACP. Wells-Barnett was shocked and incensed when her name did not make the list. Subsequently, her relationship with the NAACP was strained.

It was clear that Wells-Barnett did not have the credentials or fit the profile for entrance into the leadership of the emerging NAACP. Despite her heroic and very public anti-lynching campaign and years of experience with women's clubs and journalism, Wells-Barnett could not tout having "college degrees, professional credentials, and formal relationships to official constituencies" (Schecter, 135). Moreover, Wells-Barnett was a woman, and she was radical. The new tide of leadership, brought forth by the NAACP, was largely male and conservative. And it, ultimately, took over the anti-lynching issue, acknowledging little of Wells-Barnett's pioneering contribution. Notwithstanding the slight, Wells-Barnett moved on to other ventures.

Lone Crusader and Lynching Revisited

In the same year that the NAACP was formed, Wells-Barnett again rolled up her sleeves for protest—this time, to investigate a lynching in Cairo, Illinois. Wells-Barnett set out to ensure that the Illinois anti-lynching law, created in the aftermath of an earlier riot in Springfield, was upheld. In an unprecedented act against lynching, the state had established a law to dismiss "any sheriff who permitted a prisoner to be taken from him and lynched" (Wells, 309). Frank Davis was the sheriff in Cairo whose prisoner, an African American known as "Frog" James, was indiscriminately apprehended for the murder of a white woman. He was later seized while in custody of the sheriff, pelted with as many as 500 bullets, beheaded, and burned before a crowd of men, women, and children.

In Cairo, while trying to persuade the African American community to stand with her in her protest, Wells-Barnett appropriately called herself the "mouthpiece" of the people. Although a number of men and women signed petitions to oppose Davis' reinstatement, only one African American man, a lawyer, sat by her side, as she otherwise single-handedly testified before a throng of the former sheriff's supporters during the trial. In the end, the courts upheld the crucial anti-lynching law, and Wells-Barnett declared that there was not another case of lynching in Illinois from that moment on. Her triumph was recognized by a representative of the NAACP "as the most outstanding thing that had been done for the race during the year" (Wells, 326).

Negro Fellowship League

Wells-Barnett established the Negro Fellowship League (NFL) back in 1908 addressed crime in the African American community. Although she argued that lawlessness was, in general, a contrived excuse to abuse African Americans, she was aware that crimes among African Americans were real.

The organization's main objective was to provide a positive alternative for young African American males recently arrived in the city who might otherwise turn to idleness and crime. The original membership consisted of young African American men, ages 18 to 30, from her Sunday school class. With the help of a philanthropic white couple, the organization was able to rent a house, referred to as a reading room, in a problem section of the town on State Street where idle youth loitered or engaged in criminal activities. The house was used to lodge young men and to provide resources for assistance and employment in the city. Wells-Barnett called it the "Hull House for our people" (Wells, 356).

Wells-Barnett bore most of the financial burden of running the reading room (with the help of white benefactors who helped with the expenses for at least three years) and did much of the hands-on work herself. Wells-Barnett proclaimed proudly that the reading room provided aid for every African American who came to the NFL for help. She believed the work played a pivotal role in bettering the world for African Americans.

The Negro Fellowship League helped ordinary individuals whose stories never made the press. Among the high-profile cases was an incident involving an African American named Steve Green. Wells-Barnett and the NFL helped him to escape lynching and provided lodging for him after he killed a white man in self-defense. In another case, Wells-Barnett went to the aid of a man named "Chicken Joe" Campbell who had been accused of the death of a white woman in a fire that occurred at a penitentiary where he worked. When other papers would not give her a voice because she refused to temper her writing, Wells-Barnett went to the editor of the *Record Herald*, who allowed her to write an article of protest. Wells-Barnett's husband took on the case. Although Campbell was found guilty, he evaded a death sentence and was given a life sentence. Wells-Barnett was sorely disappointed that she was unable to garner support from the professionals in the community or from any other organizations.

In 1917, Wells-Barnett, working via the Negro Fellowship League, protested the imprisonment and hanging of African American soldiers accused of rioting in Houston, Texas. Not everyone rallied behind her. When Wells-Barnett asked local African American churches to hold a memorial for the men, she was refused. Undaunted, Wells-Barnett had buttons made, which read "In Memorial: Martyred Negro Soldiers," to protest what the American government had done. When she was accosted by two white secret service agents who accused her of treason for her stance and threatened to put her in jail and confiscate her buttons, Wells-Barnett courageously stood her ground, stating that she "would consider it an honor to spend whatever years are necessary in prison as the one member of the race who protested, rather than to be with all the 11,999,999 Negroes who didn't have to go to prison because they kept their mouths shut" (Wells, 369–370). The men, powerless to back up their threats, left, never to return.

NFL and the East St. Louis Riot

In 1918, Wells-Barnett worked congruently with the NFL and the *Chicago Defender* to protest the two-day riot that took place in East St. Louis and resulted in the death of 150 African Americans and the destruction of property worth nearly $1 million. The NFL organized a meeting, later publishing their speeches and resolutions in several newspapers. Wells-Barnett was chosen to send the resolutions to Governor Lowden. But she wanted to do more than that. She desired to do some investigating, believing that this would strengthen their protest.

Upon her arrival in East St. Louis, Wells-Barnett was astonished to find that the African American community had been left without much protection and that the people were receiving no help to reconstruct their lives. Exacerbating the situation was the fact that some leaders from the African American community met (without Wells-Barnett) with the governor, downplaying what had transpired and depicting Wells-Barnett as a troublemaker. Wells-Barnett, however, was able to press for an investigation into the causes of the riot, which, she observed, was focused unfairly on the African American men who had gone for help to avert the impending racial violence and consequently armed themselves in self-defense at the riot's onset. She wrote that it was those men who "received the brunt of the punishment meted out" (Wells, 390). Later, Wells-Barnett went to the aid of Dr. LeRoy C. Bundy, who received a life sentence for his alleged participation in the rioting. She utilized the medium, the *Chicago Defender*, to successfully raise money for Bundy's defense, and he was released from prison. Despite the numerous accomplishments made by the NFL, Wells-Barnett was forced to terminate the organization in 1920. With no money and support to draw from, she had no other choice.

African American Women's Clubs

African American women played an essential role in Wells-Barnett's activism, just as she was instrumental in their mounting power and influence and growth. She worked with and for women until her death. However, Wells-Barnett's relationship with some women, particularly those in leadership positions, who tended to perceive her tactics as abrasive and threatening, was frequently strained. And she was frequently frustrated by organizational bureaucracy.

Wells-Barnett's popularity began to show the strain when Mary Church Terrell, president of the National Association of Colored Women's Clubs in Chicago, did not invite her to a convention in 1899 because some members did not want her there. Wells-Barnett wrote of how, on another occasion, women at a meeting "hissed me off the floor," because they thought she was vying for control (Wells, 329). Some women were offended when Wells-Barnett got the Ida B. Wells Club accepted as a chartered member to the largely white Chicago Women's Club without following the proper procedures, though this was a monumental step toward integrating the women's organizations. Later, Wells-Barnett severed ties with Celia Parker Wooley and the Frederick Douglass Center (an integrated women's club). Wells-Barnett,

who had been vice president of the organization, objected to the way Wooley, the founder, treated her; Wooley challenged her stance on motherhood
and racist stereotyping of black men and attempted to prevent Wells-Barnett
from becoming president.

One of Wells-Barnett's most extraordinary adventures within the women's
clubs was her harrowing involvement in the suffrage movement. Between
1912 and 1914, "her participation in panels, dinners, canvassing, parades,
and speech making all intensified" (Schecter, 199). She and her fellow-
suffragists endured male protest and ridicule, and "tested the Jim Crowing
of African American women to the back of a major pro–woman suffrage
parade held in Washington, D.C.," in 1913 (Schecter, 200). When Wells-
Barnett stood her ground, refusing to go to the back of the parade, she was
supported by many white women, as well as the *Chicago Defender*. In the
same year, Wells-Barnett was one of the founders of the Alpha Suffrage
Club to galvanize the involvement of African American women in obtaining
voting rights (a movement launched by white women). This was the first
African American **women's suffrage** organization in the United States. This
club played a major role in the passage of the Illinois Municipal Voting Act,
which allowed women in Illinois partial voting rights.

In 1920, women obtained full voting rights in every state with the passage
of the Nineteenth Amendment. Wells-Barnett urged African American
women to use their newfound voting power to endorse black leadership and
white leaders sympathetic to the issues faced by African Americans and to
eliminate racist legislation. Despite these wins, Wells-Barnett concluded that
"all of our leading politicians proceeded to ignore those of us who had
made it possible for [them] to realize [their] ambition" (Wells, 353).

In 1927, Wells-Barnett turned her attention to politics with the hope of
empowering women, as well as her race. She formed the Third Ward Wom-
en's Political Club. This club prepared women for political positions. In the
same year, Wells-Barnett came to the aid of Mississippians who were dis-
placed in the Mississippi-Yazoo delta region in what was know as "the
greatest flood in U.S. history" (Schecter, 237). Exacerbating the situation
was that the flood broke the banks and levees of the Mississippi river.
Wells-Barnett protested the sufferings of the black victims, writing letters to
Herbert Hoover, who was the Secretary of Commerce at that time and in
charge of flood relief, and articles for the *Defender* documenting and con-
demning the conditions of black refugees" (Schecter, 237). As a result of
Hoover's responsiveness, Wells-Barnett traveled the nation to endorse his
candidacy for president and to register African American women to vote.

Lone Crusader and Birth of a Nation

Although the NAACP presented itself as a powerful champion for African
Americans, Wells-Barnett was disappointed that the organization did not

act in the case of the *Birth of a Nation* (released in 1915), a film whose portrayal of African Americans reflected southern racism. The debate over the showing of the film in Chicago ended up in court, without success. Wells-Barnett spoke in court to protest the film, but her efforts were to no avail. Wells-Barnett blamed the NAACP, which did not make an appearance in court, as well as the lack of a "leadership with a vision" (Wells, 344). She pointed out that in Philadelphia, the film was banned due to the efforts of dedicated leaders and the support of local churches, which threatened to peacefully obstruct entrance to the theater showing the film.

The Birth of a Nation

The Birth of a Nation (1915), or *The Clansman*, as it was also known, has gone down in history as one of the most racist propaganda films ever. And the name D.W. Griffith, for many blacks, is derided, since he chose to direct the film. Alarmingly, the movie was extremely popular, although it cast African Americans as villains and features a black slave (a white actor in black face) who is hunted down by the Ku Klux Klan and lynched. In one of the concluding scenes, the Klan is shown preventing black men from voting. In short, the film is a brief history of the Civil War and the end of Reconstruction when white conservatives regain control of the South. The film was based on *The Leopard's Spots: A Romance of the White Man's Burden, 1865 to 1900* (1902) and *The Clansman* (1905), two novels written by Thomas Dixon. There was a third book to that trilogy, *The Traitor* (1907). All three novels were romanticized encomiums of the Ku Klux Klan and southern life and traditions.

Blacks were outraged by the film and protests were carried out at showings in various cities. In locations such as Boston, Massachusetts and Philadelphia, Pennsylvania, the film instigated race riots. In some cities, the protestors were able to ban the film, but not everywhere. For several years following its premiere, the Ku Klux Klan actually used the film to recruit new members.

THE EQUAL RIGHTS LEAGUE

The Equal Rights League (ERL) was a thriving organization during the early twentieth century. Although Wells-Barnett was not an active participant in this organization, she supported its work from time to time. In 1915, Wells-Barnett was one of the delegates asked by the Equal Rights League to meet with President Woodrow Wilson to address discrimination in government agencies. William Monroe Trotter, president of the ERL, was one of the other delegates. The by-product of this meeting was that Wilson agreed to look into the situation. A year later, the delegates, not including Wells-Barnett (who had a previous engagement), met with Wilson again. This second meeting was a fiasco. According to Wells-Barnett, "the president became annoyed over Mr. Trotter's persistent assertion that these discriminations were still practiced and that it was his duty as president of the United States to abolish them" (Wells, 376). Wells-Barnett was one of the only leaders of the time to support Trotter's action. She, through the NFL, embarked on a campaign to regain Trotter's reputation, though many prominent African American leaders ostracized him.

ERL and the Arkansas Riot

Wells-Barnett's protest during the Arkansas riot of 1919, which ignited after African American sharecroppers refused to sell their cotton at low prices, illustrates the troublesome politics that continually frustrated her and her work. It was also the cause of her break-up with the ERL.

The Equal Rights League had appeared to be an organization after Wells-Barnett's own heart. Its purpose, she declared, was "to denounce lynching, peonage, and disfranchisement" (Wells, 397). While the extant president felt "there was nothing we can do [about the riot]," Wells-Barnett insisted that it was their duty to "protest against it and let the world know that there is one organization of Negroes which refuses to be silent under such an outrage" (Wells, 397, 398). Wells-Barnett's plan included making resolutions to the president and a senator, congressman, and governor of Arkansas and writing an article for the *Chicago Defender*. She also conducted a personal investigation into the riot, when, disguised as a family member, she visited twelve accused men. During her visit, they sang solemn spirituals to her. Wells-Barnett chastised them for being so morose and exhorted them to pray, have faith in God, and believe that they would live and be freed. Unfortunately, their resolutions (as well as those made by the NAACP and the NERL) were disregarded.

But resolutions were also created by Wells-Barnett and the People's Movement, declaring "that if those twelve men [accused of conspiring to murder whites] were electrocuted we would use our influence to bring thousands more away from Arkansas, which needed Negro labor" (Wells, 399). These resolutions were heeded, resulting in an investigation and a new trial for the accused. But the ERL was disturbed that Wells-Barnett had not shown them the resolution made by People's Movement. In her defense, she stated that this was a matter that could not be delayed. The ERL did not see her perspective, and so Wells-Barnett had nothing more to do with that organization.

Organizational politics further frustrated Wells-Barnett when a leader in the NAACP informed her that she need not publish a list of donors in the *Chicago Defender*, insisting that the NAACP had everything under control and would not need further assistance from her. In the end, the twelve men were freed, and one of them visited Wells-Barnett to thank her personally for her work. In addition, one of the attorneys on the case acknowledged Wells-Barnett's role as a pioneer in the anti-lynching movement.

Universal Negro Improvement Association

Marcus Garvey, a Jamaican immigrant who arrived to the U.S. in 1916, was the charismatic leader and founder of the Universal Negro Improvement Association (UNIA). His grand ambitions and separatist views were unpopular with the prominent African American leaders of the period. Wells-Barnett, also considered radical by her peers, was impressed by Garvey's Pan-Africanist program. Pan-Africanism is a worldview that includes all descendents of Africa, whether they be in America, Africa, South America, Europe, or elsewhere. Indeed, Garvey, in his flamboyant uniforms and Afro-centric fanfare, was outrageous in his time, and his desire to establish an independent nation for African descendents put him into a category of his own in regards to black leadership in America.

Wells-Barnett made complimentary statements about Garvey. She said, "Mr. Garvey made an impression on this country as no Negro before him had ever done" (Wells, 381). Although she supported his vision and accepted an invitation to speak before his membership, she thought that his illustrious career was cut short in 1922 because he had no substantial support and his goals were too ambitious.

Protective Association

In 1919, Wells-Barnett and the president of ERL approached local ministers to take action against the Chicago Riot. From that meeting came the Protective Association. Wells-Barnett played the role of ombudsman, collecting the stories of riot victims (who were too intimidated to go to the authorities themselves) and testifying in court on their behalf. But when it came time to appoint someone to lead on behalf of the rioters, Wells-Barnett objected to the ERL's selection of Attorney General Brundage, whose record with blacks was not good. When her objection was ignored, she dissolved her affiliation with the Association.

FINAL YEARS

In 1920, Wells-Barnett's activism was temporarily put to a halt due to ill health. She wrote how after having surgery for her gallstones, she took a year off from work to convalesce and ruminate over her life. The result of her introspection was that she felt she "had nothing to show for all those years of toil and labor" (Wells, 414). When she felt strong enough, she continued on in her vital work with the women's clubs, and in 1930, engaged in an unsuccessful race for the Illinois state legislature. On March 25, 1931, Wells-Barnett died of uremia. Her funeral service was a lavish affair. Though she was scarcely recognized or credited for her enormous contributions during much of her life, there can be no doubt that her selfless contributions to the cause of African American rights and the example she set for women's equality are unsurpassed.

See also Marcus Garvey.

FURTHER RESOURCES

The American Experience: Ida B. Wells—a Passion for Justice. Directed by William Greaves. PBS, 1989.

Decosta-Willis, Miriam, ed. *The Memphis Diary of Ida B. Wells*. Boston: Beacon Press, 1994.

Hendricks, Wanda. "Ida B. Wells-Barnett and the Alpha Suffrage Club of Chicago." In Marjorie Spruill Wheeler, ed. *One Woman, One Vote: Rediscovering the Woman Suffrage Movement*. Troutdale, OR: New Sage Press, 1995.

"Ida B. Wells-Barnett." 2006. Ida B. Wells Memorial Foundation. January 16, 2007. See http://www.idabwells.org.

McMurry, Linda O. *To Keep the Waters Troubled: The Life of Ida B. Wells*. New York: Oxford University Press, 2000.

Rydell, Robert W., ed. *The Reason Why the Colored American Is Not in the World's Columbian Exposition*. Urbana: University of Illinois Press, 1999.

Schechter, Patricia A. *Ida B. Wells-Barnett and American Reform, 1880–1930*. Chapel Hill: University of North Carolina Press, 2001.

Welch, Catherine A. *Ida B. Wells-Barnett: Powerhouse with a Pen*. Minneapolis: Carolrhoda Books, 2000.

Wells, Ida B. *Crusade for Justice: The Autobiography of Ida B. Wells*. Edited by Alfreda M. Duster. Chicago: University of Chicago Press, 1970.

Wells-Barnett, Ida B. *On Lynchings: Southern Horrors, a Red Record, Mob Rule in New Orleans*. New York: Arno Press, 1969.

Roy Wilkins (1901–1981)

Roy Wilkins was the executive director of the National Association for the Advancement of Colored People. He was also one of the so-called "Big Six." On the outside, Roy Wilkins, in his gray suit, fedora, and cigar, looked every bit the benign business man. And his autobiography, *Standing Fast: The Autobiography of Roy Wilkins* (1982), which describes a portion of his daily life as executive director of the NAACP between 1955 and 1977, is frequently mundane and deceptively uneventful. But Roy Wilkins was not ordinary, nor was the civil rights empire that he helped build and maintain through the harrowing Civil Rights Movement.

As civil rights organizations go, the NAACP is the largest, longest-running (established in 1909), and most influential. It has also notoriously been the most conservative. But that label belies the extraordinary influence of so many NAACP leaders, including Wilkins, who toiled arduously over the years to develop leverage with city officials and some of the most important leaders in the nation. It also ignores the fact that the NAACP was so disdained in parts of the South that local chapters were prohibited, that it waged "undercover operations" and demonstrations, and that as a strategy the conservative element proved to be immensely effective. In fact, the NAACP relied largely on behind-the-scenes negotiations, lobbying, and litigation. Wilkins was assistant secretary of the NAACP when the famous *Brown v. Board of Education* gave the deathblow to segregation in public schools. This was a major milestone in the early years of the Movement, though it provoked violent backlash from whites in the South who viciously opposed racial integration.

As a leader of the Civil Rights Movement, Roy Wilkins was not overly spiritual or charismatic, nor was he a ubiquitous media figure like Dr. Martin Luther King, Jr., leader of the Southern Christian Leadership Conference (SCLC). He was not recklessly daring like James Farmer of the Congress of Racial Equality (CORE) or John Lewis and James Forman of the Student Nonviolent Coordinating Committee. Wilkins was middle-class, married with no children, middle-of-the-road, and straight-laced. He could be heavy handed when he wanted to be. When the civil rights leaders combined forces, Wilkins liked to steer their meetings and was not shy about reminding others of the importance and power of the NAACP. He sometimes participated in marches and picketing, but his main task was to manage his well-organized and sophisticated organization and maintain its middle-of-the-road stance throughout the civil rights era and the militant Black Power Movement. Out of the public eye, Wilkins made profound changes and engaged in negotiations and legislative reforms that were indispensable to ensuring the freedoms and rights of African Americans. Without question, Wilkins' abilities and achievements were as important to the movement as those of the men and women who battled on the front lines.

CHILDHOOD

If it were not for a certain mishap, Roy Ottoway Wilkins would have been born in Holly Springs, Mississippi, where his parents and grandparents had lived for many years. As fate would have it, on August 30, he was born in St. Louis, Missouri, a turn of events that had a great impact on his life and outlook.

The story of Roy's birth begins with his father, William, showing his radicalness by fighting back (and fighting hard) rather than submit to racial etiquette. William came upon a white man on the road who called him a nigger and hollered at him to let him pass. Racial etiquette demanded that blacks always step aside and yield to whites. But this time the white man got a violent beating instead. To avoid white backlash, William's father, Asberry, sent him and "Sweetie" Mayfield, his new wife, out of town. They traveled to St. Louis, Missouri, which was the furthest north either one of them had ever been.

The legacy of the Wilkins' family extended back into slavery; Wilkins' great-great grandfather was a slave. As with most black slaves, the surname Wilkins originated from the white family who owned them. After the emancipation of the slaves during the Civil War (1861–1865), Roy's grandfather Asberry stayed on the plantation and married Emma, a woman who had a pronounced scar on her arm—a punishment for accidentally burning her white mistress' dress while ironing when she was a slave.

Although Asberry Wilkins acquiesced to the racist laws in the wake of Reconstruction, he was not entirely passive. Wilkins was a member of the Loyal League, a club that endorsed rights and suffrage for recently freed slaves. Although he could only sign his name with an X (in slavery, it was unlawful for him to learn to read and write), he chose to engage in the political struggle for voting rights. The Loyal League mounted numerous parades and marches at the polls, and freedmen marched in procession on election day. Voting in this period was a precarious adventure; throughout the South, whites challenged black voters with physical force, intimidation, and trickery.

"Troublemaker" and "bad nigger" were some of the labels given to African Americans who resisted the traditional way of life in the South. Willie, one of three sons and a daughter born to Asberry and Emma, was considered the family's first "troublemaker." Unlike his father, Willie received an education in a segregated school and attended Rust College (which offered a high school–level education) where he met Sweetie Mayfield. Willie customarily talked back to whites and blacks alike. When he beat the white man who had commanded him to step aside, it must have horrified his family, friends, and neighbors.

Life in St. Louis for Willie and Sweetie was difficult. To be sure, St. Louis was not completely integrated, and upon their arrival, the couple marveled at the fact that they did not have to sit in the back seats on the trolley they rode, and that there were no "black" and "white" only restrooms. But the rest of daily life in St. Louis was largely segregated, and Willie, as in the South, was forced to take the lowest-paying jobs. The experience was demoralizing. Religion helped allay much of the pain, and his burgeoning family—Roy, Armeda (1903), and Earl (1905)—was, in the beginning, a delightful escape from the grueling work day. But for the most part, William was a dour, frustrated man.

The St. Louis in which young Roy grew up took the form of blocks and blocks of hard concrete and buildings. He never had the pleasure of exploring the expansive farmland and country lanes of Mississippi, but he was sheltered from the oppressive laws and conditions of the South. Wilkins remembered friendly police officers who greeted him as they passed by him or patted his head, and days frolicking with his mother and his two siblings. His mother was a gentle, demure preacher's daughter. In St. Louis, Roy attended an all-black school kindergarten and the African Methodist Episcopal Church.

Roy was resistant to religion from the start. He did not understand the demonstrative and loud sermons, or the emotional response from the members. He endured the daily Bible readings his father insisted upon at the dinner table before the evening meal. When his mother got sick and was later diagnosed with consumption, the church women flooded the small house, cooking meals, scrubbing the floors, washing the laundry, and seeing to other household matters. Wilkins recalled their warmth and generosity, but when his mother was near death, and one of those genial women scooped up a shrieking baby Earl in her arms, Roy became angry and told her to leave him alone. Roy was shuttled off to a neighbor for the night, which was the night his mother died.

Aunt Elizabeth was the fairer-skinned sister of Roy's mother—a warm, loving, ebullient, and welcome presence for the grieving family. Elizabeth soon convinced William that the best course of action would be to follow her sister's wishes and let her and her husband, Sam Williams, take the children to St. Paul, Minnesota, rather than send them to their grandparents in the small, racially oppressive town of Holly Springs.

The train ride to St. Paul enchanted Roy. He could hardly eat he was so excited, nor was he too disappointed when the train came to a roaring stop at their destination. Uncle Sam was as wonderful and attentive as Elizabeth. The couple had no children of their own, but Roy, Armeda, and Earl filled that gap, and so received extraordinary opportunities, love, and encouragement from their adoptive parents. Uncle Sam added three new rooms and a bathroom for his new family. Home was a clean, comfortable place, nestled in an idyllic middle-class neighborhood with neat lawns and plush trees. Most of the neighbors were white, with many Irish, Swedish, German, Jewish, and French immigrants.

Williams had one of the best jobs any black man could have: he was the chief steward of the railcar that belonged to the president of the Great

Northern Pacific Railroad. This job led to many luxuries for his family, including lavish Christmases with Christmas trees that filled the sunny home with the scent of pine, boundless wrapped gifts, and turkey dinners.

Sam and Elizabeth inculcated the importance of education to Roy and his siblings. But Roy did not expect, on his first day of his school, to walk into a room full of white children. After the initial shock, he settled into school life, making friends with the other boys and interacting without incident with his teachers. Henry, his best friend, was a blonde who lived in a rougher part of town, where roguish white boys were the only ones known to use the word "nigger." The kindness that most other individuals in Roy's environment displayed was remarkable for the times. One mother in Roy's neighborhood treated him like one of her own.

Church, on the other hand, was still very much segregated, either by preference, tradition, or both. In St. Paul, Roy and his family attended the AME church. In the beginning, Roy liked going to church no more than he had in St. Louis. When Aunt Elizabeth caught him pantomiming Reverend Jones at the pulpit, she put him into the children's choir, where he had to sit in the front pews and could not act up. Roy never developed a fervent zeal for churchgoing, but he did eventually get involved. Besides the choir, he was later employed as the church janitor and then superintendent of the Sunday school, even teaching a class himself.

Roy's biological father tried to get his children back at one point. But Aunt Elizabeth and Uncle Sam hired a black attorney and became the legal guardians of the children in 1911. William, who had remarried, moved to St. Paul to be close to his children. For the most part, life continued undisturbed for Roy.

With the exception of the side of town where whites called blacks "nigger," Roy was sheltered from racism. So oblivious was he when it came to race issues that it was not until years later that he realized how much his life had been framed in protest, by his grandfather, father, as well as his Uncle Sam, who was a member of the local branch of the NAACP. The community, too, was familiar with activism. A friend of the family was the esteemed Frederick McGhee, a Minnesota attorney who joined the Niagara Movement and later the NAACP. The family doctor and the pastor of the church were instrumental in quashing the attempt to make interracial marriage unlawful in Minnesota. Roy's family had a subscription to the NAACP's organ, *The Crisis*, edited by W.E.B. Du Bois.

The issues that affected blacks in St. Paul were less intense than elsewhere in the nation, particularly the South, where lynching, riots, and legal and social oppression abounded, but there was still discrimination in employment and evidence of Jim Crow practices in hotels and restaurants. When Roy read Du Bois' *The Souls of Black Folk*, he memorized sections of it, but he could not completely relate or comprehend its full meaning.

In 1915, Roy went on to George Weitbreit Mechanical Arts High School, the top high school in his town. If it had not been for Miss Copley, his

English teacher, who pulled him aside and nurtured his natural gift for writing, he would have pursued engineering. Instead, he became the editor of the school's literary magazine, editor of the school's yearbook, and president of the Literary Society. In 1919, Wilkins graduated as salutatorian.

UNIVERSITY OF MINNESOTA

That fall, Roy began his college career at the University of Minnesota, where he studied sociology. His uncle paid for most of his expenses. Roy lived at home and worked a multitude of small jobs—at a golf club, the Union Station, Minneapolis Steel and Machinery Company, Swift and Company slaughterhouses, and the Northern Pacific's North Coast Limited. In his second year, Roy made money writing for the *Minnesota Daily*, the university's newspaper.

In the summer of 1920, racial violence came to Duluth, a town near St. Paul. The experience was traumatic for Roy who wrote that he "lost [his] innocence on race once and for all" and "felt sick, scared, and angry," causing him to finally grasp "what Du Bois had been writing about" (Wilkins, *Standing Fast*, 41, 44). What happened in Duluth was as follows: A white eighteen-year-old accused black men of putting a gun to his head and raping his girlfriend. Some twenty-two black men were apprehended as a result. Three men were abducted from jail and openly lynched in what had been a quiescent street of the small and unsuspecting town. The thirteen men who stood trial were known as the Duluth Thirteen. The national NAACP and three of the NAACP branches in Minnesota, including the one in St. Paul, raised money for their defense. All of the cases but one were either acquitted or dismissed based on lack of evidence. It took many years for one black man who was convicted and sentenced to thirty years in prison to be set free.

Roy was nineteen years old when the news of the lynching and the case of the Duluth Thirteen emblazoned papers across the nation. That he was around the same age as the men who were lynched, as well as those who were tried, rattled him. It did one other profound thing: it forced Wilkins to realize that the world was not the idyllic utopia that he had experienced in his St. Paul neighborhood.

Wilkins also experienced racism at the university. He was not allowed to join any of the fraternities on campus because of the color of his skin. And when a possible Ku Klux Klan presence on campus was talked about, the white journalists at the *Minnesota Daily* jokingly commented that there was a new university club. Every one but Wilkins laughed.

These sorts of experiences fueled Wilkins' burgeoning racial consciousness. He and other black students organized the first black fraternity on campus. He entered an Oratorical Contest, giving a presentation on "Democracy or

Democracy," a speech based on the Duluth Thirteen, and won third place. In 1922, he joined the NAACP.

Wilkins continued to work for the university paper, eventually becoming the night editor, writing the light and breezy articles on campus happenings. But in his other world, Wilkins sought to address the weightier issues that affected blacks. He edited the *Northwestern Bulletin*, a small black newspaper owned by a friend, in 1922. When the editor of the *St. Paul Appeal* died in a car accident, Wilkins became its new editor.

Through his work with the *Appeal*, Wilkins gained access into the who's who of the local black community and was initiated into the world of African American protest. Wilkins, ambitious and idealistic, explored issues he had not ever thought of before, such as the Ku Klux Klan, NAACP activities, and the trial of the controversial Marcus Garvey, leader of the Universal Negro Improvement Association and African Communities League. He was just twenty-one.

FINDING HIS WAY IN KANSAS CITY

In 1923, Wilkins graduated from the University of Minnesota with a degree in sociology. That summer, on assignment for the *Call*, a well-established black newspaper in Kansas City, he went to the 1923 NAACP's Midwestern Race Relations Conference. At the conference, Wilkins met and was awestruck by the eloquent and forceful leaders of the NAACP—James Weldon Johnson, Walter White, Du Bois, and William Pickens. The conference included a silent march, week-long daily meetings on race issues, and a stirring concluding meeting on the last day. Wilkins wrote "I had never seen anything like it. A haunting chorus of 200 Negroes in white robes sang Dett's 'Listen to the Lambs,'" and after Johnson, the general secretary of the NAACP spoke, "ten thousand black people rose to their feet. They cheered and clapped until their voices were hoarse and their hands stinging with pain. As they cheered, the soft sunlight streamed down around James Weldon Johnson, and I knew I had seen a great leader—and found my own cause" (Wilkins, *Standing Fast*, 53–54).

An excited Wilkins joined the staff of the *Call* that October, but his experience in Kansas City fell short of what he had expected. He had hoped for a thriving life in the big city. But racism was rampant and limited his access and enjoyment of the city's diversions. Wilkins was shocked to discover at his first baseball game in Kansas City that seating was segregated, and that blacks were designated the worst seats. When he politely yielded his seat on a streetcar to an aged white woman, she snapped back, not to him, but to a white passenger: "I'm not old enough yet to accept a seat from a nigger" and remained standing (Wilkins, *Standing Fast*, 60).

Racism showed itself in everyday encounters like this and elsewhere. Police officers bullied blacks, especially those who were engaged in interracial relationships. Officers ignored criminal activity in black neighborhoods. The Linwood Improvement Association worked to keep blacks confined in dilapidated homes. And the black schools were never given monetary support to improve buildings and provide up-to-date textbooks.

Whenever possible, Wilkins wrote articles to expose such atrocities, and also experimented with activism outside of journalism. He helped organize a **boycott** of Jim Crow theaters and coordinated a Paul Robeson concert with an unprecedented integrated audience. When a lynching happened near Kansas City, Wilkins' frustration got the better of him, and he uncharacteristically conceived of a radical, revolutionary plan of retaliation. He wanted "to organize a band of young Negroes to raid towns where such murders had taken place. Retaliation was my goal; what I had in mind was a black Robin Hood band that would pounce and punish with no warning" (Wilkins, *Standing Fast*, 72). But he came to his senses and never implemented that plan. Wilkins did join a group of progressive professionals that met to discuss race issues, but eventually stopped going, exasperated that the intense dialogs never produced any action. He then created "Talking It Over," a column in the *Call* that existed for the purpose of blasting racism, discrimination, and racial injustices.

As Wilkins established himself as a writer, tragedy struck in his family. In 1927, his sister, a sophomore at Hamline College, died of tuberculosis. In 1928, his aunt and uncle both died within a short period of time, Uncle Sam dying from a stroke on his way home after hearing his wife had had a heart attack. Aunt Elizabeth died while recovering from her heart attack and preparing for her husband's funeral. Earl moved to Kansas City to be near Roy.

But Wilkins' was reconsidering his life in Kansas City. Other black professionals, disheartened by Jim Crow, packed up their bags and left town for Chicago, New York, or other cities. Wilkins' first visit to New York in 1929 made it harder to stay in Kansas City. The most memorable aspect of the trip to New York was when he sat side-by-side with whites and blacks at a concert on Broadway and at the famed Harlem neighborhood of the Harlem Renaissance. Wilkins pondered over the question of whether to leave or stay in Kansas City. Should he keep on with the lonely fight in Kansas City? Would he find a better job than the *Call* in New York?

Minnie Badeau was a welcome distraction from his constant brooding over this question and from his grief over the recent loss of his family members. Badeau was a doe-eyed beauty; an independent and critical thinker like himself, who had recently arrived from St. Louis to begin her career as a social worker with the Urban League. They met at a fashion show benefit in 1928. Although Badeau's mother was initially unimpressed by the young journalist, they married on September 15, 1929, at the office of the justice of the peace.

Married life was blissful and exciting, filled with concerts and activity, but Wilkins was still on edge due to racial tensions in Kansas City. Minnie was concerned when one day, Wilkins, in an uncharacteristic move, aggressively approached a white man who asked her for directions. Wilkins had misunderstood, seeing only a white man approaching a solitary black woman. When Wilkins uncovered a local scam against African Americans and boldly printed it on the front cover of the *Call*, his life was threatened. Minnie insisted on going with Wilkins wherever he went. It was believed at that time that gangsters would not murder victims in front of spouses.

In 1930, the NAACP led a campaign against the nomination of Judge John J. Parker to the U.S. Supreme Court. Voting power was one of the most powerful weapons available to blacks, and the NAACP hoped to sway the vote against Parker, who had publicly uttered racist comments, such as "Negroes in politics is a source of evil and danger to both races" (Wilkins, *Standing Fast*, 91).

Wilkins was instrumental in the NAACP's quest. By now, he had acquired much acclaim through his work at the *Call* (he helped raise the newspaper to second in popularity to the *Chicago Defender*) and as secretary of the local NAACP chapter. Wilkins wrote articles exposing the judge's racist remarks and sent one to President Herbert Hoover. The campaign was a success, and Wilkins' contribution was acknowledged by the national office of the NAACP. W.E.B. Du Bois, editor of *The Crisis*, extended an offer to Wilkins to become the business manager of his paper. But Wilkins declined. He did not feel he had the credentials to meet the needs of that position.

Wilkins remained at the forefront of local issues and protests. He launched a successful boycott to challenge the employment discrimination of white businesses frequented by blacks, targeting a local bakery. In the nearby town of Clinton, where there was talk of an impending lynching, he conducted an investigation of his own and published a report of the incident from the point of view of the black victims.

In 1931, Walter White, in his first year as executive secretary (the title changed to executive director in 1964) of the NAACP, sent an invitation to Wilkins to fill his former position as assistant secretary. Wilkins could scarcely keep his cool. Wilkins, and anyone else who followed the NAACP, knew about White. One of his most famous exploits was to go to the South disguised as a white man to investigate lynchings. Since White had straight hair, fair skin, blue eyes, and blonde hair, he had passed easily as white. Wilkins accepted the invitation because of his admiration for White and the reputation of the NAACP "at last was a fighting organization, not a tame band of status quo Negroes" (Wilkins, *Standing Fast*, 93).

THE NATIONAL ASSOCIATION FOR THE ADVANCEMENT OF COLORED PEOPLE

The National Association for the Advancement of Colored People (NAACP) job was a prime opportunity for Wilkins. Not only was it the leading organization for protest work, but Wilkins would be second in command, making more money than he had at the *Call*. It also offered him the opportunity to move to New York and escape the Jim Crow culture of Kansas City.

In the early days after his arrival in New York, Wilkins' social calendar was full. He and Minnie enjoyed dinners with White and his wife, Gladys, and they received invitations to hear the latest bands and attend premier concerts. But as the days progressed, work became his priority.

He did not make many friends at the office, which he characterized as a stilted place. There was little in the way of light office humor or banter. It was work, work, work, punctuated by the hammering of typewriters and the perpetual ringing of telephone calls. Du Bois, the editor of *The Crisis*, was withdrawn and serious, brooding over the magazine that was his life's work. White was often away on business, which added to Wilkins' responsibilities.

In the evenings, it was off to the movies, to see a musical featuring the mercurial Cab Calloway, to the Harlem Opera House, or to visit a museum. Sometimes, Wilkins would share a drink with a friend before hustling home; sometimes he went straight home and dissolved the cares of the high-paced day by playing the radio softly and reading a book. Come morning, Wilkins was off and running again, dressing carefully in a gray suit, then bounding off to catch the train to work.

Wilkins' walk from the train to the office conjures the image of an unassuming man, alone with his thoughts, anonymous in gray suit and fedora, passing pedestrians who—at first—had no idea that he was a man wrestling with mountainous and bewildering problems without the cooperation of the city, state, or federal government. Almost everything the NAACP labored to accomplish was done with great struggle.

There was struggle within the NAACP leadership too. In those early days, even the notoriously straight-laced Wilkins thought the organization was too conservative. And there were other tensions, most notably between White and Du Bois, two strong-willed men with frequently conflicting objectives.

From the Office to the Field

Wilkins wrote that his earliest duties "involved a little bit of everything—writing, lecturing, organizing new branches, raising money for a treasury that was always Depression-dry, running the office while Walter was touring around the country" (Wilkins, *Standing Fast*, 113). In 1932, Wilkins, itching for something more thrilling than the humdrum tasks of writing, managing, and lecturing (and the daily grind of the office), plotted a scheme to investigate conditions in Mississippi, where, according to an undercover investigation, "the army was paying Negroes a dime an hour for shifts as long as twelve hours a day [for the construction] of flood-control dams and levees along the Mississippi delta" (Wilkins, *Standing Fast*, 119).

Walter White, a known swashbuckler, knew the perils of going to the deep South under any conditions, and considering that Wilkins was a dewy-eyed activist who only knew the South from reading about it and had no first-hand experience, he was not easily persuaded. When he finally agreed, he sent George Schulyer along with Wilkins.

The two men traveled to Mississippi, masquerading as poor blacks, then separated upon arrival. Wilkins almost blew his cover with one woman, who rented him lodging, who observed the smoothness of his hands (not that of a country laborer) and looked askance at him when he asked her where he could find a fire to warm himself in the morning. That question would cost him, because most blacks working in the camps went straight to work without the luxury of warmth, even though it was freezing cold and snowy in December.

Hidden dangers and close calls abounded for Wilkins and Schulyer. Schulyer almost went to jail, after being wrongly accused of a crime committed by other blacks. Once, when Wilkins and Schulyer were together, they were stopped by a car filled with white men. Luckily, the men continued on and did not molest them.

Wilkins was moved by the evidence of poverty around him—and by the generosity of the people he met despite their poverty. One black family took him in, offering him the shelter of a home that was "an unpainted shack in the woods. The cracks in the floorboards were so wide I could see chickens scratching on the ground below" (Wilkins, *Standing Fast*, 123). The mother gave him a meal from what she had and a place to sleep. Wilkins gave her $3 when he left the next day. The money was more than she could have scraped together in a year.

In January, the duo scuttled back to New York, where they reported their findings at the crowded Abyssinian Baptist Church in Harlem. Meanwhile, in Washington, D.C., Senator Robert F. Wagner, one of the NAACP's few white allies, pressured the Senate to increase wages for black workers. It was a modest raise, but the win was encouraging.

Wilkins wrote a letter to Arthur Spingarn, chairman of the national committee, stating that the NAACP should "hold itself up as a defender of the rights of Negroes everywhere and under all circumstances" (Wilkins, *Standing Fast*, 147). Spingarn wrote back, stating that his ideas were good and noble but required more resources than were currently available, unless they were able to mobilize volunteer attorneys and one full-time attorney to do the job. He concluded by saying he would think about it.

Demonstration and Arrest

When Franklin D. Roosevelt began his first year as the president in 1933, many were aglow with optimism, for he represented hope for those who had suffered most from the Great Depression. It had been a stark period for all Americans, and yet African Americans benefited the least from Roosevelt's New Deal Program. Wilkins was highly critical of Roosevelt over this fact. However, in Eleanor Roosevelt, the president's wife, African Americans found a champion. Although she could be overly cautious many times, and there were limitations to her influence, the support she gave was radically different than what blacks had historically experienced. Wilkins called her "a loyal and effective friend" (Wilkins, *Standing Fast*, 128).

Roosevelt, a tall, confident, and progressive woman, believed in equality among the races, and said so at a speech she gave (in Harlem at White's invitation) at an anti-lynching art exhibition to mobilize support for the Wagner-Costigan anti-lynching bill. In that day and age, black issues were not popular. Roosevelt's bold support of the NAACP's anti-lynching campaign was deeply appreciated. But even the support of the First Lady was not enough. In October of 1934, there was a particularly outrageous lynching in Florida. Though the local authorities knew in advance about the lynch mob, they did nothing to prevent it beforehand or to punish the perpetrators after the fact.

Through the pioneering agitation of Ida B. Wells-Barnett in the late nineteenth century and other organizations (including the NAACP) in the twentieth, lynching—the South's abominable secret—was coming under increased scrutiny. However, the federal government remained unresponsive. The NAACP supported legislation such as the Dyer and Wagner-Costigan anti-lynching bills, but the South's influence blocked the passage of both bills. When, in 1934, Attorney General Homer S. Cummings announced a national crime conference to be held in Washington, D.C., Wilkins was astonished to learn that lynching was not one of the issues to be addressed. White wrote a letter to the attorney general. The reply was, in short, the same response the NAACP had always gotten on lynching. The government, due to the influence of politicians from the South, would not budge.

Wilkins came up with an idea that he felt would finally give lynching the attention it deserved, though there were many who scoffed at him. "Picketing," he wrote later "was a radical act" to most of the NAACP, while friends of Walter White suggested that the idea of a demonstration was hackneyed and ineffectual (Wilkins, *Standing Fast*, 134). Wilkins thought otherwise. With White's approval, Wilkins drew support from others, including Virginia R. McGuire, president of the local NAACP branch in Washington. Wilkins made up slogans to paint on picket signs such as "5,068 Lynchings in U.S.A. in 52 Years," and "Al Capone Got 11 Years. Lynchers Get Cheers."

On a bitter cold day in December, Wilkins and three other men marched in front of Constitution Hall, where the conference on crime was taking place. Because they had not followed the code or received parade permits, the cops loaded them off to jail. The arrest of these men prompted a second demonstration. This time, the signs were of the correct dimensions (the issue that had caused Wilkins and the others to be arrested). Seventy men and women (including one blind man) participated, wearing, for a theatrical touch, nooses around their necks. The cops could do nothing to stop the demonstrations as the signs were all under code. The demonstration made headlines. Wilkins had found a way to make lynching an issue, with or without the federal government's support, and in doing so was making a name for himself, and coming out from under the shadow of Walter White.

Amenia Conference

Wilkins showed his radical side in other ways. When the NAACP began to plan for its second Amenia Conference in 1932, Wilkins brazenly suggested that only African Americans attend. Since the focus of that conference was to assess the current situation of African Americans, he felt there was no one better to participate in that discussion than African Americans. A compromise was made. Whites were allowed to attend, but only a small number and only for a limited amount of time.

At the conference, Wilkins presented the idea he had submitted to Spingarn following his Mississippi assignment. He suggested that the NAACP broaden its programs to assist African Americans throughout the nation, and not just regarding civil rights cases. The matter was discussed, but it would not be implemented until years later.

Du Bois Controversy

Wilkins' radicalism paled in comparison to what Du Bois published in *The Crisis* in the beginning of 1934. Du Bois' startling endorsement of voluntary separatism in 1934 was in stark contrast to the NAACP's stance on integrationism. Since 1910, Du Bois had been entrusted with publishing anything he saw fit. However, when Walter White took charge, he tightened the reins on Du Bois and insisted on overseeing the newspaper's content.

That Du Bois and White butted heads was obvious to Wilkins. The two strong-willed men bickered at meetings, and Du Bois often used *The Crisis* to lash back at White. *The Crisis* had become, for Du Bois, his own soapbox, which he used not only to fight racial injustice but to express his disagreement with White. It took everybody at the NAACP by surprise when Du Bois resigned in the summer of 1934. Wilkins was sorry to see him go and intimidated by the fact that he fell heir to the responsibility of editing *The Crisis*.

Scottsboro Case

The Scottsboro Case presented another heady challenge for Wilkins. The case began in 1931, following the arrest of nine African American youths, age thirteen to nineteen, accused of rape by two white women. This was not the first case of this kind, but it was certainly among the most sensational. The legal arm of the Communist Party and the International Labor Defense organization stepped up quickly in defense of the youths.

The NAACP did not get involved until 1935, when it combined its efforts with the American Civil Liberties Union, the Methodist Federation for Social Service, the International Labor Defense, and the League for Industrial Democracy. This was a radical move. For one thing, the NAACP generally shied away from sex cases like this one. For another, everyone was less than thrilled to work side by side with the communists. During the period of the Red Scare, the NAACP had worked hard to distance its organization from communists. A common charge from southerners was that any protest organization that challenged the life and laws of their region was affiliated with the Communist Party.

The Scottsboro Case was bitterly fought and dragged on for years. The trials themselves were a long ordeal. In the end, charges were dropped for four of the youths (two of them were underage, one was ill at the time of the crime, and the other one was legally blind) after they had served six years in prison on death row. The other five youths received lengthy sentences.

The remainder of the decade was filled with non-stop activism for Wilkins. Beginning in 1934, the NAACP launched a legal campaign to desegregate schools. This was run by the newly formed Legal Department (Wilkins' letter to Spingarn played a role in this development), headed by Charles Hamilton Houston. Both Houston and Thurgood Marshall played vital roles in these cases. In 1957, Marshall formalized the legal arm of the NAACP by establishing the NAACP Legal Defense and Educational Fund as a separate entity. Wilkins took great pleasure in watching the NAACP's star attorney, Thurgood Marshall, chisel steadily away, case by case, at Jim Crow.

In 1936, Wilkins helped coordinate a campaign against presidential hopeful William E. Borah, a senator from Idaho. Although he was considered a progressive Republican, his track record with blacks was poor. And he refused support to anti-lynching bills. The picketing campaign worked like a charm. Most African Americans voted against him, and he lost his bid for the nomination.

WORLD WAR II AND THE NAACP

The war years were complicated for the NAACP. On a personal note, they began unhappily for Wilkins, too, for in 1941, when America officially entered the war, Wilkins' brother died.

Throughout the 1940s, Wilkins fought on the front lines of an all-out challenge against racial discrimination. African Americans faced discrimination in all areas of life. Discriminatory laws were most apparent in the

South, but the North had its problems too. Blacks faced injustice in the judicial system, anti-black violence, and joblessness due to racism and discrimination. These problems raised the question of why blacks would support America in its war effort to bring democracy abroad when they were deprived of full equality and equal rights at home. But support it they overwhelmingly did.

The NAACP supported the war effort and encouraged blacks to do the same, despite the bitter fact that blacks served in segregated units, a fact that confounded Wilkins and other leaders. The hope was that through participation and demonstration of patriotism, blacks would effect greater gains at home. Wilkins accepted a government appointment to serve on a draft board, where he was an eyewitness to class preference and race discrimination. A large proportion of wealthy whites evaded the draft.

The NAACP's support of the war did not keep Wilkins from expressing his sour opinion of Jim Crow in the armed forces. When Wilkins made a presentation at an Urban League event, he was told to not speak against military segregation, since his audience would be mostly white and one of the men in attendance was an African American colonel. Wilkins gritted his teeth and gave his speech, lambasting discrimination in the military. To his surprise, the audience exploded in applause.

A. Philip Randolph, a tall, lean, and staid figure in his early fifties who had been a firebrand in the early century and had come to fame as the leader of the Brotherhood of Sleeping Car Porters, suggested a large-scale demonstration: a march on Washington, D.C. to press the government to abolish segregated armed forces. Wilkins was more than up for it. The march, however, did not happen, for the threat alone was enough to pressure President Roosevelt to create Executive Order 8802. This order did not desegregate the military forces, but it did prohibit discrimination in federal agencies and departments. It was viewed as a meaningful start.

The war helped create job opportunities for African Americans. This was a good thing, but there were disastrous ramifications. As more blacks from the South migrated to the North to fill the new jobs, racial tensions between whites and immigrants escalated in the urban neighborhoods. Competition for housing and employment, as well as racism, inflamed the competitors and caused race riots throughout cities in the North such as Detroit, Michigan and Harlem, New York. Wilkins and his wife were caught in a riot that occurred in Harlem in 1943. The Wilkinses were on a bus on their way home when a brick crashed through the window. One passenger was injured and had to be taken to the hospital. Wilkins joined White shortly thereafter at the police station. The men went with Mayor La Guardia into the streets to help quell the rioting.

The war presented special challenges for African Americans, as well as for the NAACP. Yet the NAACP prospered. By the time peace was declared, the organization had accumulated 500,000 members and 1,200 branches.

While Wilkins contemplated this great success and made plans for the future of the organization, he received troubling news. His doctor informed him that he had colon cancer. On June 20, 1946, Wilkins, who had fought so hard for the public good, awakened from surgery knowing he faced a personal battle.

Wilkins spent the summer recuperating and returned to work in October, in time to celebrate Executive Order 9808, which White and others had been canvassing for during Wilkins' long convalescence. White also brought Wilkins up to date on the new issues the organization had taken on, such as improving housing conditions and raising the minimum wage.

Wilkins was not the only NAACP leader who took ill. As the organization flourished, others faltered, undoubtedly falling prey to the rigorous schedules their work demanded. Thurgood Marshall was ill in 1946. In the following year, White suffered a heart attack. Then the doctors informed Wilkins that his cancer had returned. Wilkins was not expected to survive this second bout. But Minnie did not accept the doctors' grim prognosis. She put her husband on a strict regimen of fun and relaxation, including plenty of baseball and football games—and most importantly, no NAACP work. Wilkins' cancer went into remission.

One of Wilkins' main objectives during this period was to push the federal government to produce strong legislation towards civil rights. Not since Reconstruction (1863–1877) had African Americans witnessed substantial laws that granted them equal rights and protection. By the end of Reconstruction, with state governments again under the control of white southerners, those few laws had been eroded and the racial climate had worsened. The federal government moved sluggishly, despite the urgent demands put forward by civil rights leaders and the rampant violence and abuses African Americans suffered in the South.

President Truman appeared to be a promising ally. When he appeared and spoke at the NAACP's 38th Annual Convention in 1947, he "became the first President to do so" (Wilkins, *Standing Fast*, 198). In October 1947, he established a Commission on Civil Rights and, in 1948, issued Executive Order 9980 (ordering the desegregation of the federal workforce) and 9981 (ordering the desegregation of the armed forces), and spoke brazenly about a plan to advance civil rights during the 1948 presidential campaign. Wilkins and his colleagues were elated. It appeared that the moment they had toiled and sacrificed for was at hand. Truman won the 1948 campaign, but his promises fell dismally short.

At the same time, the NAACP underwent an internal crisis. In 1949, Walter White divorced his wife Gladys and married a white woman named Poppy Cannon and decided to take a year-long leave of absence. This meant that Wilkins would be in charge of the NAACP, and his first task would be to resolve the unrest that White's sudden news had created within the organization. While at the national convention (which he was, for the first time, in charge of) in Los Angeles, California, Wilkins permitted a discussion over White's recent marriage. The "final argument [was] how could an organization committed to integration fire its chief executive for marrying a white woman?" (Wilkins, *Standing Fast*, 205). Wilkins also addressed Paul Robeson's comment that African Americans would not participate in a war against the communist Soviet Union and the recent resignation of Du Bois.

CIVIL RIGHTS MOVEMENT

Beginning in 1949, and throughout the 1950s and 1960s, the NAACP initiated a number of strong civil rights gains and was a high-profile participant in the historic Civil Rights Movement. In 1949, Wilkins coordinated the "largest mass lobby ever to fall upon Washington" (Wilkins, *Standing Fast*, 209). The mobilization effort included some 4,000 people, representing various associations, unions, churches, and other organizations. The outcome of this effort included the establishment of a Leadership Conference on Civil Rights (of which Wilkins was the chair) and a meeting with President Truman. Truman received them coolly and remained unresponsive. Nonetheless, the NAACP rejoiced over that small step.

The first of the major legislative achievements of the Civil Rights Movement occurred in 1954, with the monumental ruling of *Brown v. Board of Education* which desegregated public schools. When Walter White died in that same year, Roy Wilkins became the new executive secretary of the NAACP. Also in that year, Martin Luther King, Jr. led an extraordinary campaign, the Montgomery Bus Boycott, which led to an Alabama state ruling that declared segregated laws for buses unconstitutional.

One of Wilkins' primary objectives as the leader of the NAACP was to pursue further civil rights legislation. This was a daunting task, requiring long and intense negotiations. One of his great frustrations was being constantly told that the NAACP was pressing too hard—moving too fast—for change.

Another difficulty was gaining a victory, only to have to deal with the intense and often violent resistance that welled up in the aftermath of that victory. After the *Brown v. Board of Education* ruling, Wilkins helped advocate for the first black students to integrate the Little Rock Central High School. This was a harrowing experience. Tensions were so hostile that President Eisenhower had to call in federal troops.

As time wore on, Wilkins divided his time between lobbying, civil rights rallies, and keeping a close eye on mounting civil rights demonstrations. The NAACP was notorious for being a conservative organization, limiting its demonstrations to rallies, marches, and picketing. But Wilkins was not a complete fan of the nonviolent direct action tactics King had popularized. Although he knew its importance in the grand scheme of things, he saw real changes in society coming about through changes in the laws.

The hostility to blacks spread to the NAACP itself. Beginning in 1956, several states resorted to legal action to stop the NAACP from setting up chapters in their states. One such state, Louisiana, tried to force the NAACP to report its members. Alabama was permitted a restraining order to prevent any NAACP organizations from forming in its state or engaging in fundraising activities. Other states to initiate similar ordinances were Georgia and Texas.

When, at long last, the Civil Rights Act of 1957 was enacted, Wilkins referred to it as a "crumb." The Act was largely directed toward strengthening voting rights for blacks. However, it had little substance and its overall effect was anemic.

Wilkins explained in his autobiography that sit-ins and other demonstrations were nothing new; there had been isolated sit-in demonstrations staged by individuals as early as the nineteenth century. Adam Clayton Powell led boycotts in the 1930s. The Congress of Racial Equality (CORE) staged demonstrations in the 1940s. He was proud of the NAACP youth council when it staged sit-ins in 1958, but he felt differently about the large-scale sit-in movement and the widely staged demonstrations of the 1960s.

When, in 1960, several college students in North Carolina staged a sit-in that sparked numerous youth-led sit-ins throughout the nation, Wilkins received the news with wariness. And he was skeptical when King helped mobilize these youths to establish the Student Nonviolent Coordination Committee (SNCC). Wilkins wrote that

> the students were young, committed, and valiant, but ... they would have no staying power beyond a few short years' time. My own experiences had taught me that the struggle would still be going on long after they were out of college and immersed in other concerns. Only a strong organization like the NAACP could survive the wear that went on year after year after year. (Wilkins, *Standing Fast*, 270)

Indeed, SNCC collapsed at the end of the decade, while the NAACP remains active today.

Nonetheless, Wilkins assisted SNCC, raising money to pay bail following the numerous arrests and to help pick up the pieces when the their students were expelled from colleges and universities because of their activism.

Wilkins participated in the Civil Rights Movement in a variety of ways. He joined leaders like Randolph and King, who were leading marches, at a large rally at the Democratic Political Convention in 1960. A young, fresh-faced, Hollywood-handsome Harvard graduate named John F. Kennedy was at this rally, hoping to win support for his presidential election campaign. When his presentation turned to voting rights, desegregating schools, and combating discrimination, everyone's curiosity was piqued.

John F. Kennedy

Wilkins had casually tracked Kennedy while he was a senator between 1953 and 1960. Wilkins was a little perplexed by him. An aura of glamour enveloped him, which affected African Americans as well as whites. Wilkins admitted that when he was around Kennedy, even he found it hard to resist Kennedy's magnetism.

Kennedy's support of blacks was legendary. One of his most well-known achievements was bringing about King's release when he was jailed in 1960. When Kennedy became president, he put African Americans in positions of power within the government.

Yet despite one meeting after another, Kennedy resisted Wilkins' pleas to implement a strong civil rights bill. The truth was that Kennedy did not want to upset the southern politicians; he wanted to make gradual changes that would not lose votes for the Democrats.

Wilkins observed that it took a combination of racial violence and media coverage to spur Kennedy to action. When racists attacked the Freedom Riders in 1961, the press were there to cover the horrific story. With television, newspapers, and radio stations broadcasting the shocking violence to the rest of America and the world, the government was forced to respond.

Wilkins himself was more than once on the front lines during this period. Once, during a picketing demonstration in Jackson, Mississippi, in the spring of 1963, Wilkins was arrested. Minnie was beside herself. But Wilkins was released a few hours after his arrest and returned home unharmed. An arrest in those harrowing days was almost like a rite of passage for civil rights activists. This was Wilkins' second arrest. That summer, Wilkins was one of the main speakers at the March on Washington for Jobs and Freedom.

Following demonstrations led by the SCLC in Birmingham, Alabama in 1963, Kennedy finally came through with what he knew was right, giving a compelling speech that declared, in no uncertain terms, that African Americans deserved equal rights. This speech gave Wilkins confidence that Kennedy just might be bold enough to demand the passage of a meaningful civil rights bill.

While Wilkins watched Kennedy's speech on television, he received a phone call. Medgar Evers, a NAACP field secretary, whom he had seen only days earlier, had been murdered. In November, Kennedy, a man in his prime and on the brink of one of the most important pieces of legislation for African Americans, was assassinated. His vice president, a tall Texan wholly lacking the charismatic charm and appeal that had defined Kennedy, took his place.

Lyndon B. Johnson

Wilkins portrayed Johnson as, as he put it, "the greatest civil rights President of our lifetime" (Wilkins, *Standing Fast*, 297). Johnson was an upfront man who took an instant liking to Wilkins, as was evidenced by the numerous phone calls that took place between them.

Though Johnson inherited the unfinished civil rights bill of 1964 by default, he quickly followed it through to completion. Johnson was helped by individuals like Wilkins and others within the NAACP who lobbied behind the scenes and organized demonstrations at the grassroots level.

Riots of 1964

When the first wave of riots broke out in the summer of 1964 in the impoverished black communities of the North, Wilkins recalled that Johnson was alarmed. The president feared that the riots would hurt any chances for additional civil rights legislation. Wilkins called together other civil rights leaders and held a meeting, at which he suggested a moratorium, or a cessation of direct action demonstrations, until Election Day. Everyone, with the exception of CORE and SNCC, agreed. Wilkins and other civil rights leaders publicly denounced the riots.

Wilkins was appreciative of the help of the FBI, whose statements laid to rest any misconceived ideas that the Civil Rights Movement had anything to do with the riots, or that during the riots blacks attacked whites. The race riots that occurred during this period were unique: blacks primarily vandalized and looted stores and buildings restricted to their communities.

Mississippi Freedom Democratic Party

One of Wilkins' most uncomfortable hours was during the Democratic National Convention in Atlantic City, New Jersey in 1964. In that year, black and white Mississippians formed the Mississippi Freedom Democratic Party (MFDP) to challenge the all-white, ultra-conservative Democratic Party in that state. But when they arrived at the national convention, they were frustrated and angry over Johnson's apparent obstruction of their aim. At the conclusion of extremely stressful negotiations, it was decided that the MFDP should concede to a less-than-favorable compromise: as Johnson wanted, the MFDP was only allowed two seats, and those were nominal at best. As with so many national white politicians before him, Johnson's aim was to not upset the southerners to secure his election. But the one-sided compromise triggered a falling out with many of the young activists who had attended the convention and "did terrible damage to relations between white liberals and black organizers in the South. [Some MFDP delegates and SNCC supporters] thought they had been sold out. [Bob Moses, a SNCC activist] took a vow never to talk to whites again ... I watched and worried for the future" (Wilkins, *Standing Fast*, 306).

Long Hot Summer

The Long Hot Summer refers to the hundreds of riots that occurred between 1965 and 1967 during the hottest days of summer in the urban ghettos of numerous northern cities.

To black leaders, whether they were militant separatists or nonviolent integrationists, the riots in New Jersey, New York, California, and Michigan came as no surprise. Black Power proponents called the riots "revolts" or "rebellions." Indeed, black youths were frustrated with conditions in the ghettos, and the riots were evidence that conditions had reached a critical point. State and federal investigations into the riots affirmed what blacks already knew: dire poverty, overcrowded and dilapidated slums, unemployment, crime, racism, and discrimination, compounded by some triggering incident (usually a recent case of police brutality or killing of a black), were a recipe for disaster.

Unlike the race riots of the late nineteenth and early twentieth centuries, where whites went into black communities and destroyed homes and property, frequently killing innocent blacks, the riots of the 1960s were largely isolated in black communities. Few deaths occurred, but innocent whites in the vicinity of the riots were known to be physically assaulted. Most deaths, when they did occur, resulted from the involvement of police officers sent in to enforce the law and quell the riots. Black youths directed their destruction inward—into their own communities and against white-owned businesses.

Conservative blacks did not condone the riots but understood the pathology behind it and interpreted the violence as a cry for help. Some militant blacks endorsed the violence and were inspired by the demonstrations of what they perceived to be revolutionary protest. They believed that this was the only viable way to bring about positive change. Most conservative whites interpreted the riots as something entirely different—as criminal acts by thugs and gangs.

President Lyndon B. Johnson, who was president during the Long Hot Summer riots, responded by establishing social-reform programs by way of the War on Poverty program. However, America's growing involvement in the Vietnam War drastically cut funding towards addressing poverty and discrimination.

Voting Rights

The next major campaign, a joint venture between the SCLC and SNCC for voting rights, took place in Selma, Alabama. The campaign began on March 7, 1965, a day that became known as Bloody Sunday after police officers violently attacked marchers. The second attempt to carry out the march occurred on March 9. But this one was cut short, because King did not want to challenge an injunction placed on the march by a judge. With the injunction lifted, the march continued with success on March 25. Wilkins was there for that last march, what he called "the civil rights movement's last great parade of the 1960s," and recalled that "it was a fine moment, the best since the March on Washington. I flew back home feeling rejuvenated" (Wilkins, *Standing Fast*, 308, 309). Shortly thereafter, Johnson signed the prestigious Voting Rights Act of 1965.

Riots of 1965

Despite the passage of two major civil rights bills, it was no surprise to Wilkins when more riots erupted in 1965. He saw these riots as the result of the gross neglect of the government and officials, as well as one of the ramifications of the NAACP's and other organizations' focus on the South. As he put it, "we had not even touched the misery and desperation of the urban ghettos outside the South" (Wilkins, *Standing Fast*, 313).

But many whites in the nation blamed the violence on criminals and gang members, and as a result city officials imposed harsher laws and strengthened their law enforcement. Johnson responded quickly by establishing a commission to investigate the true cause of the riots. The commission determined that racism played the biggest role in fueling the frustrations that produced the riots in the cities. Johnson followed up by implementing a prodigious War on Poverty program.

Moving the civil rights struggle to the North was an imposing challenge. Wilkins and his fellow civil rights leaders did not know how to approach, mobilize, or initiate a program in the North. King's campaigns in the North achieved only mild success. However, his Operation Breadbasket, under the helm of Jesse Jackson, was hugely beneficial to blacks in Chicago. Still, that was only one program. While civil rights leaders dawdled and floundered, a new movement was rising that had its own answer to the problem.

BLACK POWER

Wilkins was flustered by the Black Power Movement. He was at odds with its call for separatism and militancy, as well as aggressive talk that fed into racial hostility and animosity. Because of Wilkins' unique experience growing up in St. Paul, he could not be convinced that blacks and whites could not live peaceably together. He wrote that

> perhaps I'm a sentimentalist, but no one can tell me that it is impossible for white people and black people to live next door to one another, to get along— even to love one another. For me integration is not an abstraction constructed

on dusty eighteenth-century notions of democracy. I believe in it not only because it is right but because I had lived it all my life. Where there are decent, loving people like the Hendricksons, integration works. Where decent white people are missing—that's where the trouble begins. (Wilkins, *Standing Fast*, 30)

The black power proponents did not particularly like Wilkins or the other civil rights leaders. In black power speeches, these leaders were criticized and called Uncle Toms. They had an unflattering moniker for Wilkins, "Roy Week-knees." The civil rights leaders were considered to be a part of the establishment—out of touch, sellouts. In 1967, the FBI informed Wilkins that they had uncovered a plot to assassinate him. The plotters were members of the militant organization, RAM.

RAM

A "ram" is defined as any device used for crushing, driving, or forcing something. It is also the abbreviation for the Revolutionary Action Movement, otherwise known as RAM. RAM was one of multiple black militant and separatist organizations to emerge during the 1960s.

RAM was founded in 1963 by Max Stanford (also known as Muhammad Ahmad) and Queen Mother Audley Moore. During the riots of the 1960s, RAM attempted to organize the young rioters into what was known as the Black Guards.

Publicly, RAM advocated armed self-defense and provided protection for Malcolm X after he left the Nation of Islam. However, in 1967, Stanford and other RAM members were arrested when the Federal Bureau of Investigation (FBI) uncovered a plot to assassinate Roy Wilkins and Whitney Young.

Wilkins and Young were targeted because they were deemed by members of RAM to be "enemies to the race." The militants felt that their acceptance by whites as well as their conservatism were antithetical to the black revolutionary philosophy. Stanley's heinous plot is an example of ultra-extremism. Most militants and separatists limited their disapproval of conservative black leaders to name-calling and scathing criticism.

It was a violent time. So many lost their lives during the Civil Rights Movement, including those who stood for peace and hope for a better future, like John F. Kennedy. In 1968, two more high-profile assassinations would shock the world. On April 4, 1968, King was assassinated. On June 6, 1968, Robert Kennedy, President Kennedy's brother, was also assassinated.

VIETNAM WAR

Before King's death, he had been one of the few civil rights leaders to protest against America's involvement in the Vietnam War. Wilkins, on the other hand, refused to lead the NAACP into the peace movement that, he felt, fueled the hippie subculture.

During this period, Wilkins watched in dismay as the war absorbed all the national funding and resources that had previously gone into Johnson's War on Poverty program. Wilkins was painfully aware that the Civil Rights Act of 1964 and Voting Rights Act of 1965 had not magically cured the ills of the country, nor had they addressed racism. Laws could be changed, but hearts were an entirely different matter. With the election of Richard Nixon, Wilkins saw the inevitable erosion of many gains he personally had fought for.

Lyndon B. Johnson

Lyndon B. Johnson is not the first name that comes to mind when blacks consider which president has made the most contributions to civil rights. John F. Kennedy's name is heard most, although he primarily endorsed civil rights in word and not necessarily in deed. Kennedy did play a significant role in the initiation of one of history's most important enactments, the Civil Rights Act of 1964, which outlawed segregation in any form. But it was Johnson who rose to the occasion and made sure the act was implemented, signed the Voting Rights Act of 1965, and implemented several poverty and affirmative action programs to address racism and discrimination.

Ironically, Johnson, the man who would make such enormous contributions to civil rights and dare to tackle the issue of poverty in America, was a southerner. Born August 27, 1908 in Stonewall, Texas, Johnson was one of five siblings who lived in a farmhouse in an impoverished community. When, in 1926, Johnson attended Southwest Texas State Teachers College (now known as Texas State University–San Marcos), he had to work to finance his education himself. While teaching Mexican students, Johnson gained insight and compassion for those outside his own race.

In 1934, Johnson married Claudia "Lady Bird" Taylor, with whom he had two daughters. Three years later, he was elected to the U.S. Congress and served six years. He joined the Navy during World War II (1941–1945). In 1948, he was elected to the Senate. When John F. Kennedy became president in 1961, Johnson served as his vice president. Following Kennedy's assassination, he was thrust into the presidency during the period of tumult that included the Civil Rights Movement, the rising Black Power Movement, and the Vietnam War. Johnson was president from 1963 to 1969. He died of a heart attack on January 22, 1973.

To compound Wilkins' worries, his cancer returned in 1969. After another surgery, the doctor was optimistic that he would live many more years. Wilkins contemplated retirement. Minnie retired in 1971 from social work, and it offered them the chance to spend more time together. However, Wilkins was not ready to give up the fight. It was not until 1977 that, at seventy-six years old, Wilkins officially retired.

IN RETIREMENT

It seemed that everyone wanted to honor Wilkins at his retirement. The Library of Congress asked for his papers. The Smithsonian wanted some of his mementos. And there was still an audience for the great man. Wilkins continued to write newspaper columns and occasionally meet with presidents. He had scarcely finished his autobiography, when on September 8, 1981, he died.

Wilkins had a long and extraordinary career. He lived to see the fruits of his labors ripen and to watch the waning public fascination with the Civil Rights Movement and the Black Power Movement. He lived to see America enter a new era of freedom and equality, however incomplete, and despite the threats raised by the rise of conservative leadership in the 1980s.

See also W.E.B. Du Bois; James Farmer; Marcus Garvey; Jesse Jackson; Martin Luther King, Jr.; John Lewis; A. Philip Randolph; and Ida B. Wells-Barnett.

FURTHER RESOURCES

Hughes, Langston. *Fight for Freedom: The Story of the NAACP.* New York: Berkeley Medallion, 1962.

NAACP (April 2008). See http://www.naacp.org/home/index.htm.

"Roy Wilkins Center for Human Relations and Social Justice." Hubert H. Humphrey Institute of Public Affairs (April 2008). See http://www.hhh.umn.edu/centers/wilkins.

Wilkins, Roy. *Standing Fast: The Autobiography of Roy Wilkins.* New York: Da Capo Press, 1994.

Wilkins, Roy. *Talking It Over with Roy Wilkins: Selected Speeches and Writings.* Norwalk, CT: M & B Publishing, 1977.

Robert F. Williams
(1925–1996)

Robert F. Williams was president of the NAACP chapter in Monroe, North Carolina and founder of the Black Armed Guard. In Williams' hometown of Monroe, North Carolina, racial violence was rampant. Exacerbating the situation was the fact that African Americans received no protection from the local authorities or justice in the all-white courtrooms. In the absence of any other form of protection, Williams, in his late twenties, following a brief stint in the Marines, organized blacks in his community in self-defense against attacks by whites during his tenure as NAACP president. He also staged demonstrations against the local Jim Crow swimming pool and led a high-profile campaign to protest the jailing of two young boys who had been arrested for kissing two white girls. In 1959, shortly after publicly endorsing armed self-defense, he was suspended by the NAACP. Two years later, Williams was falsely charged with kidnapping a white couple who had been caught up in the turbulence following a demonstration staged by visiting Freedom Riders. Williams and his family fled to Canada, Cuba, and later to China.

Williams' activism did not stop after his departure from America. In Cuba, he started a radical radio station, Radio Free Dixie, from which he broadcast his incendiary criticism of white racism and violence. He supported the militant climate of the Black Power Movement and the rioting by black youths in their communities. His smoldering slogans "Freedom! Freedom! Freedom now, or death!" epitomized the spirit of a new generation of militant blacks who were fed up with racism, poverty, and discrimination, as well as social, economic, and political oppression. To the militant leaders, like Huey P. Newton, who emerged in the mid-1960s, Williams was a pioneer, a hero, and an archetype of the Black Power Movement.

However, Williams was an anomaly compared with leaders like Roy Wilkins of the NAACP and Dr. Martin Luther King, Jr. of the Southern Christian Leadership Conference. Whereas Wilkins favored, almost exclusively, courtroom litigation and genteel meetings with city officials and presidents in tranquil office rooms, and King led a mass movement that yielded passively before violent confrontation, Williams embraced armed self-defense.

When Williams and his family returned to America in 1969, he carried on with his civil rights work, but he kept a low profile. His lectures about his involvement in the Civil Rights Movement were devoid of the forceful radicalism that had made him popular and inspired so many youthful firebrands. He died on October 15, 1996.

CHILDHOOD

When Robert Franklin, the fourth of five children of John and Emma Carter Williams, was born on February 26, 1925 in Monroe, North Carolina, every one commented on his striking resemblance to his grandfather Sikes Williams. His grandmother, Ellen Williams, liked to talk to the grandchildren about her husband Sikes and their experiences in slavery. She and her late husband had been slaves until 1865, when North Carolina ratified the Thirteenth Amendment.

Ellen Williams' tales taught her grandchildren important lessons of African American protest. Robert, more than the others, was captivated. He seemed to internalize the mythical figure of the grandfather who had died before his own birth. Sikes was a rebel, and more importantly, he was a legendary figure who had really lived. Born in slavery, Sikes defied the laws that prohibited him from learning how to read and write, with the result that he could do both by the time his freedom came in 1865. He and his wife later attended the all-black Biddle Institute, a school famous for its "leadership that rejected accommodation to white supremacy," and would later become "a center of the black freedom movement in North Carolina a century after Emancipation" (Tyson, 12). But not much had changed: getting a formal education, then becoming a teacher (which both husband and wife accomplished), flew in the face of the post-war climate of white supremacy in the South.

Sikes' entrance into politics continued his step-by-step commitment to challenging white supremacy. He joined the Republican Party, which was responsible for much progressive legislation for the recently freed slaves during the **Reconstruction** period in the South (between 1862 and 1877). Sikes aligned himself with blacks and whites to strengthen the Republican influence in his home state. He made speeches and, with another African American man named Darling Thomas, established the newspaper *People's Voice* with their own printing press.

But these were violent times, aptly labeled the Black Nadir of American race relations. Racist whites formed informal and formal white vigilante groups and organizations to wage an all-out war against sympathetic whites and, especially, African Americans. Violence permeated not only North Carolina, but most of the South, as whites violently seized back political, economic, and social control, undoing much of the progress that Reconstruction had barely begun to achieve for blacks. The North turned a blind eye to the vicious crimes: beatings, riots, murders, lynching, and the destruction and illicit seizure of property owned by African Americans. African Americans, with nowhere to turn for help, learned early on to acquiesce to white oppression. Their survival depended on it.

But African Americans like Sikes were a rarity. Sikes had his own rifle, which he kept at the house to defend himself and his family. Ellen Williams inherited his rifle, and every now and then she removed it from its hiding place to exhibit it to her grandchildren. She would show Robert the ancient printing press stored away in the barn, thus authenticating the legendary Sikes in young Robert's mind. He was spellbound.

Robert could have listened to stories about Sikes all day long. But there were chores to do, the local Jim Crow school to go to, and church to attend every Sunday at Elizabeth Baptist Church. His mother attended regularly, with Robert and his four siblings trailing behind her. Robert's father was not a churchgoer.

John Williams was not made of the same material as Sikes. Robert observed this early on, and it bothered him. Like most African Americans, Williams kowtowed to whites in public, averting his gaze, instead of staring directly into their eyes, and deferred to them in a hundred other ways. If he acknowledged the existence of lynching or racism, it was in private. He would not think of protesting or challenging the racist practice of Jim Crow and racial etiquette.

The closest example of a living rebel in Robert's life was his Uncle Charlie. Uncle Charlie was rebellious in more ways than one. He was a World War I veteran and had been educated at two historically black institutions, Florida A&M College and Wilberforce University. Like his father Sikes, he returned to North Carolina and taught. His activism seems to have been limited to one incident, but that may have magnified his importance to Robert. The story goes that Charlie "put up a fierce fight for [his cousin] to take" a typing test at a federal agency (Tyson, 9). As Charlie expected, the cousin was barred from taking the test because she was black. Charlie did this to demonstrate what he knew was a case of discrimination. Robert may have also admired Uncle Charlie because he was a man who challenged the proper code of conduct his mother upheld at home: Uncle Charlie drank alcohol and even secretly shared some with his nephew. He also complained bitterly about the passive stance of the black church with regards to procuring civil rights and protection for African Americans.

The Williams family lived in a house that had been bestowed to Robert's grandmother in exchange for her lifetime of servitude to a white family. It was a spacious house built atop a hill. Robert's father had a good job, working as a boiler washer with Seaboard Air Line. Thus, Robert's economic status was a measure better than other African Americans in Monroe, as most African Americans in their community were sharecroppers. Notwithstanding this economic benefit, Robert was still forced to live in the segregated part of town and had to abide by the same laws and customs as any other African American.

Life in Monroe, while Robert was growing up, was not as violent or racist as in some states in the Deep South, but it was still perilous. When Robert was eleven, he witnessed Big Jesse Hems, a white police officer, beat an African American woman. On another occasion, rumor traveled from house to house that a mob was planning to lynch an African American man named Boyce Richardson who had "whipped out a knife and nearly sliced the collar off [Chief of Police Elmsley Armfield's] throat, threatening to kill him" after Armfield kicked him off a curb where he was sitting with his son (Tyson, 18). African American men were warned to stay indoors. John

Williams went to work that very night, but he carried his pistol. However, violence was thwarted for that time due to the diligence of a number of whites who did not condone racist behavior.

COMING OF AGE

Ellen Williams' guidance was crucial to Robert's development. In addition to her storytelling, she taught Robert to take pride in himself and not to hate whites. She also taught him about history and influenced him to think critically about world events. As a teenager, there was no awkwardness or insecurity about Robert F. Williams. He grew quickly into the towering and burly frame of his grandfather. As he took on more responsibilities he became, like Sikes, more radically minded.

In 1939, Robert got his first job: delivering newspapers. This suited him, undoubtedly because of his grandmother's influence. Williams was interested in the events that unfurled around him. He began to frequent a local spot where African American men gathered to enjoy one another's company. There he talked to the older men about local and world news, such as the Holocaust in Germany.

Sometime during Williams' adolescence he formed a vigilante-style organization called X-32 "'to make war on white philanderers who fancied Black women after dark'" (Tyson, 20). They wore white masks so no one could identify them and patrolled the streets at night to prevent these taboo trysts, even if they were consensual. In Robert's mind, he was defending and protecting the honor of the women in his community and attacking the perceived enemy: white men who frequently took advantage of black women. Undoubtedly the memory of the attack on the black woman he had witnessed as a child influenced him as a young adult. X-32 served as a vehicle for action, which was much more desirable to him than the sense of powerlessness he had felt years before. Williams knew that justice would not be found in a court of law. On one occasion, the group hurled bricks and rocks at a car that had parked at a popular nighttime stop. The white driver peeled away.

A definitive moment in Williams' development occurred shortly before his grandmother's death, when she bequeathed her husband's rifle to him. That rifle was a symbol of his burgeoning manhood and a transferal of power from one radical to another. That Ellen Williams gave the rifle to Robert implies that she knew he was different from the other children and was indeed becoming increasingly more like her husband.

Williams Leads a Strike

In 1941, sixteen-year-old Williams enrolled in a National Youth Administration job-training program near his hometown. This job was one of scores that opened up for African Americans during World War II. The problem was that Williams and the other black youths were forced to do menial tasks like digging ditches, while the white youths were trained for technical skills like stone masonry. Exacerbating the situation was the fact that the black youths were expected to drink water from used Coca-Cola bottles. After some discussion, Williams led a walk-out from the premises. The young men beseeched a high school teacher to help them contact the state office, which intervened and corrected the problem. This was a sweet victory for Williams, but there would be consequences. The FBI began to watch him closely. He would be kept under surveillance well into his adult life.

Detroit Riot

Williams was only seventeen in 1942 when he moved to Detroit. His oldest brother had found lucrative work with the Ford Motor Company and suggested Williams might give it a try. Williams worked on the assembly line and joined an interracial union.

The city itself was an unfriendly place. Racism and fierce competition over jobs, housing, and other resources were rampant and contributed to the frequent fist fights at work and in the streets. Whites were embittered against the African Americans who poured into the North, eagerly searching for the job opportunities created by the war and anxious to leave the oppressive South. The hostile, competitive, and racial climate of the urban North also appeared to foster aggression in blacks who, like Williams, would not back down from a fight. White supremacist groups like the Ku Klux Klan regularly cruised through African American neighborhoods harassing the inhabitants or sparking fights.

When Williams was not working, he indulged in two pastimes: reading and observing the activists in the city. Williams particularly enjoyed reading Langston Hughes, a major figure during the Harlem Renaissance. Williams desired to one day see New York City for himself. As for the radical political front, socialists and communists were common fixtures in Detroit. Most of them were white, and they frequently spoke out against racism in a bold way that Williams appreciated. But Williams was not so interested in their brand of politics.

In 1943, Williams, his brother, and another friend were driving to the popular Belle Isle Amusement Park when they found themselves in the middle of a fight. A black man stood alone against several white men. Williams suggested they help him. They broke up the fight only to learn that a racial riot had spread throughout the city.

The Detroit riot of 1943 lasted for three days, beginning on July 20. The riot was sparked by a fight between blacks and whites over a card game at Belle Isle. The riot was spurred on, undoubtedly, by the rumors that rippled through African American and white communities, as well as pre-existing tensions between working-class whites and blacks recently transplanted from the South in search of work and opportunity. Whites and blacks were frequently at odds due to racial **prejudice** and competition over housing, jobs, and other resources. At the end of the riot, 34 were reported dead and 760 were injured. This was just one of many riots that erupted in the North in this period.

These riots highlighted a major shift in the white-black conflict. Prior to the mid-century, African Americans were generally the target of riots, not participants. Despite this, African Americans suffered the most deaths and received the most damage to their personal property. Now, for the first time, blacks began to participate in racial riots.

CALIFORNIA NIGHTMARE

When an opportunity to move to California presented itself, Williams thought it would be in his best interests to go. California seemed a better alternative to the hostility of Detroit. Since the end of slavery, African Americans had been drawn to the North, the Midwest, and the West—the farthest reaches of the new and provocative frontier. Like whites, African Americans were caught up in the notion of the West and its promise of a new life, open spaces, and unlimited freedom.

But the West was a disappointment to Williams. Rampant racism and police harassment made life difficult. Williams was unhappy, and the headaches he began to experience made life in California unbearable. After only three months, Williams decided to move back home.

BACK TO NORTH CAROLINA AND INTO THE ARMY

Monroe, North Carolina, in 1944, was in worse shape than when he had left as a teenager. The influx of African American soldiers to nearby Camp Sutton presented a challenge to whites who were accustomed to black compliance to the way of life in the South. These soldiers were primarily from the North and were not accustomed to the laws and customs of the South. Scuffles between whites and black soldiers were rife throughout the South, including Monroe. Williams and his family heard tales of racial conflict all too frequently, such as when an African American soldier stabbed a white man after having been told to leave a white-only cafe and then being shoved by a white patron outside. Conflicts such as these threatened the safety of black males who resided in North Carolina, because whites often retaliated against any available black male. Williams was a likely target, because it was well-known that he was not a passive type. Williams' parents, fearing for his life, "began to think that Robert should not stay in

Monroe" (Tyson, 45). Williams decided to pursue his dream and move to New York. Three months later, after arriving in New York, Williams was drafted.

World War II

America's involvement in the Second World War appeared, at first, a beacon of hope for African Americans. During the war years, blacks not only served the war effort, but remained at the forefront of the struggle for racial equality and justice.

As part of the propaganda campaign for the war, the Axis powers (Germany, Italy, and Japan, who were the enemies of the Allies, including the U.S., Great Britain, the U.S.S.R., and others) were depicted as evil, since it was their goal to literally rule the world and conquer the democratic nations. Throngs of blacks were eager to participate in the war, as they had participated in all major conflicts since America's founding. Moreover, prominent leaders such as W.E.B. Du Bois as well as ordinary citizens were hopeful that by helping in the fight for democracy abroad, they might achieve the same for themselves on the home front. But the ominous Jim Crow showed its ugly head in the war, and men (and later women) served in segregated units.

Blacks made it no secret that they were unhappy with this. Articles on the subject were published in black presses across the nation. Leaders like A. Philip Randolph made desegregation of the military a crusade. Randolph, president of the Brotherhood of Sleeping Car Porters, gathered several leaders and threatened President Roosevelt with a march on Washington that would flood the nation's capitol with some 100,000 demonstrators. Roosevelt issued Executive Order 8802, which desegregated defense industry and government jobs but did not desegregate the military (that would not come until 1948 with Executive Order 9981).

Notwithstanding the indignities of segregation and the racism experienced while in the military, black men and women served with distinction. The Tuskegee Airmen, so-named for the training program at Tuskegee Army Air Field in Alabama, were among the most well-known heroes of the war, though many whites had scoffed at the idea that blacks could learn how to fly an airplane. Significantly, all the officers of that unit were black and not white, as was the custom for other all-black units. The Tuskegee Airmen flew some 200 missions to escort bombers into enemy territory and did not lose one bomber.

Important films that depict the black experience during World War II include *A Soldier's Story* (1984) and *The Tuskegee Airmen* (1995). *Miracle at St. Anna* (based on a novel by James McBride) premiered in September 2008.

The innately rebellious Williams did not assimilate well into the army, where Jim Crow culture was sustained. Williams was vexed when only the white soldiers were given coffee and donuts. He clashed with his superiors and refused orders outright. The only aspects of military life that were appealing to Williams were learning how to use weapons and taking a creative writing course. After a year and a half, the army had had enough of the intractable Williams and let him go with an honorable discharge. Once again Williams returned home to North Carolina.

THE FIRST DEMONSTRATION OF ARMED SELF-DEFENSE

Williams' return home was bittersweet. At twenty-one years of age his life had just begun, but no one would hire him. Opportunities for blacks in general were limited, but for a well-known radical like Williams, a career was close to impossible. But if work was hard to find, he found something else: camaraderie, love, and a grand purpose.

Bernie Montgomery, a boyhood friend, had just returned home from the war. Montgomery had not been known as a radical. But the war changed him. It changed most black men by making them fearless and aware of their own strength. Back in the South, Montgomery had a difficult time submitting to the indignities of Jim Crow and boldfaced oppression without fighting back, either verbally or physically. Montgomery's situation was complicated by the fact that he had sustained a serious head injury, which may have adversely affected him mentally. He struck his boss during an argument over his pay and then killed him with a knife. His clothes were still stained with blood when they found him.

Williams and other vets protested the death penalty that Montgomery received, but to no avail: he died in a gas chamber in 1947. The local Ku Klux Klan made plans to take Montgomery's lifeless body and ordered the African American funeral homeowner to remove the U.S. flags that adorned his casket. He refused to do so. When the Klan rode out in their infamous motorcade (which was often escorted by local police officers) to the Harris Funeral Home, they were met by a group of forty African American men—with rifles. Williams was among them. Steely-eyed and defiant, the men watched the hooded Klan members scurry away from the scene.

The men that stood off the Klan were mostly veterans, like Williams. These men saw each other frequently at the barbershop or the unemployment office, where they went to collect their weekly payment of $20, a part of their veterans' benefits. Despite their service to their country, these men were frequently disrespected at the unemployment office, because racist whites did not like the fact that African American men received benefits from the government. These were the very men who collaborated in the effort to grant Montgomery clemency, pointing out that during the trial it was not even considered how his head injury might have affected his mental state or that he could have acted in self-defense.

Mabel Ola Robinson was just fifteen when she met the strapping Robert F. Williams. She lived in a different black section of town, but not too far from Williams' home. They knew each other through her sister and his best friend, who were married. They often went dancing, and he walked her home from school. They married in 1947. Shortly thereafter, his mother died, and they moved in with Williams' father.

At first, Mabel did not understand Williams. His radicalness unnerved her. It was inconceivable to her that someone would willfully challenge the system of white supremacy and Jim Crow. She had never known anyone like Williams. But when Williams' father told her the story of Sikes, she began to understand.

When the couple's first child, Robert Jr., was born in 1948, Williams moved the family to Detroit, Michigan. The move was necessary, for his unemployment payments had ended, and he could find no work in his hometown.

IN SEARCH OF A LIFE

Between 1948 and 1955, Williams struggled to pursue his personal dreams and to provide for his family. Williams knew he would have no trouble finding work in Detroit, even if he had to take jobs he did not want. What he really wanted to do, however, was to become a writer, like his literary idol Langston Hughes. But he took a job on the night shift for the Cadillac Motor Company. While Mabel attended Northwestern High School, Williams took care of the baby and composed poems and other stories inspired by his experiences growing up in the South. His fictional story, "Someday, I'm Going Back South" was published in the Detroit *Daily Worker* in 1949. In this story, the protagonist, a native of the South, moves North, but plans to return to the South to wage a struggle to free his people.

Williams had not cared for the grimy, overcrowded, and unfriendly city back in 1942. His feelings did not change. Racism at work was a problem. And the work itself was loud, monotonous, and unsatisfying. Williams' headaches returned. When Williams was fired, there was no question as to whether he should stay in Detroit. An FBI report stated that Williams "was discharged from his job with the Cadillac Motor Car Company in Detroit because of excessive absenteeism and threatening his supervisors with bodily harm" (Tyson, 63).

In 1949, the Williams family returned to Monroe, North Carolina. It appeared that Williams was going to get to study writing after all—with the indirect help of the FBI. Williams had been a person of interest to them since his teens, and as an adult, he drew more attention to himself by having communist friends. The FBI scoured his hometown looking for incriminating information. They found none. Unbeknown to Williams, the FBI was able to convince businesses not to hire him. Since he could not find any work, he went to school.

Williams enrolled in West Virginia State College in Institute, West Virginia. This college was one of the only African American institutions that offered creative writing courses. Williams studied writing and got involved with the university newspaper and literary magazine. He took a course from the militant Dr. Herman G. Candy, who encouraged radicalism. Williams complained that the other students were too interested in material and self-centered pursuits. At every opportunity, Williams traveled back to his father's home, where his wife and son lived. When Williams' second son, John Chalmers, was born, he moved back home.

He attended North Carolina College for Negroes in Durham, North Carolina in 1950, but then, in 1951, switched to Johnson C. Smith College, the alma mater of his grandfather, in Charlotte, North Carolina.

If Williams expected to find other militants like himself and his grandfather, he was sorely mistaken. Indeed, as an excerpt from a piece that was published in Paul Robeson's newspaper *Freedom*, reveals, Williams was shocked to realize that the student body and the professors were "passive" in regard to protest; that the teachers endorsed "Uncle Tomism," and that the opportunity to "be the most militant agitators for democracy" were squandered on materialistic pursuits (Tyson, 69). The highlight of his enrollment at Johnson C. Smith was going to a lecture by Langston Hughes.

In 1953, Williams' GI bill ran out and he had to drop out of college. Still no one would hire him. Williams left his wife and two sons in Monroe and trekked alone to New Jersey, where he found employment at Curtiss Wright Aeronautics. While in New Jersey, he gravitated towards a host of radicals, some of whom were involved in the American Labor Party and the Communist Party. These friends provided an environment where he was permitted to express his views without censure. However, Williams did not intend to join either party, because he did not agree with their nonreligious bent or their emphasis on class over race.

Williams was eventually able to move his family to an apartment in New York, but the neighborhood was almost more volatile than Monroe. Mabel Williams caged herself indoors, fearful of going out. She kept a 9-mm Luger pistol within arm's reach. Her fear was not unfounded. Neighbors harassed the Williamses, calling them "niggers" and vandalizing their property. The family moved back to Monroe.

Williams desperate search for work led him to Los Angeles, California, where he heard there were aircraft workers needed. He was not hired. He roamed from place to place in search of any kind of work. Nearly destitute, Williams entered a recruiting office for the U.S. Marine Corps. In the 1954 photo of Private First Class Robert F. Williams, he is smiling—and he rarely smiled in pictures. This time he had a lot to be optimistic about: the marine recruiting office had promised him an opportunity to take journalism classes and to pay for three more years of college in exchange for three years of enlistment.

Williams completed basic training with a good feeling. He enjoyed the rigorous exercise, and he was treated well, at first. But when it came time for him to start his new job in information services as promised, he was assigned duties as a supply sergeant. Williams was crushed and angry. He launched a writing campaign to Charles Diggs, Congressman of Michigan, Adam Clayton Powell, President Dwight Eisenhower, and the NAACP. After only sixteen months Williams left the Marines with "an undesirable discharge and a smoldering bitterness" (Tyson, 73).

ACTIVISM

National Association for the Advancement of Colored People

Williams wrote in his autobiography, *Negroes with Guns*, "When I got out of the Marine Corps, I knew I wanted to go home and join the NAACP" (14). However, the local National Association for the Advancement of Colored People (NAACP) was in dire straits, largely as a result of the 1954 Supreme Court decision to desegregate schools. In response to that ruling, there had been violent backlash. In some areas of the South, the NAACP was made illegal. Some members lost their jobs. Others were harassed, viciously attacked, or murdered. Williams attended the meeting where the remaining six members wanted to close the Monroe chapter. Williams tried to persuade them against this. The members decided to vote Williams in as the new president, and then all but one or two members stayed on. Williams asserted that they "turned [the organization] over to me to die … so it would not die in their hands" (80). Dr. Albert E. Perry was one of the original members, and he was elected the vice president.

Negroes with Guns

Negroes with Guns (1962) is the title of the autobiography of Robert F. Williams. The title evokes black empowerment on one hand, and fear and fury on the other.

Beginning in slavery, blacks were bound by sundry laws. Enslaved blacks could not marry, read, or write. They could not travel without permission from the plantation owner. And they had no voting or any other civil rights. Blacks were not allowed to carry arms—for obvious reasons. Blacks without guns could not easily rebel against their white masters.

Historically, the gun, in any setting, has symbolized power. With a gun, one can protect self, family, and property, as well as exert a threat toward

---

(continued)

someone else. White Americans, since the foundation of the nation, have made free use of this empowering tool. In this context of international war, the victor and the image of military might are glorified. In the American frontier, the gun symbolized unbridled freedom and represented an exciting, though hazardous, period in history. Notwithstanding the lore of gun-wielding black cowboys and frontiersmen, the idea of blacks with guns has been as problematic for conservative whites in the post-emancipation years as it was during slavery.

At the end of Reconstruction in 1877, racist whites in the South viewed blacks with guns as an anomaly, an oddity, or an atrocity. For one thing, blacks were for the most part docile under the heavy pressure of economic and political control fortified by physical intimidation. Racist organizations such as the Ku Klux Klan helped to monitor and suppress black resistance. For another thing, blacks were not permitted to exercise power, and as such, blacks *and* guns were incongruous to the preexisting social construction that prescribed racist white supremacy and privilege. The few isolated occasions when blacks attempted to arm themselves and protect themselves and their community from anti-black violence and criminal activities were fruitless.

During the two World Wars of the twentieth century, blacks, particularly the soldiers, projected an unprecedented confidence and militancy. A number of racial conflicts emerged as a result of black soldiers not kowtowing to social expectation. Williams was one of a number of black soldiers who returned to their communities and physically fought back. Williams' demonstration of organized armed power was successful in North Carolina. Whites were often flabbergasted by the "audacity" of blacks to challenge *them* with guns, but they were also forced to back down from what had previously been the unbridled terrorizing of blacks.

However, when organizations like the Black Panther Party for Self-Defense armed themselves during the Black Power Movement of the 1960s, the reaction, for many conservative whites, was outrage and fear. The media portrayed "Negroes with guns" in this context as criminals. But the original purpose of guns for the Black Panthers was to protect the community from police harassment and abuse. And it worked.

When Williams became president of the Monroe chapter of the NAACP, he undoubtedly planned to give the chapter a makeover, as it had something of a poor reputation. Nor was it actively challenging discrimination, injustice, or racial violence. Under Williams' leadership, the Monroe chapter took a turn for the better. Membership boomed. The NAACP tended to draw from the black middle class, but Williams recruited new members from unorthodox places, such as barbershops, pool halls, and street corners.

The NAACP was not the only organization undergoing a resurgence in Monroe. The Klan experienced a revival, due in large part as a response to the desegregation of public schools. The Klan became increasingly visible about town, holding rallies and acting out violently against local blacks.

Union County Council on Human Relations

Williams also helped establish the interracial Union County Council on Human Relations. The aim of this organization was to "promote equal opportunity for all citizens in employment, education, recreation, and all other phases of community life" (Tyson, 83). Dr. Perry was elected president, J. Ray Shute was vice president, and Williams' wife Mabel was the secretary. Shute, a white liberal and former mayor of Monroe, was generous to Williams, helping him find a job with a textile factory as a security guard and gifting him a used car so that he could make the commute.

Williams' association with whites, through the Council on Human Relations, with his communist friends, and at the mostly white Unitarian church he attended, set him apart from future militants. Williams was not a separatist. But his radicalism would eventually alienate him from many of his white supporters.

Swimming Pool Campaign

The young African American boy who drowned in a lake near Monroe in the summer of 1957 was not the first to die in that way. Scores of African American boys drowned each summer because they had no safe swimming pool available to them. The local swimming pool at the Monroe Country Club was for whites only.

Emboldened by his newfound organizational strength, Williams launched a campaign to desegregate the Monroe Country Club swimming pool. As he saw it, the pool was funded by federal money, and, therefore, whites had no right to prohibit African Americans from using it. Though Williams felt that something drastic needed to be done to prevent the unnecessary drowning of black children, he began by using techniques that were vintage NAACP, such as sending letters to the city and to the Parks and Recreation Commission, rather than by staging dramatic demonstrations.

The Commission agreed to meet with a small delegation of African Americans. Among them was Dr. Perry. The delegates requested a separate time for African American children to use the pool. The Commission rejected that idea because they would not allow blacks to use the same pool as whites. They said it would be too expensive to maintain separate pools, but promised some day, when there were funds to do so, to build a separate swimming pool.

Williams next sought assistance from the Council on Human Relations, but their response was not at all what he had expected. Although at the inception of the organization, the members had bravely vowed to support integration in all its forms, the white members objected to the swimming pool campaign. Even these progressive whites had been tainted by the system of racism. Mabel Williams cynically commented to her husband that "White fools don't want you to sit beside them on the bus ... you really think they're gonna let you jump in the water with them half-naked?" (Tyson, 84). Other whites on the council believed "the campaign impolitic and untimely" (Tyson, 85). This polarization between the blacks and whites contributed, in a large way, to the dissolution of the organization.

When negotiation failed to produce any results, Williams turned to demonstration. Williams and Dr. Perry led eight youths to the pool, where they stood in protest at the gate. The objective was to force a test case, allowing the NAACP to lead a battle in the court system. However, their protests caused the Klan to implement its own campaign. In Williams' words, they schemed "to get rid of us, to drive us out of the community, directed primarily at Dr. Albert E. Perry, our vice-president, and myself" (Williams, *Negroes with Guns*, 16).

Black Armed Guard

Williams and others tried various means of protecting themselves and the black community from Klan intimidation and violence. Local ministers went to county and city officials for help. Williams wrote that their pleas were rejected "on the grounds that the Klan was a legal organization having as much constitutional right to organize as the NAACP" (Williams, *Negroes with Guns*, 17). Williams led a futile campaign to bring an end to Klan activities by sending appeals to the governor and the president.

Williams reasoned that if the government would not help, or even enforce the Fourteenth Amendment, blacks had to defend themselves. Williams received a charter membership to the National Rifle Association (NRA), and organized the Black Armed Guard, consisting mostly of black veterans.

Confrontation with the Ku Klux Klan

The summer of 1957 sizzled with tension. In the wake of numerous death threats and several motorcades featuring rancorous whites wearing white robes and hoods shooting into the air, Williams prepared the Black Armed Guard. The group assembled numerous weapons, especially rifles and helmets, and dug foxholes. Training sessions were held and the Guard members participated in nightly vigils. The women crafted a system for passing messages by phone for emergencies. Mrs. Crowder, a kindly, bespectacled elderly woman, kept rifles behind the walls of her house. Williams himself taught his wife and two boys how to use a gun. But the gun offered Mabel Williams little comfort. She later recalled the frightening times "when the four of us—me, Rob's father, and the two boys—we'd sit up all night with our guns, afraid someone would come kill us while Rob was at Dr. Perry's" (Tyson, 88).

Ku Klux Klan

The Ku Klux Klan (KKK) is the most notorious racist or white supremacist organization in America. But it is not the only one, nor is it, as some believe, a phenomenon restricted to the South. Although the organization was founded in the South in Tennessee, in the wake of the Civil War (1861–1865), there are KKK groups throughout America.

One of the main purposes of the KKK when it was founded was to help maintain social, economic, and political control over blacks in the South. When the organization migrated to other areas, the objectives stayed much the same. Prime targets of the KKK were individuals who tried to resist or challenge white supremacy. Sometimes the KKK conducted nightly visits, wherein "nightriders" rode through black sections of town on horses wearing hooded masks and robes. Sometimes they augmented their rides with scare-inducing ghastly effects, like howls, gunshots, and the use of a gibberish language. Sometimes the KKK left frightening symbols upon the property of blacks, like burning crosses or nooses to serve as a warning or threat. Although they conducted most of their activities after dark (reinforcing the superstition of evil spirits that appear only after sundown), they also held marches through the town during the day.

The KKK was not beyond implementing actual violence against blacks. In fact, a number of brutal attacks and murders were implemented by the KKK. Lynchings were carried out by unmasked white mobs and town citizens or the KKK.

The use of masks by the KKK was employed for the fear factor, as well as to hide the identities of whites from blacks and, in some cases, from other whites. KKK members were known to comprise most of the white male citizens in a town, including law enforcement and town officials.

The KKK maintains its membership even today, But most members do not wear masks or robes and, because of laws and the fact that the KKK is looked down upon by mainstream society, the vicious crimes have been reduced drastically. Yet hate crimes still happen, though various groups and formal agencies maintain a watch over racism and racist organizations such as the KKK.

The moment the Black Armed Guard had been preparing for arrived that fall. Someone heard that the Klan planned to attack Dr. Perry at his home. When the motorcade roared into Dr. Perry's neighborhood, firing their guns at his house, they saw a stunning sight. Some sixty African Americans, hunkering in fortifications and entrenchments, pointed their rifles and fired—cautiously, as they had been instructed—at the ground, sending the Klan scurrying out of the neighborhood. It was only then that the city council stepped in, banning the Ku Klux Klan from staging motorcades in Monroe.

This victory was momentous for blacks in Monroe, as well as for the history of African American protest. It was an unprecedented organized demonstration of self-defense against racial violence. But Williams reported that "only three Negro publications—the *Afro-American*, the *Norfolk Journal and Guide*, and *Jet*—reported the fight" (Williams, 21). Shortly after this demonstration, Dr. Perry was falsely charged with and convicted of having performed an abortion on a white woman. He was sentenced to five years in prison.

Desegregating Monroe Schools

Three years prior to the climactic confrontation at Dr. Perry's home, the NAACP had achieved a great feat by winning the famous *Brown v. Board of Education* case. The result was the eradication of separate schools for blacks and whites. The celebrations were brief, however, for integrating schools in the South proved to be an ordeal in itself, another harrowing chapter in the struggle for civil rights.

The ruling meant little to many whites in the South. Indeed, in most towns, whites completely ignored the ruling. And opposition was vicious. Sweet-faced youths shouted and spewed venomous words at the first group of black students. In places like Little Rock, Arkansas, the national guard had to be called in, but they did little to shelter the African American students from the cruel taunting and harassment that continued throughout the school year. African American teachers also suffered, as they were rarely hired in the predominately white schools.

In early October 1958, Robert and Mabel Williams were the first to attempt to integrate the East Elementary Schools in Monroe with their two young boys. They sent a letter protesting the lack of inclusion of black students and teachers in Monroe schools to the school board. The letter surreptitiously wound up in the local paper for all to see. The town was up in arms. But the Williamses were unable to follow through with enrolling their children into the local white school due to a subsequent campaign that absorbed their time and focus.

The Kissing Case

In late October, Williams was consumed with an entirely different issue. Two young African American boys, aged seven and nine, were roughly ushered into the county police station, where they were first beaten and then tormented by police officers during the course of their detainment. The young boys, David Ezell Simpson and James Hanover Grissom Thompson, had quite innocently kissed or (to their peril) been kissed by white girls while at play. Despite their young ages, the boys were accused of rape.

There were numerous variations to the story of what happened on that fall day in October. According to Thompson, he and Simpson were playing in water with some white children, when one of the boys suggested they play the kissing game with some white girls nearby. Sissy Sutton, one of the girls, agreed and sat in his lap, and on the lap of one of the white boys, and kissed them on the cheek. Later, at home, the girl told her mother. The dramatic events that ensued would haunt Simpson and Thompson for the rest of their lives.

Historically, black males would have been lynched for merely touching, looking at, or speaking to a white woman. Williams instructed the armed guard to watch over the boys' mothers. Although a mob formed shortly after word circulated through the white community about what happened, they did not wage an attack. A sensationalized scandal followed, and the two mothers' reputations were smeared, resulting in the loss of their jobs.

The *London News Chronicle* broke the story in a sympathetic manner. The story spread quickly to the continent where outraged Europeans launched several demonstrations on behalf of the two young boys. Williams remembered that "only then did many American newspapers begin to express 'concern' about the 'Kissing Case' " (Williams, *Negroes with Guns*, 24).

Williams downplayed his contribution to the case in his autobiography, but his actions greatly elevated his status in the civil rights community. Williams went first to the NAACP office, but they would not take on a controversial case involving rape. Without the support of the NAACP, Williams embarked on a whirlwind speaking tour, making television and radio appearances to expose and protest the outlandish charge against the two boys. Thus, the world first took notice of Robert F. Williams, the small-town hero.

Williams and other members of the local NAACP formed the Committee to Combat Racial Injustice. Through this organization, Williams provided further support to the two boys. Only later, when the case gained notoriety, did the NAACP get involved. Meanwhile, the children were sentenced to up to fourteen years at a reformatory and were transferred to Morrison Training School. Overwhelming public pressure forced the judge to change his verdict. When the boys were freed in 1959, their families left Monroe.

NAACP Suspension

The episode that marked Williams forever as a militant, a man to be feared, and got him in trouble with the national office of the NAACP, started with two upsetting court cases involving black victims. In one, a white man was acquitted after he kicked a black maid down a flight of stairs at a hotel. In the other, a white man was acquitted of an attempted rape charge against a pregnant black woman, even though a white neighbor testified on the woman's behalf. During that trial, the defendant's attorney referred to the white man's wife as a "pure flower of life," and pandered to the racism that was prevalent among local whites when he asked rhetorically, "Do you think this man would have left this pure flower for that?"

Frustrated and angry, the African American women who sat with Williams in the courtroom verbally attacked him. He was the one who had persuaded the victim's brothers not to retaliate, telling them to take legal recourse instead. The women heaped blame on Williams. After that trial, Williams faced reporters and made the following notorious statement:

> We must be willing to kill if necessary. We cannot take these people who do us injustice to the court and it becomes necessary to punish them ourselves. In the future we are going to have to try and convict these people on the spot. [These court decisions] open the way to real violence. We cannot rely on the law. We get no justice under the present system. If we feel that injustice is done, we must right then and there on the spot be prepared to inflict punishment on these people. I feel this is the only way of survival. Since the federal government will not bring a halt to lynching in the South and since the so-called courts lynch our people legally, if it's necessary to stop lynching with lynching, then we must be willing to resort to that method. (Tyson, 149)

Williams' words outraged and horrified whites and sent an uneasy ripple through the civil rights leadership. Ultimately, the NAACP sought to distance itself from the militant Williams. His public endorsement of self-defense endangered the organization's hard-won reputation and compromised its leverage with city, state, and federal contacts.

Williams felt he was justified in what he said, especially considering the circumstances. But his opinion was not supported by any of the prominent civil rights leaders. He was informed that he was suspended from the NAACP. Williams tried to defend himself, explaining to Roy Wilkins, executive secretary of the NAACP, in a telephone conversation, that he was reflecting his own views and opinions, not those of the NAACP. On June 3, 1950, Williams appealed to the Committee on Branches in New York. Williams was reprimanded and informed that he would be suspended for six months.

The Crusader *Weekly Newsletter and Other Campaigns*

Temporarily expelled from the NAACP, Williams undertook a venture of his own. Debuting on July 26, 1959, *The Crusader* featured his philosophy on self-defense, as well as the civil rights struggle in Monroe, North Carolina and abroad, international news, and articles that countered the prevalent negative portrayals of blacks and Africa.

After Williams was reinstated to the NAACP and resumed the presidency of the chapter in Monroe, the national office had little more to do with him. He did not much care. He had proved that he could be productive without national support. So he continued on, wielding his rifle and demonstrating his belief that community work, nonviolence, and self-defense could go hand in hand.

In 1960, Williams provided pivotal support for a women-led project called CARE, or Crusaders Association for Relief and Enlightenment. CARE provided food, clothes, and other essential items to poor blacks in the community. Williams went on a lecture tour to request financial assistance and donations. Williams was a favorite in Harlem. His supporters there assisted with the CARE program and also helped fund his arsenal of guns. Malcolm X, a prominent militant and Muslim minister, frequently invited Williams to speak at his temple. Other supporters included actors Ossie Davis and Ruby Dee (both deeply involved with the conservative contingent of the Civil Rights Movement), W.E.B. Du Bois' wife, Shirley Graham Du Bois, and the black historian John Hendrik Clarke.

In 1960, after the famous sit-in at a Woolworth's store in Greensboro, North Carolina, Williams led his organization in a sit-in campaign of its own. Williams and a dozen blacks staged the first sit-ins at Gable's Drug Store and Jones Drug Store. At both locations, the managers closed the lunch counters.

Williams' activists were never violently attacked by whites in Monroe. Williams reasoned that this was because whites knew that he and his group had guns. During one demonstration, Williams was arrested for trespassing. While Williams was occupied with the resulting legal proceedings, Monroe blacks continued to stage sit-ins, and *The Crusader* encouraged blacks to boycott the various lunch counters at downtown stores that refused to serve them. The sit-in movement in Monroe continued throughout the next year, but its success was questionable. The authorities were not easily persuaded to open up the town's lunch counters to blacks.

In contrast to other sit-ins taking place elsewhere in the nation, there were a limited number of participating activists, few arrests, and not a lot of media attention. Martin Luther King, Jr. utilized violent backlash against those participating in the sit-ins to engender sympathy and force the American government to intervene. However, Williams used armed self-defense to *prevent* violent attacks. Thus, there was very little if any actual violence attending the Monroe sit-ins, which reduced their newsworthiness. Moreover, Williams' message did not draw the sort of attention that won legions of white and black admirers to King's camp. Whites tended to be highly leery of Williams' volatile statements and his endorsement of self-defense, as they found him threatening.

Meanwhile the swimming pool campaign had begun to bear fruit. One Sunday in 1961, a mob of several thousand whites descended upon Monroe to halt the demonstrations of black picketers who were still demanding that they be allowed to swim in the only swimming pool in town. Williams described in his book *Negroes with Guns* (1962) how he was driving on the highway when someone from the white mob hit his car, causing both cars to get trapped in a ditch. Williams and some teenagers were in the car when they were approached by a white man with a bat, while the mob chanted "Kill the Niggers!" Williams brandished his Army .45. The mob hurled rocks at his car, while three police officers who were already at the scene watched and did nothing. Williams got out of the car with his weapon, then punched an officer who tried to take his gun. Another officer took out his gun. A teenager, who was in the car with Williams, convinced the officer otherwise when he leveled his .45 at him. The white mob let Williams and the teens go when the chief of police gave orders at the behest of Steve Presson, a member of the Monroe City Council. Williams eventually joined the picket line at the swimming pool. As a result of this demonstration, the pool was closed for the rest of the year.

Violence against the blacks of Monroe escalated following the swimming pool campaign. Armed whites drove through black neighborhoods, firing off their rifles. Volunteers of the Armed Black Guard frequently fired back with warning shots. Williams' home was attacked one night by the State National Guard. Williams approached the FBI. Congressman Frank Kowalski of Connecticut beseeched Attorney General Robert Kennedy to help. Kennedy called for an investigation, resulting in an interview with the chief of police, who denied that there was anything going on.

In the wake of this blaring injustice, Williams prepared his chapter to launch a broad campaign. He created a ten-point program that included a demand for the city to end employment discrimination, build an additional swimming pool, and initiate the desegregation procress of public schools. On August 15, 1961, Williams read those demands to the Monroe Board of Aldermen, to no avail. But Williams had a backup plan. He would stage more demonstrations. In the meantime, he invited a group of young Freedom Riders to come to Monroe.

FREEDOM RIDERS

The seventeen Freedom Riders who arrived in Monroe were confident that nonviolence was the best approach for protest. The Freedom Riders, black and white activists, comprised a group of nervy college students who challenged a law that upheld segregation on interstate travel and facilities and were devoted to the principles of nonviolence and direct action. They wanted an opportunity to show Williams just how effective nonviolence was. Though highly skeptical, Williams watched them as they established "Freedom House" to train new recruits and formed the Monroe Non-Violent Action Committee. When the activists breezily commented on the friendliness of the police officers and told Williams that he had, perhaps, misgauged the climate of his community, Williams warned them that the cordiality they had experienced in their limited time in Monroe was a ruse.

The demonstrations started out peaceably enough with the **picketing** of the Monroe Courthouse. On the third day, all that changed. Whites spat in the faces of the activists and jeered at them. One of the activists was arrested. In the days to follow, isolated outbreaks of violence were reported throughout the community. One activist was shot in the stomach; another went missing. Williams contacted the governor's office, attempting to get help to find the missing youth. The governor's office blamed him for the violent eruption.

What had transpired confirmed to Williams that nonviolence provoked violence. Williams' armed demonstrations had never produced such horrific violence. In the wake of the nonviolent demonstrations, he scrambled to protect the activists and his community.

But conditions were steadily worsening, with the violence spilling out into the community, affecting residents who had nothing to do with the demonstrations. Williams returned home to figure out his next strategy. Increasing numbers of outsiders streamed into the community, exacerbating the situation. Williams' phone rang constantly—parents looking for their children; people calling to inform Williams that some of the activists had been arrested or were in need of medical attention. Whites roared through the neighborhood randomly firing shots.

Williams had more than enough to deal with when, one Sunday, a white couple who had driven into his neighborhood was brought to him. They said they were lost. Williams was told that the couple had been seen the previous day driving through the neighborhood emblazoning a sign on their car that read "Open Season on Coons." The term "coons" was used by whites to refer to blacks. Although Williams was suspicious of the couple, he felt he could not leave them alone with the restive black crowd outside his door. He insisted that the couple come into his home and stay until the situation cooled down.

Before long, Williams received a call from the police chief, who threatened that he would be lynched before the night was over. Williams had had death threats many times before, and had always responded by rounding up his guards, or by keeping armed vigil with his family. This time was different. Monroe was in chaos, presenting an opportunity for racist cops to get rid of him. Someone alerted him to a television report about troops being assembled to besiege his home. Williams feared this would provide a prime opportunity for the police chief to carry out his threat. He and his family fled to New York that night.

Once in New York, Williams, thinking he had averted disaster, began to plan a publicity campaign to expose the roots of the pandemonium that had broken out in Monroe. He had no idea that he was a wanted man until, watching the news on television, he found out that he was being charged with kidnapping the white couple he had sheltered in his home.

He could hardly believe that it was his photo, grim-faced, glaring back at him on the screen. Last Williams remembered, he had seen the couple off to safety after he offered them refuge in his home. In hindsight, Williams figured that the couple had been part of a plot to frame him. As told by the white couple, the account of what happened that night in Monroe shifted constantly.

Williams did not think there was any possible way he would turn himself in, knowing all too well that the court system did not mete out justice for blacks. He decided he could not stay in America, for there would be no place to hide. Williams and his family would flee the country.

IN EXILE

Canada

Canada was Williams' first choice for exile. It had been a haven of choice for black slaves who had braved the treacherous journey to freedom. With the assistance of several socialist friends, Williams and his family arrived there safely, and lived for a while with a white family. But they were in constant fear. FBI "Wanted" posters of Williams hung in public places, and one white couple who briefly hid the Williams was visited by the FBI as well as Royal Canadian agents. They left a warning for Williams that he would, undoubtedly, make it back alive to America when they found him. It became clear that Canada was not a safe place. Williams' friends helped put together an escape plan to Cuba.

Cuba

Williams' first two trips to Cuba were recent. On his first visit, in 1960, he went as a delegate of the Fair Play for Cuba Committee, an organization established in New York to support Fidel Castro's regime. During that trip he had the opportunity to meet Castro. In his late twenties, Castro had led an armed revolution to overthrow the dictator Fulgencio Batista. During Batista's reign, years of protest and civil disobedience demonstrations had been met with arrests, torture, violence, and greater limitations on freedom. In 1959, when Castro took over power in Cuba at the age of thirty-three, the Cubans were overjoyed. Castro, however, was an enemy of the American government. Despite this, he was an idol to many black militants. Williams admired him and even emulated him in small ways, like growing out his beard and taking up the habit of smoking cigars. During Williams' second trip to Cuba—a personal invitation from Castro—he had been offered permanent residency, which he declined.

Williams and his family arrived in Cuba in 1961. Though he longed to be in America, Williams could relax somewhat and resume his activism. He started a radical radio station, Radio Free Dixie, which featured a fusion of racial commentary with soulful ballads, jazz, and protest music. He continued the publication of *The Crusader* in America. During the race riots of the 1960s, Williams attacked the system and institutions of racism with blistering commentary and praised the young rioters for lashing out at the white oppressor. During this period he displayed a radicalism that was more dramatic than before. In America, Williams became a cult figure to emerging black militants. His book, *Negroes with Guns* (1962), was written during his exile in Cuba. It had a significant influence on organizations such as the Black Panther Party for Self-Defense and the Deacons for Defense and Justice, for whom it was considered essential reading. Both organizations engaged in armed resistance to defend their communities.

But the situation in Cuba was far from ideal and getting worse. Communists residing in Cuba presented a problem. "I find many of [the Cuban Communists and Communist Party USA members in Cuba] to be very notorious racists" he wrote to one former communist, and it was reported by the FBI that "Williams 'has stubbed his toes with the Communist Party of Cuba' because of his 'criticism of [the] Communist Party for barring Negroes from leadership' " (Tyson, 292, 294). It became increasingly difficult to continue his broadcasts and his work due to the attempt of the Cuban government to censor him. It was not long before Williams knew that his future was not in Cuba. But it would be no easy task to leave.

China

In 1965, Castro allowed Williams to go to North Vietnam to speak to black troops. The Cuban leader fully expected him to return, but Williams had other plans. The trip was a ruse. After addressing the troops, he and his family moved to Beijing, China. Both Cuba and China were enemies of the U.S. during this time—a fact that was not going to make Williams' status back in the States easy. Williams enjoyed greater freedoms in China and was treated like a celebrity, provided with a chauffeur, limo, and personal attendants.

In China, Williams carried out his activism without interference. He continued his radio program and stayed in touch with black liberation movements in America. He regularly donated money to individuals (such as Fannie Lou Hamer, a black civil rights activist who was heavily involved in voter registration and social welfare programs in Mississippi) and organizations (such as the militant Revolutionary Action Movement [RAM] and the

Republic of New Afrika [RNA], a black nationalist group founded in 1968). The RNA elected Williams as president-in-exile. Following Malcolm X's assassination, "Richard Gibson, editor of *Now!* magazine in New York, wrote to Williams in 1965, 'Malcolm's removal from the scene makes you the senior spokesman for Afro-American militants'" (Tyson, 297).

Mao took no offense when Williams decided it was time to return to America. Williams made a deal with the United States: he would be able to return in exchange for valuable information on the cultural, social, and political life in China. Mao was hopeful that Williams would help prepare the way for a new relationship between the two countries. Williams visited Africa and London before he made his final return to America.

RETURN TO THE UNITED STATES

On September 12, 1969, a group of black militants waited with bated breath as Williams climbed off the plane in Detroit, Michigan. Detroit was a place of huge significance for the times. In 1967, a race riot had culminated in a mass exodus of whites, leaving the city mostly black. For the first time in the city's history, a black mayor was elected. The black leaders of Williams' day had been proponents of nonviolence, but the leaders of African American protest in the late 1960s were edgy, ultra-radical, and militant like Williams. As they waited at the airport, they fully intended to accept Williams as their leader, although they expected him to adjust his ideology whenever his did not match up to their own. However, Williams surprised them all, including the media who greeted him with questions and befuddled expressions.

Neither Robert nor Mabel Williams fit the image of a black power proponent. For one thing they did not wear afros, and for another, Williams appeared "almost embarrassed by his status" (Tyson, 302). Most significantly, Williams appeared subdued. Gone was the fiery rhetoric that made his admirers marvel. And to black militants' dismay, he was critical of their programs. He was not anti-American. He did not endorse black separatism. He had white friends and was not averse to their participation in the movement. He was open to forging alliances with conservative black leaders and organizations. And most surprising of all, he did not appreciate the reckless and romanticized manner in which some of the militants wielded guns.

A few months later, Williams canceled his memberships in RAM and the RNA, and retreated to live the quiet life. Williams' son offered one reason for Williams' withdrawal from public activism: he simply desired to live a long life without drama. With the assassinations of Martin Luther King, Jr., Malcolm X, and other activist leaders, Williams had no interest in becoming a martyr or getting embroiled in the fractious organizations of the Black Power Movement or political or cultural programs in which he did not believe.

Williams' new life appeared to be everything he wanted it to be. He worked for a year at the University of Michigan at the Center for Chinese Studies. After a year, he and his family moved to Baldwin, Michigan, an oasis of abundant lakes and rivers, where Williams could spend countless hours fishing and enjoying the lush wilderness. He supported himself and his family with lecturing—though he spoke for no charge at prisons. Mabel became a social worker, and later took a job as the project director at St. Ann's Lake County Senior Meals and Human Services Programs. They both remained committed to activism through their NAACP membership and were heavily involved in their small-town community. In 1976, Williams' kidnapping charges were finally dropped.

The last years of Williams' life, as well as his death, were tranquil. On October 15, 1996, Williams lay on his bed on the brink of death, surrounded by his loved ones. His wife, who had stood by his side through violent times and peaceful times, tenderly held his hand. He died from Hodgkin's disease at the age of seventy-one.

See also Stokely Carmichael; W.E.B. Du Bois; Fannie Lou Hamer; Martin Luther King, Jr.; Malcolm X; Huey P. Newton; and Roy Wilkins.

FURTHER RESOURCES

Negroes with Guns: Rob Williams and Black Power. Directed by Sandra Dickson and Churchill Roberts, 2004.

Sabir, Wanda. "Growing Up Revolutionary: An Interview with John Williams, Son of Mabel and Robert F. Williams." *Freedomarchives.org* (December 2007). See http://www.freedomarchives.org/Reviews/Growing%20up%20Revolutionary.pdf.

Tyson, Timothy B. *Radio Free Dixie: Robert F. Williams and the Roots of Black Power.* Chapel Hill: University of North Carolina Press, 1999.

Williams, Mabel. *Robert F. Williams: Self Respect, Self Defense, and Self Determination.* San Francisco: Freedom Archives, 2005.

Williams, Robert F. *Negroes with Guns.* Detroit: Wayne State University Press, 1962.

Library of Congress

Whitney Young
(1921–1971)

Whitney Young was the executive director of the National Urban League from 1961 to 1971 and a member of the Civil Rights Big Six. When the gregarious and extroverted Young became the executive director of the National Urban League in 1961, he did so just as the wave of student sit-ins and other demonstrations of the Civil Rights Movement was taking the world by storm.

No one expected Whitney Young to be a civil rights leader. But everyone knew he was destined for big things. Growing up in Lincoln Ridge, Kentucky, he dreamed of becoming a doctor. After playing a pivotal role as a mediator between black soldiers and white officers while in the army, he realized that his gifts might be better used elsewhere. He earned a master's degree in social work in 1947 and began a long and lucrative career with the Urban League. But the primary aim of this organization was to find work for blacks, not to engage in civil rights activism.

Over the next twenty years, Young built a considerable reputation among blacks and whites. His genial personality won the trust of white businesses and important philanthropic organizations. He was a natural, shrewd, and charismatic leader. He effortlessly opened up unprecedented opportunities for blacks in the workforce, attracted the support of wealthy philanthropists to fund various programs and the operation of Urban League offices, and facilitated steady and sometimes staggering growth of whatever project was set before him. In 1961, at the age of forty, he became the executive director of the National Urban League. Once at the helm, Young orchestrated a radical course correction, an act that boggled the minds of his colleagues and affluent allies.

Young decided that in addition to doing the social work, the Urban League should become a civil rights organization. More impressively, he convinced conservative whites that that was the right thing to do and that they ought to fund it. He managed this same feat during the height of the Black Power Movement.

As a civil rights leader, Young did not fit the mold. His style was subtle, moderate, and exceedingly polite and friendly. If it were not for the fact that he was openly aligned with the major civil rights organizations of the day, one could easily confuse him with Booker T. Washington, the famous accommodationist and influential black leader of the nineteenth century. This made Young all the more intriguing, because, unlike Washington, he was not an enemy of the radicals—he was their friend. Despite this, his reputation with conservative and wealthy whites did not suffer. In fact, it flourished.

CHILDHOOD

Whitney Moore Young, Jr. was born July 31, 1921 on the campus of the Lincoln Institute in Lincoln Ridge, Kentucky, the second of three children

(Arnita was born in 1920, and Eleanor was born in 1922). The Lincoln Institute was an all-black school set up like a college campus. The mostly white teachers lived on campus, as did the principal of the school, who lived in a three-story house. Like most black schools in the early twentieth century it was geared towards vocational training, offering courses in home economics, nursing, agriculture, construction, industrial arts, and steam and maintenance engineering.

Both Whitney's parents, Whitney Sr. and Laura Young, attended the Institute as youths. Whitney Sr. even taught there for a year before moving to Detroit, Michigan, where, thanks to his engineering degree, he found work at the American Car and Foundry Company and the Detroit United Railway. In 1918, Young married Laura and fought in the armed forces during the latter stages of World War I. After the war, he returned to Detroit and worked as an engineer for the Ford Motor Company. Young seemed settled, until the administration of the Lincoln Institute coaxed him back, telling him they wanted him to join the faculty.

Young returned to Kentucky a few years later with his wife and Arnita, but the job he was promised turned out to be a ruse. The white principal explained that they actually wanted him to work on campus as the janitor. Young did not get upset. He was an old pro at accommodating whites, as were most blacks in the early twentieth century. It would prove to be his greatest weapon.

Young agreed to work as the campus janitor, but only if he was allowed to teach a course in "janitorial engineering." The principal liked the idea. But unbeknown to him and the rest of the campus, Young also taught straight engineering, bringing in experts to supplement his lectures.

Whitney Jr. grew up in a splendidly placid world, knowing very little of the racism that was rampant beyond the borders of the Lincoln Institute. But he never forgot his first glimpse of it at the age of five when he and his parents went to the movies. Whitney Jr. wandered off from his parents into the white-only section of the theater, and the whites got upset with this outrageous behavior. Whitney's parents reprimanded him, and Whitney Jr. felt the sting. Off campus, public facilities and places were segregated by custom, not by law.

The socialization of a black child was as imperative as any other aspect of human development. Survival depended upon "staying in your place" and "by not talking back" (Weiss, 6). Whitney Sr. practiced this shrewdly, because his status depended upon it. For example, when Whitney Sr. returned home from shopping and discovered that the clothes he had bought for his son did not fit, it was Laura, not Whitney Sr., who complained to the store. In those days, blacks were not allowed to try on clothes in stores. Nor could they talk back. But it was more acceptable if a woman complained than a man. Retribution for blacks violating the codes of racial etiquette did not affect black women to the degree it did black men.

Of the two parents, Laura was the most overtly radical. She regularly ignored the white and black signs posted on restroom doors and water fountains. She defiantly used the restrooms for "whites" and also drank from fountains that were clearly marked for "whites." She had a forceful energy and an immense heart.

Laura was known around campus as someone to go to when in need. Laura fed the homeless, nursed the sick and shut-ins back to health, sent money with notes, and made good manners a top priority. Whitney Jr. was once spanked for not greeting a black person they passed in the street. The Youngs would never be considered wealthy, but they had more than most, and they were extremely generous with their resources.

Family time and education were both stressed in the Young household. The family spent a lot of time together, going on walks, socializing with other upwardly mobile black families, playing baseball and cards, and singing around the piano.

The Youngs began educating their three children as early as possible. All the children were tutored by a white woman before they entered school. Because of this jump start, Whitney Jr. entered the second grade at the Lincoln Model School at only five years old, and stayed till he was twelve. During his school years, he encountered men who impressed him because of their material achievement and aura of success. He met Julius Thomas, the industrial relations director of the National Urban League and a physician. It was the encounter with the physician that made young Whitney decide he wanted to be a doctor when he grew up. In 1933, he entered Lincoln Institute.

In the same year, Whitney Sr. became the first black principal of Lincoln Institute. So much for being a janitor—his patience, likeability, and contributions to the school had paid off. However, the new job was not particularly desirable, for the Institute was in dire straights. Because of lack of money, it was debatable if it would last another year. But Whitney Sr. was a remarkable strategist and a talented fundraiser. He established a "Faith Plan," in which teachers agreed to receive a cut in pay while he worked on getting the Institute back in shape. He traveled around the state with a group of teachers, students, and the school choir, visiting churches and organizations to beseech financial assistance. He devised a scholarship fund that would benefit both blacks and whites. He worked closely with the state legislature to receive help from the state and implement other measures. In a short time, Whitney Sr. had turned the institute's finances around and actually increased enrollment.

As a man in a position of authority, Whitney Sr. was treated differently from other blacks. This was largely because whites knew that he had leverage in the black community. Treating him with a slightly greater measure of respect was an advantage for them, especially if, for example, a white business owner wanted to cater to black customers.

Whitney Jr. appeared to thrive at Lincoln Institute—even if he did experience some pressure because his father was the principle. Whitney Sr. certainly expected the best from his children—as he did from the entire student body. He "preached to his students [and his children]: read books, work hard, and strive for excellence ...' if you want to improve yourself, your community, your state, your country, and the world, start with yourself'" (Weiss, 13).

As far as building friendships was concerned, Whitney Jr. exhibited a natural easy-going personality that made him popular with everybody. His grades were above average, and he was active in sports, especially enjoying tennis and basketball.

In 1937, Whitney Jr. graduated. He was only fifteen years old and had bested everyone academically, including his sister, who was the Institute's salutatorian.

KENTUCKY STATE INDUSTRIAL COLLEGE

There was no question as to whether or not any of the Young children would attend college. All three attended Kentucky State Industrial College in Frankfurt. Despite the fact that Young had been groomed for this next phase of his education, his school grades took a shocking nosedive. During his first year, he received several Cs, Bs, and one D. Perhaps his poor grades can be attributed to his overwhelming popularity, for Young was a jocular, friendly guy. He was involved in sports and he worked to earn extra money, though tuition was free for locals. And one can imagine he was the type of guy who was easily distracted by any and all activity on campus.

Kentucky State Industrial, an all-black school, was similar to the Lincoln Institute. There were rules to abide by: no drinking alcohol or smoking, attendance at chapel services was required once a week, and students had to attend the first three Sundays of each month.

Young had a breezy college career. After he started dating, his grades improved somewhat. But they dipped again in his junior year, when he was heavily involved again in extracurricular campus activities and was vice president of the Alpha Phi Alpha fraternity. That year he met Margaret Buckner from Aurora, Illinois. Young pursued her, but she did not give in quickly to his advances, as she was already in a relationship. So, in fact, was Young. But their friendship grew. In his senior year, they started seeing each other exclusively, quickly becoming inseparable. Everyone called them "Junior and Pookie," like they were a couple starring on a popular television show. And indeed they were both very popular. He was so well-liked that he was elected class president in his senior year. At graduation in 1941, Mary McLeod Bethune, the indefatigable civil rights activist and leader in black women's organizations, gave the commencement address.

ARMED FORCES

Young still wanted to be a doctor, but there were obstacles to overcome. And he needed to save money, so he took several odd jobs during the summer, working as a busboy and a dishwasher at a hotel in Louisville, Kentucky. He also taught math and coached basketball at Rosenwald High School in Madisonville, Kentucky. When he was able, he visited Margaret, who was in her last year at Kentucky State Industrial College.

When America entered World War II after the bombing of Pearl Harbor on December 7, 1941, Young decided to enlist. This decision was undoubtedly bolstered by the fact that as a soldier he would receive money for education. He also hoped to receive medical training for free. However, all the black medical schools were full, and so he had to go to the Massachusetts Institute of Technology (MIT) to study electrical engineering.

Young arrived at MIT with three other black men. They had talked among themselves and decided that they were not going to be segregated. In the early twentieth century, the armed forces were not yet desegregated. Surprisingly, the white officers obliged and assigned them to quarters with whites.

Only one of Young's roommates gave him any trouble. He was from Mississippi, where the color line was rigidly enforced in every aspect of life, and was visibly uncomfortable with Young. He complained to an officer on the first day, and returned sulking. He said not a word to Young for three weeks.

But thanks to Young's disarming personality, it would not be long before he penetrated his roommate's rough exterior and made a friend. Their relationship bloomed in small ways: Young helped him with some math problems, and they exchanged a few words, then they were laughing together. But even Young was shocked when he was asked to be the best man at his wedding.

In 1944, Young took a five-day leave for his own wedding, and he and Margaret married on January 2. They honeymooned for one night at a Chicago hotel and spent some time together the next day before Young was off to Rhode Island State College in Kingston. Margaret went back to Kentucky State, where she was teaching freshman composition.

That spring, Young was reassigned to the 1695th Engineer Combat Battalion. The soldiers of the battalion were all black, but the officers were white. The white officers did not know what to expect when they first laid eyes on Young, who at over six feet tall and weighing close to 200 pounds was impressive looking. But they had not expected him to have a college degree.

Young was promoted to first sergeant, given administrative duties, and was in charge of relaying orders. He no longer had to do any of the grunt work that the black soldiers were doing. One of his most important unofficial jobs was to serve as a liaison between the black soldiers and white officers. The relations in Young's battalion were similar to those that existed throughout the military, and were representative of the hostile racial climate in America. Whites treated the black men poorly and rarely rewarded them.

Black soldiers, in turn, could be belligerent, refusing to obey orders and grumbling back at their officers. After a time, white officers began to fear them. Indeed, they were outnumbered, and the blacks were armed.

This was where Young stepped in, effectively negotiating a working relationship between the soldiers and the officers. For example, he spoke to the officers about the men's needs and demands. He then went to the soldiers and got them to agree to follow orders or to remedy whatever problems they had. Sometimes the black men voiced their issues with Young himself, because he had leverage with the whites and worked so easily with them. Thanks to these experiences, Young began to reconsider his life's work. He had a knack for negotiating, and it concerned him to see how blacks were being treated. He wanted to do something about it.

Getting to know the black soldiers was enlightening too. Young's own life in Kentucky had been drastically different from theirs. Most of them came from poor communities. Many of them were in the army because there were few opportunities for work elsewhere. Upward mobility was not a consideration, given the fact that they were inadequately equipped to compete in the workforce due to the poorly funded schools in the North. Teachers cared little about empowering their black students to strive for lives that would take them out of the ghetto, where those who came from the North lived. Young was frustrated to observe that these soldiers had little self-respect or interest in self-improvement.

UNIVERSITY OF MINNESOTA

Young arrived in New York in early January 1946 and was honorably discharged on January 12. Home was now in Minnesota, for Margaret was studying for her master's degree in educational psychology at the University of Minnesota. Young did not know for certain what he wanted to do next, but he knew he wanted to go to graduate school. He also knew something else: he wanted to help improve the social conditions of blacks. He had a vague notion that social work was the place to start, if only because that was the direction his friends kept pressing him to take.

Young went to John C. Kidneigh, the associate director of the University of Minnesota School of Social Work, to flesh out his ideas and discuss what opportunities might fit his experiences and interests. Kidneigh was pleased to meet an ambitious young man so deeply interested in helping his race. After several minutes, Kidneigh knew exactly what Young had been grasping for, and he had the answer: the Urban League.

The Urban League was founded in 1910 in New York City at the start of what is known as the **Great Migration** (1910–1970), the mass migration of blacks from the South to locations throughout the North, primarily to the major cities. Although segregation was prohibited in the North, most blacks lived in overcrowded and cheaply built slums or ghettos.

Housing was not the only problem blacks faced; unemployment was a serious dilemma. Without jobs, blacks could not buy food, clothes, or other necessities for themselves or their families. Poverty and lack of opportunity gave way to other issues, like high crime and frustration. The Urban League was one way to address joblessness.

The Urban League was a collaborative effort between blacks and whites, involving three main organizations: the Committee on Urban Conditions among Negroes, the Committee for the Improvement of Industrial Conditions among Negroes in New York, and the National League for the Protection of Colored Women. Two of the key players in the early formation of this organization were Ruth Standish Baldwin, the widow of an extremely wealthy railroad magnate, and Dr. George Edmund Haynes, the first African American at Columbia University to receive a Ph.D.

The National Urban League had made significant headway in negotiating with white business owners to employ blacks and train blacks to be prepared for the workforce. During the Great Depression, the organization lobbied on behalf of blacks, who were not included in many of the relief and recovery reforms of President Franklin D. Roosevelt's New Deal.

Young agreed with Kidneigh that the Urban League would fit his aspirations. Kidneigh undoubtedly realized that Young would do well in whatever career he choose to pursue. Getting admitted to the master's program was another challenge. If Young had done better in undergraduate school he would have had an easier time getting accepted. But his grades were not spectacular. And, he had taken very few courses dealing with social work. Nonetheless, Young was accepted, largely because he included an impressive letter from a white captain he had met in the military, who glowingly gave account of how Young kept peace aboard the ship that carried the soldiers home.

Young started taking classes in the spring of 1946. He was able to pay for his studies through the GI Bill, which covered tuition and living expenses. He supplemented this money with a job at an athletic club.

During the next two years, Young was assigned to two different social agencies. The first was the Hennepin County Welfare Board, where he worked on cases of whites and blacks. In his second year, he was placed at the Minneapolis Urban League, where he shadowed the industrial secretary to various meetings and to employment bureaus, gaining considerable experience on the administrative side of the organization. He met with and interviewed individuals seeking work, and he made reports to the board.

When Young sat down to write his thesis on the history of the St. Paul Urban League, he had a surfeit of information and experience from which to draw. But Young went several steps further by conducting interviews in the community, doing research at the local library, and scouring old newspapers. The final product totaled ninety pages.

ST. PAUL URBAN LEAGUE

Young's attention to detail, sincerity, and professionalism gained him an easy foothold into a position with the National Urban League. Out of graduate school, he took a job as industrial relations secretary to the St. Paul Urban League in the fall of 1947. Young worked under S. Vincent Owens, who had a reputation for turning out stellar leaders.

Young was immediately put to the test. Not only was his job to find work for blacks, but he was charged with the task of improving the quality of those jobs and to ensure that blacks who had found employment were being promoted.

Young saw to it that blacks received training. He also went into businesses and studied them. For example, when he entered Schuneman's department store, he observed high numbers of black clientele but no black workers. He convinced the president of that company to hire blacks, then undoubtedly helped supply the employees.

Young's volunteer work kept him involved in the community, sustained his ability to network, increased his visibility, and helped develop him as a leader. Young was a board member of the NAACP, the Associated Negro Credit Union, and the Crispus Attucks Home. He joined the YMCA Men's Club, the Alpha Phi Alpha fraternity, and the No Name Club. This last organization, made up of black professionals, was particularly important because it permitted Young and the other members to address social concerns, to problem-solve, and to encourage one another's personal development.

Despite his many obligations, Young made family and friends a priority. Margaret managed the home front, splitting her time between being a homemaker and director of teenage and young adult activities at the Hallie Q. Brown Community House. In the evenings, Whitney and Margaret talked over their days, played with the new baby, and dreamed of a successful future. The weekends were largely filled with social activities with other couples. There were parties, dances, picnics, and jaunts to the theater or a concert.

Young was a man deeply committed to his community. He believed in being involved at the grassroots level. But he also knew that his work and his busy schedule were preparing him for something grander. Making friends with Lester Granger, then leader of the National Urban League, fed Young's ambition.

When Young met Granger, the latter was in his fifties, bespectacled and balding, and a well-seasoned leader. But word had it that Granger was becoming less progressive and more moderate in his management of the organization. Also, funds were dwindling. In contrast, Young was tall and robust and full of energy and optimism, with a head full of wavy black hair. He approached his work with zeal and had a fresh outlook. But he was still learning.

OMAHA URBAN LEAGUE

Granger watched Young's professional growth with pleasure. When, in 1949, M. Leo Bohanon transferred from the Omaha Urban League to a chapter in St. Louis, Young was one of six candidates Granger recommended to fill Bohanon's position as executive director. Young seemed destined for the job, and started his first day on February 1, 1950.

Part of Young's approach as the executive director was to increase the NUL's exposure in the community, as well as to tackle head-on those businesses that prohibited the hiring of blacks. Young had to ramp up his negotiation skills. Many whites had no interest in hiring blacks at all. But Young was successful with a substantial number of companies by pointing out that employing blacks would benefit them financially. Young backed up his arguments with facts and impressed the managers with his personality. Young's confident and optimistic persona and temperament helped immensely during these negotiations, and helped encourage whites to step out of their comfort zone. For many white business owners, Young was the first black they had sat down and talked with.

Although Young's work was not directly involved in grassroots social activism, his job had the same objective and yielded the same results. The focus of the NAACP (and future organizations) was to integrate society. The NUL strove to integrate the workforce, while addressing the financial needs of the black community. Young relied on negotiation, rather than direct action, to break new ground in all-white companies and businesses. All in all, Young secured ninety-three firsts for blacks in a variety of occupations in Omaha.

On most days, Young did not go straight home from work. Instead he made time for his volunteer interests. He continued his involvement as a board member of the local chapter of the NAACP. He added to his commitment to the Boy Scouts by becoming a board member. Whitney and Margaret made new friends from the church they attended, St. John's A.M.E. Church, and participated in many church activities.

Young was a staunch integrationist. Although he attended an all-black church, he struggled to integrate Omaha's businesses, as well as its neighborhoods. He and his wife specifically looked to purchase a home in a mostly white neighborhood. They found one they liked and moved in, which encouraged more blacks to move in. But eventually, this caused the whites to move out. Integration was not an easy process.

In 1951, Young played a leading role in the move to desegregate low-rent federal public housing in Omaha. This was a long, grueling process that involved a lengthy series of meetings and talks. But Young's tactics worked—"by the end of 1952, [he] reported that all hotels and eating places in the downtown area, as well as motels and tourist camps on the outskirts of the city, served blacks without discrimination" (Weiss, 50).

Young did not always rely on negotiations alone. There was a local grass-roots organization called the De Porres Club that Young called upon in times of need. The De Porres Club utilized direct-action demonstrations. One of the reasons the Urban League did not undertake these tactics themselves was because they were a non-confrontational and conservative organization, and as such, they were able to attain more success with whites. Whites would have been less inclined to associate with a radical organization. Radical demonstrations would have undermined their efforts.

But this did not stop Young from shrewdly seeking out the predominately white De Porres Club. When he was able to get a cab company to hire black workers, members of the De Porres Club rode in the cabs and told the cab drivers that they supported the hiring of black drivers. Young wanted to make a point with the cab company that whites would be comfortable with driving in cabs with black drivers.

On other occasions, Young and the De Porres Club worked as a team. During negotiations, as a last resort, if he saw that a discussion was not going well, he would mention that he had heard that the De Porres Club was considering staging a demonstration against the company. This indirect threat normally produced instantaneous results in Young's favor. Other times, as when the club boycotted the Coca-Cola Bottling Company to demand the hiring of black workers, Young appeared and handled negotiations.

Young was careful to limit his interactions with the club. He might go to a meeting or stop by briefly at a demonstration to show his support, but he was not among the picketers, and he never officially joined the group. Because Young was a leader of the NUL, he stayed clear of any behavior that might undermine his good standing with the Urban League or with white business leaders.

ATLANTA UNIVERSITY

Young was not certain what to do when, in 1953, he received an offer to become the new dean of the Atlanta University School of Social Work in Georgia. Young went to his friend, Art McCaw, who was on the board of the Urban League and someone whose opinion he respected, to help him work through his dilemma. There was a part of Young that felt this was an opportunity not to be considered lightly, and yet the pay was less than what he received as the executive director at the Omaha Urban League. Furthermore, if he stayed, he stood a chance to fill the position of executive directorship in Philadelphia. But McCaw told Young to take the Atlanta job, and so he did.

In December 1953, Lauren, Young's second daughter, was born. In the following month, the Youngs were unpacking boxes, putting up framed photographs on the walls, and settling into their new brick home for faculty in Atlanta, Georgia. Margaret was not happy about the move to Atlanta, mostly because she did not want to live in a Jim Crow environment, and she particularly did not want to raise her children under such oppressive laws and rules. She worried over the affect of segregation on their girls. But Margaret made the most of a miserable situation. She taught courses in education and psychology at Spelman College, an institution for black women, and avoided Jim Crow buses and facilities if at all possible. She made the children use the restroom at home before leaving for an outing so they did not have to use the "black-only restrooms," and she did not use the parks or go to certain other segregated places.

Young faced similar challenges, but he responded to them differently. If anything, Young thrived in the face of adversity. One challenge entailed the School of Social Work itself. The school was floundering. Like his father two decades ago just starting out as the principal of Lincoln Institute, Young set out to save the school. He made huge changes: he integrated the student body, increased faculty salaries, and adjusted the curriculum. His changes brought forth significant growth.

Young also tackled Jim Crow in the community. He was a board member of the NAACP in Atlanta. He also founded the Atlanta Committee for Cooperative Action and was involved in the Atlanta Citizens Committee on Economic Opportunity and Employment. He was co-chairman of the Greater Atlanta Council on Human Rights.

The Greater Atlanta Council on Human Rights was formed in 1958. One of its major campaigns for that year was to desegregate public libraries in Atlanta. After negotiations failed, the organization pursued legal recourse. Young and a professor who taught at Spelman College in Atlanta spearheaded efforts to find appropriate plaintiffs. That was no easy task, because the plaintiffs not only had to be beyond reproach, but they had to be fearless or at least willing to face unknown dangers. It was common knowledge that plaintiffs faced threats, intimidation, and harassment. Many lost their jobs and could be barred from employment everywhere in the city. However, on May 19, Young received an unsuspecting and pleasant surprise. A member of the library board called, asking for Young's group to hold off on the lawsuit. On that same day, the board held an emergency meeting and agreed to desegregate the libraries. At the end of that week, black students from the local colleges and universities tested the libraries. No one reported any problems or hassles.

The Atlanta Committee for Cooperative Action (ACCA) comprised young black leaders from the Atlanta community. This organization presented a bold new alternative to the general acceptance of accommodationism in the community. Since Booker T. Washington had made accommodationism extremely popular in the nineteenth century, these blacks continued to practice it. In one sense, it was an effective way to get along with whites. And it was the one ideology that (historically) both whites and blacks approved. Whites permitted blacks to enjoy some sense of achievement (though drastically limited compared to the limitless economic and social mobility of whites), and blacks could live with little fear of violent backlash or intimidation.

Young gave a speech at the Urban League's annual conference in 1959. Despite the move to Atlanta for a job unaffiliated with the Urban League, Young had remained in contact with people he knew from his old office, as well as with its executive director, Lester Granger. The speech that he gave was important not only for its content, but because of what would come of it.

Lindsley F. Kimball was in the audience that day. Kimball was the vice president of the General Education Board. He had significant connections with major philanthropic organizations. Later, he would serve as the executive vice president of the Rockefeller Foundation. When Kimball heard Young speak and saw the effect he had on the audience, he was more than impressed. It was well-known that Granger was no longer as effective as he had once been. The time for him to retire was drawing near. Kimball figured Young would be a marvelous candidate to succeed Granger.

Kimball got in touch with Young and started to work on getting him thinking about leaving Atlanta. Young was receptive. As much as he enjoyed being in the thick of the action, his wife was not happy there, largely because of the Jim Crow laws, and she was concerned that their daughter was not getting the best education possible or the best opportunities. Young considered Kimball's suggestion: take a sabbatical (an extended period away which faculty take for rest or pursuit of other projects or academic interests) from the university and attend graduate school for a year. Both knew that the sabbatical would transition Young into possible leadership of the NUL, ideally the position of executive secretary (if Granger could ever agree to retire). The break would give Young time to refresh himself, as well as to prepare himself for greater responsibilities. Young agreed.

As he made preparations to leave, Young participated in another ACCA campaign in Atlanta. He helped publish *A Second Look: The Negro Citizen in Atlanta* (1960). White Atlantans had worked long and hard to project a positive image to the rest of the nation, especially the North. The Civil War (1861–1865) had devastated all hopes of ever returning to the Old South, or antebellum period, which depended upon black slave labor and was based mostly on an agricultural economy. Journalist and long-standing editor of the *Atlanta Constitution* Henry W. Grady popularized the term "New South" to refer to its industrial advancements, economic growth, and purported improvement in race relations. Leaders in Atlanta were particularly proud of their alleged progress in terms of industrial growth and black-white relations. But ACCA's publication exposed several "inequalities that black Atlantans experienced in education, health services, housing, employment, justice, law enforcement, and policy making" (Weiss, 64).

Before ACCA distributed the publication to local businesses and prominent white leaders in the city, the members asked the conservative black leaders to look it over. Surprisingly, the accommodationist leaders approved of it and were relieved that a group bolder than they had the courage to undertake such a campaign. ACCA was even more pleased when major newspapers, such as the *Atlanta Constitution* and the *Atlanta Daily World*, published in-depth articles about the book.

ACCA had not anticipated that the publication would inspire a new generation of activists. Following the famous sit-in at a Greensboro, North Carolina Woolworth's lunch counter involving students from North Carolina A&T College, black and white students took part in sit-ins throughout the South. A number of students, including those who studied under Young, participated in local sit-ins in Atlanta, Georgia. Young was extremely supportive of these young activists. It was Young to whom they turned for advice and encouragement.

Young's support of the local sit-in movement was no secret to anyone. Because of his support, there were those who accused Young of masterminding the demonstrations. But Young acted largely as a resource for the students (not a leader like King was to the black citizens in the Montgomery Bus Boycott). His role involved cheering them on and offering advice along the way. Others implored Young, because of his influence, to persuade the students to stop demonstrating. But he would not. He was proud of what the students were doing, and was more than thrilled to be of any kind of assistance.

HARVARD UNIVERSITY

Young's colleagues, his students, and the administration were sad to see him go north after seven years in Atlanta. They sensed that Young was off to greater ventures and would not be returning. Margaret enjoyed the atmosphere in Harvard so much better. It was a welcome break for her from the heaviness of the social climate in Atlanta.

Young began his studies in the fall of 1960. He studied social sciences, thanks to a General Education Board Fellowship, which gave him monies to cover his tuition and living expenses. That spring, right on schedule, the Urban League launched its campaign to hire a new executive director. There were seven candidates, including Young. Most of the others were in their fifties and had served in top positions with the Urban League. Young was the youngest and currently on leave from his duties at a university, taking classes at Harvard University. On paper, Young had the least experience and was not currently actively involved in the League. Against those odds, Young got the job, with an official start date of October 1, 1961.

EXECUTIVE DIRECTOR OF THE NATIONAL URBAN LEAGUE

Employees and leaders in the Urban League craved change, and they certainly got that under Young's leadership. Young brought the sort of energy to his job that made everyone feel secure and relieved. Emboldened by the challenges ahead, Young formulated steps to restructure the affiliate offices, improve the organization's public image, raise more money, and—most radically—facilitate the transition of the Urban League into an active partner in the Civil Rights Movement. These objectives would require the skill of a steady, confident, and skilled hand.

Young's first test was the move to a predominately white neighborhood. The first black family that had tried to move in was deterred when whites who did not want them in their neighborhood broke all the exterior windows of the house. The black family changed its mind and moved to another neighborhood. Young's real estate agent contrived a brilliant plan to avert resistance. He told the neighbors that they were fortunate to have a neighbor like Young. He told them that the Youngs were wanted in other upscale and prominent neighborhoods, but he chose this one. The ploy worked, and the Youngs moved in. White neighbors poured on the kindness, offered to help them unpack, brought cookies, and asked for play dates with their children and Young's two girls. Young was personally invited to join the neighbors' association.

Young was not the only one to face challenges in the community. When Marcia started her first day at the integrated New Rochelle High School she faced a dubious situation. Not only was she the new girl, but her father had instructed her to not fall into the pattern of associating only with blacks. At high school, the blacks and whites generally socialized separately, so when Marcia declined the offer to sit with the other black girls at lunchtime, she had to sit alone. Eventually, she was welcomed to sit with a group of white girls.

At work, Young displayed nonstop energy and expected everyone to keep up. He saw to it that all the affiliate offices adjusted their programs to be in alignment with the national office. This structure had worked well for the NAACP. Rather than allow each affiliate office to make up its own objectives, they had to follow instructions from one central office. Although this did away with the individual character of each organization (sometimes at the cost of neglecting local issues and needs), it increased productivity and efficiency.

Bringing about uniformity to the Urban League also enhanced its public image. Young believed that the image that the Urban League projected was critical to its success, for it was important to attract blacks in the community as well as philanthropists and corporate sponsors. During a pep talk to Urban League executives in Young's first year, Young advocated professionalism. He developed new programs, demonstrating the UL's commitment to the community and the fact that the organization was active, lively, and thriving. Some of the programs included after-school tutoring, workshops targeting high school dropouts (to prepare them for college), counseling for black families, homes for special needs children, assistance to black veterans, and a host of other projects.

Uncle Tom

Uncle Tom is an epithet used commonly by radical blacks to describe conservative blacks. The term was derived from the Harriet Beecher Stowe novel *Uncle Tom's Cabin* (1852), but the meaning used by radical blacks has little to do with the character from that book. That Tom, a black slave, was portrayed as a martyred hero.

Over time, the definition of Uncle Tom has altered to refer to a black person who is subservient to whites, especially one who would not ever oppose, defy, or challenge whites in any way. Along with this definition comes the idea that the "Uncle Tom" has assimilated white behavior and speech. Blacks who call other blacks "Uncle Tom" challenge the authenticity of the other person's racial identity and portray him to be something of a "sellout," another epithet for someone who betrays his own group.

During the years that saw the rise of the Black Power Movement and the dimming of the popularity of civil rights leaders, the term was immensely popular. Among the prominent leaders to be called Uncle Toms were Dr. Martin Luther King, Jr., James Farmer, Roy Wilkins, and Whitney Young.

The term and its implicit condemnation appear to be an ill match with such civil rights luminaries, since these men's lives and careers were dedicated to fighting against racism, oppression, and discrimination, and to seeking social justice. As a result, black radicals appear to have created a new meaning for the term "Uncle Tom": an objection to the policies of conservative blacks. Thus, the term began to be used to describe any black who did not embrace the black power agenda. In time, conservatism, pacifism, integrationism, and even middle classism began to be associated with the image of a sellout or Uncle Tom. Conservative black leaders shake their heads at this phenomenon, which so thoughtlessly dismisses their ideals.

The Urban League was profoundly helped by the donations that Young raised. Young was a powerful fundraiser. He exuded confidence at meetings with donors. His straight talk was tempered by his charisma and the trust that he built so easily with many wealthy whites and philanthropic organizations. Young knew the right words to speak, and he was able to adjust his message according to his audience. By this time he had fine-tuned and gone beyond the abilities he had first exhibited while in the military, and could convince both blacks and whites to come to agreement on just about any issue. Young's efforts "paid off" handsomely in the following year, as the numbers reflect:

Bethlehem Steel, which had contributed $2,500 in 1961, gave $4,000 in 1962; General Electric and General Motors both raised their gifts from $2,500 to

$5,000; Kaiser Industries' donation jumped from $100 to $5,100; Western Electric's gift rose from $2,500 to $7,000; and IBM's donation went from $1,650 to $7,500. U.S. Steel, which had not contributed at all in 1961, gave $5,000 for 1962. All told, corporate gifts totaled $153,000 in 1962 and $527,000 the year after. (Weiss, 93)

While Young spearheaded changes and improvements to the NUL, he kept an eye on the progress of the Civil Rights Movement. He privately pondered his organization's role in the events that were unfurling, events that had captured the attention of America and the world. Due to his personal interest as well as the fact that he felt it was the responsible thing for his organization to do, Young wanted desperately to be a part of the struggle. Given the historic goals of the organization to raise the economic status of blacks and to desegregate workplaces, civil rights were not, in his mind, extending too radically beyond their scope. Young did realize that to many in his organization—as well as his donors—this step would be seen as a drastic undertaking.

CIVIL RIGHTS MOVEMENT

The Civil Rights Movement was, arguably, the largest and most important period of African American protest. It was led predominately by blacks themselves. The NAACP made significant contributions with a series of legal wins, the most well-known being the *Brown v. Board of Education* case in 1954 that ended the legal practice of segregation in public schools in the South. The next milestone was the Montgomery Bus Boycott, which spawned a wave of similar demonstrations in other areas across the South. The sit-in movement began in 1960 and continued through the decade in the South. In 1961, black and white college students, representing the Congress of Racial Equality (CORE) and the Student Nonviolent Coordinating Committee (SNCC), launched the Freedom Rides, which challenged—and ultimately put an end to—segregated interstate transportation and facilities.

Because of the tremendous media attention, most anyone could list the major organizations involved in the struggle for civil rights, as well as their leaders: James Forman, the executive secretary of SNCC; James Farmer, head of CORE; and Martin Luther King, Jr., the president of the Southern Christian Leadership Conference (SCLC). Women were also active participants in the movement, notably Dorothy Height, who was at the helm of the National Council for Negro Women (NCNW). Young knew them all, but he was closest to Roy Wilkins, since he had been a long-standing member of the NAACP.

As early as 1962, Young began to prepare the soil for the Urban League's entrance into the Civil Rights Movement. In that year, he told an audience at the "annual convention of the Southern Christian Leadership Conference [that the Urban League was] 'a necessary and important ally' in the civil rights struggle" (Weiss, 101). Also, in 1962, Young and a former trustee of the NUL met with President John F. Kennedy to discuss pressing social issues in black communities such as education, equal employment, housing, and health care. These were also concerns of the prominent civil rights organizations, although segregation and voting rights were what largely drove the mass demonstrations.

Kennedy in his first year as president was a symbol of hope for blacks, as well as for the nation as a whole. He was youthful, charismatic, and winsome. He had the sort of star quality that could disarm conservative southerners who, in that period, were as resistant to change as civil rights organizations were forceful in their demands for it. Blacks believed Kennedy would be the one to usher in racial progress.

But Kennedy proved to be a guarded supporter. Though the ills of segregation were obvious, he moved cautiously and slowly. He feared that if he took a strong and active role in achieving progress for blacks, he might provoke a national crisis, given the opposition and resistance of whites in the South. He also thought overt and speedy change might compromise the security of his presidency. Although Kennedy listened attentively to what the two men had to say and even appeared agreeable to the idea that the federal government should take an active role in addressing the social problems that blacks faced, the meeting made little, if any, tangible headway towards a definitive program for blacks.

Young did not give up on building a relationship with the president, but his unproductive meeting motivated him to forge ahead with his own plans. In a 1963 memo to League executives, Young detailed the criteria for NUL involvement in the Civil Right's Movement and why it should contemplate joining the struggle. He stated that

> affiliates ought not to initiate or participate actively in picketing and boycotting, but that they needed to be visible and to communicate effectively with the protesters. It was essential for the league to be sufficiently involved to maintain the respect of the black community and to take a leadership role in resolving some of the crises. (Weiss, 101)

Not everyone in the League backed Young from the start. As the skeptics saw it, the NUL was a social-service agency, not a social-activist organization. In that day, civil rights demonstrations were perceived as radical and revolutionary. The naysayers were also concerned that the radicalization of the Urban League might undo pivotal connections to and relationships with government officials and financial contributors. Most donors to the League based their support on its moderate stance as much as on the good works it accomplished in black communities. To convince the skeptics within the League as well as tentative white financial contributors, Young had the success of the ongoing stream of demonstrations, such as the campaigns King waged in the Deep South that forced the involvement of President Kennedy. Growing pressure from blacks within the community also swayed the skeptics. Soon the question the executives asked one another was not "Should we join?" but "When will we join?" Eventually, they looked to Young for the answer. But his approach was calculated and cautious; there would be no sudden and drastic action from Whitney Young.

Council for United Civil Rights Leadership

The year 1963 began with an unprecedented meeting, and Young was invited. Stephen Currier was well-known among elite foundations and philanthropic organizations. He and his wife, Audrey Bruce Currier, had established the Taconic Foundation in 1958. This foundation was different from most in that it reflected Currier's interest in the "radical" civil rights organizations of the day. It was his idea to put the heads of the organizations into one room and to facilitate the establishment of an elite group called the Council for United Civil Rights Leadership (CUCRL). There were several participants, but the most famous were Martin Luther King, Jr., Roy Wilkins, James Forman, John Lewis, Dorothy Height, and the newcomer Whitney Young.

The importance of that meeting and subsequent get-togethers is highlighted by the fact that each organization until that moment had acted independently. Although the organizations remained autonomous, the effort to come together to talk, to acknowledge each other's role, and to combine forces for fundraising endeavors proved indispensable.

But the meetings were also at times contentious. The various leaders often vied for money and media attention, and it was often difficult to come together on a plan of attack. For example, if Wilkins called for a moratorium (the cessation of demonstrations), he was hard-pressed to convince the front-line organizations like SNCC and CORE to agree. Conflict was often caused by personality differences, especially between Wilkins and Forman. Wilkins and Young were the most conservative leaders in the group, mainly because their organizations did not engage in direct action as the others' did. But Wilkins was less diplomatic than Young during the meetings and exuded overbearing qualities (the NAACP was the longest running and, arguably, the mightiest of the organizations in terms of numbers and political influence). James Forman of SNCC was as dogmatic as Wilkins, but from the opposite perspective. His youthful idealism and aggressiveness showed itself at most meetings. John Lewis, Forman's alternate, was much more composed and amicable. Young played an instrumental role in these meetings; he utilized his negotiating and mediating skills to forge truces and help settle disputes.

March on Washington for Jobs and Freedom

The objectors were not completely silent the day Young announced that he had been contacted by A. Philip Randolph, the leader of the Brotherhood of Sleeping Car Porters. Randolph wanted Young to participate in a march he was planning. In the years before the Civil Rights Movement, Randolph was legendary for his role in procuring wage increases and better hours for black porters and for the desegregation of the U.S. armed forces.

In 1963, Randolph, at seventy-four, was as noble in his appearance as he was esteemed for his contributions to the cause. Randolph was a portrait of elegance—tall and lean, with a crown of snow-white hair that was a striking contrast to his brown skin. When he spoke, it was with the profound resonance of the Harvard elite, although he had actually attended City College in New York. No one could refuse Randolph. Young did not plan to either, even if his decision created some dissonance among some in the League.

From the start, Young made it clear that he would only participate in the march if all the leaders involved agreed to a conservative demonstration. It was thus largely Young's doing that the forthcoming march set a light and non-malevolent tone. Young participated in the planning meetings and had private conversations with President Kennedy, who was anxious about the gathering. He worried that the march might provoke strife in the nation or ignite a riot. But Young and others reiterated over and over that the purpose of the march was to conduct a large-scale demonstration for a peaceful call to racial equality and for improvements in employment and other areas. Kennedy gave the okay, but he was not completely at ease.

Kennedy was not the only one who was anxious about the march. Young had a lot riding on the event as well. He had his own reputation, as well as that of his organization to think about. If the march failed, his career and quite possibly the Urban League itself might be done for. Young's vigilance over the planning of the march and the speeches that each leader would give bothered the leaders of the other organizations, and SNCC most of all. SNCC had hoped for a more aggressive approach to the march, for they saw it as an opportunity to let loose and exert radicalness. Although the actual march played out majestically and without violence, SNCC activists grumbled that the day was too passive, too watered down. Nonetheless, Kennedy was relieved. He was also so excited by the demonstration that he invited the major leaders back to his office afterward. This paved the way for a good working relationship between civil rights leaders and subsequent presidents that continues to this day.

Urban League Tactics

Young returned to the NUL office in triumph. The day had been a momentous one for the nation, as well as for Young and the League. As one of the speakers, Young's status as a civil rights leader had been sealed, initiating the League's entrance into the Civil Rights Movement. In the next few years, the Urban League did not organize or participate in direct-action demonstrations. But it did participate vicariously through Young's acknowledged role and symbolically through the public support it garnered. This approach was arguably insignificant. But as Young had explained back in 1962, the League represented an important ally, affirming the interests of the blacks they reached and legitimizing the movement to rich, ultra-conservative philanthropists. Young personally lent his negotiating power to meetings with more than one president. His high visibility only helped strengthen the League.

March on Selma, Alabama

The Selma march, a campaign launched by King's SCLC, took place in 1965. The first attempt was marked by violence, as police officers beat demonstrators as they tried to march to the Alabama capital. That day was so violent it became known as "Bloody Sunday." The second attempt was shortened because King did not want to defy a local court injunction prohibiting the march. The media reported on the violence in graphic video and words, gaining immense national attention. When the march finally occurred, Young was there, fresh and inspiring as he spoke under the shadow of the Alabama state capitol. He was one of many prominent leaders who gave a presentation that day.

BLACK POWER MOVEMENT

Black Power Ideology

Young watched in despair as his youngest daughter, Lauren, grew her hair out into a billowy brown afro. Lauren's inspiration was Angela Davis, an activist associated with the Black Power Movement. The afro was more than a trendy hairstyle; it was a powerful symbol of resistance, of race consciousness, of everything that threatened to undermine all of Young's work.

Young knew the man, Stokely Carmichael, who had coined the term "Black Power" at a 1966 rally in Greenwood, Mississippi. Carmichael had once been a part of the civil rights struggle as a prominent SNCC activist. The term alarmed civil rights leaders, including Young, and irreparably tore a rift between older and younger generations. Although young black militants insisted the term was a positive call for black pride and self-determination, Young knew well that it was heavily laden with anger and a radicalness he could not embrace. The fiery term infused an ideology of black separatism and a militancy that had been simmering in the nation's ghettos since the 1940s.

The Riots

The riots that erupted in 1964 and lasted through the remainder of the decade in the northern cities reflected the militant spirit of the Black Power Movement. Although black power leaders like H. Rap Brown instigated some of the riots, other militant organizations, like the Black Panther Party for Self-Defense, tried to calm blacks down and, in some cases, prevent the outbreak of riots within the confines of black communities.

The riots were largely a result of the frustrations of young black youths who were overwhelmed by the racism, despair, and hopelessness engendered by living in overcrowded, dilapidated, and rat-infested ghettos and exacerbated by incidences of police brutality and harassment. The race riots were largely contained within black environments. The riots could last for days and involved looting, the destruction of local businesses and property, and the setting on fire of cars and buildings. Few deaths occurred during the actual riots. More deaths resulted when police officers or national guardsmen arrived to restore order.

The riots stoked fear and confusion in the hearts of whites—including those who gave money, year after year, to organizations like the Urban League to improve their chances for a better life—who did not understand the underlying problems that caused the riots. In this perilous hour, Young became an advocate for the rioters. He endeavored to articulate their needs to the media, to the president, and to others of influence and power. In numerous speeches, Young tried to show his doubting audience an alternative way of looking at what was happening, and why. "The riots made white Americans aware of the problems faced by blacks and brought them face-to-face with the realization that those problems threatened the future of the nation" (Weiss, 130).

Young plunged into action. He published *To Be Equal* (1967), which put forward in-depth solutions to the many social and economic problems of blacks in America. He developed the idea of compensatory action and, in discussions with President Lyndon B. Johnson, contributed to ideas that resulted in Johnson's War on Poverty program and the formation of affirmative action.

Shifting Focus

Young tried to forge connections with Black Power organizations. He attended black power conferences. But generally, black militants were critical of Young. They called him "Whitey Young," and castigated him for aligning himself with whites rather than with militant blacks, for pushing integration, and for refusing to subscribe to "blackness," as it was culturally exemplified.

But Young was a creative opportunist, making the most of the new times, doing his best to stay in step with the new movement without compromising

Affirmative Action

Affirmative action is a hotly contested issue in America. The first instance of this concept can be found in Executive Order 10925, issued in 1961 by John F. Kennedy. This initial attempt was bolstered by Lyndon B. Johnson when he issued Executive Order 11246, which resulted in the establishment of an Equal Employment Opportunity Commission. Johnson continued to push for equality for blacks through his own interests and through discussions with such civil rights leaders as James Farmer of the Congress of Racial Equality and Whitney Young of the National Urban League. Johnson coined the term "affirmative action" during a speech at Howard University in 1965.

The purpose of affirmative action was to help diversify institutions, workplaces, and other public spaces. It was also employed to address the practice—deliberate or not—and law-enforced custom of barring blacks and other minority groups, including white women, from exclusively white-male environments. As Young conceived it, affirmative action was to be a temporary remedy to the disparities and problems blacks faced.

The term provokes mixed emotions to this day. Many conservative whites excoriate affirmative action policies, claiming that to give preference to one race over another is in itself discrimination. The term "reverse discrimination" was coined to describe situations in which affirmative action favors the marginalized. Some conservative blacks agree, and feel that the policy is degrading. Other blacks recognize it is not the best solution but feel that it has engendered progress and is still very much needed to ensure that marginalized groups are not discriminated against.

In the 1990s, a black man named Ward Connerly launched a nationwide campaign to eliminate affirmative action. In 1997, California banned all forms of affirmative action in the state. In 1998, the state of Washington followed suit. In 2000, Governor Jeb Bush (President George W. Bush's brother) abolished affirmative action in college admissions in Florida.

Civil rights leaders are dismayed over these recent developments. To them, it is not yet time to dismantle the pivotal gains that have been achieved. Economic, political, and social disparities are still serious problems in black communities. They fear that to take away policies that level the playing field might prove disastrous.

his beliefs or the premise of the NUL. He established a New Thrust program "to develop a range of special projects aimed at building economic and political power where most blacks were concentrated" (Weiss, 181).

At the 1968 annual CORE convention, he outlined his shift in tactics. CORE and SNCC were formerly integrationists, but in 1966, these organizations became militant due to dissatisfaction with pacifist techniques, conflict with white members of their organizations, and a desire to exert more control over the direction of the movement and their lives. During his speech, Young referred to his audience as "brothers and sisters," and affirmed the audience's advocacy of black power. His speech "astonished and delighted them." He later had to justify his speech on a radio program, explaining that his support of black power did not include endorsement for violence or black separatism (Weiss, 183).

Great Society

The Great Society Program was an ambitious and laudatory step taken to address poverty and racism in America. Put into place in the mid-1960s by President Lyndon B. Johnson (although John F. Kennedy had wrestled with some of the concepts prior to his assassination), the program was specifically created to meet the needs of disadvantaged minorities.

A number of programs operating today are by-products of Johnson's program, including the Job Corps (to provide job training), the Peace Corps, Upward Bound (to prepare inner-city youths for college), Food Stamps, and Head Start (for children). An array of anti-poverty programs was created under the banner of the "War on Poverty."

Johnson's programs were both visionary and timely, especially considering the barrage of race riots that inflamed black communities in the North in the same decade. These riots occurred due to neglect and rampant problems associated largely with poverty and racism.

However, America's increasing embroilment in the Vietnam War siphoned away monies that had previously funded Great Society programs and dominated the president's attention. As a result of this, augmented by the political conservatism of the 1980s, many of the gains that had been achieved were diminished.

Young closed out the decade with controversy. He went to Vietnam in 1966, to investigate how black soldiers were being treated. Young reported problems, such as blacks being prohibited from advancement, to President Johnson. In 1967, he went again to Vietnam, this time at Johnson's behest as a member of a delegation charged to report on the elections that took place there. Young's report was positive, but civil rights leaders felt he should not have gone, since they were in disagreement with America's involvement in the war. Despite the dissension he created among black leaders, the decade ended on a tremendous note when, in 1969, Johnson awarded Young the Medal of Freedom.

INTO THE 1970S

Young was still a major figure at the start of the new decade. As a result, he continued to be away from home frequently, which put a strain on his wife and children who missed him and wanted to see more of him. Although Young was enamored of his role and the attention he generated, he sometimes agonized over not having more time for his family. He thought seriously about leaving the NUL for some other opportunity.

It was during this time of reflection that Young accepted an invitation to join several delegates to participate in a dialogue between African Americans and Africans in Lagos, Nigeria. During the conference, Young and several others wandered to the beach for a swim. On March 11, 1971, Young tragically drowned. He was forty-nine years old.

See also Stokely Carmichael; Angela Davis; James Farmer; Dorothy Height; Martin Luther King, Jr.; John Lewis; A. Philip Randolph; and Roy Wilkins.

FURTHER RESOURCES

Dickerson, Dennis C. *Militant Mediator*. Lexington: University Press of Kentucky, 1998.

National Urban League (April 2008). See http://www.nul.org/history.html.

Weiss, Nancy J. *Whitney M. Young, Jr., and the Struggle for Civil Rights*. Princeton, NJ: Princeton University Press, 1989.

Young, Whitney. *Beyond Racism: Building an Open Society*. New York: McGraw-Hill, 1969.

Young, Whitney. *To Be Equal*. New York: McGraw-Hill, 1964.

Appendix 1: Executive Order 8802

Signed by President Franklin D. Roosevelt on June 25, 1941, less than six months before the American entry into World War II, Executive Order 8802 prohibited government contractors from engaging in employment discrimination based on race, color, or national origin.

REAFFIRMING POLICY OF FULL PARTICIPATION IN THE DEFENSE PROGRAM BY ALL PERSONS, REGARDLESS OF RACE, CREED, COLOR, OR NATIONAL ORIGIN, AND DIRECTING CERTAIN ACTION IN FURTHERANCE OF SAID POLICY

June 25, 1941

WHEREAS it is the policy of the United States to encourage full participation in the national defense program by all citizens of the United States, regardless of race, creed, color, or national origin, in the firm belief that the democratic way of life within the Nation can be defended successfully only with the help and support of all groups within its borders; and

WHEREAS there is evidence that available and needed workers have been barred from employment in industries engaged in defense production solely because of considerations of race, creed, color, or national origin, to the detriment of workers' morale and of national unity:

NOW, THEREFORE, by virtue of the authority vested in me by the Constitution and the statutes, and as a prerequisite to the successful conduct of our national defense production effort, I do hereby reaffirm the policy of the United States that there shall be no discrimination in the employment of workers in defense industries or government because of race, creed, color, or national origin, and I do hereby declare that it is the duty of employers and of labor organizations, in furtherance of said policy and of this order, to provide for the full and equitable participation of all workers in defense industries, without discrimination because of race, creed, color, or national origin;

And it is hereby ordered as follows:

1. All departments and agencies of the Government of the United States concerned with vocational and training programs for defense production shall take special measures appropriate to assure that such programs are administered without discrimination because of race, creed, color, or national origin;

2. All contracting agencies of the Government of the United States shall include in all defense contracts hereafter negotiated by them a provision obligating the contractor not to discriminate against any worker because of race, creed, color, or national origin;

3. There is established in the Office of Production Management a Committee on Fair Employment Practice, which shall consist of a chairman and four other members to be appointed by the President. The Chairman and members of the Committee shall serve as such without compensation but shall be entitled to actual and necessary transportation, subsistence and other expenses incidental to performance of their duties. The Committee shall receive and investigate complaints of discrimination in violation of the provisions of this order and shall take appropriate steps to redress grievances which it finds to be valid. The Committee shall also recommend to the several departments and agencies of the Government of the United States and to the President all measures which may be deemed by it necessary or proper to effectuate the provisions of this order.

Franklin D. Roosevelt
The White House
June 25, 1941

Appendix 2: Executive Order 9981

On July 26, 1948, President Harry S. Truman signed Executive Order 9981, establishing the President's Committee on Equality of Treatment and Opportunity in the Armed Services. Although segregation in the military services did not officially end until President Dwight Eisenhower's secretary of defense announced the abolition of the last all-black unit on September 30, 1954, Executive Order 9981 began the process of desegregating the armed forces of the United States.

Whereas it is essential that there be maintained in the armed services of the United States the highest standards of democracy, with equality of treatment and opportunity for all those who served in our country's defense:

Now, therefore, by virtue of the authority invested in me as President of the United States, and as Commander in Chief of the armed services, it is hereby ordered as follows:

1. It is hereby declared to be the policy of the President that there shall be equality of treatment and opportunity for all persons in the armed services without regard to race, color, religion or national origin. This policy shall be put into effect as rapidly as possible, having due regard to the time required to effectuate any necessary changes without impairing efficiency or morale.

2. There shall be created in the National Military Establishment an advisory committee to be known as the President's Committee on Equality of Treatment and Opportunity in the Armed Services, which shall be composed of seven members to be designated by the President.

3. The Committee is authorized on behalf of the President to examine into the rules, procedures and practices of the armed services in order to determine in what respect such rules, procedures and practices may be altered

or improved with a view to carrying out the policy of this order. The Committee shall confer and advise with the Secretary of Defense, the Secretary of the Army, the Secretary of the Navy, and Secretary of the Air Force, and shall make such recommendations to the President and to said Secretaries as in the judgement of the Committee will effectuate the policy hereof.

4. All executive departments and agencies of the Federal Government are authorized and directed to cooperate with the Committee in its work, and to furnish the Committee such information or the services of such persons as the Committee may require in the performance of its duties.

5. When requested by the Committee to do so, persons in the armed services or in any of the executive departments and agencies of the Federal Government shall testify before the Committee and shall make available for use of the Committee such documents and other information as the Committee may require.

6. The Committee shall continue to exist until such time as the President shall terminate its existence by Executive Order.

Harry S. Truman
The White House
July 26, 1948

Appendix 3: Selected Excerpts from the Civil Rights Act of 1964

An Act to enforce the constitutional right to vote, to confer jurisdiction upon the district courts of the United States to provide injunctive relief against discrimination in public accommodations, to authorize the Attorney General to institute suits to protect constitutional rights in public facilities and public education, to extend the Commission on Civil Rights, to prevent discrimination in federally assisted programs, to establish a Commission on Equal Employment Opportunity, and for other purposes.

> Be it enacted by the Senate and House of Representatives of the United States of America in Congress assembled, That this Act may be cited as the "Civil Rights Act of 1964."

TITLE I—VOTING RIGHTS

Section 101

(2) No person acting under color of law shall—

(A) in determining whether any individual is qualified under State law or laws to vote in any Federal election, apply any standard, practice, or procedure different from the standards, practices, or procedures applied under such law or laws to other individuals within the same county, parish, or similar political subdivision who have been found by State officials to be qualified to vote;

(B) deny the right of any individual to vote in any Federal election because of an error or omission on any record or paper relating to any application, registration, or other act requisite to voting, if such error or omission is not material in determining whether such individual is qualified under State law to vote in such election; or

(C) employ any literacy test as a qualification for voting in any Federal election unless (i) such test is administered to each individual and is conducted wholly in writing, and (ii) a certified copy of the test and of the answers given by the individual is furnished to him within twenty-five days of the submission of his request made within the period of time during which records and papers are required to be retained and preserved pursuant to title III of the Civil Rights Act of 1960 (42 U.S.C. 1974-74e; 74 Stat. 88): Provided, however, That the Attorney General may enter into agreements with appropriate State or local authorities that preparation, conduct, and maintenance of such tests in accordance with the provisions of applicable State or local law, including such special provisions as are necessary in the preparation, conduct, and maintenance of such tests for persons who are blind or otherwise physically handicapped, meet the purposes of this subparagraph and constitute compliance therewith.

TITLE II—INJUNCTIVE RELIEF AGAINST DISCRIMINATION IN PLACES OF PUBLIC ACCOMMODATION

Section 201

(a) All persons shall be entitled to the full and equal enjoyment of the goods, services, facilities, privileges, advantages, and accommodations of any place of public accommodation, as defined in this section, without discrimination or segregation on the ground of race, color, religion, or national origin.

(b) Each of the following establishments which serves the public is a place of public accommodation within the meaning of this title if its operations affect commerce, or if discrimination or segregation by it is supported by State action:

(1) any inn, hotel, motel, or other establishment which provides lodging to transient guests, other than an establishment located within a building which contains not more than five rooms for rent or hire and which is actually occupied by the proprietor of such establishment as his residence;

(2) any restaurant, cafeteria, lunchroom, lunch counter, soda fountain, or other facility principally engaged in selling food for consumption on the premises, including, but not limited to, any such facility located on the premises of any retail establishment; or any gasoline station;

(3) any motion picture house, theater, concert hall, sports arena, stadium or other place of exhibition or entertainment; and

(4) any establishment (A) (i) which is physically located within the premises of any establishment otherwise covered by this subsection, or (ii) within the premises of which is physically located any such covered establishment,

and (B) which holds itself out as serving patrons of such covered establishment.

(d) Discrimination or segregation by an establishment is supported by State action within the meaning of this title if such discrimination or segregation (1) is carried on under color of any law, statute, ordinance, or regulation; or (2) is carried on under color of any custom or usage required or enforced by officials of the State or political subdivision thereof; or (3) is required by action of the State or political subdivision thereof.

(e) The provisions of this title shall not apply to a private club or other establishment not in fact open to the public, except to the extent that the facilities of such establishment are made available to the customers or patrons of an establishment within the scope of subsections (b).

Section 202

All persons shall be entitled to be free, at any establishment or place, from discrimination or segregation of any kind on the ground of race, color, religion, or national origin, if such discrimination or segregation is or purports to be required by any law, statute, ordinance, regulation, rule, or order of a State or any agency or political subdivision thereof.

Section 203

No person shall (a) withhold, deny, or attempt to withhold or deny, or deprive or attempt to deprive, any person of any right or privilege secured by section 201 or 202, or (b) intimidate, threaten, or coerce, or attempt to intimidate, threaten, or coerce any person with the purpose of interfering with any right or privilege secured by section 201 or 202, or (c) punish or attempt to punish any person for exercising or attempting to exercise any right or privilege secured by section 201 or 202.

Section 204

(a) Whenever any person has engaged or there are reasonable grounds to believe that any person is about to engage in any act or practice prohibited by section 203, a civil action for preventive relief, including an application for a permanent or temporary injunction, restraining order, or other order, may be instituted by the person aggrieved and, upon timely application, the court may, in its discretion, permit the Attorney General to intervene in such civil action if he certifies that the case is of general public importance. Upon application by the complaint and in such circumstances as the court may deem just, the court may appoint an attorney for such complainant and may authorize the commencement of the civil action without the payment of fees, costs, or security.

(b) In any action commenced pursuant to this title, the court, in its discretion, may allow the prevailing party, other than the United States, a reasonable attorney's fee as part of the costs, and the United States shall be liable for costs the same as a private person.

(c) In the case of an alleged act or practice prohibited by this title which occurs in a State, or political subdivision of a State, which has a State or local law prohibiting such act or practice and establishing or authorizing a State or local authority to grant or seek relief from such practice or to institute criminal proceedings with respect thereto upon receiving notice thereof, no civil action may be brought under subsection (a) before the expiration of thirty days after written notice of such alleged act or practice has been given to the appropriate State or local authority by registered mail or in person, provided that the court may stay proceedings in such civil action pending the termination of State or local enforcement proceedings.

Section 205

The Service is authorized to make a full investigation of any complaint referred to it by the court under section 204(d) and may hold such hearings with respect thereto as may be necessary. The Service shall conduct any hearings with respect to any such complaint in executive session, and shall not release any testimony given therein except by agreement of all parties involved in the complaint with the permission of the court, and the Service shall endeavor to bring about a voluntary settlement between the parties.

Section 206

(a) Whenever the Attorney General has reasonable cause to believe that any person or group of persons is engaged in a pattern or practice of resistance to the full enjoyment of any of the rights secured by this title, and that the pattern or practice is of such a nature and is intended to deny the full exercise of the rights herein described, the Attorney General may bring a civil action in the appropriate district court of the United States by filing with it a complaint (1) signed by him (or in his absence the Acting Attorney General), (2) setting forth facts pertaining to such pattern or practice, and (3) requesting such preventive relief, including an application for a permanent or temporary injunction, restraining order or other order against the person or persons responsible for such pattern or practice, as he deems necessary to insure the full enjoyment of the rights herein described.

(b) In any such proceeding the Attorney General may file with the clerk of such court a request that a court of three judges be convened to hear and determine the case. Such request by the Attorney General shall be accompanied by a certificate that, in his opinion, the case is of general public importance. A copy of the certificate and request for a three-judge court shall be immediately furnished by such clerk to the chief judge of the circuit (or in his absence, the presiding circuit judge of the circuit) in which the case is pending. Upon receipt of the copy of such request it shall be the duty of the chief judge of the circuit or the presiding circuit judge, as the case may be, to designate immediately three judges in such circuit, of whom at least one shall be a circuit judge and another of whom shall be a district judge of the court in which the proceeding was instituted, to hear and determine such case, and it shall be the duty of the judges so designated to assign the case for hearing at the earliest practicable date, to participate in the hearing and determination thereof, and to cause the case to be in every way expedited. An appeal from the final judgment of such court will lie to the Supreme Court.

In the event the Attorney General fails to file such a request in any such proceeding, it shall be the duty of the chief judge of the district (or in his absence, the acting chief judge) in which the case is pending immediately to designate a judge in such district to hear and determine the case. In the event that no judge in the district is available to hear and determine the case, the chief judge of the district, or the acting chief judge, as the case may be, shall certify this fact to the chief judge of the circuit (or in his absence, the acting chief judge) who shall then designate a district or circuit judge of the circuit to hear and determine the case.

It shall be the duty of the judge designated pursuant to this section to assign the case for hearing at the earliest practicable date and to cause the case to be in every way expedited.

TITLE III—DESEGREGATION OF PUBLIC FACILITIES

Section 301

(a) Whenever the Attorney General receives a complaint in writing signed by an individual to the effect that he is being deprived of or threatened with the loss of his right to the equal protection of the laws, on account of his race, color, religion, or national origin, by being denied equal utilization of any public facility which is owned, operated, or managed by or on behalf of any State or subdivision thereof, other than a public school or public college as defined in section 401 of title IV hereof, and the Attorney General believes the complaint is meritorious and certifies that the signer or signers of such complaint are unable, in his judgment, to initiate and maintain appropriate legal proceedings for relief and that the institution of an action will materially further the orderly progress of desegregation in public facilities, the Attorney General is authorized to institute for or in the name of the United States a civil action in any appropriate district court of the United States against such parties and for such relief as may be appropriate, and such court shall have and shall exercise jurisdiction of proceedings instituted pursuant to this section. The Attorney General may implead as defendants such additional parties as are or become necessary to the grant of effective relief hereunder.

TITLE IV—DESEGREGATION OF PUBLIC EDUCATION: DEFINITIONS

Section 401

(b) "Desegregation" means the assignment of students to public schools and within such schools without regard to their race, color, religion, or national origin, but "desegregation" shall not mean the assignment of students to public schools in order to overcome racial imbalance.

SURVEY AND REPORT OF EDUCATIONAL OPPORTUNITIES

Section 402

The Commissioner shall conduct a survey and make a report to the President and the Congress, with two years of the enactment of this title, concerning the lack of availability of equal educational opportunities for individuals by reason of race, color, religion, or national origin in public educational institutions at all levels in the United States, its territories and possessions, and the District of Columbia.

TITLE VI—NONDISCRIMINATION IN FEDERALLY ASSISTED PROGRAMS

Section 601

No person in the United States shall, on the ground of race, color, or national origin, be excluded from participation in, be denied the benefits of, or be subjected to discrimination under any program or activity receiving Federal financial assistance.

Section 603

Any department or agency action taken pursuant to section 602 shall be subject to such judicial review as may otherwise be provided by law for similar action taken by such department or agency on other grounds. In the case of action, not otherwise subject to judicial review, terminating or refusing to grant or to continue financial assistance upon a finding of failure to comply with any requirement imposed pursuant to section 602, any person aggrieved (including any State or political subdivision thereof and any agency of either) may obtain judicial review of such action in accordance with section 10 of the Administrative Procedure Act, and such action shall not be deemed committed to unreviewable agency discretion within the meaning of that section.

TITLE VII—EQUAL EMPLOYMENT OPPORTUNITY: DISCRIMINATION BECAUSE OF RACE, COLOR, RELIGION, SEX, OR NATIONAL ORIGIN

Section 703

(a) It shall be an unlawful employment practice for an employer—

(1) to fail or refuse to hire or to discharge any individual, or otherwise to discriminate against any individual with respect to his compensation, terms, conditions, or privileges of employment, because of such individual's race, color, religion, sex, or national origin;

(2) to limit, segregate, or classify his employees in any way which would deprive or tend to deprive any individual of employment opportunities or otherwise adversely affect his status as an employee, because of such individual's race, color, religion, sex, or national origin.

(b) It shall be an unlawful employment practice for an employment agency to fail or refuse to refer for employment, or otherwise to discriminate against, any individual because of his race, color, religion, sex, or national origin, or to classify or refer for employment and individual on the basis of his race, color, religion, sex, or national origin.

(c) It shall be an unlawful employment practice for a labor organization—

(1) to exclude or to expel from its membership, or otherwise to discriminate against, any individual because of his race, color, religion, sex, or national origin;

(2) to limit, segregate, or classify its membership, or to classify or fail or refuse to refer for employment any individual, in any way which would deprive or tend to deprive any individual of employment opportunities, or would limit such employment opportunities or otherwise adversely affect his status as an employee or as an applicant for employment, because of such individual's race, color, religion, sex, or national origin; or

(3) to cause or attempt to cause an employer to discriminate against an individual in violation of this section.

(d) It shall be an unlawful employment practice for any employer, labor organization, or joint labor-management committee controlling apprenticeship or other training or retraining, including on-the-job training programs to discriminate against any individual because of his race, color, religion, sex, or national origin in admission to, or employment in, any program established to provide apprenticeship or other training.

(e) Notwithstanding any other provision of this title, (1) it shall not be an unlawful employment practice for an employer to hire and employ employees, for an employment agency to classify, or refer for employment any individual, for a labor organization to classify its membership or to classify or refer for employment any individual, or for an employer, labor organization, or joint labor-management committee controlling apprenticeship or other training or retraining programs to admit or employ any individual in any such program, on the basis of his religion, sex, or national origin in those certain instances where religion, sex, or national origin is a bona fide occupational qualification reasonably necessary to the normal operation of that particular business or enterprise, and (2) it shall not be an unlawful employment practice for a school, college, university, or other educational institution or institution of learning to hire and employ employees of a particular religion if such school, college, university, or other educational institution or institution of learning is, in whole or in substantial part, owned, supported, controlled, or managed by a particular religion or by a particular religious corporation, association, or society, or if the curriculum, of such school, college, university, or other educational institution or institution of learning is directed toward the propagation of a particular religion.

(f) As used in this title, the phrase "unlawful employment practice" shall not be deemed to include any action or measure taken by an employer, labor organization, joint labor-management committee, employment agency with respect to an individual who is a member of the Communist Party of the United States or of any other organization required to register as a Communist-action or Communist-front organization by final order of the Subversive Activities Control Board pursuant to the Subversive Activities Control Act of 1950.

(i) Nothing contained in this title shall apply to any business or enterprise on or near an Indian reservation with respect to any publicly announced employment practice of such business or enterprise under which preferential treatment is given to any individual because he is an Indian living on or near a reservation.

OTHER UNLAWFUL EMPLOYMENT PRACTICES

Section 704

(a) It shall be an unlawful employment practice for an employer to discriminate against any of his employees or applicants for employment, for an employment agency to discriminate against an individual, or for a labor organization to discriminate against any member thereof or applicant for membership, because he has opposed any practice made an unlawful employment practice by this title, or because he has made a charge, testified, assisted, or participated in any manner in an investigation, proceeding, or hearing under this title.

EQUAL EMPLOYMENT OPPORTUNITY COMMISSION

Section 705

(a) There is hereby created a Commission to be known as the Equal Employment Opportunity Commission, which shall be composed of five members, not more than three of whom shall be members of the same political party, who shall be appointed by the President by and with the advice and consent of the Senate. One of the original members shall be appointed for a term of one year, one for a term of two years, one for a term of three year, one for a term of four years, one for a term of five years, beginning from the date of enactment of this title, but their successors shall be appointed for terms of five years, except that any individual chosen to fill a vacancy shall be appointed only for the unexpired term of the member whom he shall succeed. The President shall designate one member to serve as Chairman of the Commission, and one member to serve as Vice Chairman. The Chairman shall be responsible on behalf of the Commission for the administrative operations of the Commissions, and shall appoint, in accordance with the civil service laws, such officers, agents, attorneys, and employees as it deems necessary to assist it in the performance of its functions and to fix their compensation in accordance with the Classification Act of 1949, as amended. The Vice Chairman shall act as Chairman in the absence or disability of the Chairman or in the event of a vacancy in that

TITLE VIII—REGISTRATION AND VOTING STATISTICS

Section 801

The Secretary of Commerce shall promptly conduct a survey to compile registration and voting statistics in such geographic areas as may be recommended by the Commission on Civil Rights. Such a survey and compilation shall, to the extent recommended by the Commission on Civil Rights, only include a count of persons of voting age by race, color, and national origin, and determination of the extent to which such persons are registered to vote, and have voted in any statewide primary or general election in which the Members of the United States House of Representatives are nominated or elected, since January 1, 1960. Such information shall also be collected and compiled in connection with the Nineteenth Decennial Census, and at such other times as the Congress may prescribe. The provisions of section 9 and chapter 7 of title 13, United States Code, shall apply to any survey, collection, or compilation of registration and voting statistics carried out under this title: Provided, however, That no person shall be compelled to disclose his race, color, and national origin, or questioned about his political party affiliation, how he voted, or the reasons therefore, nor shall any penalty be imposed for his failure or refusal to make such disclosure. Every person interrogated orally, by written survey or questionnaire or by any other means with respect to such information shall be fully advised with respect to his right to fail or refuse to furnish such information.

Source: Civil Rights Act (1964). *Historical Documents in United States History.* April 1, 2008. See http://www.historicaldocuments.com/CivilRights Act1964.htm.

Appendix 4: Selected Excerpts from the Voting Rights Act of 1965

An Act to enforce the Fifteenth Amendment to the Constitution of the United States, and for other purposes.

> Be it enacted by the Senate and House of Representatives of the United States of America in Congress assembled, That this Act shall be known as the "Voting Rights Act of 1965."

Section 2

No voting qualifications or prerequisite to voting, or standard, practice, or procedure shall be imposed or applied by any State or political subdivision to deny or abridge the right of any citizen of the United States to vote on account of race or color.

Section 3

(a) Whenever the Attorney General institutes a proceeding under any statute to enforce the guarantees of the fifteenth amendment in any State or political subdivision the Court shall authorize the appointment of Federal examiners by the United States Civil Service Commission in accordance with section 6 to serve for such period of time and for such political subdivisions as the court shall determine is appropriate to enforce the guarantees of the fifteenth amendment (1) as part of any interlocutory order if the court determines that the appointment of such examiners is necessary to enforce such guarantees or (2) as part of any final judgment if the court finds that violations of the fifteenth amendment justifying equitable relief have occurred in such State or subdivision: Provided, That the court need not authorize the appointment of examiners if any incidents of denial or abridgement of the right to vote on account of race or color (1) have been few in number and have been promptly and effectively corrected by State or local action, (2) the continuing of effect of such incidents has been eliminated, and (3) there is no reasonable probability of their recurrence in the future.

Section 4

(a) To assure that the right of citizens of the United States to vote is not denied or abridged on account of race or color, no citizen shall be denied the right to vote in any Federal, State, or local election because of his failure to comply with any test or device in any State with respect to which the determinations have been made under subsection (b) or in political subdivision with respect to which such determinations have been made as a separate unit, unless the United States District Court for the District of Columbia in an action for a declaratory judgment brought by such State or subdivision against the United States has determined that no such test or device has been used during the five years preceding the filing of the action for the purpose or with the effect of denying or abridging the right to vote on account of race or color: *Provided*, That no such declaratory judgment shall issue with respect to any plaintiff for a period of five years after the entry of a final judgment of any court of the United States, other than the denial of a declaratory judgment under this section, whether entered prior to or after the enactment of this Act, determining that denials or abridgments of the right to vote on account of race or color through the use of such tests or devices have occurred anywhere in the territory of such plaintiff.

An action pursuant to this subsection shall be heard and determined by a court of three judges in accordance with the provisions of section 2284 of title 28 of the United States Code and any appeal shall lie to the Supreme Court. The court shall retain jurisdiction of any action pursuant to this subsection for five years after judgment and shall reopen the action upon motion of the Attorney General alleging that a test or device has been used for the purpose or with the effect of denying or abridging the right to vote on account of race or color.

If the Attorney General determines that he has no reasons to believe that any such test or device has been used during the five years preceding the filing of the action for the purpose or with the effect of denying or abridging the right to vote on account of race or color, he shall consent to the entry of such judgment.

(b) The provisions of subsection (a) shall apply in any State or in any political subdivision of a state which (1) the Attorney General determines maintained on November 1, 1964, any test or device, and with respect to which (2) the Director of the Census determines that less than 50 per centum of the persons of voting age residing therein were registered on November 1, 1964, or that less than 50 per centum of such persons voted in the presidential election of November 1, 1964.

A determination or certification of the Attorney General or of the Director of the Census under this section or under section 6 or section 13 shall not be reviewable in any court and shall be effective upon publication in the Federal Register.

(c) The phrase "test or device" shall mean any requirement that a person as a prerequisite for voting or registration for voting (1) demonstrate the ability to read, write, understand, or interpret any matter, (2) demonstrate any educational achievement or his knowledge of any particular subject, (3) possess good moral character, or (4) prove his qualifications by the voucher of registered voters or members of any other class.

(d) For purposes of this section no State or political subdivision shall be determined to have engaged in the use of tests or devices for the purpose or with the effect of denying or abridging the right to vote on account of race or color if (1) incidents of such use have been few in number and have been promptly and effectively corrected by State or local action, (2) the continuing effect of such incidents has been eliminated, and (3) there is no reasonable probability of their recurrence in the future.

(e) (1) Congress hereby declares that to secure the rights under the fourteenth amendment of persons educated in American-flag schools in which the predominant classroom language was other than English, it is necessary to prohibit the States from conditioning the right to vote of such persons on ability to read, write, understand, or interpret any matter in the English language.

(2) No person who demonstrates that he has successfully completed the sixth primary grade in a public school in, or a private school accredited by, any State or territory, the District of Columbia, or the Commonwealth of Puerto Rico in which the predominant classroom language was other than English, shall be denied the right to vote in any Federal, State, or local election because of his inability to read, write, understand, or interpret any matter in the English language, except that in States in which State law provides that a different level of education is presumptive of literacy, he shall demonstrate that he has successfully completed an equivalent level of education in a public school in, or a private school accredited by, any State or territory, the District of Columbia, or the Commonwealth of Puerto Rico in which the predominant classroom language was other than English.

Section 10

(a) The Congress finds that the requirement of the payment of a poll tax as a precondition to voting (i) precludes persons of limited means from voting or imposes unreasonable financial hardship upon such persons as a precondition to their exercise of the franchise, (ii) does not bear a reasonable relationship to any legitimate State interest in the conduct of elections, and (iii) in some areas has the purpose or effect of denying persons the right to vote because of race color. Upon the basis of these findings, Congress declares the constitutional right of citizens to vote is denied or abridged in some areas by the requirement of the payment of a poll tax as a precondition to voting.

Section 11

(a) No person acting under color of law shall fail or refuse to permit any person to vote who is entitled to vote under any provision of this Act or is otherwise qualified to vote, or willfully fail or refuse to tabulate, count, and report such person's vote.

(b) No person, whether acting under color of law or otherwise, shall intimidate, threaten, or coerce, or attempt to intimidate, threaten, or coerce any person for urging or aiding any person to vote or attempt to vote, or intimidate, threaten, or coerce any person for exercising any powers or duties under section 3(a), 6, 8, 9, 10, or 12(e).

(c) Whoever knowingly or willfully gives false information as to his name, address, or period of residence in the voting district for the purpose of establishing his eligibility to register or vote, or conspires with another individual for the purpose of encouraging his false registration to vote or illegal voting, or pays or offers to pay or accepts payment either for registration to vote or for voting shall be fined not more than $10,000 or imprisoned not more than five years, or both: *Provided, however,* That this provision shall be applicable only to general, special, or primary elections held solely or in part for the purpose of selecting or electing any candidate for the office of President, Vice President, presidential elector, Member of the United States Senate, Member of the United States House of Representatives, or Delegates or Commissioners from the territories or possessions, or Resident Commissioner of the Commonwealth of Puerto Rico.

(d) Whoever, in any matter within the jurisdiction of an examiner or hearing officer knowingly and willfully falsifies or conceals a material fact, or makes any false, fictitious, or fraudulent statements or representations, or makes or uses any false writing or document knowing the same be fined not more than $10,000 or imprisoned not more than five years, or both.

Source: Voting Rights Act 1965. *Historical Documents in United States History.* April 1, 2008. See http://www.historicaldocuments.com/Voting RightsActof1965.htm.

Appendix 5: Excerpt from the Black Panther Party Ten Point Platform and Program (October 1966)

What We Want
What We Believe

1. We want freedom. We want power to determine the destiny of our Black Community.
2. We want full employment for our people.
3. We want an end to the robbery by the capitalist of our Black Community.
4. We want decent housing, fit for the shelter of human beings.
5. We want education for our people that exposes the true nature of this decadent American society. We want education that teaches us our true history and our role in the present-day society.
6. We want all black men to be exempt from military service.
7. We want an immediate end to police brutality and murder of black people.
8. We want freedom for all black men held in federal, state, county, and city prisons and jails.
9. We want all black people when brought to trial to be tried in court by a jury of their peer group or people from their black communities, as defined by the Constitution of the United States.
10. We want land, bread, housing, education, clothing, justice, and peace.

Source: Hilliard, David. *Huey: Spirit of the Panther.* New York: Thunder's Mouth Press, 2006, pp. 31–35.

Appendix 6: Icons in Their Own Words

The following section contains quotes pulled from the essays, autobiographies, speeches, interviews, and other publications of the twenty-four icons of African American protest featured in these two volumes.

W.E.B. DU BOIS: ON THE POWER OF PROTEST, 1907

W.E.B. Du Bois wrote the essay "The Value of Agitation" in 1907. In this essay, Du Bois defended his endorsement of African American protest, and, in doing so, challenged the prevailing anti-black attitudes, laws, and practices in the United States.

> We are confirmed in our belief that if a man stand up and tell the thing he wants and point out the evil around him, that this is the best way to get rid of it. May we not hope then that we are going to have in the next century a solid front on the part of colored people in the United States, saying we want education for our children and we do not have it today in any large measure; we want full political rights and we never have had that; we want to be treated as human beings; and we want those of our race who stand on the threshold and within the veil of crime to be treated not as beasts, but as men who can be reformed or as children who can be prevented from going further in their career.
>
> If we all stand and demand this insistently, the nation must listen to the voice of ten millions.

Source: Foner, Philip S., ed. *W.E.B. Du Bois Speaks: Speeches and Addresses, 1890–1910.* New York: Pathfinder Press, 1970, pp. 174–178.

IDA B. WELLS-BARNETT: A SOLUTION TO THE LYNCHING EPIDEMIC, 1909

Ida B. Wells-Barnett spoke the following words in "Lynching, Our National Crime," a speech she gave at the National Negro Conference in New York in 1909—almost two decades after she singlehandedly pioneered an anti-lynching campaign.

> Is there a remedy, or will the nation confess that it cannot protect its protectors at home as well as abroad? Various remedies have been suggested to abolish the lynching infamy, but year after year, the butchery of men, women, and children continues in spite of plea and protest. Education is suggested as a preventive, but it is as grave a crime to murder an ignorant man as it is a scholar. True, few educated men have been lynched, but the hue and cry once started stops at no bounds, as was clearly shown by the lynchings in Atlanta, and in Springfield, Illinois.
>
> Agitation, though helpful, will not alone stop the crime. Year after year statistics are published, meetings are held, resolutions are adopted. And yet lynchings go on....
>
> The only certain remedy is an appeal to law. Lawbreakers must be made to know that human life is sacred and that every citizen of this country is first a citizen of the United States and secondly a citizen of the state in which he belongs. This nation must assert itself and protect its federal citizenship at home as well as abroad. The strong men of the government must reach across state lines whenever unbridled lawlessness defies state laws, and must give to the individual under the Stars and Stripes the same measure of protection it gives to him when he travels in foreign lands. Federal protection of American citizenship is the remedy for lynching.

Source: Wells-Barnett, Ida B. "Lynching, Our National Crime." In *Can I Get a Witness?: Prophetic Religious Voices of African American Women: An Anthology.* Edited by Marcia Y. Riggs and Barbara Holmes. Maryknoll, NY: Orbis, 1997, pp. 146–150.

MARCUS GARVEY: RADICALISM DEFINED, 1923

Marcus Mosiah Garvey's second wife, Amy Jacques-Garvey, published the *Philosophy and Opinions of Marcus Garvey* in 1923 during an intense campaign to deport him back to Jamaica by those who opposed his views on black separatism and nationalism and his ambitious programs to empower blacks. Garvey, the leader of the massively popular Universal Negro Improvement Association (UNIA), was eventually deported in 1927. The following quote comes from an essay entitled "Radicalism."

> 'Radical' is a label that is always applied to people who are endeavoring to get freedom.

Jesus Christ was the greatest radical the world every saw. He came and saw a world of sin and his program was to inspire it with spiritual feeling. He was therefore a radical.

George Washington was dubbed a radical when he took up his sword to fight his way to liberty in America one hundred and forty years ago.

All men who call themselves reformers are perforce radicals. They cannot be anything else, because they are revolting against the conditions that exist.

Conditions as they exist reveal a conservative state, and if you desire to change these conditions you must be a radical.

Source: Jacques-Garvey, Amy, ed. *The Philosophy and Opinions of Marcus Garvey.* New York: Arno Press and the New York Times, 1923, pp. 18–19.

THURGOOD MARSHALL: ON SECURING AND ENFORCING CIVIL RIGHTS, 1942

Thurgood Marshall, who later argued before the U.S. Supreme Court in the monumental *Brown v. Board of Education* case that declared segregated schools unconstitutional in 1954, spoke the following words in his speech "The Legal Attack to Secure Civil Rights" during the NAACP's Wartime Conference in 1942.

Thus it seems clear that although it is necessary and vital to all of us that we continue our program for additional legislation to guarantee and enforce certain of our rights, at the same time we must continue with ever-increasing vigor to enforce those few statutes, both federal and state, which are now on the statute books. We must not be delayed by people who say "the time is not ripe," nor should we proceed with caution for fear of destroying the "status quo." Persons who deny to us our civil rights should be brought to justice now. Many people believe the time is always "ripe" to discriminate against Negroes. All right then—the time is always "ripe" to bring them to justice. The responsibility for the enforcement of these statutes rests with every American citizen regardless of race or color. However, the real job has to be done by the Negro population with whatever friends of the other races are willing to join in.

Source: Marshall, Thurgood. "The Legal Attack to Secure Civil Rights." In *The American Civil Rights Movement: Readings and Interpretations.* Edited by Raymond D'Angelo. New York: McGraw-Hill, 2001, pp. 189–194.

ROY WILKINS: ENCOURAGING YOUNG ACTIVISTS, 1959

Roy Wilkins, Executive Secretary of the NAACP (1955–1977), was among the speakers who addressed young demonstrators at a Youth March for Integrated Schools in 1959. Following is an excerpt from his speech.

So you are here to say by your presence and in your resolutions that you want integrated schools for all American children. You have every right to say this to your government and to all among the citizenry who will listen. No one has a better right, for in so speaking, you are demanding only that the high pronouncements and glorious traditions of this beloved bastion of freedom be vindicated, and that we be about the business of building the kind of world in which your generation can preserve freedom.

Source: Wilkins, Roy. *Talking It Over with Roy Wilkins: Selected Speeches and Writings.* Norwalk, CT: M & B Publishing, 1977, pp. 21–23.

JOHN LEWIS: ON GETTING ARRESTED FOR THE FIRST TIME, 1960

John Lewis, SNCC chairman (1963–1966), faced violence and was arrested numerous times during civil rights demonstrations. In the following excerpt from his autobiography, *Walking with the Wind: A Memoir of the Movement* (1998), he explains the rush he felt following his first arrest in 1960 while participating in a sit-in in Nashville, Tennessee.

But I felt no shame or disgrace. I didn't feel fear, either. As we were led out of the store single file, singing "We Shall Overcome," I felt exhilarated. As we passed through a cheering crowd gathered on the sidewalk outside, I felt high, almost giddy with joy. As we approached the open rear doors of a paddy wagon, I felt elated.

It was really happening, what I'd imagined for so long, the drama of good and evil playing itself out on the stage of the living, breathing world. It felt holy, and noble, and good.

That paddy wagon—crowded, cramped, dirty, with wire cage windows and doors—seemed like a chariot to me, a freedom vehicle carrying me across a threshold.

Source: Lewis, John. *Walking with the Wind: A Memoir of the Movement.* New York: Simon & Schuster, 1998, pp. 100–101.

FANNIE LOU HAMER: THE STRUGGLE FOR THE BALLOT, 1962

Civil rights activist Fannie Lou Hamer described in the following excerpt from her autobiography, *To Praise Our Bridges* (1967), the moment she decided to register to vote in 1962.

Until then I'd never heard of no mass meeting and I didn't know that a Negro could register and vote. Bob Moses, Reggie Robinson, Jim Bevel and James Forman were some of the SNCC workers who ran that meeting. When they asked for those to raise their hands who'd go down to the courthouse the next day, I raised mine. Had it up high as I could get it. I guess if I'd had any sense I'd a-been a little scared, but what was the point of being scared. The only thing they could do to me was kill me and it seemed like they'd been trying to do that a little bit at a time ever since I could remember.

After leaving the registration office, Hamer lost her home, her job, and nearly her life.

Source: Hamer, Fannie Lou. "To Praise Our Bridges." In *Mississippi Writers: Reflections of Childhood and Youth*. Edited by Dorothy Abbott. Jackson: University Press of Mississippi, 1985, pp. 321–330.

MARTIN LUTHER KING, JR.: IN DEFENSE OF NONVIOLENT DIRECT ACTION, 1963

In 1963, Dr. Martin Luther King, Jr., president of the Southern Christian Leadership Conference (1957–1968), wrote "Letter from Birmingham City Jail" (1963) while imprisoned for his participation in a demonstration. The letter was a response to a public statement given by Alabama clergy who denounced his organized remonstrations. The following is an excerpt from that letter.

> You may well ask, "Why direct action? Why sit-ins, marches, etc.? Isn't negotiation a better path?" You are exactly right in your call for negotiation. Indeed, this is the purpose of direct action. Nonviolent direct action seeks to create such a crisis and establish such creative tension that a community that has constantly refused to negotiate is forced to confront the issue. It seeks so to dramatize the issue that it can no longer be ignored.

Source: King, Martin Luther, Jr. "Letter from Birmingham City Jail." Philadelphia: American Friends Service Committee, 1963, p. 5.

MALCOLM X: MILITANCY RECONSIDERED, 1963

At the onset of Malcolm X's activism, his radicalism was evident in the following words from his 1963 speech "Message to the Grass Roots." In this address, Malcolm X gives his definition of a revolution—something he believed at that time was necessary to address the grievances of African Americans.

> A revolution is bloody. Revolution is hostile. Revolution knows no compromise. Revolution overturns and destroys everything that gets in its way. And you, sitting around here like a knot on the wall, saying, "I'm going to love these folks no matter how much they hate me." No, you need a revolution. Whoever heard of a revolution where they lock arms, as Reverend Cleage was pointing out beautifully, singing "We Shall Overcome"? Just tell me. You don't do that in a revolution. You don't do any singing; you're too busy swinging. It's based on land. A revolutionary wants land so he can set up his own nation, an independent nation. These Negroes aren't asking for no nation. They're trying to crawl back on the plantation.

Source: Malcolm X. "Message to the Grassroots." *American Rhetoric: Top 100 Speeches*. November 10, 2007. See http://www.americanrhetoric.com/speeches/malcolmxgrassroots.htm.

WHITNEY M. YOUNG, JR.: ADVOCATING FOR AFRICAN AMERICANS BEYOND BASIC CIVIL RIGHTS, 1964

Following the explosion of race riots in African American communities in the North, Whitney M. Young, Jr., Executive Director of the National Urban League (1961–1971), published a plan of action in his book *To Be Equal* (1964) to address the needs of African Americans extending beyond the landmark Civil Rights Act of 1964. The following is an excerpt from that book.

> The basic issue here is one of simple logic and fairness. The scales of justice have been heavily weighted against the Negro for over three hundred years and will not suddenly in 1964 balance themselves by applying equal weights. In this sense, the Negro is educationally and economically malnourished and anemic. It is not "preferential treatment" but simple decency to provide him for a brief period with special vitamins, additional food, and blood transfusions.

Source: Young, Whitney M. *To Be Equal*. New York: McGraw-Hill, 1964, p. 25.

MALCOLM X: RECONSIDERING BLACK SEPARATISM, 1965

Following a life-changing pilgrimage to Mecca, the sacred city in Islam, Malcolm X, who once called whites "blue-eyed devils," reconsiders his black separatist philosophy in this excerpt from a 1965 interview with acclaimed African American photographer Gordon Parks.

> Remember the time that white college girl came into the restaurant—the one who wanted to help the Muslims and the whites get together—and I told her there wasn't a ghost of a chance and she went away crying? … Well, I've lived to regret that incident. In many parts of the African continent I saw white students helping Black people. Something like this kills a lot of argument.

Source: Ali, Noaman. "Interview with Gordon Parks." *Malcolm-x.org.* November 10, 2007. See http://www.malcolm-x.org/docs/int_parks.htm.

ROBERT F. WILLIAMS: ON THE WATTS RIOT IN LOS ANGELES, 1965

Robert F. Williams established the radical radio station, Radio Free Dixie, while exiled in Cuba. The following is an excerpt from a 1965 broadcast concerning the Watts Riot, one of many that erupted in the 1960s.

> Yes, Los Angeles, Los Angeles is a warning to oppressor racist beasts that they can no longer enjoy immunity from retribution for their brutal crimes of

violence and oppression of our people. Let them be apprised of the fight. That we are going to have justice or set the torch to racist America. The masses of our people want relief from their misery.... We must protect ourselves. We must defend ourselves. We must meet violence with violence....

Let us resist tyranny to the death. Resist, resist, resist! Burn, burn, burn! Death to the oppressor! Down with the thug cops! To the streets and let our battle cry be heard around the world! Freedom, freedom, freedom now or death!

Source: Mosley, Walter. "Aug. 11, 1965: The Day Oppression Exploded." *The Freedom Archives*. November 10, 2007. See http://www.freedomarchives. org/pipermail/news_freedomarchives.org/2005-August/001332.html.

STOKELY CARMICHAEL: ON BLACK POWER, 1966

Stokely Carmichael, chairman of SNCC (1966–1967), was a harbinger of the Black Power Movement. The following excerpt comes from a speech, entitled "Black Power," which he gave in 1966 in Berkeley, California.

We cannot have white people working in the black community—on psychological grounds. The fact is that all black people question whether or not they are equal to whites, since every time they start to do something, white people are around showing them how to do it. If we are going to eliminate that for the generation that comes after us, then black people must be in positions of power, doing and articulating for themselves. That's not reverse racism; it is moving onto healthy ground; it is becoming what the philosopher Sartre says, an "anti-racist racist." And this country can't understand that. If everybody who's white sees himself as racist and sees us against him, he's speaking from his own guilt.

Source: Carmichael, Stokely. "Black Power." *Sojust.net*. November 10, 2007. See http://www.sojust.net/speeches/stokely_carmichael_blackpower. html.

HUEY P. NEWTON: ON ARMED RESISTANCE, 1967

Huey P. Newton was the minister of defense for the Black Panther Party beginning in 1966. The following excerpt comes from his article, "In Defense of Self Defense," published on June 20, 1967, in the Black Panther newspaper.

Black people must now move, from the grass roots up through the perfumed circles of the Black bourgeoisie, to seize by any means necessary a proportionate share of the power vested and collected in the structure of America. We must organize and unite to combat by long resistance the brutal force used against us daily. The power structure depends upon the use of force within retaliation. This is why they have made it a felony to teach guerrilla warfare. This is why they want the people unarmed.

The racist dog oppressors fear the armed people; they fear most of all Black people armed with weapons and the ideology of the Black Panther Party for Self-Defense. An unarmed people are slaves or are subject to slavery at any given moment. If a government is not afraid of the people it will arm the people against foreign aggression. Black people are held captive in the midst of their oppressors. There is a world of difference between thirty million unarmed submissive Black people and thirty million Black people armed with freedom, guns, and the strategic methods of liberation.

Source: Hilliard, David, and Donald Weise, eds. *The Huey P. Newton Reader.* New York: Seven Stories Press, 2002, pp. 134–137.

A. PHILIP RANDOLPH: MILITANCY FROM THE PERSPECTIVE OF AN ADVOCATE OF NONVIOLENCE, 1969

In a 1969 oral history interview, preserved in the L.B.J. Library, A. Philip Randolph, the distinguished leader of the Brotherhood of Sleeping Car Porters and a civil rights pioneer, explained militancy in the following excerpt.

Militancy consists largely in their idea of achieving an objective by any means necessary. That's what they're for. Now that involves violence and so forth, and I am definitely opposed to calculated organized violence in order to achieve our civil rights objective. In the first place, after you have had violence you still have the problem. Violence doesn't solve the problem. It may attract attention to it but then you still have the problem, because the problem is involved in relationships between forces and groups with respect to an idea.... Many of [the militants] have no concept of the history of revolution. They haven't given time to try to find out what the mechanism, the structure, and so forth of revolutionary developments are. But they've grasped this, and some of them misconstrue riots for revolution....

[The militants are] quite impatient and they perhaps are making a contribution, because the older Negro leaders are not disposed to enter upon new adventures and things of that sort, you know; and you need this new force to come in and through dialogues if you can have them, why, ideas are changed, points of view are modified, tactics and strategy will undergo transformation....

Source: Transcript. A. Philip Randolph Oral History Interview I, 10.29.69, by Thomas H. Baker, Internet Copy, L.B.J. Library.

ELLA BAKER: ON THE ROLE OF WOMEN IN THE CIVIL RIGHTS MOVEMENT, 1969

In her speech, "The Black Woman in the Civil Rights Struggle" (1969), Ella Baker gives her distinctive perspective on a controversial topic. Historians, as well as some women activists of the civil rights era, frequently criticized the lack of inclusion of women in the male-dominated Civil Rights Movement.

> I was a little bit amazed as to why the selection of a discussion on the role of black women in the world.... I have never been one to feel great needs in the direction of setting myself apart as a woman. I've always thought first and foremost of people as individuals ... [but] wherever there has been struggle, black women have been identified with that struggle.

Source: Grant, Joanne. *Ella Baker: Freedom Bound.* New York: John Wiley & Sons, 1998, pp. 227–231.

ANGELA DAVIS: AN ACTIVIST DESCRIBES HER CALLING TO ACTIVISM, 1969

In *Angela Davis: An Autobiography* (1974), Angela Davis, following several years of extensive study in New York, Massachusetts, France, and Germany, recounts her desperate longing to be a part of the Black Power Movement while a graduate student at the University of California, San Diego (1968/69). She subsequently joined the Black Panther Political Party, the Student Nonviolent Coordinatin Committee (SNCC), and the Che-Lumumba Club.

> I was like an explorer who returns to his homeland after many years, with precious bounty and no one to give it to. I believed my energy, my commitment, my convictions were the treasure I had accumulated, and I looked high and low for a way to spend it. I roamed the campus, examined the bulletin boards, read the newspapers, talked to everyone who might know: Where are my people? It was as if I would be churned up and destroyed inside by these irrepressible desires to become a part of a liberation movement if I did not soon discover an outlet for them. Therefore, I turned to the radical students' organization on campus....

Source: Davis, Angela. *Angela Davis: An Autobiography.* New York: International Publishers, 1974, pp. 152–153.

ELAINE BROWN: POLITICAL AGENDA OF THE BLACK PANTHER PARTY, 1973

In 1973, before Elaine Brown became the minister of defense of the Black Panther Party, she made an unsuccessful bid for the Oakland City Council, along with the organization's co-founder Bobby Seale. In the following excerpt from her autobiography, *A Taste of Power* (1992), Brown asserts the party's objective.

> Our agenda was to overthrow the United States government. It was to defend the humanity of our people with armed force. It was to institute socialist revolution. That was not the program of the Republican Party. It was not the program of the Democratic Party. It was not the program of the traditional white-endorsed, black-faced candidates. It was not the program of the

NAACP or the Urban League. It was not even the program of the black nationalists or SNCC or the radical Peace and Freedom Party. It was still the program of the Black Panther Party.

Source: Brown, Elaine. *A Taste of Power: A Black Woman's Story.* New York: Pantheon Books, 1992, p. 323.

JAMES LEONARD FARMER, JR.: REMINISCING ON THE CIVIL RIGHTS MOVEMENT, 1985

James Leonard Farmer, Jr. was the national director of CORE (1961–1966) and one of the leaders of the Freedom Rides, which were conducted to test legislation that prohibited segregation in intrastate travel and public facilities. In the following excerpt from *Lay Bare the Heart: An Autobiography of the Civil Rights Movement* (1985), Farmer reflects on Dr. Martin Luther King's Montgomery Bus Boycott and his program of nonviolence.

Here was a movement of black Americans flying in the face of the American cult of "the big fist wins." Here was a movement dedicated to the proposition that one could win without using any fists at all, except those pounding within the soul.

King's Montgomery protest not only repudiated the violent machismo of America; it also stirred to awakening another America—the America of Emerson and Thoreau, of the Quakers, of the abolitionists, the America of principle and compassion. A part of America was born again, one might say, and the rebirth lasted through the decade of the sixties.

Source: Farmer, James. *Lay Bare the Heart: An Autobiography of the Civil Rights Movement.* Fort Worth: Texas Christian University Press, 1985, p. 186.

ROSA PARKS: ON PROGRESS SINCE THE CIVIL RIGHTS MOVEMENT, 1992

Rosa Parks, the woman who was arrested and lionized for not giving up her seat on a Jim Crow bus in 1955, expressed her thoughts on the impact of the Civil Rights Movement in her autobiography, *Rosa Parks: My Story* (1992).

My life has changed a great deal since 1955.... I look back now and realize that since that evening on the bus in Montgomery, Alabama, we have made a lot of progress in some ways. Young people can go to register to vote without being threatened and can vote without feeling apprehensive. There are no signs on public water fountains saying "Colored" and "White." There are big cities with black mayors, and small towns with black mayors and chiefs of police.... All those laws against segregation have been passed, and all that progress has been made. But a whole lot of white peoples' hearts have not been changed. Dr. King used to talk about the fact that if a law was changed, it might not change hearts but it would offer some protection. He was right. We now have some protection, but there is still much racism and racial violence.

In recent years there has been a resurgence of reactionary attitudes. I am troubled by the recent decisions of the Supreme Court that make it harder to prove a pattern of racial discrimination in employment and by the fact that the national government does not seem very interested in pursuing violations of civil rights. What troubles me is that so many young people, including college students, have come out for white supremacy and that there have been more and more incidents of racism and racial violence on college campuses. It has not been widespread, but still it is troublesome. It seems like we still have a long way to go.

Source: Parks, Rosa, with Jim Haskins. *Rosa Parks: My Story.* New York: Scholastic, 1992, pp. 186–187.

LOUIS FARRAKHAN: MANY PATHS, ONE GOAL, 1995

Louis Farrakhan, Nation of Islam Minister, is one of the most controversial black leaders of the twenty-first century. Historically, he has been a critic of prominent protest organizations. In the following excerpt of a speech Farrakhan gave at the 1995 Million Man March, he demonstrates a change of heart.

We must belong to some organization that is working for and in the interest of the uplift and the liberation of our people.

Go back, join the NAACP if you want to, join the Urban League, join the All African People's Revolutionary Party, join us, join the Nation of Islam, join PUSH, join the Congress of Racial Equality, join SCLC—the Southern Christian Leadership Conference, but we must become a totally organized people and the only way we can do that is to become a part of some organization that is working for the uplift of our people.

Source: "Minister Farrakhan Challenges Black Men: Transcript from Minister Louis Farrakhan's Remarks at the Million Man March." *CNN.com.* November 10, 2007. See http://www-cgi.cnn.com/US/9510/megamarch/10-16/transcript/index.html.

JESSE JACKSON: ON THE EDUCATION OF AN ACTIVIST, 2000

The following is an excerpt from a 2000 *Teen Ink* interview with Jesse Jackson in which he discusses his preparation for protest work.

Many who left school [to join the Civil Rights Movement] never came back; I was tempted to do the same thing. I was just as fascinated; it became a very personal thing because of my own pain and rejection and denial of access based on the race law.

[Dr. Samuel DeWitt Proctor] called me in one day and said, "I know you're inspired by Mike." (That's what he called Dr. King.) "But," he said, "Mike has his Ph.D. And a lot of guys are talking, protesting and doing a good job. But because Mike is so prepared with his B.S. degree and his doctorate, having read the great books, his sense of philosophy and history, his contributions will outlast theirs. He's prepared for the struggle."

"So, if you are as committed as you say you are, you must decide now to be a student of the movement, not just a student in the movement. You will cease to be a student at some point, and so your commitment to the struggle must be your commitment to prepare to offer something of substance to it."

And so I did not leave school; actually I became president of the student body. Then I went to graduate school, which was enormously important to me in terms of preparation.

And the irony of all is that—the ultimate irony—after finishing two years of seminary, Dr. King came to Chicago. I had six more months to finish. He said to me, "You will learn more theology right here in this room with me in six months than you'll learn in six years of seminary."

I said, "It's easy for you to say, you have your Ph.D."

And I asked my wife who said, "I know you want to finish, but the unique opportunity to work with Dr. King may be such that if you remain focused it may be worth the risk."

So, I left the seminary to work with him.

Source: Interview with Rev. Jesse Jackson, Civil Rights Leader. *Teen Ink.* November 10, 2007. See http://www.teenink.com/Interviews/article/5456/Jesse-Jackson-Civil-Rights-Leader.

AL SHARPTON ON AL SHARPTON, 2002

Al Sharpton emerged as an activist during the Civil Rights Movement and continues to maintain a vigilant watch over issues that matter to and affect contemporary African Americans. His omnipresent crusade to smite racism in the twenty-first century has made him a figure of ridicule to some and a modern hero to others. Sharpton's perspective on his importance is summarized in the following statement.

If there were no injustice, if there were no racism, there would be no need for an Al Sharpton.

Source: Sharpton, Al. *Al on America.* New York: Kensington Publishing, 2002, p. 190.

DOROTHY HEIGHT: WHAT WOMEN OF COLOR WANT, 2003

Dorothy Height, president of the National Council of Negro Women (1957–1998), wrote the following in her autobiography, *Open Wide the Freedom Gates: A Memoir* (2003).

Women of color around the world have common problems and common dreams. Whether affluent or needy, living in the northern industrialized world or the developing South, educated or illiterate, we all want to improve the quality of life for our loved ones and our communities. We want to participate in our nations' development. We long for loving child care and access to nutritious food and good health for our families. We seek training and skills for better-paying jobs. We expect equal wages for equal work....

And yet black women universally have been denied education and barred from political power. The systematic denial of women's central role in nation-building has been as costly to the nations concerned as it has been harmful to women and their families.

Source: Height, Dorothy. *Open Wide the Freedom Gates: A Memoir.* New York: Public Affairs, 2003, pp. 232–233.

SPIKE LEE: EXPOSING THE PROBLEM IS PART OF THE SOLUTION, 2005

Spike Lee has produced films for the big screen that explore racism, the lives of radical activists such as Huey P. Newton and Malcolm X, and the African American experience. He is notorious for stirring up controversy. In the following excerpt from Lee's *That's My Story and I'm Sticking to It*, he explains part of his function as a filmmaker.

And that's something I've been accused of: of raising questions without having answers. But I've never felt it was the film-maker's job to have all the answers. I think, for the most part, if we choose to do so, we have more of a provocateur role, where we ask these questions and hopefully they will, by the way that they are asked, stimulate and generate some discussion and dialogue. But to find answers for racism and prejudice in films? You can't do that.

Source: Lee, Spike. *That's My Story and I'm Sticking to It.* New York: W.W. Norton, 2005, p. 3.

Glossary

accommodationism. A philosophy in which blacks concede to the attitudes, traditions, or practices of opposing views or policies, such as segregation.

apartheid. The system of racial segregation practiced in South Africa between 1948 and 1993.

Black Nadir. A period of extreme adversity for blacks that occurred between 1877 and the early twentieth century, marked by anti-black violence such as lynchings and race riots, the establishment of Jim Crow laws, and the erosion of civil rights gained during Reconstruction. "Nadir" was coined by an African American scholar named Rayford Logan in his book *The Negro in American Life and Thought: The Nadir, 1877–1901* (1954).

black nationalism. An ideology that promotes black social, economic, and political independence from whites and the establishment of black self-government.

Black Power Movement. A period, which occurred concurrent with the Civil Rights Movement, of political activity by black organizations that espoused any combination of the following: racial pride, black separatism, black nationalism, and militancy, and/or actively promoted the protection and political, economic, and social needs of blacks in impoverished communities.

boycott. The act of abstaining from using, buying, or dealing with some one or some other institution, organization, or establishment as a form of protest.

Buddhism. A major religion in Asian countries that venerates the teachings of Gautama Buddha, an Indian religious leader of the sixth century B.C.E.

capitalism. An economic system in which investment in and ownership of the means of production, distribution, and exchange of wealth is made and maintained chiefly by private individuals or corporations.

Christianity. A major religion in the United States and in the West, which is based on the life and teachings of Jesus Christ as revealed in the Holy Bible.

civil disobedience. The refusal to obey certain laws for the purpose of influencing legislation or policy, characterized by the employment of nonviolent demonstrations.

Civil Rights Movement. A period spanning the 1950s and the 1960s of large-scale black protest for full legal, social, and economic equality.

Cold War. A state of political hostility and tension that existed from 1945 to 1990 between the Soviet Union and the United States and their respective allies.

colonialism. The control of a nation over another country. Colonialism in Africa, particularly during the nineteenth century, often resulted in the mistreatment and subjugation of indigenous peoples and the exploitation of land and resources. This phenomenon sparked many liberation movements. In 1956, Tunisia was the first country in Africa to gain its independence. Today, there are 53 independent African countries.

communism. A system of social organization based on the holding of all property in common, actual ownership being ascribed to the community as a whole or to the state.

Confederate flag. A twentieth-century symbol of the South. The term Confederate refers to the eleven southern states that seceded from the United States of America (the Union), largely over the issue of slavery, and then engaged the Union in the American Civil War (1861–1865). The Union's victory ended slavery in the United States.

cracker. A pejorative used by blacks to refer to a white person; the term is believed to have originated from the sound of the "crack" of the bullwhip the plantation overseer used to punish black slaves.

demonstration. A public display of protest that takes a variety of forms, such as rallies, sit-ins, picketing, boycotts, and marches.

direct action. Any demonstration employed to achieve an immediate or direct result.

discrimination (or racial discrimination). The making of a distinction, generally against a person, based on race.

disfranchisement. The state of being deprived of the right to vote.

Fifteenth Amendment. A modification to the U.S. Constitution, ratified in 1870 during Reconstruction, for the purpose of prohibiting the restriction of voting rights for recently freed black slaves. Applies to any U.S. citizen regardless of race, color, or previous state as a slave.

Fourteenth Amendment. A modification to the U.S. Constitution, ratified in 1868 during Reconstruction, for the purpose of granting recently freed black slaves due process of law and equal protection.

Garveyism. The philosophy of Marcus Garvey, the founder of the Universal Negro Improvement Association-African Communities League (UNIA-ACL). The three tenets of Garvey's philosophy include the concepts of race first, self-reliance, and nationhood.

ghetto. A section of a city characterized by substandard housing and inhabited by disadvantaged and impoverished residents; also referred to as a slum.

Great Migration. A period between 1910 and 1950 characterized by large-scale relocation of blacks from the South to the North to escape segregation, antiblack violence, racism, and catastrophes, like a boll weevil infestation and flooding, in some parts of the South. Southern blacks went North to follow the employment opportunities that increased as a result of World War I.

Harlem Renaissance. A renewal and flourishing of black literary and musical culture between 1912 and the 1930s in the Harlem section of New York City.

Hinduism. A major religion of India that emphasizes freedom from the material world through purification of desires and elimination of personal identity.

Holocaust. A systematic mass slaughter of mostly Jews in Nazi concentration camps beginning with Adolf Hitler's rise to power in Germany in 1933 and ending with the victory of the United States and its allies in World War II (1939–1945).

integrationism. A belief or philosophy that supports the inclusion or incorporation of blacks into white society and the elimination of racially segregated public institutions and facilities.

Islam. The religious faith of Muslims, based on the teachings and life of the prophet Muhammad as recorded in the Qur'an.

Jim Crow. Term originating from a minstrel show song in the early nineteenth century referring to a practice and legal policy of segregating or discriminating against blacks in public places, public transportation, employment, etc.

Judaism. A religion of the Jews based on the writings of the Old Testament and teachings in the Talmud.

Ku Klux Klan (KKK or the Klan). One of numerous white supremacist organizations established to terrorize, intimidate, and attack blacks, as well as whites who sympathized with blacks, Jews, Catholics, and other groups. This organization was established in 1866 by veterans of the Confederate Army and remains active throughout the United States. Historically, members wore white robes and white cone-shaped masks.

lynching. A term mostly used to refer to a killing by hanging, but it can indicate any illicit murder by any other means. Lynchings were most common during the American frontier (1865–1890) between whites and other whites or immigrants over alleged crimes, competition, or disputes. During the late nineteenth and early twentieth centuries, blacks were primarily, but not exclusively, targeted in the South. Black males were charged for alleged rape crimes whether or not an actual crime had been committed. Racial lynching was largely employed to maintain the social, economic, and political supremacy of whites.

Middle Passage. The forced voyage of enslaved Africans across the Atlantic Ocean to the Americas. Treated as cargo and transported in horrendous conditions, many Africans died on the journey. The term "middle" refers to the area of the triangular trade voyage that occurred between West Africa, the West Indies, and colonies in North America.

militancy. The quality of being aggressive or combative.

nigger. An ethnic slur used to refer to black slaves. During and after slavery, blacks also used the term to refer to one another. Employed by blacks, the term can be used in a familiar, neutral, or derogatory manner. Those who protest the use of the word by whites or blacks will frequently use the term "N-word" instead.

nonviolence. The policy, practice, or technique of refraining from physically harming another person or defending oneself from a physical attack.

Pan-Africanism. A philosophy that advocates the political alliance or union of all African nations and African descendents.

passive resistance. Opposition to a government or to governmental laws by the use of non-cooperation and other nonviolent demonstrations, such as boycotts, sit-ins, and marches.

picketing. The presence of a person or group of persons stationed outside an establishment to express grievance and to discourage entry by patrons. Picketers, or participants in a picket, will often vocalize slogans and carry signs.

prejudice (or racial prejudice). An unfavorable opinion or feeling towards someone based on race.

racial consciousness (or race consciousness). The awareness and advocacy of racial heritage, culture, and traditions.

racial etiquette. Informal rules, practices, customs, and traditions that regulate social relations, conduct, and speech behavior between blacks and whites.

racial profiling (or racial stereotyping). The practice of making a negative or positive judgment based on an individual's race. For example, to pass a black male on a street and assume he is a criminal or perpetrator is a form of racial profiling.

racism. Hatred or intolerance of another racial group.

Reconstruction. The effort following the end of the Civil War (1861–1865) to provide assistance and legal reform for recently freed blacks in the South. In this period, American soldiers enforced black male suffrage (women were not yet allowed to vote) and the establishment of black politicians in the South. Through violence and intimidation, white southerners gradually retook political control over the region. By 1877, all the gains achieved for blacks were lost and Reconstruction officially ended. One of the longest lasting effects of Reconstruction was in education and the establishment of numerous historically black colleges and universities (HBCU)

Red Scare. Two periods in U.S. history, between 1917 and 1920 and 1947 and 1957, that were characterized by a heightened state of fear and suspicion of Communist infiltration of the American government.

redneck. One of several pejoratives used by blacks to refer to whites. One speculation is that the term originated from a description of poor southern whites whose skin, particularly the neck region, turned red as a result of working out under the sun.

reparations. Term referring to a popular issue among some blacks who feel the descendents of slaves in the U.S. should receive monetary or other restitution.

segregation. The legalized separation of blacks and whites in the United States.

self-defense. A philosophy that endorses the protection of oneself and one's community or property if attacked.

separatism (or black separatism). The advocacy of withdrawing socially, economically, and/or politically from the white establishment.

sit-ins. A form of demonstration made popular during the 1960s with youths who entered white-only public places, like restaurants, where they sat down at lunch counters and refused to leave to protest Jim Crow laws.

slavery. The phenomena of forcing individuals into a state of bondage, where they are deprived of all freedom and made to work without payment. American slavery lasted from 1654 to 1865. It is estimated that twelve to fifteen million slaves were transported from Africa to America, mostly coming from the West Coast of Africa. Because records were not kept on the slaves, African Americans are unable to track their lineage. Slavery sustained the economic system of the antebellum South, where blacks toiled on plantations or in white homes. Slavery was generally abandoned in the North. Northern abolitionists, or individuals calling for the end of slavery, made critical contributions in helping slaves escape to the North.

socialism. A system of social organization based on the collective ownership of production and distribution of goods and property. According to the philosopher

Karl Marx (1818–1883), the development of a society included the stages of capitalism, socialism, and communism.

Uncle Tom. A pejorative to describe blacks who are subservient to whites. This term was frequently applied by black power proponents to refer to civil rights leaders who advocated integrationism.

white supremacy. The belief that whites are superior to other races; this belief includes the advocacy of social, economic, and political domination by whites.

whitecapping. With regard to race relations, the term refers to the late nineteenth- and early twentieth-century phenomenon in the South in which white farmers used violence and intimidation to prevent black land ownership and to control the black population.

women's suffrage. The struggle for women's right to vote. White women led this struggle, but blacks, like Ida B. Wells-Barnett, made contributions. The Nineteenth Amendment to the U.S Constitution was ratified in 1920, granting all women full voting rights.

Bibliography

BOOKS

Abu-Lughod, Janet L. *Race, Space, and Riots in Chicago, New York, and Los Angeles*. New York: Oxford University Press, 2007.

Appiah, Kwame Anthony, and Henry Louis Gates, Jr., eds. *Africana: The Encyclopedia of the African and African American Experience*. 5 vols. New York: Oxford University Press, 2005.

Asante, Molefi Kete, and Mambo Ama Mazama, eds. *Encyclopedia of Black Studies*. Thousand Oaks, CA: Sage Publications, 2005.

Berry, Mary Frances. *Black Resistance/White Law: A History of Constitutional Racism in America*. New York: Penguin Group, 1994.

Bonilla-Silva, Eduard. *White Supremacy and Racism in the Post-Civil Rights Era*. Boulder, CO: Lynne Rienner, 2001.

Brundage, W. Fitzhugh, ed. *Under Sentence of Death: Lynching in the South*. Chapel Hill: University of North Carolina Press, 1997.

Buckley, Gail. *Strength for the Fight: A History of Black Americans in the Military*. New York: Random House, 2001.

Carson, Clayborne, Emma J. Lapsansky-Werner, and Gary Nash. *African American Lives: The Struggle for Freedom*. New York: Pearson/Longman, 2005.

Chafe, Williams, H., ed. *Remembering Jim Crow: African Americans Tell about Life in the Segregated South*. New York: New Press, 2001.

Chalmers, David M. *Hooded Americanism: The History of the Ku Klux Klan*. Durham, NC: Duke University Press, 1987.

Chalmers, David Mark. *Backfire: How the Ku Klux Klan Helped the Civil Rights Movement*. Lanham, MD: Rowman & Littlefield, 2003.

Clark, Kenneth B. *Dark Ghetto: Dilemmas of Social Power*. New York: Harper & Row, 1965.

Clark, Robert F. *The War on Poverty: History, Selected Programs and Ongoing Impact*. Washington, D.C.: University Press of America, 2002.

Collier-Thomas, Bettye, and Franklin, V.P. *Sisters in the Struggle: African-American Women in the Civil Rights-Black Power Movement*. New York: New York University Press, 2001.

Dobratz, Betty A. *The White Separatist Movement in the United States: "White Power, White Pride!"* Baltimore: The Johns Hopkins University Press, 2000.

Dovidio, J.F., and S.L. Gaertner, eds. *Prejudice, Discrimination, and Racism.* New York: Academic Press, 1986.

Fairclough, Adam. *Better Day Coming: Blacks and Equality, 1890–2000.* New York: Viking, 2001.

Feagin, Joe R. *Racist America: Roots, Current Realities, and Future Reparations.* New York: Routledge, 2000.

Gates, Henry Louis, Jr., and Cornel West. *The African-American Century: How Black Americans Have Shaped Our Country.* New York: Touchstone, 2002.

Guerrero, Ed. *Framing Blackness: The African American Image in Film.* Philadelphia: Temple University Press, 1993.

Helsing, Jeffrey. *Johnson's War/Johnson's Great Society: The Guns and Butter Trap.* Westport, CT: Praeger Publishers, 2000.

Jacobs, Ronald N. *Race, Media, and the Crisis of Civil Society: From Watts to Rodney King.* Cambridge: Cambridge University Press, 2000.

Joseph, Peniel E. *Black Power Movement: Rethinking the Civil Rights-Black Power Era.* New York: Routledge, 2006.

Lincoln, C. Eric. *The Black Muslims in America.* 3rd ed. Grand Rapids, MI: Eerdmans Publishing Company, 1994.

Lincoln, C. Eric. and Lawrence H. Mamiya. *The Black Church in the African American Experience.* Durham, NC: Duke University Press, 1990.

Perry, Barbara. *In the Name of Hate: Understanding Hate Crimes.* New York: Routledge, 2001.

Robinson, Cedric J. *Black Movements in America.* New York: Routledge, 1997.

Smiley, Tavis. *Doing What's Right: How to Fight for What You Believe—and Make a Difference.* New York: Anchor, 2000.

Upton, James N. *Urban Riots in the 20th Century: A Social History.* Bristol, IN: Wyndham Hall Press, 1989.

Van Debert, William L., ed. *Modern Black Nationalism: From Marcus Garvey to Louis Farrakhan.* New York: New York University Press, 1997.

Ward, Brian E. *Media, Culture, and the Modern African American Freedom Struggle.* Gainesville: University Press of Florida, 2001.

West, Cornel. *Race Matters.* Boston: Beacon Press, 1993.

WEB SITES

African American Web Connection. *AAWC.com* (June 2008). See http://www.aawc.com/paa.html.

Black History. *Archives Library Information Center* (June 2008). See http://www.archives.gov/research/alic/reference/black-history.html.

McElrath, Jessica. "African American History." *About.com* (June 2008). See http://afroamhistory.about.com.

Taylord, Quinard. *Blackpast.org* (June 2008). See http://www.blackpast.org.

"The Story of the Movement—26 Events." *PBS.org* (June 2008). See http://www.pbs.org/wgbh/amex/eyesontheprize/story/01_till.html.

Index

ABOUT THE AUTHOR

GLADYS L. KNIGHT has written extensively on individuals, issues, and topics relevant to African American history. She has contributed to numerous Greenwood publications, including *The Greenwood Encyclopedia of African American Literature* (2005), *The Greenwood Encyclopedia of African American Folklore* (2005), *Encyclopedia of the Reconstruction Era* (2006), *Encyclopedia of American Race Riots* (2006), and the forthcoming *Encyclopedia of African American Popular Culture*.